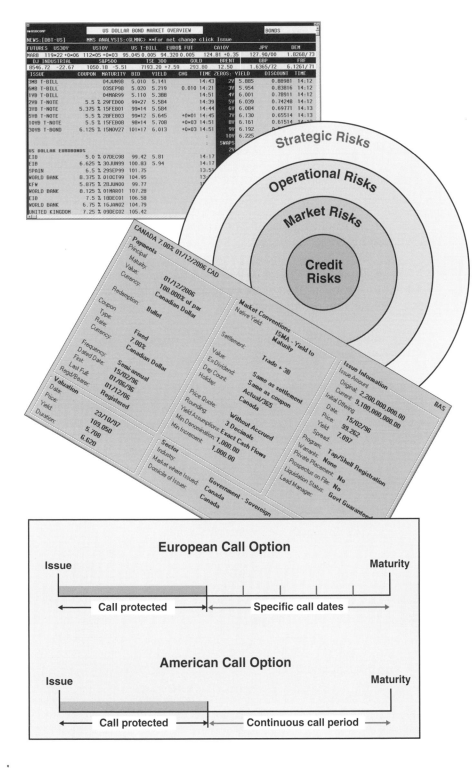

An Introduction to

Bond Markets

John Wiley & Sons (Asia) Pte Ltd

Singapore New York Chichester
Brisbane Toronto Weinheim

Other titles in the series

An Introduction to Technical Analysis *0-471-83127-1*
An Introduction to Derivatives *0-471-83176-X*
An Introduction to Foreign Exchange & Money Markets *0-471-83128-X*
An Introduction to Equity Markets *0-471-83171-9*
An Introduction to Commodities, Energy & Transport Markets *0-471-83150-6*

You can get more information about the other titles in the series from the Reuters Financial Training series companion web site at *http://www.wiley-rft.reuters.com.*

Acknowledgments

The publishers and Reuters Limited would like to thank the following people for their invaluable assistance in this book:

Dr. Jonathan Batten from the Nanyang Technological University, Singapore (NTU) for his review of the book and constructive feedback.

Keith Rogers who wrote and produced the original version of the book.

Tom Windas from Reuters Limited who wrote some of the material found in this book.

Professor Brian Scott-Quinn of the ISMA Centre – the Business School for Financial Markets, University of Reading, UK (see page 28) for supporting this project.

The London Stock Exchange Limited for use of their Glossary at the back of this book.

Numa Financial Systems Ltd for use of their Directory of Futures & Options Exchanges at the back of this book.

Published in 1999 by John Wiley & Sons (Asia) Pte Ltd
2 Clementi Loop, #02-01, Singapore 129809, Singapore.

This publication is designed to provide accurate and authoritative information in
regard to the subject matter covered. It is sold with the understanding that the
publisher is not engaged in rendering professional services. If professional advice or
other expert assistance is required, the services of a competent professional person
should be sought.

Other Wiley Editorial Offices
John Wiley & Sons, Inc., 605 Third Avenue, New York, NY 10158-0012, USA
John Wiley & Sons Ltd, Baffins Lane, Chichester, West Sussex PO19
1UD, England
John Wiley & Sons (Canada) Ltd, 22 Worcester Road, Rexdale,
Ontario M9W 1L1, Canada
Jacaranda Wiley Ltd, 33 Park Road (PO Box 1226), Milton,
Queensland 4064, Australia
Wiley-VCH, Pappelallee 3, 69469 Weinheim, Germany

Library of Congress Cataloging-in-Publication Data
An introduction to bond markets.
        p.   cm. — (The Reuters financial training series)
    Includes bibliographical references (p.).
    ISBN 0-471-83174-3
    1. Bond market.   2. Bonds.   I. Reuters ltd.   II. Title: Bond markets.   III. Series.
HG4651.I574   1999   99-37481
332.63'23 — dc21   CIP

ISBN 0-471-83174-3

Typeset in 10/12 point New Baskerville
Printed in Singapore by Craft Print Pte Ltd
10 9 8 7 6 5 4 3 2 1

An Introduction to

Bond Markets

Contents

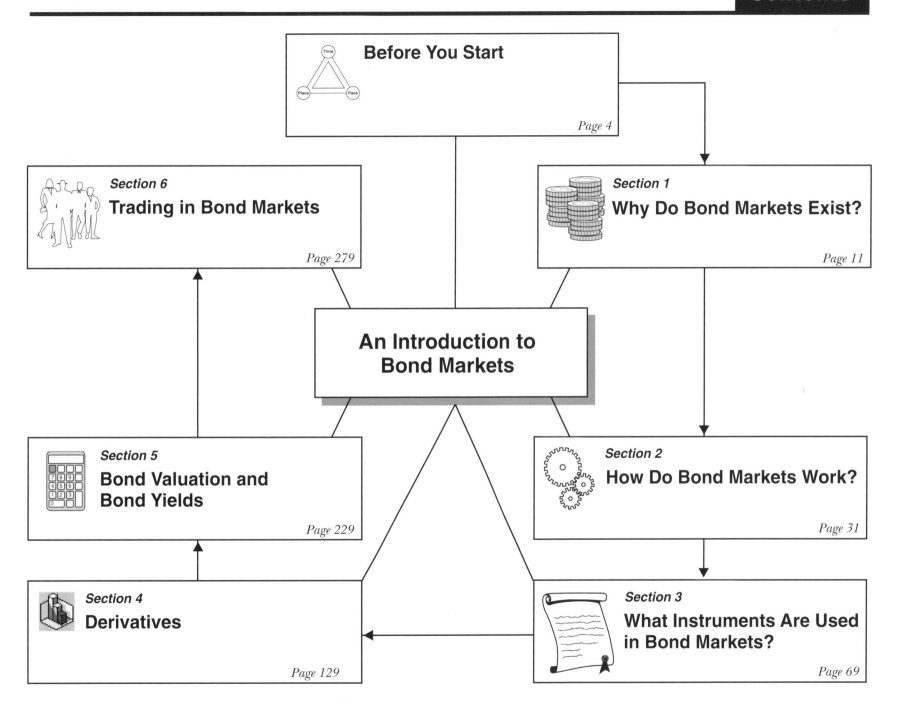

Before You Start
Page 4

Contents

Contents

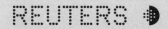

Who Should Use This Book?

This book is designed to provide an overview of the bond markets for a variety of readers: salespeople, support and operations staff, trainers, managers or investors who want to learn more about the markets to refine their investing strategies. Also, anyone beginning an in-depth study of the markets will find this book to be a very useful primer.

Despite the complexity of the financial markets, more and more people need a working knowledge of what the basic instruments are and how the markets are structured, for for professional and personal pursuits. Such readers will find this book to be helpful as it provides not only the fundamental definitions, but also exercises and examples to make markets more accessible.

This book will take you through the basics of the bond markets, from what the instruments are and why the markets exist, to who the market players are, to how the markets are structured and regulated and how information is used. By the time you have completed this book, you should be able to participate in the bond markets in an informed fashion.

An Introduction to Bond Markets is one in the Reuters Financial Training series, designed to provide readers with an overall understanding of the financial markets. Other titles cover equities, derivatives, technical analysis, and foreign exchange and money markets.

What Will You Find in This Book?

This book provides a new approach to gaining some basic familiarity with the essential concepts of the bond markets. The book is written in a very accessible style with jargon kept to a minimum, but with market language clearly explained.

Most importantly, the book includes a range of materials to help you reinforce what you are learning. Each section offers a solid explanation of basic concepts, followed by actual examples for the reader to work through. Additional exercises and quick quizzes enable the reader to further enhance learning. To enable the reader to better understand how market players use financial data, screens from Reuters electronic information services are provided. Finally, each section concludes with a graphic overview – a visual outline – of what has been covered for quick yet thorough review, and ends with a listing of additional reference materials.

> In addition, the **RFT Web Site** has been created as this book series' companion web site, where additional quiz questions, updated screens and other information may be found. You can find this web site at:
> **http://www.wiley-rft.reuters.com**

This text focuses primarily on the UK and US bond markets for detailed descriptions, issuing and trading procedures, and so forth. This is done to keep as much consistency as possible throughout the text and in recognition that these markets, given their size and standing, often set precedents for other markets. For the specifics of different markets throughout the world, the reader is advised to refer directly to the various international associations (eg, the Bond Market Association, the International Securities Market Association) and self-regulatory bodies for more detailed information. While contact information for exchanges around the world is provided at the back of this book, virtually all bond market trading is done Over-The-Counter (OTC) – that is, off the exchanges. Also refer to the **Further Resources** listings at the end of each section.

How is This Book Organised?

This book contains the following sections:

Before You Start

This section!

Why Do Bond Markets Exist?

This section covers the history and purpose of the market.

How Do Bond Markets Work?

This section explains operation or "mechanics" of the market and addresses market "jargon" and conventions.

What Instruments Are Used in Bond Markets?

This section provides a brief overview of all the instruments used in the market. Each instrument is defined and accompanied by sample screens from Reuters' electronic information services to illustrate how information is provided to market players via data terminals.

Derivatives

This section provides a substantial review of the basic concepts of derivatives, and how they are used and traded.

Bond Valuation and Bond Yields

This section explains how bond values – the most common ratios, for example – are determined by market players.

Trading in Bond Markets

This section describes market players and their trading techniques. The section also provides examples of market player conversations so you can get a better idea of what they do in their jobs.

Throughout the book you will find that important terms or concepts are shown in **bold**, for example, **dividend**. You will also find that activities included to enhance your learning are indicated by the following icons:

 This indicates the definition of a term that you must know and understand to master the material.

 This means stop and think about the point being made. You may also want to jot a few words in the box provided.

 This indicates an activity for you to do. It is usually something written – for example, a definition, notes, or a calculation.

 This is the answer or response to an activity and it usually follows the activity or is close to it.

 This indicates the main points of the section.

 This indicates questions for you to answer to help you to review the material. The answers are also provided.

 This indicates the one-page summary that provides a quick overview of the entire section. This page serves as an excellent study tool.

Additional reference material is listed in **Further Resources** at the end of each section.

How to Use This Book

Before you start using this book, decide what you want from the material. If you are using it as part of your work, discuss with your manager how she will help by giving time for study and giving you feedback and support. Although your learning style is unique to you, you will find that your learning is much more effective if you allocate reasonable sized periods of time for study. The most effective learning period is about 30 minutes – so use this as a basis. If you try to fit your learning into odd moments in a busy schedule you will not get the best from the materials or yourself. You might like to schedule learning periods into your day just as you would business meetings.

Remember that the most effective learning is an interactive process and requires more than just reading the text. The exercises in this book make you think through the material you have just read and then apply your understanding through basic activities. Take time to do the exercises. This old Chinese saying sums up this concept:

> I hear and I forget
> I see and I remember
> I do and I understand

Try to make sure your study is uninterrupted. This probably means that your workplace is not a good environment! You will need to find both the time and place where you can study – you may have access to a quiet room at work, you may have a room at home, you may need to use a library.

Market Developments as This Book Was Published

The financial markets are constantly evolving and as this book was going to print in July 1999, changes of extraordinary significance were taking place. Individual sections of this book include some of these changes, but the below paragraphs highlight the key events the reader should bear in mind.

The Introduction of the Euro

Already in 1999, though the euro currency itself has gotten off to a mixed start, its place in the Eurobond market has been significant. The volume of euro-denominated new issues has greatly exceeded expectations, with eurobond issuances up over last year at the same time and dollar-denominated issues down slightly. The ramifications of these changes are potentially significant, as the euro-dominated eurobond market's increases in volume and liquidity will change both issuers' and investors' view of the bond markets overall. Analysts expect a new and strong rival to the mighty US Treasury bond market and fundamental changes in how bond risk is determined will take place.

Readers should bear these changes in mind particularly when reading Sections 3 and 5. While nothing about the financial markets ever stands still, the euro in particular is accelerating change as we reach the year 2000.

Changes at the Exchanges

1998 and 1999 have already been witness to the merging of some major exchanges, the announcement of collaborative agreements among others and an overall trend toward expanding services. These include:

- October 1998   The NASDAQ and AMEX exchanges merged
- January 1999   Paris and Swiss exchanges agree to allow cross membership to enable members to access both exchanges on the same screen
- February 1999   NYSE announces consideration of beginning trading earlier in the day and extending hours to midnight, to accommodate European and Asian investors and the individual investor
- March 1999   LSE and Frankfurt announce plans to consider creating a pan-European exchange; talks include Paris, Zurich, Milan, Madrid, Amsterdam and Brussels

These unions are occurring as the exchanges must address the same competitive and cost pressures as many other organisations do. The exchanges must find ways to collaborate to enable them to meet the demands of their clients, the market players, who want to reduce the cost of trading and have as broad access as possible to other exchanges. For example, the cost of developing and employing technology to keep up with a 24-hour marketplace are significant, and exchanges are finding that collaboration is a cost-effective way to address these issues. In addition, the exchanges must also address what the arrival of the euro means to their operations, as the characteristics of trading instruments and currencies alters and new instruments are created. While this has the most obvious impact on the equity markets, as an overall market trend it also has bearing on the bond markets.

The Role of the Internet for the Individual Investor

Perhaps one of the greatest changes to take place in the investing world is the empowerment of the individual investor to trade on her own behalf through access to the Internet. Once the ability to trade around-the-clock was the sole privilege of institutional investors or very wealthy individuals with access to advisors around the globe.

Today, the average investor may place buy and sell orders 24 hours a day, obtain market research information around the clock, and track and calculate the ever-changing value of her portfolio throughout the day and night. Thus, the average investor demands more information about investments and wants assurances that the trades will be executed. The failure of one online trading service in early 1999 highlighted what happens when the system breaks down and investors – thousands of investors – are left hanging at their keyboards. These events will no doubt affect how these activities are regulated and the growth in how many of these services become available.

This section of the book should take about 60 minutes of study time. You may not take as long as this or you may take a little longer – remember your learning is individual to you.

As Bill Simon used to shout at his traders, 'If you guys weren't trading bonds, you'd be driving a truck. Don't try to get intellectual in the market place. Just trade.' When a trader is long and wrong he cuts and runs. He drops his position, cuts his losses, and moves on. He only hopes he hasn't sold at the bottom, which is what people do who buy at the top.

Michael Lewis – 'Liar's Poker'

Introduction

What is "debt"? You may have borrowed money from a bank to pay for something you need but for which you do not have enough money. You may have heard the term "the national debt". Are personal debts the same as the debt of a nation? This section is concerned with introducing the concept of debt and those markets – specifically, the "bond markets" – in which money can be borrowed and loaned. In particular the following are covered:

- The meaning of the term debt in the context of the capital markets

- The relationship among money, bond and equity markets, their purposes and uses

- The relationship between risk and return, and how bonds and equity are positioned with respect to them

- An overview of the bond market players and the primary and secondary markets in which they operate

- An overview of the components of a debt instrument, that is, of a bond.

Before moving on, try the activity opposite to check your current understanding of the terms mentioned above. No specific answers are given as the following text covers all the terms.

Can you think of the two main reasons why the capital markets exist?

In simple terms, what are the main differences among the money, bond and equity markets?

Why Do Bond Markets Exist?

An Overview of Bond Markets

Most governments, corporations, international organisations, supranationals, banks, financial institutions and individuals at some time need to raise money to fund their activities for many different reasons.

The term **Capital Markets** refers to the financial markets in which money is raised and traded, that is, where funds may be ultimately exchanged between issuers of bonds and securities ("borrowers") and investors ("lenders"). However, the ways in which organisations raise capital separates the capital markets into three main areas:

- **Money Markets**
  These are characterised by borrowing and lending large amounts of money for **short periods** – typically overnight up to, and including, 12 months.

- **Bond Markets**
  These are characterised by instruments that generally pay interest for a fixed period of time for loan periods over 12 months up to 30 years. For this reason, these markets are also known as the **Fixed Income Markets** and involve medium- to long-term borrowing. Generally, one-to-ten year instruments are called **notes** and instruments exceeding ten years in maturity are called **bonds**.

- **Equity Markets**
  These markets also involve medium- to long-term borrowing but in this case interest is not paid to the lender. Instead the organisation borrowing the money issues **stocks** or **shares** to investors who become part owners of the organisation. Investors may or may not be paid a dividend on their shares depending on how well the organisation performs.

The following diagram summarises the relationship among the money, bond and equity markets.

Money Markets	Bond Markets	Equity Markets
Short-term debt	Medium- to long-term Non-permanent funding	Long-term Permanent funding
0　　　　1		
Years		

The capital markets can also be represented by the following diagram, although as you will see, it will be refined later.

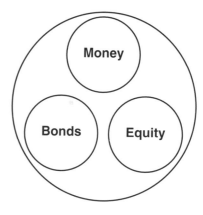

This book has been designed primarily to help your understanding of the bond markets. If you need to know more about the other markets, then you may find it useful to refer to the other books in this series, in particular, *An Introduction to Foreign Exchange and Money Markets*, ISBN 0-471-83128-X.

REUTERS

There are two fundamentally different ways in which bonds or fixed income instruments are traded – they are either **negotiable** or **non-negotiable**.

- **Negotiable Debt Instruments** are those which can be bought or sold in a secondary market once they have been issued by a borrower – in effect they are IOUs. The instruments include bonds and notes, and structured securities such as asset-backed and mortgage-backed instruments. Another class of instruments called derivative securities have their value determined by the value of an underlying market variable such as the interest rate on other simple negotiated instruments like bonds. For more detailed information about derivatives, refer to *An Introduction to Derivatives*, ISBN 0-471-83176-X.

- **Non-negotiable Loans** are private transactions between counterparties – such as banks and corporations or governments – and are not generally traded in the markets. The details of the interest rate payable, repayment dates for interest payments, etc are not formally made available publicly. For more information about non-negotiable instruments, which are both short- and long-term, refer to *An Introduction to Foreign Exchange and Money Markets*, ISBN 0-471-83128-X.

Although most trading for bonds and notes takes place **Over-The-Counter (OTC)**, trading can take place on a stock exchange such as the **London Stock Exchange (LSE)** or the **New York Stock Exchange (NYSE)**. Futures and options derivatives are traded on exchanges such as the **London International Financial Futures and Options Exchange (LIFFE)** and the **Chicago Board of Trade (CBOT)**, whereas swaps are traded OTC.

This book concentrates on negotiable instruments, and in particular, on notes and bonds. For this reason, this book uses the term "bond market", as that is the most common term used in the financial industry.

Bond Markets deal in financial instruments such as bonds and notes which represent loans to large organisations that investors believe will be able to honour their obligations to repay the loan and interest payments due.

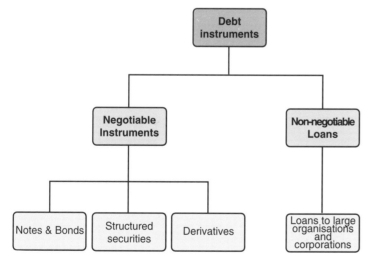

Government and Corporate Bonds

Look at the Reuters screens below that display commentary about the US Treasury Market and an index for new Eurobond issues.

```
GovPX      GovPX 3:00 Market Diary for Tuesday, October 28, 1997        GVWW
                                                               3:00

Today's volume will surpass the previous $139.4 bln record set on March 26

 ×By 3pm $135.4 bln traded, 115% above average Tuesday in 4Q 1996
 ×Bill volume was 40% above average; coupon volume was 149% above average
 ×Morning volume was 132% above average; afternoon was 80% above average

Comments
Today continues to break the records.  In addition to record overnight and
morning volume, today's total volume by the close will break the $139.4 bln
record made on March 26, 1997, the day after the Fed tightened.  (See Page 9
for list of top ten volume days.)  Like the morning, 2-yr trading dominated
the afternoon.  By 1pm, 2-yr volume had exceeded the $14 bln record for an
entire day; this was on January 10, 1997 after the employment data.  By 3pm,
$16.8 bln 2-yrs had traded, more than triple the volume on recent Tuesdays.
The $13.3 bln 5-yrs was also a record and was more than double recent levels.
For more information call GovPX(212)693-1200, Maureen Mooney(x209)
10/28 15:34 EST Today is Top Volume Day, Breaking $139.4 bln Record on 3/26.
```

```
14:34  RTRS-Reuters mark Eurobond new issue index
14:32  RTRS-Greece sets 300 million mark 10-year FRN
14:30  RTRS-GREECE SETS 300 MLN MARK 10-YEAR FRN, 6M LIBOR +35 BP, AT 100.30 -LEHMAN
14:25  RTRS-Reuters dollar Eurobond new issue index
14:24  RTRS Pera Financial prices $350 mln 5 year bond
14:
14: 14:34  07 Oct  RTRS-Reuters mark Eurobond new issue index
14: (Click on the Z-code in brackets to access data for an issue)
14:LAUNCH AMT BORROWER / COUPON / MATURITY / ISSUE PRICE
14:OCT.28 1BN DEUTSCHE HYPO 4.75 PCT 2001 AT 99.095....[nFLLFAS00V]
13:OCT.27 207 NETIA 11.0 PCT 2007 AT 65.198.................<Z3HV>
13:OCT.23 250 ARBED (CONVERTIBLE) 3.25 PCT 2004 AT PAR......<Z3GO>
10:OCT.23 200 SUNNAMERICA INST FUNDING FRN 2002 99.99.......<Z3GJ>
10:OCT.23 150 KEPCO (FRN) 2002 AT 99.775....................<Z3FU>
09:OCT.23 500 CAJA MADRID (FRN) 2002 AT 100.068.............<Z3GF>
15:OCT.21 500 PSK 5.25 PCT 2002 AT 101.99....................<Z3DU>
14:OCT.21 1BN EIB 5.25 PCT APRIL 2004 AT 100.471............<Z3DV>
00:OCT.20 500 SUEDWESTLB UNIT 5.5 PCT 2004 AT 101.71.........<Z3DG>
08:OCT.20 500 BCO BOZANO 8.25 PCT 2005 AT 101.475...........<Z3CO>
   OCT.17 300 TUB FINANCE 5.375 PCT 2002 AT 101.46..........<Z3CH>
   OCT.16 1.5B TURKEY 8.125 PCT 2007 AT 100.625.............<Z33V>
```

These screens show that huge sums of money are involved in issuing and trading debt instruments. Before considering why governments and corporations issue so much debt, a look at the following statistics to put the amounts into perspective.

- At the end of March 1999 the total outstanding UK central government marketable sterling debt (including official holdings by government) is estimated to be £300 billion. *Her Majesty's Treasury: Debt Management Report 1999–2000, March 1999*

- At the end of March 1999 the amount of US Public Debt was $5.6 trillion of which nearly 60% was marketable. *US Treasury: Monthly Statement of the Public Debt March 1999*

The US national debt is displayed in real time in New York City's Time Square.

- In 1998, $768 billion equivalent of international bonds were issued by corporations, governments and international agencies. *International Securities Market Association (ISMA) Annual Report 1998*

- For 1998, the turnover for US dollar denominated Eurobonds of all types was $12,259 billion. *International Securities Market Association (ISMA) Annual Report 1998*

Recognise that an investor acquires a financial **asset** when purchasing a debt instrument. There are always two ways of looking at the instrument – from the perspective of the **issuer**, or **borrower**, and from that of the **investor**, or **lender**.

Government Bonds

Governments usually spend more money in running their countries than they receive in revenue from taxes. To finance this deficit governments sell debt instruments – these are often called **Treasury securities**. Every year governments need to borrow money for new requirements and to repay loans that are **maturing** – reaching the end of the fixed period for the loan.

In order to raise the money required, governments issue marketable bonds and notes. The difference between these instruments is usually only a matter of maturity period – **bonds** are usually **long-term** (more than ten years) whereas **notes** are usually **medium-term** (one to ten years).

In their simplest forms bonds and notes are **IOUs** for a **principal amount** of loan made by investors to the government for a specified period of time – maturity period. The loan is repaid in full on maturity. For the privilege of lending the money, investors receive **interest** of a fixed or floating amount known as the **coupon payment**. The coupon is usually paid at specified intervals – annually or semi-annually.

Investors are willing to buy government-issued instruments because they are considered to be free from default **risk** (discussed later in this section), that is, the government can always meet its obligations even if it has to raise taxes to pay interest payments or repay loans. Thus, government instruments have a **high credit rating** (credit ratings are reviewed in detail in *Section 6, Trading in Bond Markets*), and a lower rate of return. It is worth noting that not all governments have the same credit rating. For example, US, UK and German bonds have high credit ratings whereas instruments issued by developing country governments may not be so high. This is because these latter governments do not have the same ability to back their debt.

In general the bonds and notes issued by a government have the highest credit rating for the denomination of that country.

Once issued, a government's debt instruments can be bought and sold freely in the bond markets worldwide. The process is summarised in the diagram below.

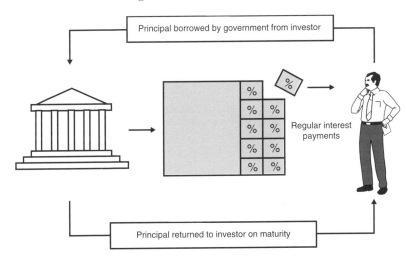

Below is a table showing some countries' bond credit ratings.

Country	Bond Credit Rating
Australia	Aa2
Brazil	B2
China	A3
France	Aaa
Germany	Aaa
Hong Kong	A3
Japan	Aa1
India	Ba2
Russia	B3
Singapore	Aa1
United Kingdom	Aaa
United States	Aaa

Source: Moody's Investors Service Ratings, June 1999

Corporate Bonds

In principle, once a bond or note has been issued by a corporation, then it functions in exactly the same way as an instrument issued by a government. The instruments can be bought and sold freely as they are negotiable instruments.

However, corporations do not have to use the bond markets exclusively to raise funds – they can also use the equity markets.

There are fundamental differences between the bond and equity markets from both the issuers' and investors' perspectives. By issuing equity, an organisation is selling part of itself. Investors holding shares own a part of the organisation and they will expect a reward if it is profitable. An organisation issuing debt is raising a loan, and will have to repay the loan in full, with interest, over a set period. Investors typically know how much interest they will receive and that their initial investment will be repaid.

Corporate bonds generally pay a higher rate of interest than government bonds because they are considered to be a riskier investment, that is, the investor relies on the corporation's ability to repay the debt, which depends upon its profitability. However, the risk in equity is greater still, as bond holders are paid before stockholders if a corporation goes into liquidation.

The daily volume of bond trading is very difficult to estimate owing to the diverse nature of trading and reporting methods. For example, the International Securities Market Association (ISMA) reported that the average daily turnover in the Eurobond and related markets in the week to July 1, 1999 was $267.2 billion. The daily volume of turnover traded through GOVPX in the news item at the beginning of the section was over $70 billion – the true figure was probably much greater as this figure only records trades from GOVPX contributors.

As you will see, the capital markets are very innovative and the distinctions among the money, bond and equity markets may not be quite as clear as you may think. For example, swap derivatives involving debt instruments can span the money and bond markets, and hybrid instruments such as equity-linked debt instruments exist. (For more information, see *An Introduction to Derivatives*, in this series.)

In reality the capital markets diagram illustrated previously looks more like this.

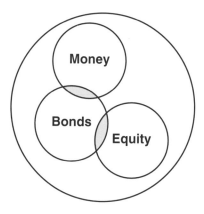

Before moving on, look at the following table summarising the main features of bonds and equity instruments.

Bonds	Equity
• Defined lifetime	• Shared ownership, assets and profits
• Maturity date	• Variable dividend
• Normally pays a known rate of interest	• Normally voting rights
• Negotiable	• Negotiable

Risk and Return

There is a direct relationship between risk and return for both issuers and investors. Investors in equities are taking a high risk by putting their money into part ownership of an organisation. They expect a high return, either through the growth in value of their shares, or through the dividend paid on the shares, or both. On the other hand the organisation may not make a profit, in which case no dividend may be paid. The organisation may under-perform in which case the value of its shares may fall rather than rise. Worst of all the organisation may collapse leaving the investors with a worthless investment.

Investors in the bond market are looking for more security. They will lend money to a government or large international company, reasonably secure in the knowledge that the organisation will exist for the term of the loan and will not default on its debt. In return for this security, investors are willing to accept a return on their investment which is lower than they might get from higher risk investments such as equities. The lesser the level of risk, the lower the return the investor requires as compensation to that risk.

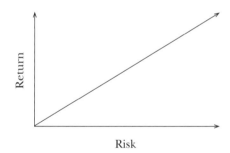

You have now seen the risks and rewards from the investor's perspective – now try the following activity and look at matters from the issuer's point of view.

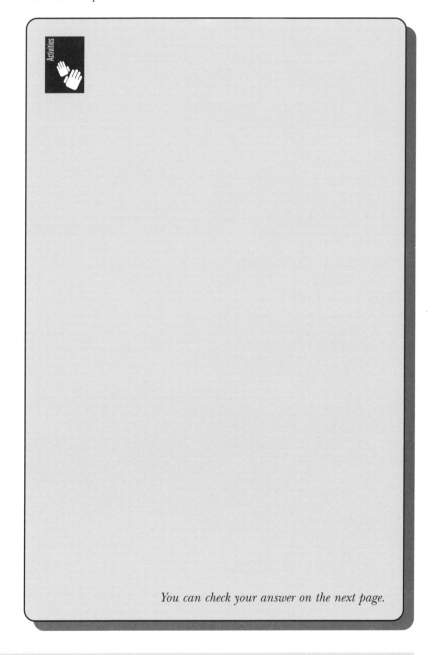

You can check your answer on the next page.

Why Do Bond Markets Exist?

You may have listed many reasons in your responses, however the key issues are outlined here:

 Imagine you are the financial director of a large company. You need to raise capital for a major project. List as many reasons as you can why you might decide to issue equity rather than bonds.

Your list may have included the following reasons:

- To dilute the risk of owning the organisation by sharing ownership.

- To raise risk capital which does not need to be repaid and does not require a fixed rate of interest to be paid at regular intervals.

Who Needs Bond Markets?

Different organisations need to borrow money for different purposes and for different lengths of time. As you have seen, the financial markets provide a range of instruments for short to long-term borrowing. As has already been mentioned, this book is only concerned with the bond markets – who uses them and why?

There are three main types of market-player involved in the bond markets who are briefly described here and in more detail in *Section 6, Trading in Bond Markets*. These market-players are:

- Issuers

- Investors

- Intermediaries

Issuers

Organisations that have sufficient security and creditworthiness to attract investors issue debt. Investors need to feel confident that their money is safe, that they will be paid the interest due to them and that their principal will be repaid at the end of the loan.

The four main categories of issuers are identified in the table below:

Category	Examples
• Banks and other financial institutions	Australian & New Zealand Bank, Banque Paribas
• Corporations	General Electric Company, ICI, Glaxo, Siemens, Ford, GM, Toyota, Hyundai
• Governments and quasi-government bodies	UK Treasury, Federal National Mortgage Association (FannieMae), City of Vienna, Kingdom of Sweden
• Supranational organisations	European Investment Bank, World Bank, Council of Europe

REUTERS

Firms issue bonds rather than borrow money using negotiable loans because:

- The sums of money raised in the bond market are usually larger than a single bank would be prepared to lend – often the loan runs into billions of dollars

- The borrowers are usually looking for the most competitive finance rates, which are not always available from banks

- They may wish to borrow over a longer period of time than a bank is prepared to lend. For example, to support long term investment plans

- Money can be raised **quickly** in the bond market – sometimes within 24 hours

Investors

These market players lend capital for the issue. As a reward for the use of their money, investors expect to receive regular interest payments throughout the loan period and they expect the loan to be repaid at a specified date in the future. As you have seen the amount of reward is closely linked with the amount of risk taken.

There are two main types of investor you will need to know something about:

- Institutions

- Individuals

Institutions, including mutual funds, pension funds, life assurance companies, insurance companies and savings institutions are the biggest investors in the bond markets, holding some 80% of the market. These institutions have fund managers who look after large sums on behalf of individual investors, who are indirectly investing in the bond market through the purchase of, for example, life insurance policies or pensions. High net worth individuals may invest directly in bonds to obtain a guaranteed income from their investment.

But how do issuers, who are raising capital, meet the investors, who are looking for a safe and profitable return on their investment?

Why Do Bond Markets Exist?

Intermediaries

In the bond markets, **intermediaries** – the merchant banks, investment banks, brokers, market makers, financial advisers – match buyers and sellers to ensure a transaction that is beneficial to all parties, including themselves. The intermediaries are also responsible for managing the whole process of issuing and trading bonds.

The market-players in the bond markets are illustrated in the diagram below.

Issuers borrow money from investors

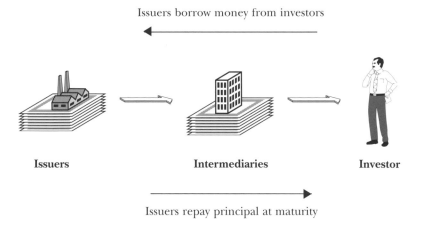

Issuers   **Intermediaries**   **Investor**

Issuers repay principal at maturity

Primary and Secondary Markets

The issuance of new debt instruments to raise funds is called the **primary market**. Once debt is issued in the form of a bond or note the instrument can then be traded – bought and sold – in the **secondary market**. These markets are described later in more detail in *Section 4*.

The largest part of debt markets activity is concerned with trading issued instruments in the secondary markets. In 1998, ISMA reported that new issues of Eurobonds and international bonds reached the 1,000 billion equivalent, but trading in the secondary markets exceeded $60,000,000,000,000 – $60,000 billion!

Trading in the secondary markets

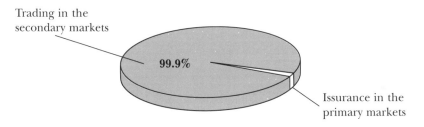

99.9%

Issurance in the primary markets

Source: ISMA Annual Report 1998

But where does trading take place? Where are the market places? Most of the trading in the primary and secondary markets takes place **Over-The-Counter (OTC)**. Deals are conducted by telephone or electronically using quote screens such as those provided by Reuters or other services. However some corporate and government bonds that are issued in their domestic markets and which are listed on stock exchanges such as the **London Stock Exchange (LSE)** and **New York Stock Exchange (NYSE)** are traded in the same way as stocks and shares on those exchanges.

Before moving on, try the following activity.

List at least two reasons why an organisation may decide to issue bonds rather than equity.

You can check your answer on the next page.

What Is a Bond?

A **Bond** is an agreement in which an issuer is required to repay to the investor the amount borrowed plus interest over a specified period of time. A bond is in effect an IOU which can be bought and sold.

If you invest in a bond, then you are **lending** money; if you issue a bond, then you are **borrowing** money. In its simplest form, a bond has four components that identify it. These components are:

- **Issuer**
  The organisation responsible for ensuring that interest and principal payments are made to bondholders, usually via a paying agent.

- **Principal**
  The amount denominated in a specific currency that the issuer wishes to borrow and agrees to repay the investor.

- **Coupon**
  The rate of interest the issuer agrees to pay the investor. This can be for a **fixed** amount as a percentage of the face value of the bond or as a **floating rate** relative to an index such as the **London Interbank Offer Rate (LIBOR)**. The frequency of the interest rate payments is usually on an annual or semi-annual basis.

- **Maturity**
  The date on which the issuer of a bond must repay the principal due and the final interest rate payment.

REUTERS

An Introduction to Bond Markets 21

Why Do Bond Markets Exist?

You may have listed many reasons in your responses; however the key issues are outlined here:

List at least two reasons why an organisation may decide to issue bonds rather than equity.

- Bonds may be a cheaper source of money than issuing equity since, as a relatively safe, low risk investment, investors do not expect as high a return as from an equity investment. Therefore the organisation may pay out less in interest than dividends.

- Bonds do not involve diluting the ownership of the company. The issue of debt does not confer any rights of ownership, such as voting rights, or a share in the company profits.

- Many bond issuers do not have a choice. They are not in the position to issue equity because the equity is not theirs to sell. For example, governments and nationalised industries cannot issue equity.

- It is faster to issue bonds than equity.

- The organisation can match the period of their debt to their funding requirements.

The Reuters screens below show details for a typical government and supranational bond.

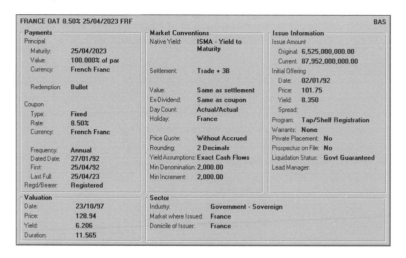

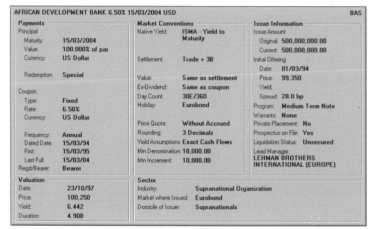

You have also been introduced to debt instruments known as **notes**. In principal there is no difference in dealing with bonds and notes – the differentiation comes from the term, or time to maturity of the instrument. In general bonds are long-term and notes are medium-term, however, different debt markets have different conventions for medium- and long-term as you will see in *Section 3*.

REUTERS

The simplest form of bond is known as a **straight** – European term – or a **bullet** – US term. Occasionally this type of bond is also known as a **plain vanilla**.

A straight or bullet bond can be imagined to be a series of future cash flows over the term of the bond.

Example

You buy a bond with a face value of $1 million maturing in five years. The bond has a coupon of 10% paid annually. The cash flow over the life of your bond looks like this:

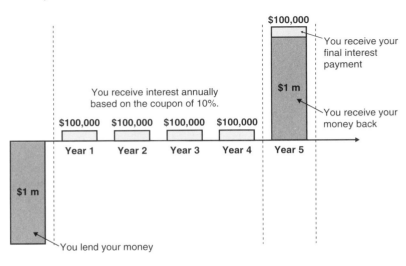

This is an example of a bearer bond and its coupons – whoever presents the coupon will receive the interest payment

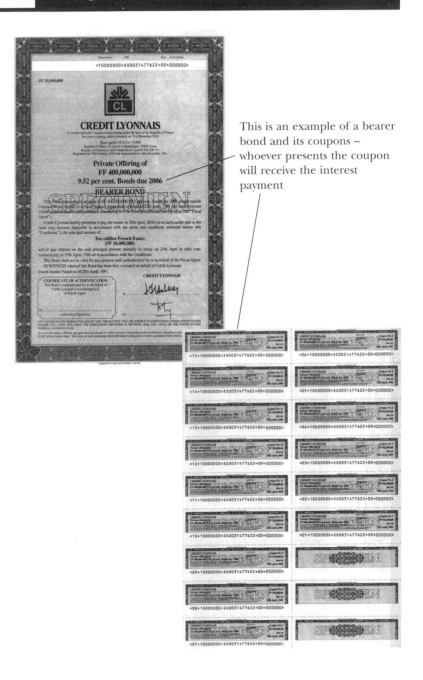

You may find it helpful to remember this simple cash flow diagram when you consider some of the calculations associated with bond valuation later in this book.

Summary

You have now finished the first section of the book and you should have a clear understanding of the following:

- The meaning of the term bond in the context of the capital markets

- The relationship among the money, bond and equity markets, their purposes and uses

- The relationship between risk and return and how bonds and equity are positioned with respect to them

- An overview of bond markets players and the primary and secondary markets in which they operate

- An overview of the components of a debt instrument, that is, a bond

As a check on your understanding you should try the Quick Quiz Questions on the next page. You may also find the Overview Section to be a helpful learning tool.

The Reuters screens below illustrate new headlines and a story about the US corporate bond market.

15:05	LDA<LUDZs.WA> plans new convertible bond issue
14:48	FOCUS-Russian borrowers delay Eurobonds in crisis
14:47	RTRS-LDA<LUDZs.WA> plans new convertible bond issue
14:46	RTRS-US corp bond primary market remains in disarray
14:42	Lithuania delays DM eurobond plans until early '98
14:41	RTRS-La CGIP émet 2,0 mds FF sur 5 an à 5,7% - SocGen
14:41	RTRS-IPO PRICING - American Residential <INV.N> at $15
14:39	RTRS-Jewett Cameron <JCT.TO> announcement/issuer bid
14:38	RTRS-IPO PRICING - Casella Waste <CWST.O> at $18
14:38	RTRS-IPO PRICING - Beringer Wine <BERW.O> at $26
14:32	RTRS-Oman stocks dip 0.8 pct, escape turmoil abroad
14:28	RTRS-IPO PRICING - Tropical Sportswear <TSIC.O> at $12
14:28	RTRS-Pioneer <PHB.N> sets $92.50/shr price in auction
14:25	RTRS-Reuters French franc Eurobond new issue index
14:24	RTRS-Royal Bank<RY.TO> announcement/debenture/note swap
14:23	RTRS-CGIP sets 2.0 billion FFR five-year bond
14:23	RTRS-IPO PRICING - ZymeTx Inc <ZMTX.O> at $8
14:23	RTRS-CGIP EMET 2,0 MDS FF SUR 5 ANS, REOFFERT A 99,94, +65 PDB - SOCGEN
14:21	RTRS-IPO PRICING - Metromedia Fiber <MFNX.O> at $16
14:20	RTRS-CGIP SETS 2.0 BLN FFR FIVE-YEAR BOND, 5.7 PCT, 99.94 REOFFER, +65 BP-

14:46 29 Oct   RTRS-US corp bond primary market remains in disarray

NEW YORK, Oct 29 (Reuters) - A major correction in the U.S. corporate bond market has left issuers and underwriters scrambling to assess price levels and demand for new issues, syndicate officials said.

As of Wednesday morning, no investment-grade deals were expected for the day. But that could easily change if calm returned to the Treasury and stock markets, they said.

"Life is coming back, but it won't take much to snuff it out," said one investment-grade syndicate official. "There are companies looking for levels in the market. But if you see a big rally or decline, they will just wait it out."

For related news, double click on one of the following codes:
[E] [U] [D] [T] [NAT] [MNI] [TEL] [US] [USC] [DBT] [MUNI] [ISU] [EUB] [LEN] [RTRS] [US/CORP]

Wednesday, 29 October 1997 14:46:08
RTRS [nN29347383]
MORE

Quick Quiz Questions

1. If an organisation issues bonds, the bond holders will normally have the right to vote at the organisation's annual general meeting.
   - ☐ a) True
   - ☐ b) False

2. Six months after a bond has been issued in which market would it normally be trading?
   - ☐ a) Primary
   - ☐ b) Secondary

3. In which of the following markets is a 10-year public bond issued?
   - ☐ a) Money market
   - ☐ b) Equity market
   - ☐ c) Debt market
   - ☐ d) Private placement market

4. What is the difference between an issuer and a borrower?
   - ☐ a) A borrower raises capital while the issuer underwrites
   - ☐ b) A borrower raises capital loaned by the issuer
   - ☐ c) None

5. If an organisation wished to borrow money for 6 months it would use the debt markets.
   - ☐ a) True
   - ☐ b) False

6. Which of the following statements is **not** true?
   - ☐ a) A bond is traded in the primary market
   - ☐ b) A bond usually has a fixed maturity date
   - ☐ c) A bond pays a known rate of interest called a coupon
   - ☐ d) A bond holder is entitled to a share of the issuing organisation's profits

7. List the four categories of organisations issuing debt.

8. What might an investor have to sacrifice in order to have the most secure type of investment?

9. What kind of trading dominates the debt markets?

You can check your answers on page 27.

Overview

The Capital Markets

- **The Capital Markets**

Money Markets	Bond Markets	Equity Markets
Short-term debt	Medium- to long-term Non-permanent funding	Long-term Permanent funding
0 1		
	Years	

- **Types of Debt Instruments**

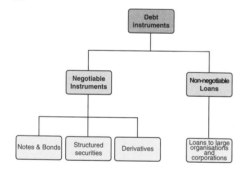

- **The Bond Markets**

The **Bond Markets** deal in financial instruments such as bonds and notes which represent loans to large organisations who investors believe will be able to honour their obligations to repay the loan and any interest payments due. This market is most commonly referred to as the **bond market.**

Government and Corporate Bonds

- **Government Bonds**

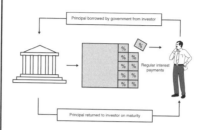

- **Bonds and Equity**

Bonds	Equity
• Defined lifetime	• Shared ownership, assets and profits
• Maturity date	• Variable dividend
• Normally pays a known rate of interest	• Normally voting rights
• Negotiable	• Negotiable

Why Do Bond Markets Exist?

What Is a Bond?

A **Bond** is an agreement in which an issuer is required to repay to the investor the amount borrowed plus interest over a specified period of time. A bond is in effect an IOU which can be bought and sold.

- **Issuer**
- **Principal**
- **Coupon**
- **Maturity**

Who Needs Bond Markets?

- **Issuers**
  - Banks and other financial institutions
  - Corporations
  - Governments & quasi-government bodies
  - Supranational organisations
- **Intermediaries**

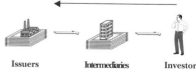

Issuers borrow money from investors

Issuers repay principal at maturity

- **Investors**
  - Institutions
  - Individuals

Primary and Secondary Markets

Secondary market accounts for 99.9% of trading in debt instruments

99.9%

Quick Quiz Answers

	✓ or ✗
1. b)	☐
2. b)	☐
3. c)	☐
4. c)	☐
5. b)	☐
6. d)	☐
7. Banks	☐
Corporations	☐
Governments	☐
Supranationals	☐
8. The return on the investment – the greater the level of security the less the return	☐
9. Over-The-Counter, OTC	☐

How well did you score? You should have scored at least 9. If you didn't, review the materials again.

Further Resources

Books

Getting Started in Bonds
Sharon Saltzgiver Wright, John Wiley & Sons, Inc., 1999
ISBN   0 471 32377 2

Forbes Guide to the Markets: Becoming a Savvy Investor
Marc M. Groz, John Wiley & Sons, Inc., 1999
ISBN   0 471 24658 1

The Reuters Guide to World Bond Markets
Martin Essex and Ruth Pitchford (Reuters Limited), John Wiley & Sons, Inc., 1996
ISBN   0 471 96046 2

All About Bond Funds
Werner Renberg, John Wiley & Sons, Inc., 1995
ISBN   0 471 31195 2

Investor's Chronicles: Beginner's Guide to Investment
Bernard Gray, Business Books Ltd., 2nd Edition 1993
ISBN   0 712 66026 7

A-Z of International Finance
Stephen Mahony, FT Pitman Pub., 1997
ISBN   0 273 62552 7

The Bond Market: Trading and Risk Management
Christina I. Ray, Irwin Professional Press, 1992
ISBN   1 556 23289 6

International Bond Markets
David H. Gowland, Routledge, 1991
ISBN   0 415 03504 X

Why Do Bond Markets Exist?

Publications

International Securities Market Association (ISMA)
- Annual Report 1998

Bank for International Settlements (BIS)
- The Development of the International Bond Market
  BIS Economic Papers No. 32, 1992

Her Majesty's Treasury
- Debt Management Report 1999–2000

US Treasury
- Monthly Statement of the Public Debt March 1999

Internet

RFT Web Site
- http://ww.wiley-rft.reuters.com

This is the series' companion web site where additional quiz questions, updated screens and other information may be found.

ISMA
- http://www.ISMA.org

The International Securities Market Association (ISMA) is the self-regulatory organisation and trade association for the international securities market.

The ISMA Centre – the Business School for Financial Markets @ The University of Reading, UK
- http://www.ismacentre.reading.ac.uk
  e-mail: admin@ismacentre.reading.ac.uk

The ISMA Centre is the only business school in Europe specialising in securities and investment. It is supported by the International Securities Market Association based in Zurich, the trade association and market regulator for the international bond (Eurobond) market. The Centre opened a new $5 million building in 1998 financed by ISMA with a 30 position, Reuters 3000 dealing room provided by Reuters. The Centre runs BSc, MSc, PhD, MBA (from 2001), Diploma and executive courses in all areas of securities and investment.

Exchanges

Refer to the back of this book for a listing of worldwide stock exchange contact information and web sites.

REUTERS

This section of the book should take about $1\frac{1}{2}$ hours of study time. You may not take as long as this or you may take a little longer – remember your learning is individual to you.

Annual income twenty pounds, annual expenditure nineteen nineteen six, result happiness. Annual income twenty pounds, annual expenditure twenty pounds ought and six, result misery.

Mr Micawber – 'David Copperfield', Charles Dickens (1812–1870)

Introduction

You should now have a clear understanding of the reasons for and the position of the bond market as part of the long-term capital markets. You should also know a bit about the issuers, investors and intermediaries – the market players. This section expands on the different elements of the bond market and how they operate. In particular this section is concerned with:

- An overview of the elements of the bond markets – government, sovereign and corporate bonds

- Domestic bond markets – government securities and corporate issues

- International bond markets – foreign bonds, eurobonds, dragon bonds and global bonds

The Reuters screens to the right show an overall guide to the global bond markets, with a more detailed index each for the US Treasury, corporate, and Eurobond markets.

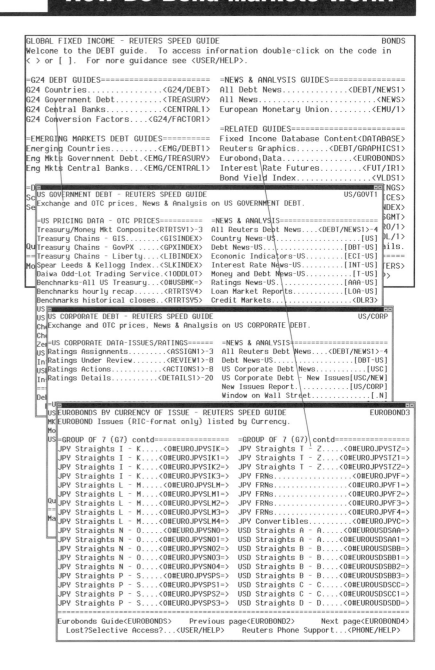

Elements of Bond Markets

It is important to realise that there is not a single, unified bond market. The bond markets are multifaceted with many types of instruments, market players and market places. To simplify matters to some extent, the following diagram illustrates the main elements of the bond markets. Some of the elements have already been mentioned in *Section 1* but are further explained in this section.

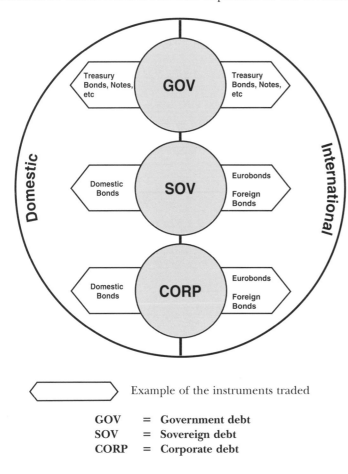

Example of the instruments traded

GOV   =   **Government debt**
SOV   =   **Sovereign debt**
CORP =   **Corporate debt**

Government Bonds

Government debt forms one of the most important elements of the bond markets. All governments raise money in the domestic bond markets to finance national schemes and major development programs – some governments, such as the UK or the US, have been raising money this way for centuries.

Some of the most famous financial scandals have occurred as the result of the national debt of one country or another. One of the best known financial collapses is the **"South Sea Bubble"** which resulted in huge losses for some investors unfortunate enough to be left with outstanding loans when the South Sea Company collapsed. The company was founded in 1711 and some time later offered to take on the UK government debt of nearly £10 millions for an interest rate of 6% per annum for a certain period. More and more stock was issued, based on false aspirations, until in 1720 the "bubble" burst entailing huge losses for most investors. However, some investors, including the company directors and influential government officials made huge profits!

Once issued, government bonds are traded in both the domestic and international markets – these are explained later. Different governments name their debt instruments in different ways – you will come across Treasury Stocks, Treasury Gilts, Treasury Bonds and Treasury Notes. In the market places, government debt instruments have simple names or abbreviations, for example, **Gilts** (UK), **T-Bonds** (US), **Bunds** (German), **OATs** (French) and **JGBs** (Japanese) – all these instruments are described later.

Sovereign Bonds

Governments and government-backed agencies use the bond market to raise money in the following ways:

- Government-backed agencies, for example, local authorities, states, municipalities and supranational organisations, can issue and trade bonds in any currency including that of the issuer

- Central government bonds can be issued in any other currency other than that of the issuer

Corporate Bonds

Corporations raise money using both the domestic and international bond markets. Within this element international banks and financial institutions now account for a considerable amount of issued debt.

It is difficult to quantify precisely the market share for these main elements within the bond markets. This is because there are different ways of trading the different types of instruments; however, the chart below indicates the position for international securities issued in 1997 as reported by the **Bank for International Settlements (BIS)**, a central banking institution that provides specialised services to central banks around the world.

All types of debt are traded in the **domestic bond market** of the country of issue. In this case, the debt instruments are issued in the domestic currency of the country of origin.

The **international bond markets**, as you might expect, deal with bonds issued by organisations in one country in the currency and territory of another. International debt is raised mainly by issuing **foreign bond** (bonds issued on the domestic capital market of another country) or **eurobonds** (bonds underwritten by international syndicates issued in more than one country simultaneously and outside any of the countries' jurisdiction).

Domestic and international bond markets are now dealt with in a little more detail.

This is an example of a bond issued in London by a Japanese organisation denominated in US dollars

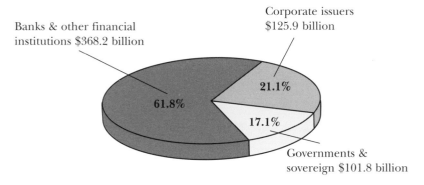

Banks & other financial institutions $368.2 billion

Corporate issuers $125.9 billion

61.8%

21.1%

17.1%

Governments & sovereign $101.8 billion

Source: BIS 1998

Domestic Bond Markets

The domestic debt market of any country comprises buying and selling debt instruments of two main types:

- Government securities

- Corporate issues

Domestic bonds are issued by borrowers in their home market in their own domestic currency. These bonds are regulated by the government of the country of issue and subject to domestic withholding tax (WHT) regulations. Examples of domestic bond issuers are Abbey National issuing a bond in sterling in the UK or General Motors raising US dollars in the US domestic markets. Corporates also issue debt in their domestic markets, but they are more likely to use the international or Eurobond markets today due to their flexibility.

The most important and liquid domestic debt markets are those in government securities. As you have already seen, government security bonds have various names in the markets – the full names are indicated in the table below.

Country	Name
United States	US Treasuries (T-Bonds, T-Notes)
United Kingdom	UK Treasuries (Gilts)
Japan	Japanese Government Bonds (JGBs)
France	Obligations Assimilable du Trésor (OATs)
Germany	Bundesrepublik bonds (Bunds)
Italy	Buoni del Tesoro Poliennali (BTPs)

Government Securities

 Government Securities are issued by sovereign states denominated in their own currency. The instruments are issued to raise capital to finance government projects, to repay maturing debt, and to pay interest on existing debt.

The Government securities market is both large and important as a benchmark against which other bonds are priced. In terms of nominal amounts of bonds outstanding, the US government bond market is the largest worldwide. In the Euro-zone fixed income markets, Italy dominates. The chart below indicates the total government debt outstanding in 1998 for each of the countries in the EMU.

The potential euro area – total government debt outstanding in 1998

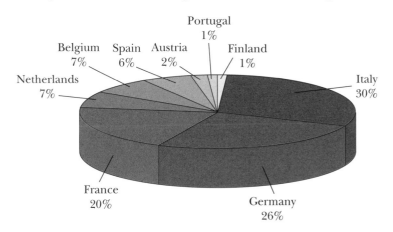

Source: Futures & OTC World, July 1999

Traditionally, most government bonds were issued as "conventional" types such as **straights**, **Forward Rate Notes (FRNs)** etc which are described in more detail later. However, more recently, with the globalisation of financial markets trading taking place 24 hours a day, changes have been necessary to ensure liquidity and attractiveness to investors and stability in bond trading for many different governments.

There are a number of important developments that have taken place since the 1980s which have affected bond trading for many of the major governments. They include:

- Repo markets
- Stripping bonds
- European Monetary Union (EMU)
- Index-linked or inflation-indexed bonds

Repo Markets

Within the financial markets, market players need to finance their activities using loans. As with most financial loans, lenders require collateral – security – for the loan.

A **Repurchase Agreement (Repo)** is an agreement for the **sale** of an instrument with the simultaneous agreement by the seller to **repurchase** the instrument at an agreed future date and agreed price.

A **Reverse Repurchase Agreement (Reverse Repo)** is an agreement for the **purchase** of an instrument with the simultaneous agreement by the seller to **resell** the instrument at an agreed future date and agreed price.

A repo is a sale and repurchase agreement which can use almost any asset as collateral; however, government-issued instruments such as T-Bonds and T-Bills are most often used because of the credit worthiness of the issues. FRNs, Certificates of Deposit (CDs) and Commercial Paper (CP) are also used for repos.

In a repo, Dealer **A** sells instruments to Dealer **B** with an obligation to repurchase equivalent instruments from B at an agreed future date. Dealer B now holds the instruments but has the obligation to deliver equivalent instruments to A at the agreed future date.

The interest rate implied by the difference between the sale and purchase price is known as the **repo rate**. If Dealer A uses a repo as a means to raise capital, the repo rate is in effect the cost of the loan.

The following diagrams illustrate the process of using a repo.

First Leg – The Sale

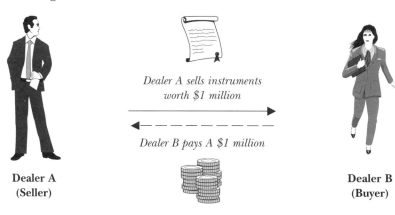

Dealer A now has $1 million for delivering the instruments worth $1 million to Dealer B.

Second Leg – The Repurchase

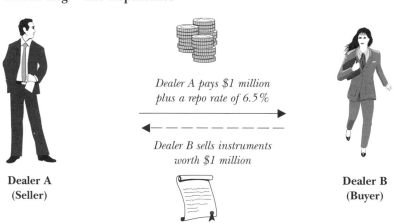

Dealer B has earned 6.5% interest on the repo.

In a **reverse repo** Dealer A agrees to buy the instruments and re-sell them back to Dealer B at an agreed price at an agreed future date.

How Do Bond Markets Work?

Repo transactions are often used by central banks as a means of monetary control. For example, in the US the largest repo market involves trading T-Bills **overnight** which spans the closing and opening times of the money markets. When the Fed uses a repo it is initially buying T-Bills to temporarily add cash to the money markets. A reverse repo is where the Fed sells T-Bills to the money markets to drain money from the system. Consider the Fed as Dealer B in the previous diagrams.

In the UK ,the Gilt repo market is relatively new and trading overnight has been used to profit when the return for longer maturity periods is higher. For example, funds are borrowed overnight on repo, the transaction is rolled over on a daily basis and the funds are lent for a week or longer. The market player thus profits from the higher rates for one week over the overnight Repo rate. In the UK, the Global Master Repurchase Agreement (GMRA) establishes what type of interest bearing instrument can be used for repos and allows dealers to substitute eligible instruments.

Dealers now run books in repos and reverse repos hoping to match counterparties and make a profitable spread in the middle. In effect this means the dealer is acting in a similar way to a bank – lending money for instruments on one side and taking deposits on the other side. Counterparties to repos are typically:

- Central banks

- Pension funds

- Insurance funds

- Large corporations

The repo market formalises to some extent the use of interest bearing instruments – particularly government bonds – as collateral for loans. In some cases, dealers use the cash raised on existing bonds to buy more bonds. In other cases dealers may have sold bonds they do not actually possess and use the tepo markets to borrow the bonds they require for cash. Repos can resemble futures contracts in that dealers can open and close large financial positions without involving too much of their capital.

The Reuters screens below show the overnight to 3-month US Treasury repo rates, as well as repo rates for other government bonds.

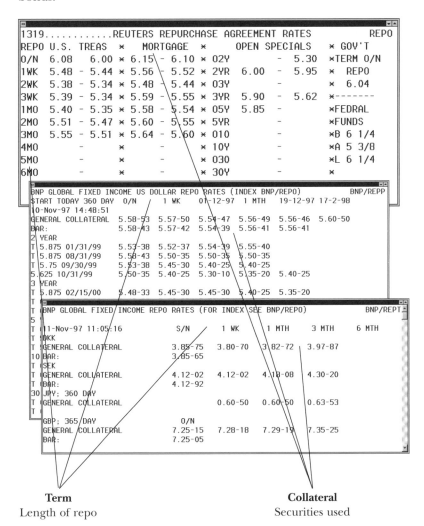

Term
Length of repo

Collateral
Securities used

REUTERS

Stripping Bonds

A stripped bond is one in which a conventional bond with coupons is separated into its component cash flows. This means that each payment of coupon and principal becomes a separate bond maturing on its particular date. The stripped bond therefore becomes a series of **zero-coupon bonds** which can be traded in their own right. Both zero-coupon and stripped bonds are described in more detail later in this book.

Stripped securities were originated in the late 1970s and early 1980s by US brokers and dealers but were not available from government issuers such as the Fed until 1985 when the Fed created the **Separate Trading of Registered Interest and Principal of Securities (STRIPS)** program which was intended to reduce the cost of funding the public debt by helping market activities. France introduced stripped government bonds in 1991, Belgium and the Netherlands in 1992, and Germany, Spain and the UK in 1997.

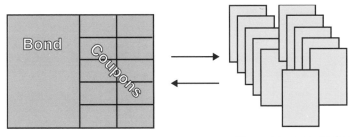

Zero-coupon strips

European Monetary Union (EMU)

The effects of EMU and the euro on the money and bond markets will be far reaching, particularly for those countries in the union. EMU does have a profound effect on how these countries' banking operations and monetary policies function, which will ultimately go hand in hand with the evolution of the eurobond market itself, both with respect to the government and corporate issues. When the euro was launched in January 1999, various structural aspects of the EMU were in place:

- The European Central Bank (ECB) is responsible for setting monetary policy for participating member states. The European System of Central Banks (ESCB) comprises the ECB and the national central banks. The ECB manages short-term debt for the member states, resulting in an integrated money market for the member states. The primary tool is repurchase agreements (refer to page 35, for a detailed explanation of repurchase agreement instruments).

- Within the participating member states' debt markets changes have taken place (referred to as harmonisation) involving the nominal value of the debt which was redenominated into euro as well as trading conventions. These more standardised procedures will lead to reduced costs in these markets over the long run. The potential size of the euro bond market is such that it will be second to the US bond market and may even surpass it. At the very least, the euro bond market should provide investors with a more comparable alternative to the US bond market.

- Governments issuing debt are likely to be rated according to their foreign currency ratings rather than according to their local currency ratings which are often AAA, the highest rating available. Debt issued in Euros is likely to be considered as a foreign currency obligation.

Index-linked or Inflation-indexed Bonds

The UK introduced index-linked bonds in 1981 when it issued bonds where both interest and principal payments were adjusted to reflect changes in the Retail Price Index (RPI). More recently, the US government issued inflation-indexed bonds linked to the Consumer Price Index for all Urban consumers (CPI-U). These types of bonds are described in more detail in *Section 3*.

This Reuters screen shows US Treasury Inflation-Indexed Note details.

```
┌─────────────────────────────────────────────────────────────┐
│12:30 20OCT97    U.S. Treasury Inflation-Indexed Notes US18742        TIPS1 │
│                                                              │
│        TREASURY 10-YEAR INFLATION-PROTECTION SECURITY        │
│        SERIES:                       A-2007                   │
│        CUSIP:                        9128272M3                │
│        DATED DATE:                   January 15, 1997        │
│        ORIGINAL ISSUE DATE:          February 6, 1997        │
│        ADDITIONAL ISSUE DATE:        April  15, 1997         │
│        MATURITY DATE:                January 15, 2007        │
│        Ref CPI on DATED DATE:               158.43548        │
│                                                              │
│                                                              │
│        CPI-U (NSA) July '97                 160.5            │
│        CPI-U (NSA) August '97               160.8            │
│        CPI-U (NSA) September '97            161.2            │
│                                                              │
│xx Note- Issue Pricing Available on Page <RTRTSY2> and RIC <US9128272M3=RR> xx │
│                                                              │
│        Treasury 10-year Inflation-Protection Auction Summary:│
│DATE   BILLION   MATURITY   COUPON   PRICE   AVG YLD    BID RANGE │
│04/08   8.00     01/15/07   3.375    98.307   3.590    3.450 - 3.650 │
│                                                              │
│       xxx See page <TIPS4> for 5-Year TIPS information xxx    │
│                                                              │
│              xxxx  CONTINUED ON PAGE <TIPS2>  xxxx           │
└─────────────────────────────────────────────────────────────┘
```

To help you better understand this important section of the markets, some of the key features of the following government debt instruments are summarised:

- US Treasuries

- UK Gilts

- French Government Securities

- German Government Securities

- Japanese Government Bonds

US Treasuries

The US government is by far the single largest issuer of debt in the world – as of March 1999, the US national debt exceeded $5.6 trillion. US government instruments are of the highest quality and therefore the lowest risk of government instruments, making this market the most liquid in the world with a daily turnover of approximately $100 billion. Investors in US Treasuries are worldwide and include foreign governments, international banks, pension funds, multinational corporations and insurance companies.

US treasuries are classified by name according to their maturity period **at the time of issue**. There are three types of instrument:

- **Treasury Bonds (T-Bonds)**
  These have original maturities of 10 – 30 years with fixed coupons paid annually. At maturity the principal is repaid as a single 'bullet' – hence the name previously referred to in *Section 1*.

- **Treasury Notes (T-Notes)**
  These are identical in structure to T-Bonds except their original maturity is between 1 – 10 years.

- **Treasury Bills (T-Bills)**
  These are discount instruments with original maturities of 12 months or less. These instruments are discussed more fully in *An Introduction to Foreign Exchange and Money Markets*.

US Treasury bonds and notes are sold by the **Federal Reserve System (The Fed)** on a regular basis using an **auction yield** system. The most recently issued instruments in each maturity are called **on-the-runs** and account for most of the trading activity. Currently, the auctions take place as follows:

- 2- and 5-year notes are issued on a monthly basis

- 3- and 10-year notes are usually announced in the first week of February, May (except 30-year bonds), August and November and auctioned in the second week of those months

- 30-year bonds are auctioned in the first week of February and August

At these auctions, bids are accepted on a **competitive** and **non-competitive** basis. Non-competitive bids are those where the investor will pay whatever the final auction price is set at and these are allocated first. The remainder of the bonds or notes are allocated to **primary dealers** (those select dealers authorized to deal in new issues of government bonds on a competitive basis – at the **lowest cost to the US Treasury**.

T-Bonds and T-Notes are held in a computerised **book-entry** form, the primary dealers which in turn is linked to the Fed. It is also possible for an investor to be issued a **registered** bond as a certificate.

Most T-Bonds and T-Notes are denominated in minimum sizes of $1 million, although it is possible to trade instruments with a face value as small as $1000.

T-Bonds and T-Notes are priced as a percentage of the face value in increment of thirty-seconds. For very liquid bonds, the price may be quoted in sixty-fourths of a percent to $^1/_{256}$ of a percent.

A price of 98−28 means $98^{28}/_{32}\%$ which is 98.875% or 0.98875.

A price of 98−28+ means $98^{28}/_{32} + {}^1/_{64} = 98^{57}/_{64}\%$. As a decimal this is 98.890625%.

Interest that accrues on T-Bonds and T-Notes is calculated on the actual number of days elapsed over the actual length of the coupon period – this is written as **Actual/Actual**. Interest is paid **semi-annually**. Although US Treasuries are listed on the NYSE, most trading is OTC.

In 1985 the Fed created the Separate Trading of Registered Interest and Principal of Securities (STRIPS) program and in early 1997 the US Treasury auctioned its first inflation-indexed bonds.

Summary of US Treasuries	
Types	T-Bonds and T-Notes
Maturities	1–30 years
Coupon	Semi-annual
Issued by	Federal Reserve Bank. Auctioned by Federal Reserve Bank of New York. Auction yield system – competitive and non-competitive
Primary market	Primary dealers
Listing	NYSE
Price	Percentage of face value in thirty-seconds of a percent
Forms of issue	Book entry and registered certificate
Tax	No withholding taxes
Accrued interest	Actual/Actual
Repo market	Yes
STRIPS programme	Yes

How Do Bond Markets Work?

The Reuters screens below show the exchange and OTC prices for US Treasuries, and closing T-Bond prices.

These Reuters screens give detailed data for the US T-Bond due in 2007, including an illustration of the price changes.

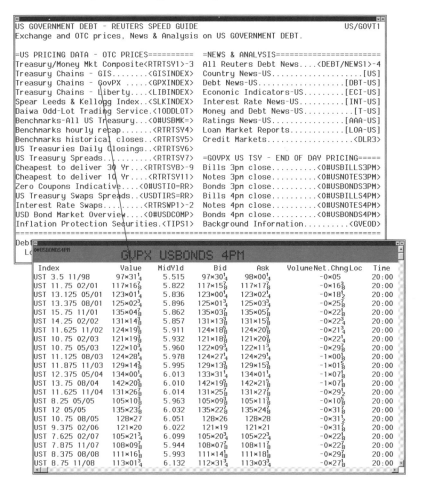

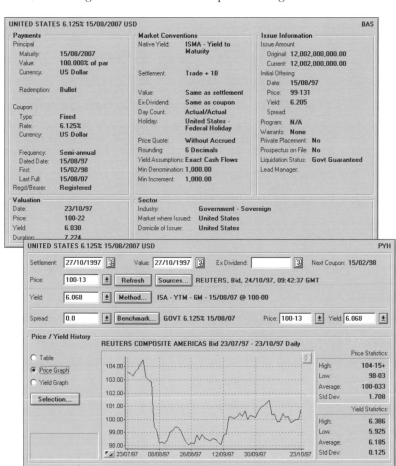

UK Gilts

Gilts are marketable securities issued by the UK government for borrowing money. The term Gilts is short for **Gilt-edged securities** which is a name the instruments acquired for their reputation as one of the safest investments. Originally the instruments were edged in gold leaf – hence the name. Gilts are issued with names such as **Exchequer, Treasury** and **Funding Stock** although the names have little significance now.

Unlike US Treasuries, UK Gilts are classified according to the **number of years remaining to redemption** not on the number of years specified at issue. There are three classes:

- **Short-dated** – 7 years or less to maturity

- **Medium-dated** – Over 7 but less than 15 years to maturity

- **Long-dated** – 15 years or more to maturity

Most Gilts pay fixed semi-annual coupons and are repaid in full at maturity in a bullet repayment. Gilts are issued in sterling and ECUs.

A Bank of England bearer bond of 1790 showing the total interest to be paid at 3% per annum

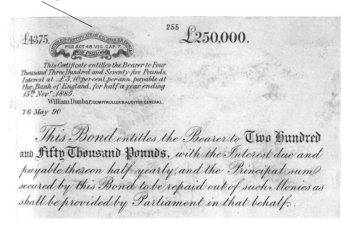

The UK government issues other types of Gilts, the amount issued is small in relation to the total market. These types of Gilts include:

- **Convertibles**
  These are short-dated bonds which offer the holder the option to convert every nominal £100 into a pre-determined nominal value of a longer dated bond, usually with a lower coupon, at a specified future date.

- **Dual dated**
  These bonds may be redeemed, at the government's option, between two redemption dates. In other words the government has the option to repay the loan earlier than the scheduled maturity date.

- **Index-linked**
  Bonds of this type have coupon interest payments and redemption proceeds linked to the Retail Price Index (RPI).

- **Undated**
  Some bond issues in the past have had no redemption date. This type of Gilt only pays a steady stream of interest payments – no capital is repaid.

Gilts usually have a minimum denomination of £1000 and are normally in registered form recorded electronically by the **Gilts Central Office (GCO)** at the Bank of England, which pays the coupons directly. Since it takes time to organise these coupon payments, Gilts go **ex-dividend** about a month before the next coupon date. Once this has happened, any buyer of a Gilt is not entitled to receive the coupon payment – the original holder will receive it. In this case the buyer has to be compensated and this is reflected in the price paid for the bond.

Most new Gilts are issued by the Bank of England under an **auction price** system where investors can bid on a competitive or non-competitive basis. Gilts are allocated to the highest competitive bidders whereas non-competitive bidders are allocated Gilts on an average price system.

How Do Bond Markets Work?

The UK auction system for competitive bids works in a similar way to the US system, such that **Gilt Edged Market Makers (GEMMs)** act as intermediaries in the primary market. The GEMMs are expected to bid on a competitive basis at auctions and are required to make continuous and effective two-way prices in all Gilts – straights, index-linked, FRNs, etc.

The GEMMs are also supported by a small number of **InterDealer Brokers (IDBs)**. These IDBs provide dealing facilities in gilts between the GEMMs which enables them to cover positions arising from their activities in the conventional and repo markets. IDB activity also includes interdealer broking on a wide range of instruments including:

- Repo borrowing/lending transactions in the same instruments

- Options on Gilts

- Exchange traded derivative instruments relating to Gilts

If circumstances dictate, the Bank of England can also sell **tranches** (different maturities) of existing Gilts or **taps** of new issues directly to the GEMMs without using the auction system.

In the past the Bank of England dealt almost exclusively with a small number of **discount houses** when auctioning Gilts. This is no longer the case and the Bank's counterparties now includes commercial banks, investment banks and building societies.

Gilts are priced in the same way as US Treasuries – in thirty-seconds of a percent of the face value. The basis for calculating accrued interest is on the actual number of days elapsed in a 365 day year – **Actual/365**. However, there are proposals to change the pricing system to a decimal percentage of face value – 0.01% and to change the basis for calculating accrued interest to Actual/Actual. Gilts are listed on the LSE but most trading occurs OTC.

There is now an active Gilt repo market and UK gilt strippable bonds were introduced in 1997.

Summary of UK Gilts	
Types	Fixed coupon, convertible, index-linked, dual dated, undated
Maturities	1–20+ years
Coupon	Semi-annual
Issued by	Bank of England Auction price system – competitive and non-competitive
Primary market	GEMMs supported by IDBs
Listing	LSE
Price	Percentage of face value in thirty-seconds
Forms of issue	Book entry and registered by GCO – although some bonds can be transferred to bearer form
Tax	Income, accrued interest and capital gains for traders
Accrued interest	Actual/365
Repo market	Yes
STRIPS programme	Yes

Below are Reuters screens showing the UK Government Speed Guide summary, with additional detail on OTC Gilt benchmark prices.

These Reuters screens show of a UK government benchmark 10-year bond, with detailed price and historical data.

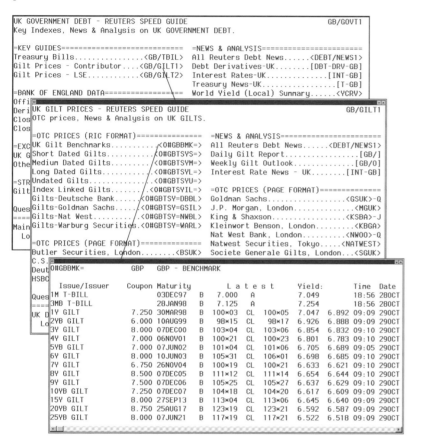

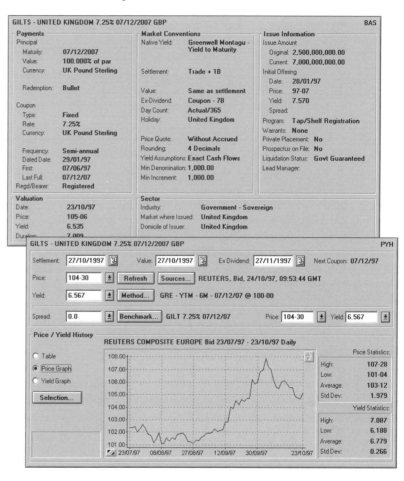

French Government Securities

The Bank of France issues bearer bonds and notes on behalf of the French government on a bid price auction system. The longer-term instruments issued are:

- **Bons du Trésor à Taux Fixe et à Interêt Annuel – BTANs**
  These are fixed-rate, medium-term, coupon-bearing instruments with 2 – 5 years' maturity from issue

- **Obligations Assimilable du Trésor – OATs**
  These are long-term bonds with maturities of 6–30 years from issue. The bonds are also **fungible**. This means that within a given year new bonds with the same maturity are issued as additional tranches to existing bonds. OATs can have fixed or floating coupons.

For both BTANs and OATs coupons are paid annually and the repayment of principal is in bullet form.

BTANs and OATs are auctioned on a monthly basis using a competitive auction system where primary dealers, brokers and other intermediaries bid on an equal footing.

The minimum denomination for BTANs is FF 1 million and OATs is FF 50 millions. Both instruments are quoted as a percentage of the face value to the nearest 0.01%.

The method for calculating accrued interest is **Actual/Actual**. However, the unique feature of the French market is that interest accrues from the **trade** date not the settlement date.

Summary of French Government Securities	
Types	BTANs and OATs
Maturities	2–30 years
Coupon	Annual
Issued by	Bank of France Auction price system – competitive
Primary market	Primary dealers, brokers, intermediaries
Listing	Paris Bourse for OATs
Price	Percentage of face value – 0.01%
Forms of issue	Bearer held by Cedel/Euroclear
Tax	No withholding tax for non-residents
Accrued interest	Actual/Actual
Repo market	Yes
STRIPS programme	Yes

Below are Reuters screens showing French government bond exchange and OTC prices and OTC benchmark prices.

These Reuters screens show of a French government benchmark 5-year bond, with detailed price and historical data.

```
FRENCH GOVERNMENT DEBT - REUTERS SPEED GUIDE               FR/GOVT1
Exchange and OTC Prices, News & Analysis on FRENCH GOVERNMENT DEBT.

=GOVT BONDS-OTC PRICES(RIC FORMAT)=====  =NEWS & ANALYSIS=====================
Government Bond Benchmarks...<O#FRBMK=>  All Reuters Debt News......<DEBT/NEWS1>
BTFs.......................<O#FRTSYS=>   Debt Derivatives-France....[DBT-DRV-FR]
BTANs......................<O#FRTSYM=>   Interest Rates News-France.....[INT-FR]
OATs.......................<O#FRTSYL=>   Money and Debt News-France......[T-FR]
BTANs and OATs-SVT Prices....<O#FRTSY=>  Today's Main Economic News.[GLANCE/FEA]
                                         Govt Bond Spreads (Europe)....[GVD/SPR]
=GOVERNMENT BOND GUIDES===============
BTANs/BTFs..................<FR/BTAN>    =TREASURY AUCTION ANNOUNCEMENTS=======
OATs........................<FR/OAT>     Auction Results/Calendars..<TRESORMENU>
French Government Loans.....<O#ETAT=PA>
General SVTs Chains.........<FR/GOVT2>
Government Bond Futures....<FR/OAT/FUT>
Government Bond Warrants......<FR/WT$5>
French Repos................<FR/REPO1>
French indices............<FR/INDICES4>


Questions/Comments: Please call French Help Desk on 01 42 21 54 55
=========================================================================
Debt Guide <BONDS>      French Debt Guide<FR/DEBT>      More Govt Debt<FR/GOVT2>
   Lost?Selective Access?...<USER/HELP>      Reuters Phone Support...<PHONE/HELP>
```

```
O#FRBMK=       FRF   FRF - BENCHMARK

   Issue/Issuer   Coupon Maturity     L a t e s t    Yield:        Time  Date
ON DEPOSIT                        B   3.320  A   3.430  3.320  3.430 07:25 29OCT
1M BTF              27NOV97  B  99.740  A  99.740  3.380  3.340 09:25 29OCT
3MB BTF             29JAN98  B  99.120  A  99.130  3.500  3.460 09:24 29OCT
6M BTF              07MAY98  B  98.090  A  98.110  3.700  3.660 09:26 29OCT
1YB BTF             03SEP98  B  96.760  A  96.800  3.920  3.870 09:25 29OCT
2YB BTAN    7.000   12NOV99  B 104.860  A 104.860  4.447  4.445 09:28 29OCT
3Y BTAN     7.000   12OCT00  B 106.080  A 106.170  4.740  4.710 09:28 29OCT
4Y BTAN     5.500   12OCT01  B 101.910  A 102.010  4.955  4.925 09:28 29OCT
5YB BTAN    4.500   12JUL02  B  97.730  A  97.850  5.050  5.020 09:28 29OCT
6Y OAT      6.750   25OCT03  B 107.690  A 107.850  5.218  5.188 09:28 29OCT
7Y OAT      6.750   25OCT04  B 107.870  A 107.970  5.367  5.350 09:28 29OCT
8Y OAT      7.750   25OCT05  B 114.510  A 114.560  5.457  5.450 09:29 29OCT
9Y OAT      6.500   25OCT06  B 106.530  A 106.680  5.556  5.535 09:29 29OCT
10YB OAT    5.500   25OCT07  B  98.810  A  98.910  5.659  5.645 09:29 29OCT
15YB OAT    6.500   25APR11  B 106.300  A 106.500  5.808  5.787 09:29 29OCT
20YB OAT    8.500   25OCT19  B 128.030  A 128.250  6.142  6.126 09:28 29OCT
30YB OAT    6.000   25OCT25  B  96.720  A  96.920  6.251  6.235 09:29 29OCT
```

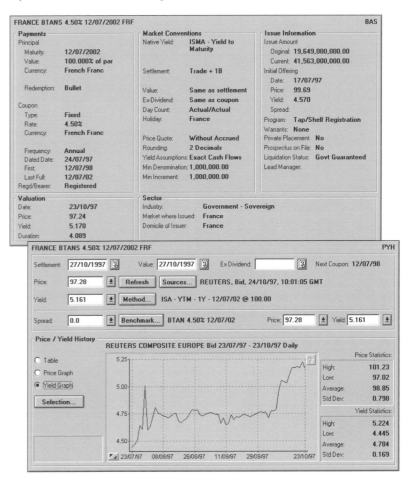

German Government Securities

■ **Deutsche Bundesbank** The German government issues a wide range of bonds on behalf of the federal government and its agencies.

Federal government bonds are known as **Bundesanleihen** or **Bunds** usually having a maturity of 10 years, although maturities from 6 – 30 years are possible. The federal government also guarantees bonds from its many agencies including:

- The Federal Railway – Bundesbahn

- The Federal Post Office – Bundespost

- The German Development Fund – Treuhand

The Bundesbank, the German central bank, issues bearer bonds on behalf of the federal government which have an annual coupon and a bullet redemption payment.

The federal government also issues medium-term notes known as **Bundesobligationen (Bobls),** and until mid-1995, federal treasury notes known as **Bundesschatzanweisungen (Schätze)**. These notes have maturities of 5 and 4 years respectively.

There are a variety of ways in which German government instruments are sold. Bunds are normally issued every month although there is no definite schedule. The method of issue uses a bid price system which takes place in two tranches.

- The **first tranche** has fixed terms indicating the issue price. A syndicate known as the **Federal Bonds Consortium**, headed by the Bundesbank, are allocated a fixed percentage of the issue. The Bundesbank retains up to 25% of the issue for day-to-day market intervention to control the government's monetary policy.

- The **second tranche** is auctioned the following day with price bids made via the syndicate group. Bids in this auction are on a competitive and non-competitive basis as used by other governments.

Both Bunds and Bobls are listed on all German stock exchanges. Although trading on the Frankfurt Stock Exchange is the most active for exchange trading, the majority of Bund and Bobl trading is OTC.

All German bonds are quoted as a percentage of face value to the nearest 0.01%. The minimum denomination for Bunds is 1000 deutschemarks and for Bobls is 100 deutschemarks. However, OTC trading for both instruments usually involves 5 million deutschemarks. The accrued interest for coupons is paid on a **30 European/360** basis. In this convention every month has 30 days and a year is therefore 360 days. The 30E means that **no** interest accrues on the 31st of any month.

Summary of German Government Securities	
Types	Bunds, Bobls, Schätze etc
Maturities	4–30 years; Bunds usually 10 years
Coupon	Annual
Issued by	Bundesbank
Primary market	Underwritten by Consortium and price bid auction
Listing	All German stock exchanges – Frankfurt most active
Price	Percentage of face value – 0.01%
Forms of issue	Bearer
Tax	30% on coupon
Accrued interest	30 European/360
Repo market	Not domestic but traded overseas
STRIPS programme	Yes

Below are Reuters screens showing the German government debt exchange and OTC prices and news headlines, with detail on benchmark OTC bonds.

These screens show a German government benchmark 30-year bond, with detailed pricing and historical data.

```
GERMAN GOVERNMENT DEBT - REUTERS SPEED GUIDE            DE/GOVT1
Exchange and OTC Prices, News & Analysis on GERMAN GOVERNMENT DEBT.

=OTC PRICES=========================    =NEWS & ANALYSIS=======================
Government Bond Benchmarks...<O#DEBMK=>  All Reuters Debt News......<DEBT/NEWS1>
German Government Bonds......<O#DETSY=>   Money and Debt News-Germany......[T-DE]
German Bunds-Short Term.....<O#DETSYS=>  D-Mark Bond Analysis.............[DE/I]
German Bunds-Medium Term....<O#DETSYM=>
German Bunds-Long Term......<O#DETSYL=>  =EXCHANGE PRICES=======================
List of Contributors.....<DE/GOVT/OTC1>  Bundesanleihe-Frankfurt......<O#DEBA=F>
=CENTRAL BANK=======================      Bundesanleihe-Dusseldorf.....<O#DEBA=D>
Bundesbank Index...........<BUNDESBANK>  Bundesobligation-Dusseldorf.<O#DEBO=D>
Lombard Rate..................<BBK04>    Bundesobligation-Frankfurt...<O#DEBO=F>
Bundesbank(Reuter-reported)....<BUBA01>  IBIS Bonds-Agency/Treasury..<O#BOND=IB>
=SEMI GOVT/AGENCY GUIDES=============     Schatz(Shot-Term)-Dusseldorf.<O#DEBS=D>
Landeranleihen/Staatsbank<DE/GOVT/SEMI>  Schatz(Short-Term)-Frankfurt.<O#DEBS=F>
Agency...................<DE/GOVT/AGEN>  Treuhand Bunds-Dusseldorf....<O#DETR=D>
=FUTURES===========================       Treuhand Bunds-Frankfurt.....<O#DETR=F>
German Government Bonds...<DE/GOVT/FUT>   Treuhand Obligs-Dusseldorf...<O#DETO=D>
Futures & Options Exchanges.<DE/FUTEX>   Treuhand Obligs-Frankfurt....<O#DETO=F>
=STRIPS===========================
Bunds Strip Data..........<DE/STRIPS1>

Debt Guide<BONDS>   German Debt Guide<DE/DEBT>   More Government Debt<DE/GOVT2>
  Lost?Selective Access?...<USER/HELP>    Reuters Phone Support...<PHONE/HELP>
```

```
O#DEBMK=        DEM   DEM - BENCHMARK

  Issue/Issuer    Coupon Maturity        L a t e s t     Yield:        Time Date
ON DEPOSIT                          B   3.380  A   3.500  3.380  3.500 09:28 29OCT
1M DEPOSIT                          B   3.400  A   3.500  3.400  3.500 08:49 29OCT
2M DEPOSIT                          B   3.460  A   3.560  3.460  3.560 09:29 29OCT
3M DEPOSIT                          B   3.580  A   3.680  3.580  3.680 09:29 29OCT
6M DEPOSIT                          B   3.720  A   3.820  3.720  3.820 09:29 29OCT
1Y DEPOSIT                          B   4.000  A   4.100  4.000  4.100 09:29 29OCT
2Y BUND SCHATZ  4.000 17SEP99       B  99.450  A  99.510  4.307  4.273 09:35 29OCT
3Y BRD OBL S.117 5.125 21NOV00      B 100.960  A 101.020  4.777  4.756 09:36 29OCT
4Y BUND BRD     8.250 20SEP01       B 111.290  A 111.320  4.973  4.965 09:35 29OCT
5Y BUND BRD     7.250 21OCT02       B 108.940  A 108.980  5.162  5.153 09:35 29OCT
6Y BUND BRD     6.000 15SEP03       B 103.600  A 103.680  5.267  5.251 09:35 29OCT
7Y              7.500 09SEP04       B 111.520  A 111.600  5.436  5.423 09:35 29OCT
8Y BUND ANL     6.500 14OCT05       B 106.000  A 106.080  5.545  5.532 09:35 29OCT
9Y BUND ANL     6.250 26APR06       B 104.340  A 104.380  5.587  5.581 09:35 29OCT
10YB BUND ANL   6.000 04JUL07       B 102.470  A 102.530  5.651  5.643 09:36 29OCT
20Y BUND BRD    6.000 20JUN16       B  99.240  A  99.340  6.065  6.056 09:35 29OCT
30YB BUND ANL   6.500 04JUL27       B 103.300  A 103.400  6.250  6.242 09:35 29OCT
```

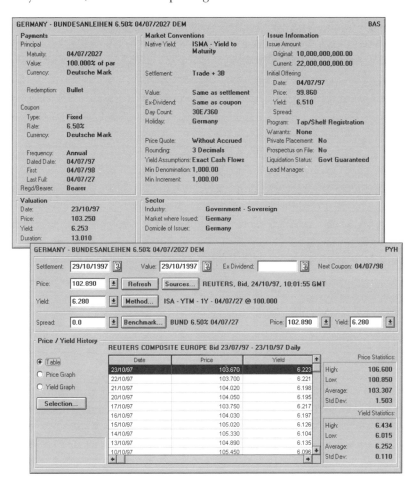

How Do Bond Markets Work?

Japanese Government Bonds

The Japanese Government issues a variety of medium- and long-term bonds (JGBs) including:

- **Medium-term bonds**
  These include 2-, 3- and 4-year instruments which are issued by competitive auction and have a fixed coupon. There are also 5 year discount instruments which are issued via a syndicate.

- **Long-term bonds**
  The most frequently issued long-term bond is for 10 years although 6- and 20-year bonds are sometimes issued. These bonds have a semi-annual fixed coupon and are issued via a syndicate.

Two methods of issuance are used in Japan:

- **Syndicate**

- **Public auction**

The syndicate method involves a syndicate of approximately 2000 banks, securities houses and other financial institutions. The system is best illustrated using 10-year JGBs as an example. The Ministry of Finance (MOF) negotiates with the syndicate for a coupon rate and amount of loan to be issued. An auction is then held by MOF for members of the syndicate in which 60% of the issue is auctioned on a price bid competitive basis. The remaining 40% is underwritten by the syndicate members according to their allocation based on an average price of the competitive auction. There is no obligation on the syndicate members to make a market in the bonds.

For public auctions, MOF invites a large number of investors to submit bids based on terms set by MOF. The procedure is as follows:

- MOF issues notices of invitation via the Bank of Japan

- The market players submit their bids and amounts to the Bank of Japan

- MOF decides the amounts of bonds for each market player

Government bonds are listed on all the Japanese stock exchanges such as the Tokyo Stock Exchange, but about 98% of all bond trading is OTC.

The normal denomination for a JGB is ¥100,000 and the price is quoted as a percentage of face value to the nearest 0.01%. JGBs are subject to a withholding tax and are either in registered or bearer form. Over 97% of bonds are registered with the Bank of Japan. The accrual of interest is based on an Actual/365 or Actual/365+1 basis.

Summary of Japanese Government Bonds	
Types	Medium- and long-term JGBs
Maturities	2–20 years
Coupon	Semi-annual
Issued by	Ministry of Finance Syndicate or auction – bids by price
Primary market	Primary dealers supported by IDBs and brokers
Listing	All Japanese stock exchanges – Tokyo most active
Price	Percentage of face value – 0.01%
Forms of issue	Registered or bearer
Tax	Withholding tax
Accrued interest	Actual/365 or Actual/365+1
Repo market	Gensaki in Japan – also traded overseas
STRIPS programme	No

REUTERS

Below are Reuters screens showing the Japanese government debt exchange and OTC prices and news headlines, with detail on benchmark OTC prices.

These screens show a Japanese government benchmark 10-year bond, with detailed pricing and historical data.

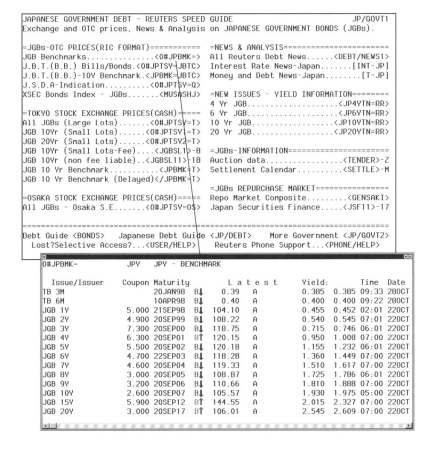

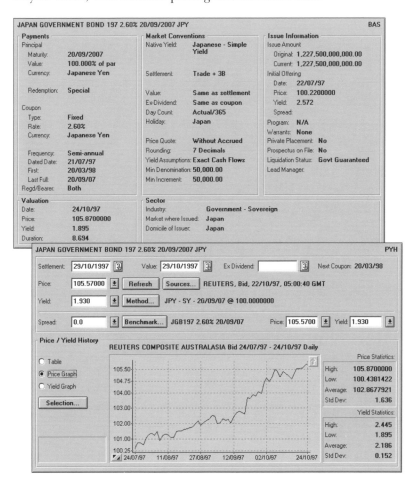

These Reuters screens show prices and yield curves for the benchmark (most actively traded) bonds for the US, UK, France, Japan and Germany.

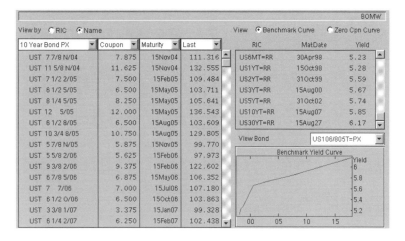

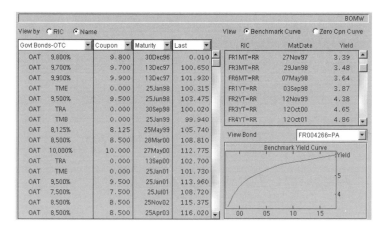

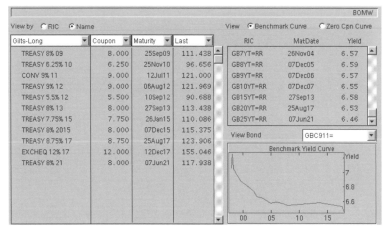

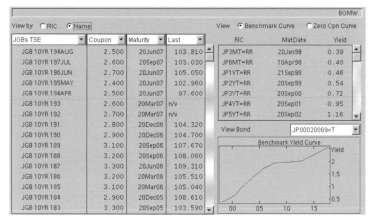

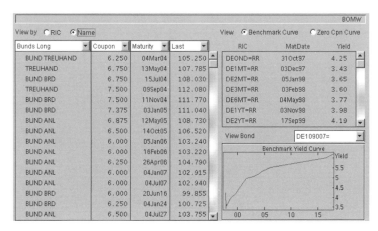

Corporate Issues

Corporate Issues are instruments issued by domestic organisations in the domestic currency. They are usually issued by a syndicate of domestic banks.

As you have seen, although both governments and corporates need to raise funds, the types of instruments used by commercial organisations may differ from those issued by governments. For example, corporate debt can be linked to its equity but governments do not have shares to sell in their countries.

Originally the domestic markets were where corporations sought to raise money by issuing stocks or shares, borrowing from banks via non-negotiable loans or by issuing debt as marketable **loan securities** or bonds.

Corporate bonds offer different risks and rewards over government issues. Investors have to be persuaded to lend money based on the creditworthiness and market expectations of the corporation concerned. Most corporate issues in the domestic markets involve a **syndicate** of domestic banks. The **lead manager** of this syndicate is appointed by the issuer. The process of issuing a bond is described in more detail in *Section 4*.

Most corporate issues involve a **trust deed** that is administered by an independent trustee. The various terms associated with issuing a bond with which you should be familiar are described in the following text. Be aware that some of the terms have different meanings in the UK and US markets.

Do you know the meaning of the following terms in the context of corporate bonds? Write down your ideas here.

- Debenture

- Zero coupon

- Convertibles

Turn to the next page to find the definition of these terms.

Debentures – Secured/Unsecured Risk

In money markets, including the UK, Australia and NZ a debenture is an acknowledgement of a debt and describes the amount which is **secured** by the assets of a corporation. The debenture can be split into units and traded on an exchange or OTC as **debenture stocks**.

Debentures usually pay semi-annual fixed coupons as a percentage of the face value and holders receive a certificate of ownership. Debentures are loans secured by fixed and/or floating charges usually based on the corporation's property or financial assets.

- **Fixed charge debentures** specify which assets the corporation is unable to dispose of. If the corporation goes into liquidation, then these assets are sold to repay the debenture.

- **Floating charge debentures** cover all the assets of the corporation. If the corporation goes into liquidation, then all the assets are sold to repay the debenture.

The distinction between these debentures is important as the type determines what priority the holder has if the corporation goes into liquidation. The order for settling claims is as follows:

1. Fixed charge debentures
2. Preferential creditors such as the government for taxes etc
3. Floating charge debentures
4. Unsecured creditors

In the US, bonds such as these are known as **collateral** or **collateral trust bonds**. In the US, **debenture bonds** are **not secured** against specific fixed or floating assets. In the UK this type of bond is known as an **unsecured loan stock**.

Guaranteed Bonds

These are **unsecured** bonds that are guaranteed by a third party, usually the parent corporation of the issuer or another organisation in the same group as the issuing corporation.

Subordinated Bonds

These are **unsecured loan stocks** subordinated to other debt. In the event of liquidation these instruments are paid after the more "senior" debts have been settled.

Floating Rate Notes (FRNs)

These are instruments which do not have fixed rate coupons but instead pay coupons at specified periods based on an index such as LIBOR.

Zero-coupon Bonds

As the name implies, these bonds neither have a coupon nor pay interest. In effect the holder receives the interest when buying the bond because it is issued at a deep discount to its face value. Maturity periods for zero-coupon bonds are usually 5 – 10 years. The issuer benefits by not having to pay interest over the maturity period but receives annual tax relief for the notional interest payments. Investors must have sufficient confidence that the corporation will be in existence at the maturity date to buy this kind of bond.

Convertibles

If a corporation issues equity as well as debt, then it is able to issue secured or unsecured debt instruments that can **convert** part or all of the debt into equity. This is effectively a call option at a specified strike price.

Usually the bond holder has the option to convert the debt, at specified times, into ordinary or preference shares of the issuing corporation at pre-stated prices. The terms of the bond usually set out the permitted number of shares for conversion, which is in proportion to the amount loaned by the investor.

This guaranteed rate of conversion is how investors hope to profit. They hope the conversion price will be lower than the future share price so that they can buy low/sell high. This potential for profit allows issuers to offer conversion instruments at a lower rate than a straight bond.

Summary of Domestic Bond Markets

Government Securities

- Money is raised for:
  - financing budget deficits
  - repaying maturing debt
  - paying interest on existing debt

- Bonds and notes are issued in domestic currency

- Most instruments are issued using an auction system and involve primary dealers for the issue in the primary market

- Government securities are the highest quality instruments issued in a country and are therefore generally used as a **benchmarks** for other bonds in that currency

- Markets in government securities are well regulated and usually very liquid

- The securities are often listed and traded on the domestic stock exchange/s but the majority of trading is OTC

- There are well established conventions for issuing, pricing, coupon payments and repayments at maturity for government securities

- The largest single government securities market worldwide is that for US Treasuries

Corporate Issues

- Domestic bonds are issued in the domestic currency by domestic corporations using a syndicate of domestic banks

- There are many different types of instruments available including bullets, FRNs, convertibles, zero-coupon etc

- Domestic markets are usually overshadowed by trading in government bonds and Eurobonds denominated in the domestic currency

- Domestic markets are well regulated governing trading and tax matters

- Corporate bonds are generally listed and traded on the domestic stock exchange/s but there are also large OTC markets

- Within the domestic markets the creditworthiness of the issuer is usually better understood than in the international markets, but the domestic markets may not be suitable for a large issue

- Coupon payments usually use the same frequency as for the domestic government securities

- The largest single domestic corporate market worldwide is that for the US

How Do Bond Markets Work?

International Bond Markets

In essence, the domestic markets are well regulated markets where bonds are issued in the domestic currency and subject to the tax laws of that country.

For many organisations wishing to raise funds, the domestic markets are too restrictive in terms of market size, regulations and taxation. In order to overcome these restrictions there has been a rapid growth in the international markets since the 1960s.

There are four main types of international bonds issued by corporations, governments, sovereigns and supranationals. These are:

- Foreign bonds

- Eurobonds

- Dragon bonds

- Global bonds

Historically, foreign bonds were the first international bonds to be issued but Eurobonds are now the most important in terms of size of the market and turnover per annum. These markets are segmented by risk. For example, even though Eurobonds are not secured, many are rated AAA or AA, while many foreign bonds are rated only A.

Foreign Bonds

 Foreign Bonds are issued by foreign borrowers in a domestic market denominated in that market's own currency. Issuing these bonds is regulated by the domestic market authorities.

These are debt instruments issued by foreign borrowers into a domestic market, in that market's own currency. For example, if Unilever issues a bond in the German market, denominated in Deutschemarks, then it would be classed a **foreign** bond.

Issuing foreign bonds has been a less popular means of raising finance for organisations than the Eurobond market for a number of years now. This has been due mainly to the tax and other restrictions imposed by national governments in the country of origin. However some governments, particularly the US have recently taken a less restrictive stance on foreign bonds in order to maximise on the enormous source of potential revenue.

The markets are regulated by the domestic authority, and the issues are given appropriate names reflecting their market. For example, IBM issuing in the Japanese domestic market is known as a **Samurai**, whereas British Gas issuing in the US domestic market is known as a **Yankee**. One of the largest foreign bond markets is the Yankee market, in which non-US issuers issue bonds according to US domestic regulations, in US dollars, mainly in New York.

Foreign bonds tend to be more strictly regulated than Eurobonds, as domestic bonds tend to be closely supervised by the country's regulatory authorities. The following table indicates the market names for some of the more important foreign bonds.

Market of Issue	Currency	Market Name
US	USD	Yankee
UK	GBP	Bulldog
Japan	JPY	Samurai
Spain	ESP	Matador

REUTERS

Where do you think the following foreign bonds are issued?

1. Matildas

2. Rembrandts

3. Navigators

You can check your answer on the next page.

To protect investors, most countries impose regulations governing foreign bond issues restricting terms such as coupon and redemption structure, creditworthiness of the borrowers etc. These bonds are usually issued in the currency of the foreign country targeted by the borrower. The advantage to foreign bond investors is that they can diversify their portfolios without any currency exposure.

Most investors in foreign bonds tend to be residents of the country in which the bonds are issued, which is one reason that they have a much smaller market share than Eurobonds, which attract investors worldwide.

Eurobonds

Eurobonds are instruments for unsecured debt issued by governments, banks, corporate entities and supranationals which are issued outside the domestic market of the currency of denomination. The bonds are issued by an international syndicate, usually as bearer bonds. As a Eurobond, the issue will be sold to an international group of investors who are beneficial owners of the currency of issue but not resident in the country of that currency.

Eurobonds are **unsecured** debt that can be issued simultaneously in different countries by an international syndicate. Most Eurobonds have maturities of 3–20 years and are denominated in Euros or US dollars. Typically the face values (minimum trading amounts) of Eurobonds are small in order to attract individual investors.

The underwriters and managers of the issue will have restrictions imposed on them during syndication ensuring that bonds are not sold to legal entities whose base currency is that of the issued currency – the **selling restrictions**. These restrictions are removed after a period, normally 90 days, when the issue is perceived to have become **seasoned**. For example, if a UK institution were to issue a Eurodollar bond through a Netherlands Antilles finance subsidiary, ICI Finance (Netherlands Antilles), then the management group would not normally be allowed to sell to US, UK or Netherlands Antilles investors during syndication.

However, it is important to note that these rules are **not** always strictly adhered to, with the exception of restrictions on sales to US citizens.

Once issued, Eurobonds may be listed on exchanges to facilitate trading, but not necessarily.

Why Eurobonds?

After World War II the world's premier capital market was the US, where foreign companies issued Yankee bonds – foreign bonds denominated in US dollars. However, by the 1960s, the US government was growing increasingly concerned at the amount, of dollars flowing to Europe into the reserves of the central banks.

The US dollars held in these tax-free bank accounts outside the US were called Eurodollars and London was one of the main centres. The trigger for Eurobond lending was the US imposition in 1962 of an "Interest Equalisation Tax" that tried to stem the dollar outflow and discourage investors from buying foreign bonds in the US. Borrowers in the Yankee market now found their issues less attractive to the US investors and so they turned to the Eurodollar market.

The first big **Eurobond** deal came in 1963 when the Italian state-owned road building company Autostrade issued the deal in US dollars and the British merchant bank SG Warburg brought the issue to the market.

In the late 1960s and 1970s, large corporations switched to the Eurobond market as a source of finance because the interest rates became more attractive. The London market developed rapidly from the early 1970s and by the 1980s it had become the second largest capital market in the world after New York. Although the Eurobond market is very large, dwarfing the other markets, many issues do not trade very often as the investors tend to hold the bonds to maturity.

Between 1990 and 1999 the Euro-market size rose from less than $1,000 US$ billion to $2,121 US$ billion. Daily, billions of dollars worth of Eurobonds are traded over the phone. The following chart shows the annual market size of the Euro market (excluding CHF and DEM issues).

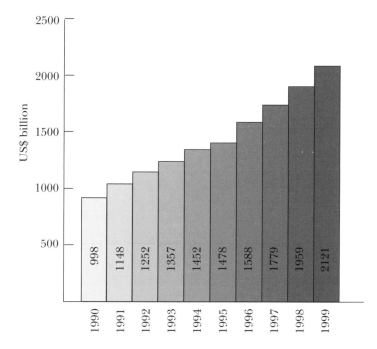

Source: ISMA Quarterly Comment Volume 37, April 1999

Where do you think the following foreign bonds are issued?

1. Matildas   – **Australia**

2. Rembrandts   – **Netherlands**

3. Navigators   – **Portugal**

Why Did the Market Grow So Rapidly?

There are two main advantages in issuing Eurobonds. The first is the less restrictive regulatory environment they enjoy. They are not subject to national laws or regulations. Eurobonds can be issued in any country and in any currency other than that of its country of issue.

This Reuters screen provides details about a British Petroleum America Eurobond issue.

Country of issue is the US

Eurobond currency is Deutschemarks   Credit ratings

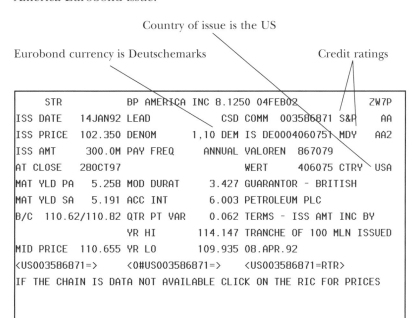

```
   STR              BP AMERICA INC 8.1250 04FEB02              ZW7P
ISS DATE    14JAN92 LEAD           CSD COMM  003586871 S&P     AA
ISS PRICE   102.350 DENOM      1,10 DEM IS DE000406075  MDY    AA2
ISS AMT      300.0M PAY FREQ     ANNUAL VALOREN  867079
AT CLOSE    28OCT97                    WERT      406075 CTRY   USA
MAT YLD PA   5.258 MOD DURAT     3.427 GUARANTOR - BRITISH
MAT YLD SA   5.191 ACC INT       6.003 PETROLEUM PLC
B/C  110.62/110.82 QTR PT VAR    0.062 TERMS - ISS AMT INC BY
                   YR HI       114.147 TRANCHE OF 100 MLN ISSUED
MID PRICE   110.655 YR LO      109.935 08.APR.92
<US003586871=>     <0#US003586871=>     <US003586871=RTR>
IF THE CHAIN IS DATA NOT AVAILABLE CLICK ON THE RIC FOR PRICES
```

So issuers can choose a country with less restrictive regulations and select a currency that best suits their needs. Eurobonds provided an unprecedented degree of flexibility – country of issue, currency and the ability to shift between currencies should the climate change.

The other main advantage is that Eurobonds are normally issued in the form of **bearer bond** in which mere possession is sufficient to prove ownership. Bond holders are not registered in the same way as holders of domestic bonds or equities. This is an advantage for investors, many of whom prefer to remain anonymous.

Eurobonds developed a reputation as an attractive proposition for tax–evading investors. This claim was probably largely unjustified as there has been little real evidence of such activity. This reputation lay behind the City (referring to London's financial centre) jokes about Belgian dentists who were unfairly seen as the kind of investors with excess funds who were looking for a safe investment out of view of the tax authorities.

In 1988, as a result of a debt-financed buyout bid for RJR Nabisco, the price of existing Nabisco debt instruments fell dramatically and bond holders' portfolios lost a lot of value. This introduced the concept of **'junk' bonds** into the markets. The term now generally refers to bonds with low credit ratings (below investment grade) and therefore, would be considered speculative investments. These bonds are also referred to as **high yield debt** – typically issuers have to offer high yields to attract investors who have to accept the higher risks associated with the lower credit rating of the issuer.

Where Is the Eurobond Market?

As you already know, there is no physical, central market place that can be held accountable to any particular government. As the City of London was historically where Eurobond trading started, largely by accident, it is the unofficial home of the Eurobond markets. The UK regulatory environment for Eurobonds, the concentration of highly skilled staff, a sophisticated system to support the market and its position in the trading time zone have all assured London's position. Banks and security houses from all over the world have set up offices in London in order to use it as a trading base for Eurobonds.

When Does the Eurobond Market Operate?

Eurobond trading takes place around the clock. This is because it is:

- A telephone- and screen-based market

- An international market

- Covering all time zones

London is an ideal geographical location as it is fortunate to be between the time zones of Tokyo and New York.

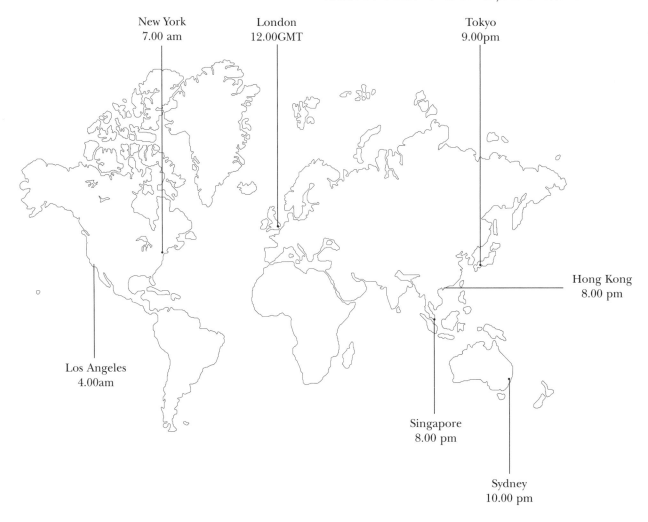

New York
7.00 am

London
12.00GMT

Tokyo
9.00pm

Hong Kong
8.00 pm

Los Angeles
4.00am

Singapore
8.00 pm

Sydney
10.00 pm

REUTERS

The Reuters screens below are an alphabetical lisitng of Eurobonds with a Finland 7.50% due 27 Jan 2000 highlighted, including detailed bond analysis.

This Reuters screen was the result of searching from all Eurobonds issued by Ford, one issued by Ford Brasil.

```
0#EURODEMSFG=          STR EUROS FG

  Issue/Issuer      Coupon Maturity      L a t e s t      Yield:        Time  Date
FARMING FINANCE       6.75 20JUL98   M 101.000                         22:06 28OCT
FEDERAL NATL MTG      6.000 23AUG00   B↑ 102.89   A 102.99   4.86   4.83 10:10 29OCT
FEDERAL NATL MTG      5.0000 16FEB01  B↑  99.99   A 100.09   4.100  4.099 10:11 29OCT
FED HOME LOAN BK      6.0000 23AUG00  B↑ 102.89   A 102.99   4.86   4.83 10:10 29OCT
FEK                   6.125 24NOV98   M 101.650                         22:06 28OCT
FEK                   3.125 15SEP99   B↑  97.47   A  98.07               10:06 29OCT
FEK                   5.250 16JAN01   M 100.300                         22:06 28OCT
FEK                   5.25 06MAR01    B        A                         :
FELDMUEHLE NOBEL      8 29DEC99        M 105.300                         22:06 28OCT
FIDELIO TRUST         15 02APR07                                         :

FIDELIO TRUST 2       11 01APR05                                         :
FIH                   8.375 05FEB99   M 104.100                         22:06 28OCT
FIH                   8.375 22APR99   M 105.200                         22:06 28OCT
FINLAND               7.75 20NOV97    M 100.100                         22:06 28OCT
FINLAND               8.5000 31JUL98  M 103.150                         22:06 28OCT
FINLAND               8.625 11DEC98   M 104.500                         22:06 28OCT
FINLAND               7.5000 27JAN00  B↓ 105.91   A 106.01   4.614      10:10 29OCT
FINLAND               5.5000 09FEB01  B↑ 101.51   A 101.61   4.961      10:10 29OCT
FINLAND               8.2500 25JUN02  B↑ 111.92   A 112.22               10:06 29OCT
FINLAND               5.5000 05FEB03  B↑ 100.74   A 100.84   5.318      10:10 29OCT
FIRST AUSTRIA BK      7 28MAR00        106.37                           20:58 04JUN
FIRST AUSTRIA BK      5.750 07MAR01   M 101.850                         22:06 28OCT
```

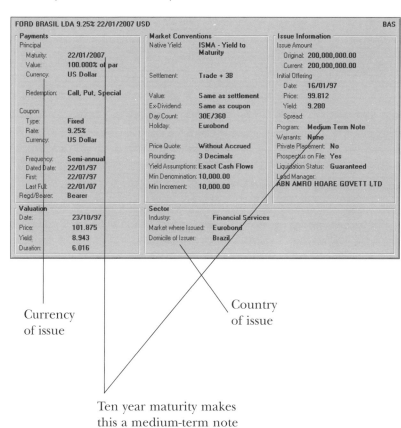

FORD BRASIL LDA 9.25% 22/01/2007 USD   BAS

Payments

Principal
Maturity:	22/01/2007
Value:	100.000% of par
Currency:	US Dollar
Redemption:	Call, Put, Special

Coupon
Type:	Fixed
Rate:	9.25%
Currency:	US Dollar
Frequency:	Semi-annual
Dated Date:	22/01/97
First:	22/07/97
Last Full:	22/01/07
Regd/Bearer:	Bearer

Valuation
Date:	23/10/97
Price:	101.875
Yield:	8.943
Duration:	6.016

Market Conventions
Native Yield:	ISMA - Yield to Maturity
Settlement:	Trade + 3B
Value:	Same as settlement
Ex-Dividend:	Same as coupon
Day Count:	30E/360
Holiday:	Eurobond
Price Quote:	Without Accrued
Rounding:	3 Decimals
Yield Assumptions:	Exact Cash Flows
Min Denomination:	10,000.00
Min Increment:	10,000.00

Sector
Industry:	Financial Services
Market where Issued:	Eurobond
Domicile of Issuer:	Brazil

Issue Information

Issue Amount
Original:	200,000,000.00
Current:	200,000,000.00

Initial Offering
Date:	16/01/97
Price:	99.812
Yield:	9.280
Spread:	
Program:	Medium Term Note
Warrants:	None
Private Placement:	No
Prospectus on File:	Yes
Liquidation Status:	Guaranteed
Lead Manager:	ABN AMRO HOARE GOVETT LTD

Currency of issue

Country of issue

Ten year maturity makes this a medium-term note

FINLAND 7.50% 27/01/2000 DEM   BAS

Payments

Principal
Maturity:	27/01/2000
Value:	100.000% of par
Currency:	Deutsche Mark
Redemption:	Special

Coupon
Type:	Fixed
Rate:	7.50%
Currency:	Deutsche Mark
Frequency:	Annual
Dated Date:	27/01/93
First:	27/01/94
Last Full:	27/01/00
Regd/Bearer:	Bearer

Valuation
Date:	23/10/97
Price:	105.600
Yield:	4.796
Duration:	1.957

Market Conventions
Native Yield:	ISMA - Yield to Maturity
Settlement:	Trade + 3B
Value:	Same as settlement
Ex-Dividend:	Same as coupon
Day Count:	30E/360
Holiday:	Eurobond
Price Quote:	Without Accrued
Rounding:	3 Decimals
Yield Assumptions:	Exact Cash Flows
Min Denomination:	1,000.00
Min Increment:	1,000.00

Sector
Industry:	Government - Sovereign
Market where Issued:	Eurobond
Domicile of Issuer:	Finland

Issue Information

Issue Amount
Original:	2,000,000,000.00
Current:	3,000,000,000.00

Initial Offering
Date:	04/01/93
Price:	102.400
Yield:	
Spread:	
Program:	N/A
Warrants:	None
Private Placement:	No
Prospectus on File:	Yes
Liquidation Status:	Govt Guaranteed
Lead Manager:	DRESDNER BANK AG

How Do Bond Markets Work?

Dragon Bonds

 Dragon Bonds can be issued in any currency, usually US dollars, on at least two of the "Dragon" exchanges – Hong Kong, Singapore or Taiwan. Trading takes place during the Asian time zone.

The first Dragon bond was issued by the Asian Development Bank in 1991.

This Reuters screen shows a Dragon bond issue, Nomura International HK. with all pertinent bond details

```
10:34 12SEP97    NOMURA INTERNATIONAL HK LTD        HK14014          NIHKC
Dennis Mak /John Woo / Davis Lai
Tel : (852)-2869-7811    Reuter Dealing : HKNI    Quotron : NIHK

US$ FIXED RATE DRAGON BOND                  Last update : 12-09-97 9:34 HK

ISSUER            COUPON   MATURITY   PRICE      YLD(S) UST   LIFE   RATING
------            ------   --------   -----      ----------   ----   ------

Astra O/S Fin BV   8.7500 S 07-08-03  99.48-98   8.750 +248  5Y11M
Indorayon Intl Fi 10.0000 A 29-03-99 100.35-65   9.230 +346  1Y 7M
Intl Indorayon Ut  9.1250 S 15-10-00  98.27-77   9.590 +350  3Y 1M
NPC                9.0000 S 05-07-02 104.82-32   7.650 +142  4Y10M
PCIB               7.7500 S 26-09-01  99.84-34   7.650 +148  4Y           Ba2
PNOC               7.2500 S 20-10-98  99.93-23   7.010 +141  1Y 1M
PNOC               8.1250 S 06-12-01  99.57-07   8.100 +192  4Y 3M
SCICI              8.0000 A 30-07-01 101.56-06   7.230 +108  3Y11M
Siam City Bk       7.3750 S 25-09-01  97.05-55   8.100 +193  4Y           Baa2
```

Currency
of issue

Time remaining
until maturity

Credit rating
by Moody's.

Global Bonds

 Global Bonds are traded simultaneously in the Euromarket and on one or more domestic markets. For example, a global bond will be registered first in the US and then traded simultaneously on the US and Asian domestic markets and as Eurobonds.

The first global bond was issued by the World Bank in 1989 when a 10-year bond was issued simultaneously in the US Yankee bond and Eurobond markets. Global bonds are issued by organisations having a consistent need for finance and who have a very high credit rating, for example, supranationals.

The title page from the Official Circular for Global Notes to be issued by the US Student Loan Marketing Association – Sallie Mae

Summary of International Bond Markets

Foreign Bonds

- Foreign bonds are issued in a domestic market by a foreign issuer and are denominated in the domestic currency

- Foreign bonds often have names associated with the country of issue, for example, Bulldogs, Yankees, Samurais etc

- This type of bond is usually subject to stricter market requirements, conditions and conventions than those for the euro markets

- Coupons are usually paid at the same frequency as used in the domestic market

- Foreign bonds may be issued as bearer bonds

Eurobonds

- Eurobonds are not subject to the same regulations as those applying to domestic bonds and are sold internationally

- Eurobonds are issued as bearer bonds – no register of bond holders is kept by the issuer

- Coupons are paid annually and no deductions are made for withholding tax

- Most Eurobonds are issued as unsecured debt by organisations with high credit ratings

- Eurobonds may be listed and traded on a stock exchange but most trading is OTC

- Prices for Eurobonds are quoted as a percentage of face value to the nearest 0.01%

- Eurobonds can be denominated in any Eurocurrency but the largest markets are for bonds issued in US dollars, deutschemarks and yen

Summary

Your notes

You have now finished the second section of the book and you should have a clear understanding of the following:

- An overview of the elements of the bond markets – government, sovereign and corporate bond

- Domestic bond markets – government securities and corporate issues

- International bond markets – foreign bonds, Eurobonds, Dragon bonds and global bonds

As a check on your understanding, try the Quick Quiz Questions on the next page. You may also find the Overview section to be a helpful study tool.

Quick Quiz Questions

1. In what sector of the debt markets would a UK local authority raise capital?
   - ☐ a) Government
   - ☐ b) Corporate
   - ☐ c) Sovereign

2. Which of the main sectors of the debt markets is the largest in terms of turnover?
   - ☐ a) Government
   - ☐ b) Corporate
   - ☐ c) Sovereign

3. What is a German government long-term bond called?
   - ☐ a) BTP
   - ☐ b) Bund
   - ☐ c) Bobl
   - ☐ d) BTAN

4. Which country has the largest government debt market?
   - ☐ a) Germany
   - ☐ b) Japan
   - ☐ c) UK
   - ☐ d) US

5. Banque Nationale de Paris have decided to issue a Eurobond. In what currency can they **not** issue the bonds?
   - ☐ a) US Dollars
   - ☐ b) Swiss Francs
   - ☐ c) Japanese Yen
   - ☐ d) French Francs

6. With which country's laws and regulations must Eurobond issues conform?
   - ☐ a) US laws and regulations
   - ☐ b) The country of issue's laws and regulations
   - ☐ c) No specific country's laws and regulations
   - ☐ d) EU laws and regulations

7. The Japanese company Sony issues bonds in New York denominated in US dollars. Which of the following describes these bonds?
   - ☐ a) Samurais
   - ☐ b) Shoguns
   - ☐ c) Yankees
   - ☐ d) Sumos

8. Which of the following currencies dominates Eurobond issue denominations?
   - ☐ a) Eurodollar
   - ☐ b) ECU
   - ☐ c) US dollar
   - ☐ d) Sterling

9. The German electronics company Siemens issues bonds denominated in sterling which can only be traded in the UK. What kind of bond is this?
   - ☐ a) Domestic
   - ☐ b) Primary
   - ☐ c) Eurobond
   - ☐ d) Foreign bond

You can check your answers on page 65.

Overview

```
How Do Bond
Markets Work?
```

Elements of the Bond Markets
- **Government debt**
- **Sovereign debt**
- **Corporate debt**

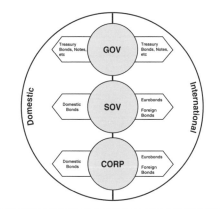

Domestic Bond Markets

- **Government Securities**
  - Repo markets
  - Stripping bonds
  - EMU
  - Index-linked/
    Inflation-indexed bonds

- **Corporate Issues**
  - Debentures – secured/
    unsecured risk
  - Guaranteed bonds
  - Subordinated bonds

Country	Name
US	US Treasuries (T-Bonds, T-Notes)
UK	UK Treasuries (Gilts)
JP	Japanee Government Bonds (JGBs)
FR	Obligations Assimilable du Trésor (OATs)
DE	Bundesrepublik Bonds (Bunds)
IT	Buoni del Tesoro Poliennali (BTPs)

The potential euro area – total government debt outstanding in 1998

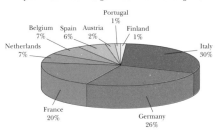

Source: Futures & OTC World, July 1999

International Bond Markets

- **Foreign bonds**

Market of issue	Currency	Market name
US	USD	Yankee
UK	GBP	Bulldog
Japan	JPY	Samurai
Spain	ESP	Matador

- **Eurobonds**

- **Dragon bonds**

- **Global bonds**

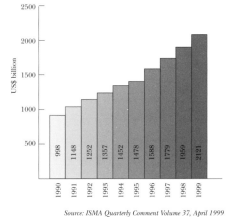

Source: ISMA Quarterly Comment Volume 37, April 1999

Quick Quiz Answers

	✓ or ✗
1. c)	☐
2. a)	☐
3. b)	☐
4. d)	☐
5. d)	☐
6. c)	☐
7. c)	☐
8. c)	☐
9. d)	☐

How well did you score? You should have scored at least 7. If you didn't, enter the materials again.

Further Resources

Books

The Reuters Guide to World Bond Markets
Martin Essex and Ruth Pitchford (Reuters Limited), John Wiley & Sons, Inc., 1996
ISBN   0 471 96046 2

All About Bond Funds
Werner Renberg, John Wiley & Sons, Inc., 1995
ISBN   0 471 31195 2

The Financial Times Guide to Using the Financial Press
Romesh Vaitilingam, FT Pitman Pub., 3rd Edition 1996
ISBN   0 273 62201 3

Bond Markets, Analysis and Strategies
Frank J. Fabozzi, Prentice Hall International, 3rd Edition 1996
ISBN   0 13 520370 8

How the Bond Market Works
Robert Zipf and John Allan (Editor), Prentice Hall Trade, 1997
ISBN   0 131 24306 3

The Guide to Investing in Bonds
David Logan Scott, Globe Pequot Press, 1997
ISBN   0 762 70060 2

Corporate Bonds: Structures & Analysis
Richard S. Wilson and Frank J. Fabozzi, Irwin Professional Press, 1996
ISBN   1 883 24907 4

EMU Explained: The Impact of the Euro
Noah Barkin and Adam Cox, Kogan Page, Second Edition 1998
ISBN   0 7494 2654 3

Publications

Bank of England
• British Government Securities: The Market in Gilt-Edged Securities

Internet

RFT Web Site
• http://www.wiley-rft.reuters.com
This is the series' companion web site where additional quiz questions, updated screens and other information may be found.

Bank for International Settlements (BIS)
• http://www.bis.org
The Bank for International Settlements (the BIS) is owned and controlled by central banks and it provides a number of highly-specialised services to central banks and, through them, to the international financial system more generally. The Monetary and Economic Department of the BIS conducts research, particularly into monetary and financial questions, collects and publishes data on international banking and financial market developments, and runs an intra-central bank economic database to which contributing central banks have automated access.

Asian Development Bank (ADB)
• http://www.adb.org
The Asian Development Bank is a multilateral development finance institution, founded in 1966.

Exchanges

Refer to the back of this book for a listing of worldwide stock exchange contact information and web sites.

Your notes

This section of the book should take about 2 to 3 hours of study time. You may not take as long as this or you may take a little longer – remember your learning is individual to you.

My customer did not like his loss, but it was just as much his own fault as mine. The law of the bond market is *caveat emptor*. That's Latin for 'buyer beware'. (The bond markets lapse into Latin after a couple of drinks. *Meum dictum pactum* was another Latin phrase I used to hear, but that was just a joke. It means 'my word is my bond'.) I mean he didn't have to believe me when I told him AT&T bonds were a good idea.

Michael Lewis – 'Liar's Poker'

Introduction

You have seen already that the innovative and fast-changing financial markets offer a wide range of instruments for investors to select from, depending upon investors' goals, requirements and capacity for risk. The same criteria apply to the issuer, adding in the factor of cost of issuance and debt payment. Since this book aims to provide a broad overview of the various instruments available, this section classifies instruments to provide a broad overview to help you understand how they are used by issuers and investors and what are the relevant advantages and disadvantages to each. (In subsequent sections you will study valuation techniques and derivatives products.)

It is difficult to classify the instruments into simple categories, as many instruments' characteristics may overlap. The diagram that follows places the instruments into a classification based on the different ways in which a bond can be viewed. Bear in mind that it is possible to combine different elements of a bond, for example, a Eurobond with a floating coupon rate. The result is that if you need to know about a particular type of bond you may have to search across classes. Also, there are a number of derivatives that are based on underlying government securities prices. For example, interest rate futures contracts on long-term bonds are also known as bond futures, options are available on physical bonds, and interest rate futures contracts and swaps on interest rates and currencies involve bonds. It is also possible to have options on Interest Rate Swaps (IRSs) known as swaptions.

In this section you will review the following bond market instruments through their organisation by various classifications, including:

- Market type (eg, domestic and international)

- Principal payment type

- Interest related features

- Types of borrower

- Redemption features

- Equity linked types of instruments

Before moving on, try the activity below. The answers are provided within the diagram on the next page.

Identify as many instruments as you can that fall within the classifications listed in the column at left.

What Instruments Are Used in Bond Markets?

Bond Market Instruments

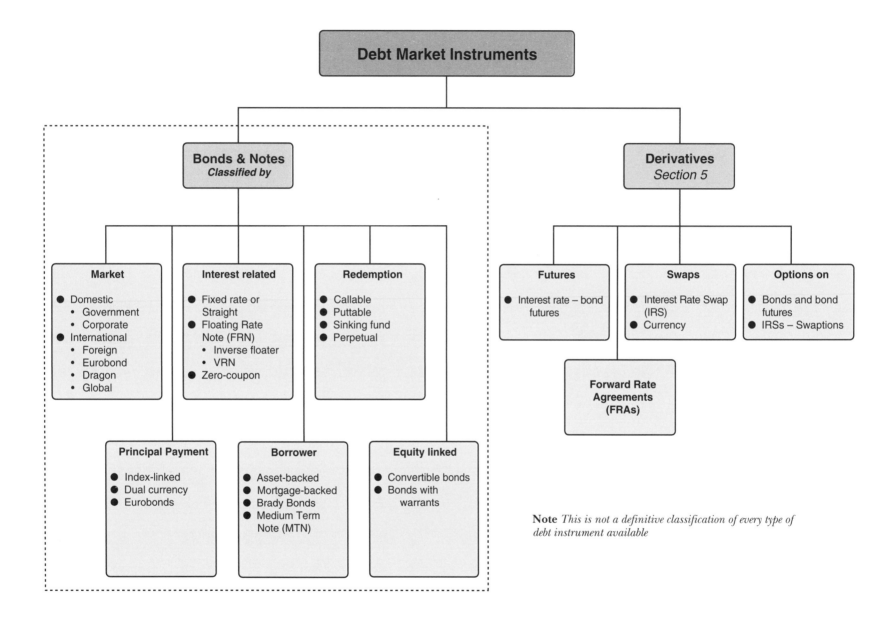

Debt Market Instruments

Bonds & Notes
Classified by

Derivatives
Section 5

Market
- Domestic
  - Government
  - Corporate
- International
  - Foreign
  - Eurobond
  - Dragon
  - Global

Interest related
- Fixed rate or Straight
- Floating Rate Note (FRN)
  - Inverse floater
  - VRN
- Zero-coupon

Redemption
- Callable
- Puttable
- Sinking fund
- Perpetual

Futures
- Interest rate – bond futures

Swaps
- Interest Rate Swap (IRS)
- Currency

Options on
- Bonds and bond futures
- IRSs – Swaptions

Forward Rate Agreements (FRAs)

Principal Payment
- Index-linked
- Dual currency
- Eurobonds

Borrower
- Asset-backed
- Mortgage-backed
- Brady Bonds
- Medium Term Note (MTN)

Equity linked
- Convertible bonds
- Bonds with warrants

Note *This is not a definitive classification of every type of debt instrument available*

Market Classification

This classification was considered in the previous section; however, the summaries of the major types have been reproduced here for your easy reference.

Domestic Bond Markets
• Government securities
• Corporate issues

International Bond Instruments
• Foreign bonds
• Eurobonds
• Dragon bonds
• Global bonds

In summary, all bonds are in effect **IOUs** for money loaned to governments and corporations by investors. Government securities are generally considered to be the safest form of investment as they are considered to be credit risk free – they are backed by the government and there is little risk of default. As such, government securities pay the lowest interest rates. Bonds issued by corporations pay higher interest rates because they are considered a riskier investment. The creditworthiness of a corporation is also important in determining the risk associated with secured and unsecured bonds. If a corporate bond is unsecured, then the investor has only the standing of the organisation on which to base any investment decision. Government securities and corporate bonds comprise the domestic bond markets which are usually well regulated, governed by rules and taxation laws.

For corporations wishing to borrow funds in a currency other than its own, foreign bonds historically were the first available. However, since the launch of Eurobonds in the early 1960s, a borrower of US dollars, for example, can now issue a Eurobond, a Yankee or a Dragon bond.

Foreign bonds have the disadvantage that they are still regulated by the domestic market in which they are issued. Eurobonds are not only issued by corporations but by governments and supranationals also. Generally they are issued as bearer bonds on unsecured debt by organisations with high credit ratings. They are sold in the international market where regulation and tax rules are different from domestic markets. Eurobonds can be launched quickly and cost effectively in a wide range of currencies, types and maturities.

Governmental Securities

- Money is raised for:
  - financing budget deficits
  - repaying maturing debt
  - paying interest on existing debt
- Bonds and notes are issued in domestic currency
- Most instruments are issued using an auction system and involve Primary Dealers for the issue in the primary market
- Government securities are the highest quality instruments issued in a country and are therefore generally used as a benchmarks for other bonds in that country.
- Markets in government securities are well regulated and usually very liquid.
- The securities are often listed and traded on the domestic Stock Exchange/s but the majority of trading is OTC.
- There are well established conventions for issuing, pricing, coupon payments and repayments at maturity for government securities.
- The largest single government securities market worldwide is that for US Treasuries.

Corporate Issues

- Domestic bonds are issued in the domestic currency by domestic corporations using a syndicate of domestic banks
- There are many different types of instrument available including bullets, FRNs, convertibles, zero-coupon etc.
- Domestic markets are usually overshadowed by trading in government bonds and Eurobonds denominated in the domestic currency
- Domestic markets are well regulated governing trading and tax matters
- Coirporate bonds are generally listed and traded on the domestic Stock Exchange/s but there are also large OTC markets
- Within the domestic markets the crediworthiness of the issuer is usually better understood than in the international markets but the domestic markets may not be suitable for a large issue
- Coupon payment usually use the same frequency as for the domestic government securities
- The largest single domestic corporate mrket worldwide is that for the US

Foreign Bonds

- Foreign bonds are issued in a domestic market by a foreign issuer and are denominated in the domestic currency
- Foreign bonds often have names associated with the country of issue, for example, Bulldogs, Yankees, Samurais etc
- This type of bond is usually subject to stricter market requirements, conditions and conventions than those for the domestic markets
- Coupons are usually paid at the same frequency as used in the domestic market
- Foreign bonds may be issued as bearer bonds

Eurobonds

- Eurobonds are not subject to the same regulations as those applying to domestic bonds and are sold internationally
- Eurobonds are issued as bearer bonds – no register of bodn holders is kept by the issuer
- Coupons are paid annually and no deductions are made for withholding tax
- Most Eurobonds are issued as unsecured debt by organisations with high credit ratings
- Eurobonds may be listed and traded on a Stock Exchange but most trading is OTC
- Prices for Eurobonds are quoted as a percentage of face value to the nearest 0.01%
- Eurobonds can be denominated in any Eurocurrency but the largest markets are for bonds issued in US Dollars, Deutschemarks and Yen
- Eurobond issues allow organisation greater flexibility to issue debt and allow rapid access to the markets
- Eurobonds accrue interest using a 30/360 basis

What Instruments Are Used in Bond Markets?

Who Uses the Domestic and International Bond Markets?

The following tables list the advantages and disadvantages for both issuers and investors for the two largest market sectors – domestic and Eurobonds.

Issuers – Domestic Bonds

Advantages	Disadvantages
• Government issues usually have a very competitive position in domestic markets because of their high credit ratings and highly liquid markets • Issuer's creditworthiness may be better understood in the domestic market rather than internationally • Certain instruments such as asset-backed and dual currency bonds may suit particular groups of domestic investors	• Government issues may not attract a large enough domestic market • Domestic markets may not be of sufficient magnitude to cater for a large domestic issue • Domestic markets are heavily regulated with conditions on matters such as registration and listing • Some domestic markets have restrictions on the types of instrument permitted, issue size and the nationality of the issuer

Investors – Domestic Bond Markets

Advantages	Disadvantages
• Most of the major currencies have well developed government treasuries markets • Some institutional investors may be constrained to invest in domestic markets • Many investors understand domestic instruments, regulation and settlement arrangements better than the international markets	• Domestic markets may be small compared with international markets and it may not be possible to invest large sums in liquid markets • International investors may not understand domestic instruments, regulation and settlement arrangements • There may be tax implications (eg, with-holding taxes) for investors from abroad which may affect the attractiveness of domestic instruments.

REUTERS

Issuers – Eurobonds

Advantages	Disadvantages
• There is a large diversified international base of investors	• Eurobond issue depends to some extent on the creditworthiness of the issue and so Eurobonds are usually issued by highly rated organisations
• Eurobonds can be issued in a wide range of types, for example, straight, FRN, callable, puttable, index-linked, asset-backed	• Eurobonds are usually bearer bonds which can exclude some groups of investors
• The issue size is not restricted or regulated and so issues can be large	• Some groups of investors are restricted to investing in the domestic markets or domestic currency
• There is a wide range of currencies in which Eurobonds are issued although the US dollar dominates	• The majority of Eurobond investors want issues whic are AAA rated, in US dollars, straight and with
• Eurobonds can be issued very quickly	
• There is a general lack o regulation and reporting restrictions although IPMA and ISMA are self-regulatory bodies providing standards, rules and regulations within which issuers should operate	
• Eurobonds may be listed on exchanges such as London and Luxembourg	

Investors – Eurobonds

Advantages	Disadvantages
• Eurobonds are available in a wide range of issue types, currencies, coupons and maturities	• The lack of regulation may expose investors to additional risk although many government agencies regulate the behaviour of market players in general
• Most Eurobonds are issued by highly rated organisations, sovereign states, governments and supranationals	• The market is mainly OTC and there are no centralised reporting requirements
• Some Eurobond issues can be highly liquid although this is not always the case	• Some Eurobonds can be illiquid – once a Eurobond has been issued there are no obligations on market makers to continue to quote two-way prices
• Eurobonds are bearer bonds paying gross coupons – this appeals to some investor groups who prefer to remain anonymous	
• Clearing houses such as Cedel and Euroclear offer simple settlement and custodial services for Eurobonds	

The following Reuters screens illustrate domestic and international markets.

Here is a screen displaying an overview of the US dollar bond market.

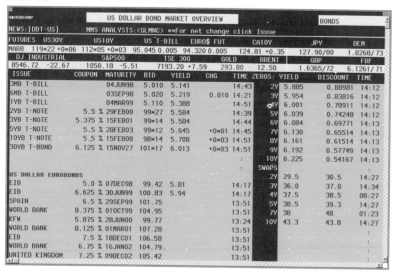

Here is an index page for France Eurobonds with detail about a specific issue.

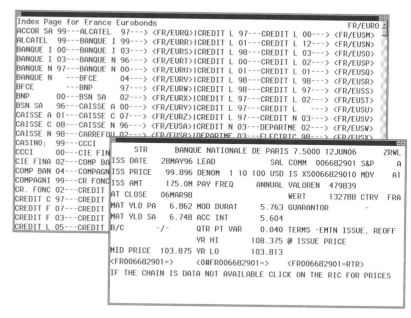

Here is a summary page for the Belgian domestic debt market with detail about corporate bonds.

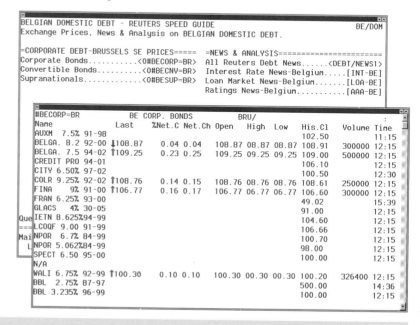

Interest Related Classification

There are three important ways in which interest payments are related to a bond issue. Payments can be made on a fixed or floating basis but there are also bonds for which no interest payments are made at all. In terms of interest payments, a bond can be classified as one of the following:

- **Fixed rate or straight bond**

- **Floating Rate Note (FRN)**

- **Zero-coupon bond**

Fixed Rate or Straight Bond

A **Fixed Rate** or **Straight** bond has no special features and pays a fixed rate of interest to investors throughout its maturity period. The bond has a final maturity date when the final interest payment is made and the principal of the loan is repaid.

The bond coupon is expressed as a percentage of the face or nominal value of the bond either as a decimal or as a fraction depending on the particular market convention for the bond. Usually interest is paid either semi-annually, for example, for US and UK government securities, or annually, for example, for Eurobonds.

Example
A $1000 face value bond has a 10% coupon and pays interest annually. On the payment date the investor receives a single payment of $100. If the same bond paid a coupon semi-annually, then the investor would receive two $50 payments per year.

A straight bond may also be termed a **plain vanilla** or **vanilla** bond – a bond with no special features. These are the most common type of bond issued. Most of the calculations and concepts associated with pricing bonds (next section — *Bond Valuation and Bond Yields*) are based on an understanding of fixed rate bonds.

Payments	
Principal	
Maturity:	15/08/2007
Value:	100.000% of par
Currency:	US Dollar
Redemption:	Bullet
Coupon	
Type:	Fixed
Rate:	6.125%
Currency:	US Dollar
Frequency:	Semi-annual
Dated Date:	15/08/97
First:	15/02/98
Last Full:	15/08/07
Regd/Bearer:	Registered

In this section of a Reuters screen for a US T-Bond, you can see that the bond has a fixed coupon of 6.125% paid semi-annually in US dollars for 10 years and at redemption the bullet payment is for 100% of the bond's face value in US dollars. The bond is registered rather than in bearer form.

The following cash flow chart may help you to remember the basic characteristics of a straight bond.

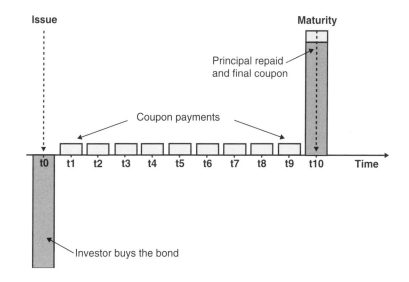

The principal is the amount the issuer agrees to repay the bondholder at maturity. If the principal is repaid at maturity in a single repayment then the bond is also known as a **bullet**.

The principal amount outstanding of a bond is the total amount of funds borrowed by the issuer. The original issue amount is specified in the issue documents. However, over time the principal amount outstanding may exceed the original amount. How can this be?

It is possible for an issuer to re-issue a particular bond and add to the existing amount outstanding. Governments and large multinational organisations with high credit ratings typically re-issue bonds. In the case of governments re-issues are often termed **taps**. In the US organisations can register securities they intend to issue in the future which is termed **shelf registration**.

The Reuters screen below gives detailed information for the original and current issues of a Canadian bond.

Within the Eurobond market, straight bonds pay an annual coupon on these mainly unsecured loans. The most important currency for Eurobond issues are those denominated in US dollars, followed by issues in deutschemarks and yen.

The first Reuters screen below illustrates details of a Daimler Benz International Finance Eurobond denominated in US dollars. The next screen shows similar data taken from a Reuters fixed income service.

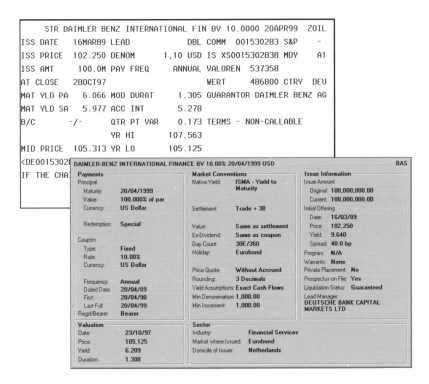

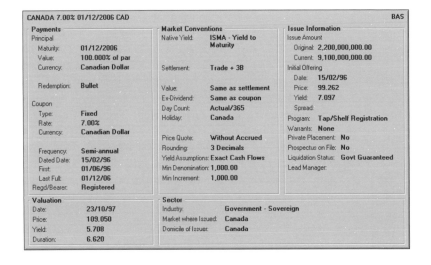

Below is a Reuters summary screen for new issue straight bonds, with details of a yen issue by Anheuser-Busch.

```
          STRAIGHT BONDS - NEW ISSUES                    STRA
CODE            ISSUER          COUPON MAT DAT      RIC
Z39W \ JPY  ANHEUSER BUSCH      4.1000 24APR01                 C
Z3HS \ USD  AMERICAN DREAMS     5.1000 04DEC00  KY008153965=   C
Z3GM  USD  ABN-AMRO HLDG        7.1250 29OCT98  NL008170266=   C
Z36I  USD  AFRICAN DEV BANK     6.2500 28OCT02  XS008133794=   S
Z36H  FRF  ASSET BACKED CAP     5.3000 05NOV07                 C
Z32V  DEM  ASIAN DEV BANK       5.5000 24OCT07  XS008116695=   S
Z32W  ZAR  AFRICAN DEV BANK    14.0000 04NOV04  XS008120315=   S
Z31P  DEM  ARGENTINA            8.0000 30OCT09  AR008115036=   S
Z31Q  NLG  ACHMEA               5.7500 22OCT07  NL008112550=   C
Z3KE  ITL  ARGENTINA            9.0000 18MAR04  AR008105758=   S

CONTINUED FROM -                      CONTINUED ON - SRTA
```

```
     STR    ANHEUSER-BUSCH COMPANIES INC 4.1000 24APR01     Z39W
ISS DATE   31OCT97 LEAD           DAT COMM     -      S&P      A
ISS PRICE  100.000 DENOM    0.5M JPY IS JP584055ATA2 MDY     A1
ISS AMT     20.0B PAY FREQ       SEMI VALOREN    -
LISTING        -         -            WERT       -   CTRY USA
AT CLOSE       -    GUARANTEE TYPE   - 1ST TRADE  31OCT97
MGT/UND    0.250 GUARANTOR             -
SELL CONC  1.250 TERMS -SAMURAI

MID PRICE      -

IF THE CHAIN IS DATA NOT AVAILABLE CLICK ON THE RIC FOR PRICES
```

Floating Rate Note (FRN)

A **Floating Rate Note** is a medium-, to long-term debt instrument which pays a variable interest rate linked to a financial index and adjusted periodically – typically every 3 or 6 months.

When interest rates are high and coupon rates are high, investors tend to buy long-term fixed rate bonds because they are attractive investments. However, when interest rates are volatile, issuers seek to pay the least coupon possible – they would like to keep coupons as close to current interest rates as possible. **Floating Rate Notes (FRNs)** provide such an instrument for issuers.

A **FRN** or **floater** differs from a fixed rate bond in that at the time of issue its interest is not fixed at an absolute rate for the life of the bond. FRNs pay a variable rate of interest. In this case the bond is issued at a fixed margin equal to, above or below a floating rate index. A typical index is **LIBOR (London Interbank Offered Rate)** – the rate at which banks borrowing in the interbank market must pay interest on a loan taken out that day, for different periods. The LIBOR index is reset on a daily basis at 11.00.

The coupon is expressed as LIBOR plus or minus so many **basis points** (bp), for example, LIBOR + 50bp. The excess over LIBOR is called the **margin** – but remember it can also be negative, for example, LIBOR –10bp.

This means that although an investor does not know the exact rate of return that will be realised on the security, the rate of return will always be in line with current market rates. The interest rate is adjusted according to the money market conditions – usually every 3 or 6 months with a minimum rate normally guaranteed. The date the new rate is set is termed the **fixing date**. In many cases this is the same date as the **reset date** which is the date the new rate becomes effective. In some cases the fixing date may precede the reset date by a specified number of business days.

You can find the current LIBORs for different currencies using this page from Reuters.

```
1121        INTNL SWAP & DERIVATIVES ASSOCIATION        ISDA
                    INTERBANK RATES FROM LONDON
         USD      GBP      JPY      CHF      DEM      XEU
       LONDON   LONDON   LONDON   LONDON   LONDON   LONDON
1M    5.63281  7.22917  0.52344  1.76042  3.51250  4.44792
2M    5.76563  7.29167  0.52344  2.00000  3.71240  4.55208
3M    5.76563  7.35417  0.52344  2.02083  3.71865  4.58333
6M    5.80469  7.44271  0.54688  2.08333  3.83115  4.65625
1Y    5.92188  7.54688  0.57811  2.27083  4.08740  4.76042

       LIBO     LIBP     JNBO     CHFO     DMBO     ECUO
     30/10/97 30/10/97 30/10/97 30/10/97 30/10/97 30/10/97
```

This Reuters screen shows the details of an FRN issued by BankAmerica Corporation.

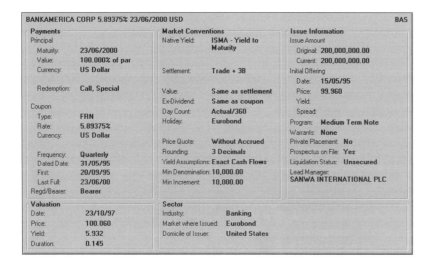

Although LIBOR is most commonly used as the floating rate index, other benchmarks which are used include the following:

- 3- or 6-month rates for money market instruments such a certificates of deposit (CDs), commercial papers (CPs) and bankers' acceptances (BAs)

- 3- or 6-month US T-Bill yields

- The US prime rate – the base rate at which commercial banks lend to their prime customers

If you need to know more about these money market instruments, then refer to *An Introduction to Foreign Exchange and Money Markets* (ISBN 0-471-83128-X).

FRNs or floaters are used by investors wishing to hedge against rising interest rates. However there are other types of FRNs which are also available for investors with a wide range of investment requirements. These instruments include:

Inverse Floaters

These instruments carry coupons which change in the **opposite** direction to the benchmark index. The first inverse FRN was issued in 1986 by the US Student Loan Marketing Association (Sallie Mae) when the coupons were set at 17.20% **minus** 6 month LIBOR.

Inverse floaters are usually issued as part of a broad financial strategy but it is worth noting:

- Inverse floaters **increase** in value when interest rates **fall** – both the price and the coupon payment increase

- Inverse floaters **decrease** in value when interest rates **rise** – both the price and the coupon payment decrease

There are many other variations of FRNs which include combination of other bonds, for example, convertible FRNs and hybrids of other bonds which are not discussed further here.

The following cash flow charts may help to remember the basic characteristics of floaters and inverse floaters.

Floater

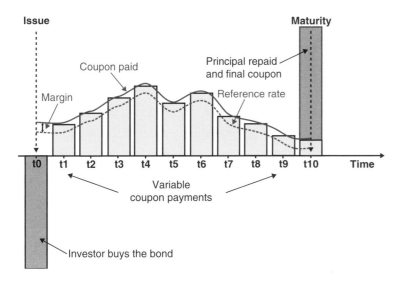

Inverse Floater

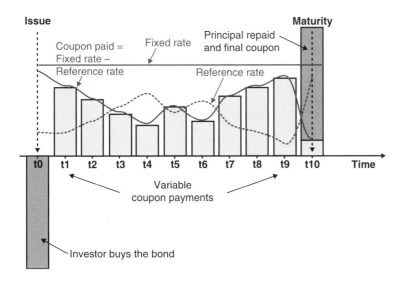

Variable Rate Notes (VRNs)

Variable Rate Notes (VRNs) have a coupon which is based on a long-term rate which resets no more than once a year.

There are many other variations of FRNs that include combinations of other bonds, for example, convertible FRNs and hybrids of other bonds not discussed in this text.

Zero-coupon Bond

A **Zero-coupon** bond pays **no** coupon during its life.

Instead of paying interest a zero-coupon bond or **zero** is issued at a deep discount to the face value and the bond is redeemed at **par** – the full face value. Investors hope to profit from the large difference between the price paid for the bond and the principal they will receive at maturity. In other words the investors are effectively receiving all their interest due when they buy the bond. But who issues and invests in bonds with no interest payments?

Issuers who want to delay repayment of cash to investors issue zero-coupon bonds. Such issuers must have the highest credit rating to satisfy investors that the organisation will still exist to repay the debt on maturity of the bond. Typically governments, sovereigns and supranationals issue this type of bond. However, some large organisations issue zero-coupon bonds – the screen below shows such a bond issued by British Gas International Finance.

Zero coupon   **Credit ratings**

```
    STR   BRITISH GAS INTERNATIONAL FINANCE 0.0000 04NOV21   ZT5B
ISS DATE   07OCT91 LEAD          GS COMM  003439470 S&P    AA-
ISS PRICE    8.770 DENOM 10,100,1M USD IS XS0034394709 MDY    A3
ISS AMT     1.5B PAY FREQ        N/A VALOREN  536359
AT CLOSE  28OCT97                WERT     405371 CTRY   GBR
MAT YLD PA   7.326 MOD DURAT  22.372 GUARANTOR - BRITISH GAS
MAT YLD SA   7.196 ACC INT        -   PLC
B/C      -/-    QTR PT VAR   0.061 TERMS - ISSUE/REOFFER
               YR HI    18.563 PRICE=8.77%
MID PRICE  18.313 YR LO    14.500
<GB003439470=>   <0#GB003439470=>   <GB003439470=RTR>
IF THE CHAIN IS DATA NOT AVAILABLE CLICK ON THE RIC FOR PRICES
```

The Reuters screen below gives the details of a zero-coupon bond issued by the World Bank.

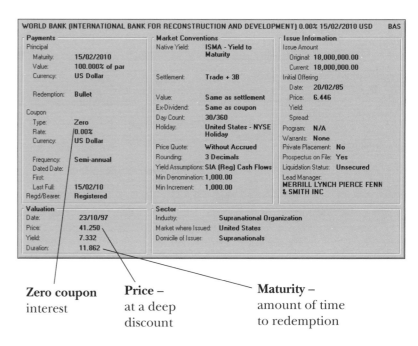

Zero coupon
interest

Price –
at a deep
discount

Maturity –
amount of time
to redemption

Investors buying zero-coupon bonds are typically pension fund managers who prefer to receive a lump sum at maturity rather than a series of coupon repayments. They use zero-coupon bonds to match investments with future payouts – there is no reinvestment risk as there is with a straight bond. The return is thus capital and not income, which can offer tax benefits to some investors and issuers. However, not all tax authorities exempt zero-coupon bonds from tax payments.

Zero-coupon bonds can also be created from a coupon bearing bond in a process of **stripping** or detaching the coupons. Stripping bonds – in particular government bonds – allows a conventional bond to be converted to a series of new zero-coupon strips which match exactly the cash flows of the original bond. This practice which was pioneered in the US during the late 1970s and early 1980s by brokers and dealers.

Many governments now have official **Separate Trading of Registered Interest and Principal of Securities (STRIPS)** programmes whereby their fixed coupon bonds may be stripped of their coupons to create zero-coupon bonds. For example, a 10-year bond with annual coupons can be stripped into 11 zero-coupon bonds – one for the principal repayment and 10 for the annual coupons. The cash flow on the zero-coupon strips is identical to the cash flow on the original

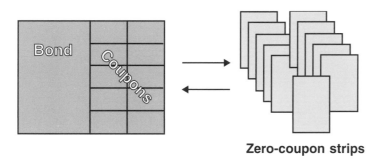

Zero-coupon strips

bond. The payment value of each coupon becomes the face value of a **strip** which has just one payment. The bond which remains is now a zero-coupon bond and is sold at a deep discount to its face value.

The zero-coupon bonds may then be sold **separately** in the markets. At the same time an appropriate bundle of strips can be exchanged for a coupon bearing bond.

For example, a 20-year bond with a face value of $10,000 and a coupon of 6.00% could be stripped into its principal repayment and 40 semi-annual interest payments. The result would be 41 separate zero-coupon instruments, each with its own maturity date. The principal instrument is still worth $10,000 at maturity and each interest coupon is worth £300. All 41 zero-coupon instruments can be traded separately in the markets.

The following cash flow chart may help to remember the basic characteristics of a zero-coupon bond.

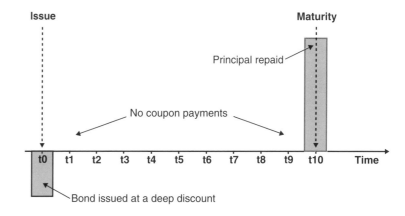

The Reuters screen below shows the **US Treasury Securities Stripped of Interest Payments.** The next two screens show detail for the same STRIPP.

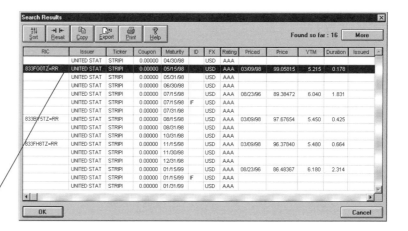

RIC	Issuer	Ticker	Coupon	Maturity	ID	FX	Rating	Priced	Price	YTM	Duration	Issued
	UNITED STAT	STRIPI	0.00000	04/30/98		USD	AAA					
833FG0TZ=RR	UNITED STAT	STRIPI	0.00000	05/15/98		USD	AAA	03/09/98	99.05815	5.215	0.178	
	UNITED STAT	STRIPI	0.00000	05/31/98		USD	AAA					
	UNITED STAT	STRIPI	0.00000	06/30/98		USD	AAA					
	UNITED STAT	STRIPI	0.00000	07/15/98		USD	AAA	08/23/96	89.38472	6.040	1.831	
	UNITED STAT	STRIPI	0.00000	07/15/98	IF	USD	AAA					
	UNITED STAT	STRIPI	0.00000	07/31/98		USD	AAA					
833B/5TZ=RR	UNITED STAT	STRIPI	0.00000	08/15/98		USD	AAA	03/09/98	97.67654	5.450	0.425	
	UNITED STAT	STRIPI	0.00000	08/31/98		USD	AAA					
833FH8TZ=RR	UNITED STAT	STRIPI	0.00000	10/31/98		USD	AAA					
	UNITED STAT	STRIPI	0.00000	11/15/98		USD	AAA	03/09/98	96.37840	5.480	0.664	
	UNITED STAT	STRIPI	0.00000	11/30/98		USD	AAA					
	UNITED STAT	STRIPI	0.00000	12/31/98		USD	AAA					
	UNITED STAT	STRIPI	0.00000	01/15/99		USD	AAA	08/23/96	86.48367	6.180	2.314	
	UNITED STAT	STRIPI	0.00000	01/15/99	IF	USD	AAA					
	UNITED STAT	STRIPI	0.00000	01/31/99		USD	AAA					

Found so far : 16

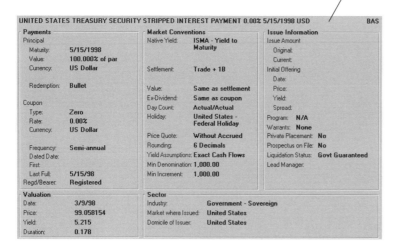

UNITED STATES TREASURY SECURITY STRIPPED INTEREST PAYMENT 0.00% 5/15/1998 USD   BAS

Payments
Principal
Maturity: 5/15/1998
Value: 100.000% of par
Currency: US Dollar

Redemption: Bullet

Coupon
Type: Zero
Rate: 0.00%
Currency: US Dollar

Frequency: Semi-annual
Dated Date:
First:
Last Full: 5/15/98
Regd/Bearer: Registered

Valuation
Date: 3/9/98
Price: 99.058154
Yield: 5.215
Duration: 0.178

Market Conventions
Native Yield: ISMA - Yield to Maturity

Settlement: Trade + 1B

Value: Same as settlement
Ex-Dividend: Same as coupon
Day Count: Actual/Actual
Holiday: United States - Federal Holiday

Price Quote: Without Accrued
Rounding: 6 Decimals
Yield Assumption: Exact Cash Flows
Min Denomination: 1,000.00
Min Increment: 1,000.00

Sector
Industry: Government - Sovereign
Market where Issued: United States
Domicile of Issuer: United States

Issue Information
Issue Amount
Original:
Current:
Initial Offering
Date:
Price:
Yield:
Spread:
Program: N/A
Warrants: None
Private Placement: No
Prospectus on File: No
Liquidation Status: Govt Guaranteed
Lead Manager:

Who Uses These Bonds?

The following tables indicate the advantages and disadvantages for both issuers and investors for fixed rate bonds, floating rate notes and zero-coupon bonds.

Issuers

Fixed Rate Bonds	Floating Rate Notes	Zero-coupon Bonds
Governments & Sovereign States These issue fixed rate bonds to finance debt and large scale projects. The markets are large and issuance is easy with regular auctions prearranged. **Corporations** These have the choice of using either the debt or equity markets to raise capital. Fixed rate bonds are issued when an organisation has a view about interest rates – future interest payments are known in advance. These organisations can also issue Eurobonds in the international markets in a foreign currency as a currency hedge to protect overseas investments or trading. **Banks and Investment Houses** These often issue subordinated fixed bonds to raise capital to finance their activities or if they have a view on interest rates. Fixed rate bonds also provide instruments for swap deals. **Supranationals** These raise capital for international projects using fixed rate domestic or Eurobonds. The bond currency is often matched to the country where the project is being financed.	**Governments & Sovereign States** These issue FRNs for much the same reasons as issuing fixed rate bonds. However, if the organisation has a particular view about interest rates, then issuing a FRN may reduce costs over fixed coupon payments. **Corporations** These issue FRNs if they have particular views on interest rates and wish to reduce costs over fixed coupon payments. Some organisations may not be sufficiently creditworthy to issue fixed rate bonds and find it easier to issue FRNs. These bonds can also be used for swaps transactions to convert floating rates into fixed. Issuing a FRN is a direct alternative to a bank loan. **Banks and Investment Houses** These are usually high quality issuers who use FRNs to raise capital to finance their activities and manage their liquidity. FRNs are also used to fund money market activities in various currencies.	**Governments/Sovereign States/ Supranationals/Corporations** Zero-coupon bonds are often issued by organisations who wish to delay repayment of cash to investors. Many governments have introduced STRIPS programmes which allow conventional fixed rate bonds to be stripped of their coupons resulting in a series of zero-coupon bonds. Stripped government bonds are not sold directly by treasuries but are stripped and traded by market makers according to rules set by the respective governments.

What Instruments Are Used in Bond Markets?

Investors

Fixed Rate Bonds	Floating Rate Notes	Zero-coupon Bonds
Pension Funds & Life assurance Fixed rate bonds provide a stable long-term asset to hedge long-term liabilities. **General Insurance** As the fixed rate is known these organisations can balance cash flows to match their financial predictions. **Fund Managers** Fixed rate bonds are used for investments when the fund manager has a particular view of interest rates. These bonds are also used to lower price volatility over equity markets and depending on the manager's view, improve performance over equity markets.	**Banks and Investment Houses** These invest in FRNs as an alternative to loans and as a means of managing liquidity and money market activities. **Corporations** These invest in FRNs if they have particular views on interest rates and wish to improve on returns over fixed coupon payments. These bonds can also be used for swaps transactions to convert floating rates into fixed. **Fund Managers** These invest in FRNs if they have particular views on interest rates and wish to improve on returns over fixed coupon payments.	**Pension Funds** Zero-coupon bonds are popular investments for these funds as tax can be deferred or may not be applicable.

REUTERS

Summary

Fixed Rate Bonds

- **Fixed rate, straight, plain vanilla** or **bullet** bonds are one of the most popular types of bond – they are easy to value, trade and swap

- This type is bond is issued in the domestic and international markets as government treasuries, corporate bonds, Eurobonds etc as **medium** to **long-term instruments** where the **principal** is repaid in a **single payment** at **maturity**

- The **coupon** is fixed throughout the life of a bond as a percentage of face value so the cash flow until maturity is known

- The coupon is usually set at launch as a **spread** above/below a government benchmark security in the same currency for the same maturity

- Depending on the market convention, coupons are paid **annually** or **semi-annually**

Floating Rate Notes

- **Floating Rate Notes (FRNs)** are medium to long term debt instruments which combine interest rate payments characteristic of short-term instruments with the maturity of fixed rate bonds

- The **coupon** is floating above or below a reference index such as **LIBOR, HIBOR** or **SIBOR**, or US Treasury Bills and is periodically reset

- If the coupon rate is set plus a margin in basis points (or percentage), then it is a conventional **floater**; if the rate is minus a margin, then it is an **inverse floater**

- The most common coupon reset periods are **quarterly** and **semi-annually**, for example, 3-month US T-Bills, 6-month LIBOR

Zero-coupon Bonds

- **Zeros** pay no coupons or interest over their life and so are bought at a deep discount from their face value

- The **return** on a zero is the difference between its purchase and redemption price

- Zero-coupon bonds can be created by **stripping** conventional bonds of their coupons and trading the resulting series of coupons and stripped bond separately

What Instruments Are Used in Bond Markets?

These Reuters screens display the UK Strips Speed Guide, with detail of OTC prices for all strippable gilts.

These Reuters screens display the Zero-Coupon Yield Curve Speed Guide, with detail of US dollar-denominated bonds' yields and discount prices for selected maturities.

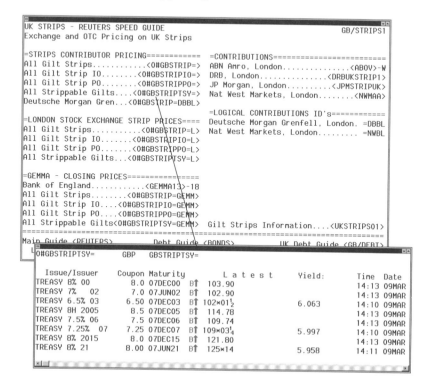

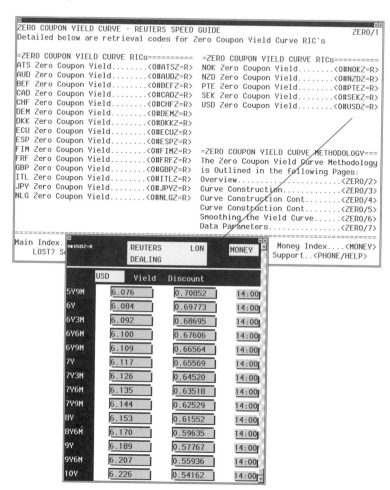

REUTERS

The Reuters Speed Guide below shows exchange and OTC listings for French OATS STRIPS, with pricing details from Paribas.

The screens below show a list of new issue FRNs, with detail about a French franc issue of FRNs from Abbey National.

```
FRENCH OAT STRIPS - REUTERS SPEED GUIDE              FR/OAT/STRIP
Exchange and OTC prices on OAT STRIPS.

=OAT SVT PRICES=====================  =OAT SVT PRICES contd==================
ABN Amro.................<AAFISTRIP>   Société Générale...............<SGFR05>
B.I.P. Dresdner.........<DRBSTRIP1>-2  U.B.S.......................<UBSFRSTRIP>
B.N.P........................<OBNE>-F  Union Européenne de CIC.......<CICSTRIP>
Banque d'Esconpte...................<>
C.C.F....................<CCFSTRIP>    =CVT PRICES=========================
C.P.R....................<CPRSTRIP>    BZW (CVT)....................<BZWTR>-S
Caisse des Dépôts........<CDCSTRIP1>-2
Crédit Agricole Indosuez<INDOSTRIP1>-2
Crédit Lyonnais..........<CLSTRIP01>   =PARIS STOCK EXCHANGE PRICES===========
Deutsche Bank.........<O#FRSTRIP=DEBP> All FRF Strips............<O#FRSTRIP=PA>
Goldman Sachs................<GSPH>-J  All FRF Principals......<O#FRSTRIPPO=PA>
J.P. Morgan..................<MGTO>-P  All April FRF Certif...<O#FRSTRIPAPR=PA>
Lehnan Brothers.....................<> All October FRF Certif.<O#FRSTRIPOCT=PA>
Merrill Lynch ...........<MLFSTRIP>    All ECU Strips........<O#FRSTRIPECU=PA>
Morgan Stanley.........<MSPE><MSPJ>-K  All ECU Principals.....<O#FRSTRIPECU=PA>
Paribas.................<PBSTRIP01>-3

Questions/Con
=============
French Debt<
  Lost?Select
```

```
14:51 09MAR98    PARIBAS PARIS SVT    TEL : 1.42.61.81 FRO1955    PBSTRIP01
Tel: 331 42.61.81.87
         APR FRF  OCT FRF   JAN DEM  JUL DEM   APR ECU    JAN ESP
98       3.23/17  3.55/49   0.03/    3.52/46   4.16/10
99       3.71/65  3.87/81   3.64/58  3.78/72   4.17/11    4.10/04
00       4.02/96  4.15/09   3.89/83  4.07/01   4.23/17    4.12/06
PO                                             4.23/17
01       4.24/18  4.36/30   4.17/11  4.32/26   4.39/33    4.33/27
PO                                             4.33/26
02       4.45/39  4.53/47   4.42/36  4.53/46   4.58/52    4.47/41
PO                                             4.58/52
03       4.60/54  4.66/60   4.60/54  4.69/63   4.70/64    4.66/59
PO       4.58/54  4.63/59                      4.69/63    4.67/61
04       4.74/68  4.79/74   4.73/67  4.82/76   4.84/78    4.83/77
PO       4.71/67  4.78/74                      4.83/77
05       4.88/82  4.93/87   4.89/83  4.93/88   4.98/92    4.94/88
PO       4.86/82  4.91/87                      4.97/91
06       4.97/91  5.02/96   4.96/90  5.03/97   5.08/02    5.08/02
PO       4.95/91  5.00/96                      5.08/02
07       5.06/00  5.11/05   5.07/00  5.10/04   5.16/10    5.22/16
PO       5.05/01  5.09/05   5.04/98  5.06/00   5.16/10

         OPEN              OPEN              OPEN              OPEN
NNN : 103.83       5Y:105.20 - 10Y:106.94   NNN : 103.24     Fut:108.88
Menu on <PBBONDS>                                    Next on <PBSTRIP02>
```

```
               FRN BONDS - NEW ISSUES                     FLOA
CODE          ISSUER           COUPON MAT DAT    RIC
Z69P   USD  AMETHYST FUNDING   5.9328 02SEP03  KY008487839=   C
Z63F   GBP  ARGENTARIA           -    04MAR03  ES008459509=   C
Z65N   FRF  ARGENATRIA           -    04FEB09  ES008395098=   C
Z5YL   USD  ADVANTA CCMT       5.8134 29JAN01                 C
Z5SV   XEU  ARGENTARIA         4.3816 19MAY03  ES008413428=   C
Z5NQ   FRF  ABBEY NATIONAL     4.3900 10FEB09  GB008398593=   C
Z5IE   DEM  AWA PAPER          1.9832 27JAN03  JP008352577=   C
Z5HJ   JPY  ASAHI CHEM IND     1.2980 27FEB06  JP008353344=   C
Z5EH   USD  ARGENTARIA           -    21JAN03  ES008353603=   C
Z57R   GBP  ANNINGTON FIN      8.0904 10JAN23  GB008307997=   C
```

```
    FRN           ABBEY NATIONAL 4.3900 10FEB09            Z5NQ
ISS DATE   21JAN98 LEAD           CL COMM  008398593 S&P    AA
ISS PRICE  100.000 DENOM          1M FRF IS XS0083985936 MDY AA2
ISS AMT     1.0B   PAY FREQ          QTR VALOREN    -
AT CLOSE     -     NEXT COUP     11MAY98 WERT      197343 CTRY GBR
NO OF DAYS   -     NEUTRAL          -   GUARANTOR    -
ACC INT      -     DISC MGN         -
B/C        -/-     SIMPLE MGN       -   TERMS -FRTEC10Y-0.7,FM(2
                   YR HI            -   ),ENG LAW,+24 OVER TEC10
MID PRICE    -     YR LO            -   25/01/09,REOFF @ ISSUE
<GB008398593=>   <O#GB008398593=>   <GB008398593=RTR>
IF THE CHAIN IS DATA NOT AVAILABLE CLICK ON THE RIC FOR PRICES
```

Redemption Classification

In the case of a straight bond, once an issuer has issued a bond the organisation is locked into paying agreed coupons. However, over time interest rates may fall and the issuer could get cheaper financing in the current market place. For investors, if interest rates rise over time, then a better return may be possible in the current markets but their capital is locked in. What can be done to overcome these eventualities?

A straight bond involves a bullet repayment at maturity but it is this capital which may be required prior to maturity. There are a number of bonds available which vary the structure of a bond such that the principal may be repaid prior to maturity. These bonds may be classified as one of the following:

- **Callable bond**
- **Puttable bond**
- **Sinking fund bond**
- **Perpetual bond**

Both callable and puttable bonds contain embedded options and sinking fund bonds may contain options available to the issuer. Perpetual bonds, as the name implies, have no maturity date although this type often includes a call option feature for the issuer.

Callable Bond

A **Callable** bond gives the **issuer** the right or option, but not the obligation, to redeem a bond at agreed specific prices and dates **before** the scheduled maturity date.

The call features are embedded in the bond and cannot be traded separately. If the call is exercised, then the principal amount outstanding is called, thus creating an early redemption.

A callable bond is therefore advantageous to an issuer if interest rates fall – the bond can be redeemed early allowing the issuer to re-finance at a lower interest rate. This feature is often less appealing to

investors and therefore callable bonds are issued with higher coupon rates.

Investors, therefore, require a higher coupon rate from callable bonds to compensate for the possibility of early redemption.

These Reuters screens show the basic details of a callable bond issued by Tenet Healthcare Corporation, with more specific details in the lower screen as to redemption features such as call dates and pricing.

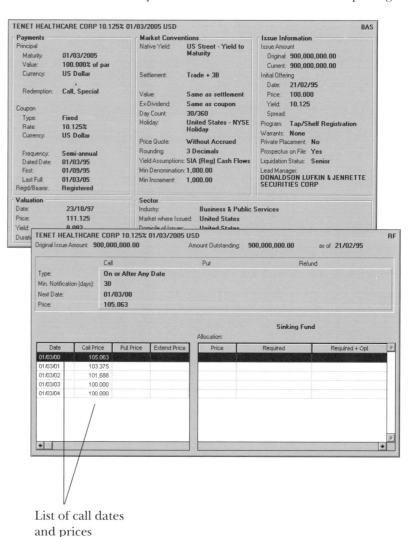

List of call dates and prices

There are a number of ways the call prices and dates can be structured. For example, call prices may decline each year, there may be only a single call date or there may be a series of call prices for each call date.

There are also different ways in which the issuer can exercise the call option – American or European style.

- **American** or **continuous style** is where the issuer can exercise the call on the call date **or** any date thereafter

- **European** or **discrete style** is where the issuer can exercise the call **only** on interest payment dates which correspond with the call dates

In the period between the issuance of the bond and the first call date the bond is said to be **call protected**. In order to exercise a call the issuer is required to give a **minimum notification period** in order to inform the investors that the bond will be called.

Puttable Bond

A **Puttable** bond gives the **investor** the right or option, but not the obligation, to sell back his/her portion of the bond to the issuer at specific prices and dates.

Puttable bonds give investors the opportunity to re-invest their funds at higher returns if rates rise. Because of this potential advantage to investors, issuers can issue this type of bond at lower rates than straight or callable bonds.

As with call options, put options can be American or European style and have minimum notification periods. Some issuers limit the amount of bonds they will redeem from an investor on a single put date.

The following cash flow chart may help to remember the basic characteristics of a callable and puttable bond. Note that if the issuer calls, or the investor puts, the bond, the final payments (marked X) do not occur.

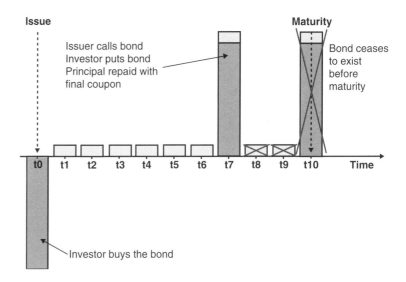

These Reuters screens show the basic details of a puttable bond issued by Coca-Cola Enterprise Inc, with more specific details in the lower screen as to redemption features such as put dates and pricing.

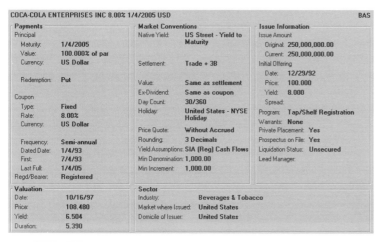

Sinking Fund Bond

 A **Sinking Fund** bond is one in which part of the total principal amount of the bond is repaid according to an agreed schedule of dates, amounts and prices.

The purpose of a sinking fund bond is to reduce the issuer's credit risk by not requiring that all of the principal be paid at maturity. A sinking fund bond is rather like a callable bond with respect to an issuer except that there is now an obligation to retire all or part of the principal according to an agreed schedule. This schedule may specify just dates and amounts or it may also include a call schedule of prices — a call option on prices.

As with the case of callable bonds, for the risk of receiving their principal back early, investors expect higher coupons than for conventional bonds. However, if interest rates are high and bond prices fall, a sinking fund could act like a puttable bond for an investor. Bonds which are surrendered cease to exist.

It is also possible for an issuer to add additional amounts to a sinking fund using a **voluntary sink**. This is rather like a callable bond where the issuer can choose whether or not to reduce the principal by more than the scheduled amount.

There are a number of ways in which an issuer can distribute sinking fund payments to investors. These include:

- **Lottery** – specific investors are selected at random by the paying agent

- **Pro-rata** – each investor receives an equal portion of the principal

- **Serial** – portions held are sunk according to the serial number of the bond

- **Trustee** – portions to be sunk are determined by the Trustee responsible for administering the conditions of the bond

Look at this Reuters screen for a sinking fund Revlon bond and the following explanation.

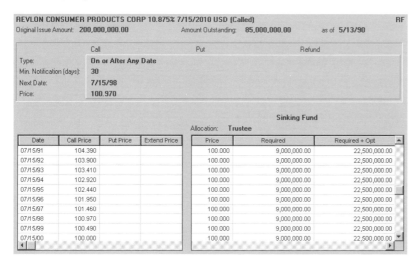

This bond has both call options on prices for the scheduled dates and an option on the sinking fund required to be retired. The first sink occurred on 15th July 1991 on which date Revlon were required to retire $9 million at 100% of par value. There was also the option to exercise a call price of 104.390 and an option to retire up to $22.5 million of the principal. You can also see that for this bond the method of allocation was by **Trustee**.

The following cash flow chart may help to remember the basic characteristics of a sinking fund bond.

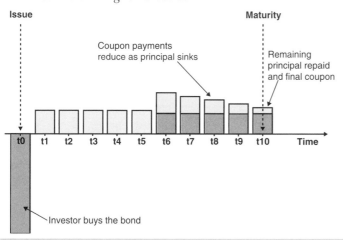

The Reuters screens below give information about a sinking fund bond issued by Rohm & Haas Company, with more specific details about its redemption features, such as dates, prices and amounts.

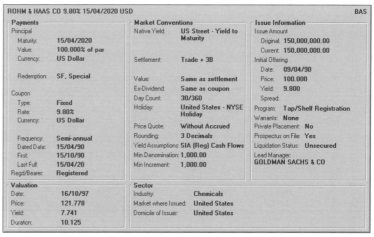

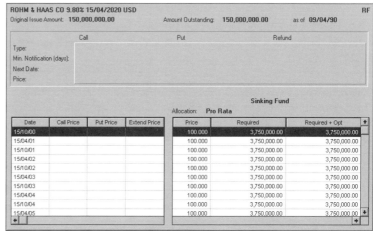

Perpetual Bond

> A **Perpetual** bond is one which has a coupon but **no** final maturity date specified.

A perpetual bond is also sometimes known as an **undated** or **irredeemable** bond. Although the bond, which can be issued by a government or corporation, pays a stream of fixed coupon payments, a perpetual bond does not conform to the normal definition of a bond in that it has no maturity date. To overcome this difficulty, some perpetuals include a call schedule allowing the issuer to pay back the bond principal and therefore remove the perpetual obligation.

The UK government has issued this type of bond in the past when yields were low. Typically these bonds had low coupons, for example, 3.5% War Loan gilts. Because the coupons are lower than current yields, it would be expensive for the UK government to repay these bonds and refinance with a new issue.

The following cash flow chart may help to remember the basic characteristics of a perpetual bond.

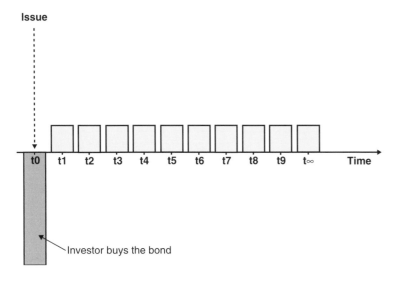

The Reuters screen below shows the details of a straight **Air Canada** perpetual bond – as you can see the bond has no maturity date.

```
      STR              AIR CANADA (PERP) 5.7500 PERP              ZLOY
ISS DATE      FEB86 LEAD              SBC COMM   001253069 S&P     -
ISS PRICE   100.000 DENOM       5,100 CHF IS CH0006621301 MDY     -
ISS AMT     200.0M PAY FREQ        ANNUAL VALOREN   662130
AT CLOSE    12NOV97                        WERT      477504 CTRY  CAN
MAT YLD PA      -    MOD DURAT        -    GUARANTOR        -
MAT YLD SA      -    ACC INT       4.472
B/C        -/-      QTR PT VAR       -    NEXT CALL         07FEB99
                    YR HI        85.950 CALL AMT          200.000M
MID PRICE   82.250 YR LO        63.650 PRICE             101.500
<CH662130=>          <O#CH662130=>        <CH662130=RTR>
IF THE CHAIN IS DATA NOT AVAILABLE CLICK ON THE RIC FOR PRICES
```

Who Uses These Bonds?

Callable Bonds
A callable bond is advantageous to the issuer if interest rates fall over time. The issuer can exercise the right to repay the principal and refinance at lower costs. This option means that investors are exposed to reinvestment risk. To compensate for this risk of early redemption the coupon rate has to be higher than for conventional instruments.

Puttable Bonds
In the case of a puttable bond the advantage lies with the investor who has the right, but not obligation, to redeem the bond or part of it earlier than the scheduled maturity date. The investor thus receives a lower coupon rate in order to offset the risk to the issuer of early redemption.

Sinking Fund Bonds
Issuers using this type of bond may find future redemption obligations easier to manage on an instalment plan and benefit from reduced interest payments over time. Rating agencies may give this type of bond a higher rating than a straight bond which may also be more cost effective for the issuer. If a bond is trading below the sinking fund price, the issuer may buy back the required amount of

bonds in the open market in a **market repurchase** and profit from the transaction.

Certain investors such as central banks may be constrained to buying bonds with a maximum maturity period. By issuing a sinking fund bond an issuer can reduce the **average life** of the bond to suit such investors.

Summary

Callable Bond

- The **issuer** has the **right**, but not obligation, to redeem the bond **before** the scheduled maturity date

- The call features are **embedded** in the bond and cannot be traded separately

- Callable bonds can be exercised **American style** – exercise on the call date or any date thereafter – or **European style** – exercise only on call dates

- Once called the bond **ceases** to exist

Puttable Bond

- The **investor** has the **right**, but not obligation, to redeem the bond **before** the scheduled maturity date

- The put features are **embedded** in the bond and cannot be traded separately

- Puttable bonds can be exercised **American style** – exercise on the call date or any date thereafter – or **European style** – exercise only on call dates

- Once put the bond **ceases** to exist

Sinking Fund Bond

- Part of the total principal amount of the bond is repaid according to a schedule of dates and amounts – hence the repayable principal amount **sinks** over time

- Sinking fund bonds have an **obligation** to repay principal amounts according to the schedule of dates and amounts

- Sinking fund bonds can have a **call option** on the prices to be paid on the scheduled dates

- **Voluntary sinks** also have an option on additional amounts which can be repaid on the scheduled dates

- Sinking fund repayments to investors may be allocated by **lottery, pro-rata, serial** or **trustee**

Perpetual Bond

- The bond has a coupon but no **maturity date** is specified

- The bond may have a **call option** which allows the issuer to repay the principal and thus remove the perpetual obligation

- Perpetual bonds are also known as **undated** or **irredeemable** bonds

Principal Payments Classification

This classification covers differing ways in which final principal payments may be made from bullet bonds. In terms of principal payments, other than a bullet bond, a bond may be classified as one of the following:

- **Index-linked bond**

- **Dual currency bond**

- **ECU bond**

Issuers have varying reasons for altering the principal repayment. Also governments are now increasing their issues of index-linked and ECU bonds in order to attract a wider number of investors.

Index-linked Bond

An **Index-linked** or **Inflation Indexed** bond has a fixed principal payment which is tied to a financial index such as the UK Retail Price Index (RPI), the US Standard & Poor 500 Stock Index, the US Consumer Price Index for all Urban consumers (CPI-U), foreign exchange rate or money market rates.

Typically this type of bond is based on an inflation index such as the RPI which provides investors with some protection against inflation and which allows issuers to use a lower rate for its bonds. Index-linked gilts are an important part of the UK government issuance of bonds.

Index-linked or inflation-indexed bonds are issued by a number of governments and organisations now as a way of reducing their borrowing costs and as a way to attract investors. Conventional bond coupons are subject to inflation risk and therefore the coupon yield incorporates a premium to compensate for such risk. By removing this risk, treasuries can issue index-linked bonds at lower coupon rates and thus reduce the cost of borrowing.

The determination of the final principal can be based on a simple ratio of the index at issue compared to the index at maturity. An issuer can also structure the principal of an index-linked bond to be adjusted for every coupon as in the case of index-linked UK gilts. The issuer can also specify that the principal only is adjusted at maturity. In the case of the index-linked UK gilts coupon payments are affected by the reset principal value.

There are three main types of index-linked bonds which have been or are currently being issued by governments. These are:

- **Capital indexed**. Most current index-linked bonds issued by governments are of this type where interest payments are made equal to a fixed coupon rate based on an inflation adjusted principal amount. At maturity both the final coupon payments and the principal repayment are adjusted for inflation.

- **Interest indexed**. This type of bond pays a fixed rate coupon and an indexation of the fixed principal every coupon date. In this case the principal repayment at maturity is not adjusted for inflation.

- **Zero-coupon indexed**. As with other types of zero-coupon bonds this type of bond pays no coupon over its life time but at maturity the principal repayments is adjusted for inflation.

The UK government has issued index-linked gilts since 1981 and is currently the largest government issuer of this type – as of March 1997 the total outstanding UK index-linked gilts was the equivalent of $84.4 billion. The first issue of US inflation-indexed bonds was in January 1997 when $7 billion of 10-year indexed bonds were issued with a real yield of 3.45%. At the same time the conventional 10-year T-Bonds were issued with a yield of 6.63%

Index-linked bonds or inflation-indexed bonds as they are termed in the US have been introduced to attract investors who are keen to protect their purchasing power in the future. For example, a $10,000 straight bond with an annual 5% coupon is not worth $10,500 in real terms after one year. Inflation will have reduced its real purchasing power by an amount depending on the level of inflation.

With an index-linked or inflation-indexed bond the rate of return is fixed at a certain percentage. So it does not matter what the inflation rate is at maturity, the return percentage on the bond remains the same.

This makes these types of bond popular with investors who need a predictable real cash flow and who wish to protect their investment from inflation, for example, pension funds and individuals. However, such bonds are not actively traded as investors buy them with the intent of holding them to maturity.

The Reuters screen below show the basic details of this UK Treasury gilt, plus the index-linked details.

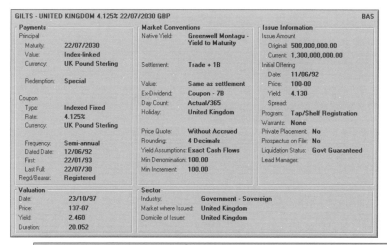

Dual Currency Bond

 A **Dual Currency** bond is one which involves a different currency for the coupon payments than that used for the repayment of the principal at maturity.

Most bonds pay both interest payments and principal repayments in the same currency. Dual currency bonds involve different currencies for these payments, for example, an Australian dollar denominated bond repaid at maturity in Australian dollars pays coupons in yen.

Dual currency bonds are typically issued by issuers who simultaneously enter into an Interest Rate Swap (IRS) which effectively locks in forward currency rates at favourable interest rates for that currency. Swap derivatives are explained in general in *An Introduction to Derivatives*. If you need a more detailed explanation of IRSs then you may need to refer to *An Introduction to Foreign Exchange and Money Markets*.

There are a number of ways in which dual currency bonds can be issued which include the following:

- The currency exchange rate used for converting the coupon repayments into a currency other than that of the principal is specified when the bond is issued

- The currency exchange rate for the coupon payments is the spot rate at the payment date

- Investors or issuers have a choice of currency for the coupon payments at some point during the lifetime of the bond – this type is often referred to as an **option currency bond**

The Reuters screen below shows the basic details of this Federal National Mortgage Association (Fannie Mae) dual currency Eurobond. The principal payment is in US dollars, whereas the coupon payments are in Japanese yen.

FEDERAL NATIONAL MORTGAGE ASSOCIATION (FANNIE MAE) 5.12% 28/06/1999 USD		BAS
Payments	**Market Conventions**	**Issue Information**
Principal	Native Yield: ISMA - Yield to Maturity	Issue Amount
Maturity: 28/06/1999		Original: 10,000,000,000.00
Value: 100.000% of par		Current: 10,000,000,000.00
Currency: US Dollar	Settlement: Trade + 3B	Initial Offering
		Date: 05/06/97
Redemption: Special	Value: Same as settlement	Price: 100.000
	Ex-Dividend: Same as coupon	Yield:
Coupon	Day Count: 30E/360	Spread:
Type: Fixed	Holiday: Eurobond	Program: Medium Term Note
Rate: 5.12%		Warrants: None
Currency: Japanese Yen	Price Quote: Without Accrued	Private Placement: Yes
	Rounding: 3 Decimals	Prospectus on File: No
Frequency: Semi-annual	Yield Assumptions: Exact Cash Flows	Liquidation Status: Unsecured
Dated Date: 27/06/97	Min Denomination: 500,000.00	Lead Manager:
First: 28/12/97	Min Increment: 500,000.00	MERRILL LYNCH FAR EAST LTD
Last Full: 28/06/99		
Regd/Bearer: Registered		
Valuation	**Sector**	
Date:	Industry: Government - Agency	
Price:	Market where Issued: Eurobond	
Yield:	Domicile of Issuer: United States	
Duration:		

European Currency Unit (ECU) Bond

Prior to the launch of the euro in January 1999, the European Currency Unit (ECU), which was a composite basket currency consisting of specified amounts of each European Union community currency, was used for euro issues.

On 1 January 1999, the ECU ceased to exist and all ECU-denominated debt was converted into euro at the rate of ECU 1 = euro 1.

Who Uses These Bonds?

Index-linked or Inflation-indexed Bonds

Most bonds of this type are issued by governments and the largest issuers in terms of total outstanding in $ billion equivalent is shown in the chart below.

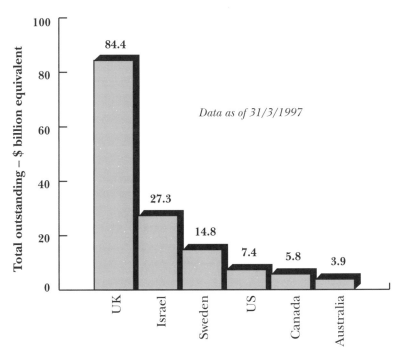

Data as of 31/3/1997

Source: Bank of England: Gilts and the Gilt Market – Review 1996/97

Corporations issuing this type of bond include commodity producers, utilities and retailers who use these bonds to hedge revenues or incomes.

Investors in these bonds typically include pension funds, investment funds and individuals who seek to protect their real purchasing power in the future. Corporations also invest in these bonds as a hedge for long-term operating costs such as fuel, utilities, rent etc.

Dual Currency Bonds

Issuers and investors in dual currency bonds often use these bonds to enter into interest rate swaps or currency swaps where forward currency exchange rates can be locked in at the same time as receiving favourable interest rates in the coupon currency. As an example, the Export-Import Bank of Korea issued a 3-year dual currency samurai bond in Tokyo. In order to hedge the currency exposure the bank entered into a currency swap at the same time. The result was an overall borrowing cost of 0.15% over 6-month USD LIBOR and cheap funding.

Summary

Index-linked or Inflation-indexed Bond

- An **index-linked** or **inflation-indexed** bond provides **protection** against inflation and is typically linked to a **market index** such as the UK Retail Price Index (RPI) or the US Consumer Price Index for all Urban consumers (CPI-U)

- Most bonds issued have fixed coupons and are **capital indexed** – coupon rates are lower than those of conventional bullet bonds of comparable maturities

- Investors are attracted to these bonds because the inflation risk of their investment is **adjusted** during the life time of the bond thus preserving their real purchasing power

Dual Currency Bond

- A **dual currency** bond uses **different** currencies for the principal repayment and the coupon payments

- **Exchange rates** for coupon payments can be fixed at issue or set at spot for each coupon date.

- Dual currency bonds provide a means of entering into currency swaps.

ECU Bond

On 1 January 1999, the ECU ceased to exist and all ECU-denominated ebt was converted into euro at the rate of ECU 1 = euro 1.

These Reuters screens are a list of index-linked gilts and the pricing for a US Treasury inflation-indexed note.

These Reuters screens below are a list of euro-denominated bonds and euro-denominated Eurobonds.

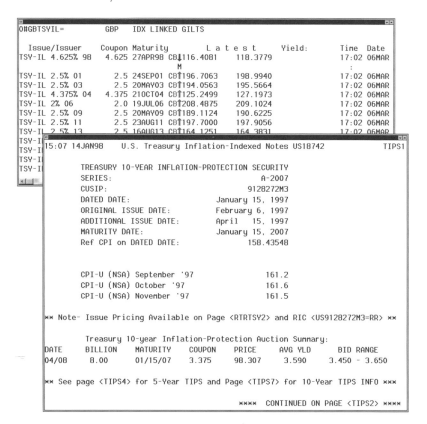

```
O#GBTSYIL=          GBP    IDX LINKED GILTS

   Issue/Issuer    Coupon Maturity      L a t e s t    Yield:     Time  Date
TSY-IL 4.625% 98   4.625  27APR98 CB↓116.4081   118.3779          17:02 06MAR
                                M                                    :
TSY-IL 2.5% 01     2.5    24SEP01 CB↑196.7063   198.9940          17:02 06MAR
TSY-IL 2.5% 03     2.5    20MAY03 CB↑194.0563   195.5664          17:02 06MAR
TSY-IL 4.375% 04   4.375  21OCT04 CB↑125.2499   127.1973          17:02 06MAR
TSY-IL 2% 06       2.0    19JUL06 CB↑208.4875   209.1024          17:02 06MAR
TSY-IL 2.5% 09     2.5    20MAY09 CB↑189.1124   190.6225          17:02 06MAR
TSY-IL 2.5% 11     2.5    23AUG11 CB↑197.7000   197.9056          17:02 06MAR
TSY-IL 2.5% 13     2.5    16AUG13 CB↑164.1251   164.3831          17:02 06MAR
```

```
15:07 14JAN98    U.S. Treasury Inflation-Indexed Notes US18742        TIPS1

       TREASURY 10-YEAR INFLATION-PROTECTION SECURITY
       SERIES:                        A-2007
       CUSIP:                         9128272M3
       DATED DATE:            January 15, 1997
       ORIGINAL ISSUE DATE:   February 6, 1997
       ADDITIONAL ISSUE DATE: April  15, 1997
       MATURITY DATE:         January 15, 2007
       Ref CPI on DATED DATE:          158.43548


       CPI-U (NSA) September '97         161.2
       CPI-U (NSA) October '97          161.6
       CPI-U (NSA) November '97         161.5

** Note- Issue Pricing Available on Page <RTRTSY2> and RIC <US9128272M3=RR> **

       Treasury 10-year Inflation-Protection Auction Summary:
DATE   BILLION   MATURITY    COUPON   PRICE   AVG YLD    BID RANGE
04/08   8.00     01/15/07    3.375    98.307   3.590     3.450 - 3.650

** See page <TIPS4> for 5-Year TIPS and Page <TIPS7> for 10-Year TIPS INFO ***

                      ****  CONTINUED ON PAGE <TIPS2>  ****
```

```
O#XETSY1=      XEU      G7 EUROS                           EUROBOND1
For European Monetary Union Overview Page please see <EMU/1>
Issue/Issuer   Coupon Maturity     Bid   Ask     BYld  AYld  Contributor    Loc Time  Date
FRANCE OAT     5.5000 25APR07    98.91-99.01     5.65-5.63   BANQUE PARIB   PAR 12:04 25NOV
FRANCE OAT     8.2500 25APR22   125.48-125.88    6.19-6.17   BIP            PAR 12:04 25NOV
ITALY          4.4570 31JUL9B  100.100-100.180      -        ISMA CLOSING       22:20 24NOV
ITALY         10.7500 18APR00  112.64-112.89        -        KREDIETBANK    LUX 10:33 25NOV
ITALY          6.0000 02APR04  102.18-102.68    5.58-5.48    DEUTSCHE BK    LON 12:06 25NOV
ITALY          4.46B8 30OCT05    99.60-99.90        -        CREDITO        MIL 08:15 25NOV
ITALY          9.2500 07MAR11  129.87-130.37        -        KREDIETBANK    LUX 10:33 25NOV
ITALY TRANCHE 7     0 07MAR9B   98.750-99.000        -       ISMA CLOSING       22:20 24NOV
ITALY TRANCHE 8     0 07MAR99   94.000-94.250        -       ISMA CLOSING       22:20 24NOV
ITALY TRANCHE 9     0 07MAR00   89.375-89.625        -       ISMA CLOSING       22:20 24NOV
ITALY TRANCHE 10    0 07MAR01   84.375-84.625        -       ISMA CLOSING       22:20 24NOV
ITALY TRANCHE 11    0 07MAR02   75.250-75.500        -       ISMA CLOSING       21:25 26MAR
ITALY TRANCHE 12    0 07MAR03   74.500-74.750        -       ISMA CLOSING       22:20 24NOV
ITALY TRANCHE 13    0 07MAR04   70.000-70.250        -       ISMA CLOSING       22:20 24NOV
ITALY TRANCHE 14    0 07MAR05   65.625-66.625        -       ISMA CLOSING       22:20 24NOV
ITALY TRANCHE 15    0 07MAR06   61.625-62.625        -       ISMA CLOSING       22:20 24NOV
ITALY TRANCHE 16    0 07MAR07   57.625-58.625        -       ISMA CLOSING       22:20 24NOV
ITALY TRANCHE 17    0 07MAR0B   47.750-49.000        -       ISMA CLOSING       21:25 26MAR
ITALY TRANCHE 18    0 07MAR09   49.500-50.375        -       ISMA CLOSING       22:20 24NOV
ITALY TRANCHE 19    0 07MAR10   46.375-47.750        -       ISMA CLOSING       22:20 24NOV
ITALY TRANCHE 20    0 07MAR11        -              -                            :
ITALY TRANCHE 21    0 07MAR11   43.250-44.000        -       ISMA CLOSING       22:20 24NOV
UNITED KINGDOM 8.0000 27JAN98  100.49-100.56    4.46-       UNION EURO P   PAR 11:46 25NOV
```

```
O#EUROXEUSAB=            STR EUROS AB

  Issue/Issuer    Coupon Maturity       L a t e s t     Yield:     Time  Date Source
ABBEY NATIONAL    4.125  21AUG9B   B   99.250  A  99.750          22:57 21NOV
ABBEY NATIONAL    5.0000 12DEC00   B↓  99.61   A 100.11  5.14 4.96 12:06 25NOV DMG61
ABBEY NATL TRSY   6.2500 26APR99   B 101.500   A 101.875          22:20 24NOV
ABBEY NATL TRSY   5.0000 12DEC00   B  99.750   A 100.125          22:20 24NOV
ABBEY NATL TRSY   5.7500 15OCT04   B↑ 105.50   A 106.25           07:32 25NOV KRBG
ABN-AMRO          6.3750 25APR07   B↑ 102.57   A 102.97           10:33 25NOV KBECU5
AMER TEL & TEL    7.250  17AUG9B   B 101.375   A 101.750          22:20 24NOV
AMER TEL & TEL    8.000  18OCT99   B↓ 104.98   A 105.23           10:37 25NOV KBECU3
AUSTRIA           7.75   20MAR9B   B 100.875   A 101.250          22:20 24NOV
BACOB             7.5    27MAY9B   B 101.125   A 102.125          22:20 24NOV
BANQUE INDOSUEZ   6.25   15OCT9B   B 101.125   A 101.500          22:20 24NOV
BAYERISCHE HYPO   8.250  07DEC9B   B 103.125   A 103.375          22:20 24NOV
BAYERISCHE HYPO   7.0000 22DEC00   B 104.875   A 105.375          22:20 24NOV
BAYERISCHE HYPO   5.0000 09JUL01   B  99.500   A 100.000          22:20 24NOV
BAYERISCHE HYPO   6.25   30OCT01   B 103.125   A 103.750          22:20 24NOV
BAYERISCHE HYPO   5.75   17DEC04      100.85   A 101.15           10:33 25NOV KBECU5
BAYERISCHE HYPO   6.0000 18MAR05   B↑ 106.60   A                  10:12 25NOV KRBH
BAY VEREINSBANK   8.250  23FEB99   B↑ 103.79   A 104.04           10:33 25NOV KBECU2
BAY VEREINSBANK   5.2500 30JUL02   M 105.000                      22:20 24NOV
BAY VEREINSBANK   5.3750 31DEC03   B↑  99.91   A 100.26           10:33 25NOV KBECU5
BELLSOUTH CORP    5.25   02FEB99   B 100.250   A 100.625          22:20 24NOV
BFCE              9.000  24MAY99   B↓ 105.59   A 105.84           10:33 25NOV KBECU3
BK NEDERL GEM     8.125  08DEC9B   B 103.125   A 103.375          22:20 24NOV
BK NEDERL GEM     8.125  08DEC9B   B↓ 103.01   A 103.21           10:33 25NOV KBECU2
BQE GEN DU LUX    5.5000 27JUN03   B↑ 100.75   A 100.90           08:12 25NOV BGLH
BQE GEN DU LUX    5.5    29OCT04   B↑  99.95   A 100.10           08:12 25NOV BGLH
```

These Reuters screens show details for a US Treasury index-linked bond and a UK index-linked bond.

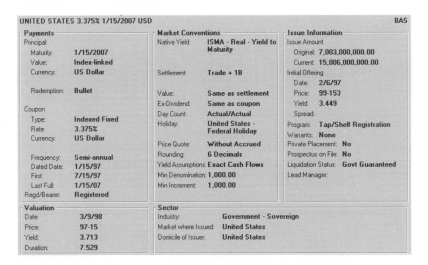

UNITED STATES 3.375% 1/15/2007 USD   BAS

Payments

Principal

Maturity:	1/15/2007
Value:	Index-linked
Currency:	US Dollar
Redemption:	Bullet

Coupon

Type:	Indexed Fixed
Rate:	3.375%
Currency:	US Dollar
Frequency:	Semi-annual
Dated Date:	1/15/97
First:	7/15/97
Last Full:	1/15/07
Regd/Bearer:	Registered

Valuation

Date:	3/9/98
Price:	97-15
Yield:	3.713
Duration:	7.529

Market Conventions

Native Yield:	ISMA - Real - Yield to Maturity
Settlement:	Trade + 1B
Value:	Same as settlement
Ex-Dividend:	Same as coupon
Day Count:	Actual/Actual
Holiday:	United States - Federal Holiday
Price Quote:	Without Accrued
Rounding:	6 Decimals
Yield Assumptions:	Exact Cash Flows
Min Denomination:	1,000.00
Min Increment:	1,000.00

Sector

Industry:	Government - Sovereign
Market where Issued:	United States
Domicile of Issuer:	United States

Issue Information

Issue Amount

Original:	7,003,000,000.00
Current:	15,006,000,000.00

Initial Offering

Date:	2/6/97
Price:	99-153
Yield:	3.449
Spread:	
Program:	Tap/Shelf Registration
Warrants:	None
Private Placement:	No
Prospectus on File:	No
Liquidation Status:	Govt Guaranteed
Lead Manager:	

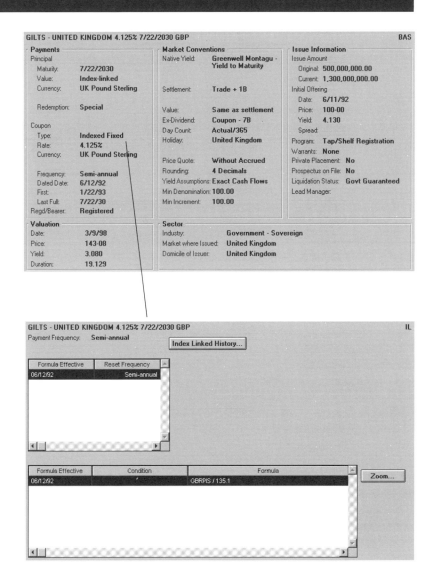

GILTS - UNITED KINGDOM 4.125% 7/22/2030 GBP   BAS

Payments

Principal

Maturity:	7/22/2030
Value:	Index-linked
Currency:	UK Pound Sterling
Redemption:	Special

Coupon

Type:	Indexed Fixed
Rate:	4.125%
Currency:	UK Pound Sterling
Frequency:	Semi-annual
Dated Date:	6/12/92
First:	1/22/93
Last Full:	7/22/30
Regd/Bearer:	Registered

Valuation

Date:	3/9/98
Price:	143-08
Yield:	3.080
Duration:	19.129

Market Conventions

Native Yield:	Greenwell Montagu - Yield to Maturity
Settlement:	Trade + 1B
Value:	Same as settlement
Ex-Dividend:	Coupon - 7B
Day Count:	Actual/365
Holiday:	United Kingdom
Price Quote:	Without Accrued
Rounding:	4 Decimals
Yield Assumptions:	Exact Cash Flows
Min Denomination:	100.00
Min Increment:	100.00

Sector

Industry:	Government - Sovereign
Market where Issued:	United Kingdom
Domicile of Issuer:	United Kingdom

Issue Information

Issue Amount

Original:	500,000,000.00
Current:	1,300,000,000.00

Initial Offering

Date:	6/11/92
Price:	100-00
Yield:	4.130
Spread:	
Program:	Tap/Shelf Registration
Warrants:	None
Private Placement:	No
Prospectus on File:	No
Liquidation Status:	Govt Guaranteed
Lead Manager:	

GILTS - UNITED KINGDOM 4.125% 7/22/2030 GBP   IL

Payment Frequency: Semi-annual

[Index Linked History...]

Formula Effective	Reset Frequency
06/12/92	Semi-annual

Formula Effective	Condition	Formula
06/12/92	'	GBRPIS / 135.1

[Zoom...]

These Reuters screens show details of a World Bank US dollar issue with coupon patments made in yen. Also shown are the details of two ECU-denominated French issues.

WORLD BANK (INTERNATIONAL BANK FOR RECONSTRUCTION AND DEVELOPMENT) 5.10% 8/27/1998 USD — BAS

Payments

Principal

Maturity:	8/27/1998
Value:	100.000% of par
Currency:	US Dollar
Redemption:	Special

Coupon

Type:	Fixed
Rate:	5.10%
Currency:	Japanese Yen
Frequency:	Annual
Dated Date:	8/27/96
First:	8/27/97
Last Full:	8/27/98
Regd/Bearer:	Bearer

Valuation

Date:	
Price:	
Yield:	
Duration:	

Market Conventions

Native Yield:	ISMA - Yield to Maturity
Settlement:	Trade + 3B
Value:	Same as settlement
Ex-Dividend:	Same as coupon
Day Count:	30E/360
Holiday:	Eurobond
Price Quote:	Without Accrued
Rounding:	3 Decimals
Yield Assumptions:	Exact Cash Flows
Min Denomination:	100,000.00
Min Increment:	100,000.00

Sector

Industry:	Supranational Organization
Market where Issued:	Eurobond
Domicile of Issuer:	Supranationals

Issue Information

Issue Amount

Original:	7,000,000,000.00
Current:	7,000,000,000.00

Initial Offering

Date:	7/24/96
Price:	100.125
Yield:	
Spread:	
Program:	Medium Term Note
Warrants:	None
Private Placement:	No
Prospectus on File:	No
Liquidation Status:	Unsecured
Lead Manager:	DEUTSCHE MORGAN GRENFELL (UK) LTD

FRANCE OAT 8.50% 3/15/2002 XEU — BAS

Payments

Principal

Maturity:	3/15/2002
Value:	100.000% of par
Currency:	European Currency Unit
Redemption:	Bullet

Coupon

Type:	Fixed
Rate:	8.50%
Currency:	European Currency Unit
Frequency:	Annual
Dated Date:	3/15/91
First:	3/15/92
Last Full:	3/15/02
Regd/Bearer:	Registered

Valuation

Date:	3/10/98
Price:	114.40
Yield:	4.492
Duration:	3.199

Market Conventions

Native Yield:	ISMA - Yield to Maturity
Settlement:	Trade + 3B
Value:	Same as settlement
Ex-Dividend:	Same as coupon
Day Count:	Actual/Actual
Holiday:	France
Price Quote:	Without Accrued
Rounding:	2 Decimals
Yield Assumptions:	Exact Cash Flows
Min Denomination:	500.00
Min Increment:	500.00

Sector

Industry:	Government - Sovereign
Market where Issued:	France
Domicile of Issuer:	France

Issue Information

Issue Amount

Original:	1,003,995,500.00
Current:	1,988,180,000.00

Initial Offering

Date:	4/27/91
Price:	96.51
Yield:	
Spread:	
Program:	Tap/Shelf Registration
Warrants:	None
Private Placement:	No
Prospectus on File:	No
Liquidation Status:	Govt Guaranteed
Lead Manager:	

BANQUE NATIONALE DE PARIS SA 6.20% 2/8/2008 XEU — BAS

Payments

Principal

Maturity:	2/8/2008
Value:	100.000% of par
Currency:	European Currency Unit
Redemption:	Bullet

Coupon

Type:	Fixed
Rate:	6.20%
Currency:	European Currency Unit
Frequency:	Annual
Dated Date:	10/8/97
First:	2/8/99
Last Full:	2/8/08
Regd/Bearer:	Both:

Valuation

Date:	3/6/98
Price:	98.500
Yield:	6.391
Duration:	7.058

Market Conventions

Native Yield:	ISMA - Yield to Maturity
Settlement:	Trade + 3B
Value:	Same as settlement
Ex-Dividend:	Same as coupon
Day Count:	Actual/Actual
Holiday:	France
Price Quote:	Without Accrued
Rounding:	3 Decimals
Yield Assumptions:	Exact Cash Flows
Min Denomination:	1,000.00
Min Increment:	1,000.00

Sector

Industry:	Banking
Market where Issued:	France
Domicile of Issuer:	France

Issue Information

Issue Amount

Original:	40,000,000.00
Current:	40,000,000.00

Initial Offering

Date:	9/16/97
Price:	101.154
Yield:	6.040
Spread:	
Program:	N/A
Warrants:	None
Private Placement:	No
Prospectus on File:	Yes
Liquidation Status:	Subordinated
Lead Manager:	

Borrowers Classification

This classification deals with bonds which may be defined broadly by the type of collateral involved including government agencies, banks, corporates to emerging economies to help refinance their debt. The most common types include the following:

- **Asset-backed security**

- **Mortgage-backed security**

- **Brady bond**

- **Medium Term Note (MTN)**

Asset-backed Security

An **Asset-backed Security (ABS)** is part of a group of fixed income debt instruments whose coupon payments are governed by the cash flow generated by an underlying asset. By convention an asset-backed security is backed by **non-mortgage** assets.

In general bonds can be secured or unsecured debt. Secured bonds have the security of an asset, or group of assets, on which bond holders have a claim in the event of an issuer defaulting on payments.

These are instruments which are based on receivable assets, such as, automobile and aircraft lease payments, credit card receivables and unsecured personal loans. In effect these securities convert loans which are non-negotiable into negotiable instruments. The interest and principal payments on the underlying assets provide the cash flow to pay coupon payments and principal on maturity for the security issued. Most asset-backed securities are bullet issues although FRNs have been issued. There are a number of types of asset-backed securities:

- **Certificates for Automobile Receivables (CARS).** These are bonds issued against automobile receivables.

- **Certificates for Amortising Revolving Debt (CARDS).** These bonds are issued against credit card receivables where the underlying debt is paid in installments

- **Home Equity Loan-backed Securities (HELS)**. These are loans rather than mortgages on homes. The difference between loans and mortgages is usually concerned with the loan repayment conditions – loans are usually required to be paid back at a much faster rate than mortgages which are often long-term.

- Student loans in the US can be made by the federally chartered **Student Loan Marketing Association – Sallie Mae**. This US corporation issues asset-backed instruments based on pools of student loans.

One of the more interesting asset-backed securities issued in 1996 used Spanish tax receipts levied to finance the dismantling of nuclear power stations as collateral.

The interest and principal repayments on the underlying loans are passed onto the holders of the bonds.

The market in this type of bond has grown considerably in the recent past – in 1998 asset-backed securities worth around $197.6 billion were launched internationally. Issuers are able to convert otherwise illiquid receivables into cash funds. Investors can buy bonds with a high credit rating, attractive coupons, good liquidity and maturities up to 7 years.

The Reuters screens show **US Asset Backed Securities** and in particular, bonds from Harley Davidson EM Trust using motorcycle receivables as collateral.

```
09:45 27OCT97    U.S. ASSET-BACKED SECURITIES        US18742           USABS1

Date   Issuer                         Tranche   Amount  Lead U/W  Detail Page
----   ------                         -------   ------  --------  -----------
10/24  DISCOVER CARD MASTER TRUST     1997-4   739.47MM  MSDW +   <USABS3>
10/23  ACCESS                         1997-3   200.00MM  PRU      <USABS3>
10/23  HARLEY DAVIDSON E.M. TRUST     1997-3   100.00MM  SAL      <USABS4>
10/22  MLMI                           1997-1   363.80MM  ML       <USABS4>
10/22  NAVISTAR FINCL OWNERS TRUST    1997-B   200..00MM CSFB     <USABS5>
10/21  FIRST CHICAGO MASTER TRUST     1997-U   400.00MM  FCM      <USABS5>
10/21  FIRST CHICAGO MASTER TRUST     1997-T   600.00MM  FCM      <USABS5>
10/21  NISSAN GRANTOR TRUST           1997-A   755.60MM  JPM      <USABS6>
10/17  AMERUS HOME EQUITY             1997-1   125.00MM  BEAR     <USABS6>
10/17  IMC HOME EQUITY TRUST          1997-6   700.00MM  PW.BEAR  <USABS6>
10/16  CHASE MAN. MARINE OWNER TR     1997-A   266.26MM  CHASE    <USABS7>
10/16  CPS AUTO RECEIVABLES           1997-4   100.57MM  GCM      <USABS7>
10/16  DISCOVER                       1997-3   684.21MM  MS       <USABS8>
10/1
10/1
10/1
```

```
09:43 27OCT97     U.S. ASSET-BACKED SECURITIES        US18742           USABS4

10/23; HARLEY DAVIDSON E.M. TRUST  1997-3
   SIZE: 100.00MM        COLLAT:MOTORCYCLES RECEIVABLES
   MNTH PAY:11/17/97     DEL:10/30   LEG: N/A     U/W:SAL
   CLASS     AMOUNT    RATING     COUPON
   A-1       62.50MM   AAA        5.98%
   A-2       31.00MM   AAA        6.16%
   A-3        6.50MM   BBB        6.60%

10/22; MLMI  1997-1
   SIZE: 363.80MM        COLLAT:HELOC
   MNTH PAY:11/25/97     DEL:10/30   LEG: N/A     U/W:ML
   CLASS     AMOUNT    RATING     COUPON
   N/A       363.80MM  AA         1M LB + 18BP
```

Mortgage-backed Security

 A **Mortgage-Backed Security (MBS)** is a specific type of asset-backed security where the bonds are backed by a pool of mortgage loans which have been made to individuals.

As with asset-backed securities, the interest and principal repayments on mortgage-backed bonds is paid for by the revenue generated from the underlying mortgage repayments of the individuals. Issuers use these to transform an illiquid asset into a negotiable debt instrument.

When an individual obtains a mortgage on a property the lending institution receives a fee for arranging the loan and a repayment of the loan plus interest over a certain period of time. These fees and interest payments are an asset to the lending institution but the funds are somewhat illiquid.

The loans to the individuals are not in themselves negotiable instruments and cannot easily be sold. However, lending institutions are able to sell portfolios of similar loans to a closed fund. This fund raises the money to buy the loans by issuing mortgage-backed securities. The process once again transfers illiquid assets into a negotiable instrument which can be traded for cash.

The US has the largest mortgage-backed securities market worldwide. Three large US government agencies regularly purchase loans from lending institutions who are therefore more willing to lend to individuals. The agencies fund their operations for the loans they buy by issuing mortgage-backed securities. Instruments from the three agencies are popularly known as:

- **Ginnie Maes** – issued by the **Government National Mortgage Association (GNMA)**

- **Fannie Maes** – issued by the **Federal National Mortgage Association (FNMA)**

- **Freddie Macs** – issued by the **Federal Home Loan Mortgage Corporation (FHLMC)**

The Reuters screens below show the 30 year **US Mortgage Backed Securities** details from GNMA, FNMA and FHLMC, and the US MBS dealer prices for these bonds.

```
0000      U.S. MORTGAGE-BACKED SECURITIES  ×30 YEAR×         MTGA

        SOURCE PAGES
30YR ISSUES ,  15YR ISSUES    GNMA       FNMA       FHLMC
<30YRMBS>  ,   <15YRMBS>      6.0%       6.0%       6.0%
<30YRMBS>  ,   <15YRMBS>      6.5%       6.5%       6.5%
<30YRMBS>  ,   <15YRMBS>      7.0%       7.0%       7.0%
<30YRMBS>  ,   <15YRMBS>      7.5%       7.5%       7.5%
<30YRMBS>  ,   <15YRMBS>      8.0%       8.0%       8.0%
<30YRMBS>  ,   <15YRMBS>      8.5%       8.5%       8.5%
<30YRPREM>                    9.0%       9.0%       9.0%
<30YRPREM>                    9.5%       9.5%       9.5%
<30YRPREM>                   10.0%      10.0%      10.0%
```

```
17:07 28OCT97      U.S. MBS DEALER PRICES- 30 YEAR      US18742        30YRMBS
GNMA   30YR Nov CHG    BEY    Dec/Jan/Feb T/W  I F  GNMA    Dec     Jan     Feb
06.0   95.29-31  -20  6.696%  04/ 04/ 04   -   I O  06.0   95.25   95.21   95.17
06.5   98.13-15  -16  6.814%  06/ 04/ 04   -   I R  06.5   98.07   98.03   97.31
07.0  100.06-08  -16  7.019%  05/ 05/ 05   -   I W  07.0  100.01   99.28   99.23
07.5  101.28-30  -17  7.224%  05/ 05/ 05   -   I A  07.5  101.23  101.18  101.13
08.0  103.17-19  -18  7.306%  05/ 05/ 05   -   I R  08.0  103.12  103.07  103.02
08.5  104.23-25  -12  7.163%  05/ 04/ 05   -   I D  08.5  104.18  104.14  104.09
FNMA   30YR Nov CHG    BEY    Dec/Jan/Feb T/W  I F  FNMA    Dec     Jan     Feb
06.0   95.22-24  -17  6.752%  04/ 03/ 04   -   I M  06.0   95.18   95.15   95.11
06.5   97.25-27  -19  6.899%  04/ 05/ 04   -   I O  06.5   97.21   97.16   97.12
07.0   99.29-31  -15  7.033%  04/ 05/ 05   -   I N  07.0   99.25   99.20   99.15
07.5  101.28-30  -13  7.126%  06/ 06/ 06   -   I T  07.5  101.22  101.16  101.10
08.0  103.11-13  -06  7.144%  06/ 06/ 06   -   I H  08.0  103.05  102.31  102.25
08.5  104.15-17  -08  6.892%  05/ 05/ 05   -   I    08.5  104.10  104.05  104.00
GOLD   30YR Nov CHG    BEY    Dec/Jan/Feb T/W  I P  GOLD    Dec     Jan     Feb
06.0   95.21-23  -17  6.790%  04/ 03/ 04   -   I R  06.0   95.17   95.14   95.10
06.5   97.28-30  -20  6.916%  04/ 04/ 04   -   I I  06.5   97.24   97.20   97.16
07.0  100.00-02  -15  7.050%  04/ 05/ 04   -   I C  07.0   99.28   99.23   99.19
```

This type of bond usually involves coupon repayments which are paid from the interest received on the underlying mortgage repayments. Each month mortgage payments are made to the issuer into the pool of funds – the payments are in effect **passed-through**. The process is illustrated in the diagram here:

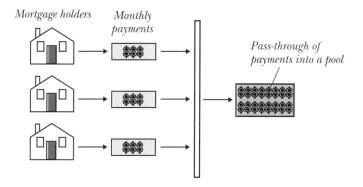

Mortgage holders   *Monthly payments*

Pass-through of payments into a pool

The pass-through system operates well with regular payments being received by the issuer until the mortgage holder decides to pay-off all of the loan or a significant part of it. This situation is known as **principal prepayment** and all mortgage-backed securities have an inherent prepayment risk. In effect MBSs are a complex callable bond with a maturity date that is not known absolutely. The result of this prepayment risk is that MBSs tend to have higher coupon rates than conventional bonds.

In order to overcome the uncertain maturity date and prepayment risk to some extent **Collateralised Mortgage Obligations (CMOs)** are often issued. In some cases these CMOs have beneficial tax advantages and in the US are known as **Real-Estate Mortgage Investment Conduits (REMICS)**. But what are they? A CMO issuance comprises the following:

- A **deal** which is backed by specific pass-through instruments and is structured as a series of bonds each with different maturities

- The bonds that comprise the deal are known as **tranches**

An index of CMOs can be found on the Reuters screen below.

Federal National Mortgage Association
(FannieMae)

```
COLLATERALIZED MORTGAGE OBLIGATIONS (REMICS) INDEX          CMOA
ISSUE            COLL   U/W   AMT   PRICED STLMT PSA WAM WALA
FNMA 1997-90    7.00%    NM  300.0MM 11/20  12/30 NA  NA  NA
FNMA 1997-89    7.00%    GC  500.0MM 11/20  12/30 NA  NA  NA
FNMA 1997-88    7.00%   LEH  500.0MM 11/20  12/30 NA  NA  NA
FNMA TRUST 293  6.00%   LEH  370.0MM 11/20  12/18 NA  NA  NA
FNMA 1997-T2   MULTI MBS SAL  50.0MM 11/19  12/16 NA  NA  NA
FNMA 1997-W2   MTG LOANS CSC 187.5MM 11/18  N/A   NA  NA  NA
FNMA 1997-87    6.50%    GS  180.0MM 11/14  11/26 NA  NA  NA
FNMA TRUST 292  7.50%   UBS  600.0MM 11/13  11/28 NA  NA  NA
FHLMC C064    30YRSFFR   PW  434.0MM 11/05  11/28 NA  NA  NA
FHLMC 2012     C064      PW  635.0MM 11/05  11/28 NA  NA  NA
21-NOV-1716. FEP103 N05405407
                                            MORE
```

Coupon

The difference between a MBS and a CMO is that the principal repayment and coupon payments for the CMO are now structured according to a set of rules as to how any prepayments are allocated to individual tranches (bonds) in the deal.

There are a number of ways tranches have been devised in order to provide investors with stable cash flows. **Planned Amortised Class (PAC)** tranches are designed for a wide range of prepayment situations and are customised using other tranches. CMOs may also be structured into **Interest Only (IO)** and **Principal Only (PO)** tranches.

- **IO** tranches pay a stream of interest only payments from the interest payments generated from the underlying mortgage loans

- **PO** tranches pay one or a limited number of payments from the principal derived from the underlying mortgage loans – in effect these are zero-coupon bonds

To add to the complexity of MBSs it is also possible to strip these bonds into IO and PO securities.

Another type of MBS which is available where the actual maturity is shorter than the issued period involves **balloon mortgages**. In this case the mortgage holder has a loan which is has its terms renegotiated at specific future dates, for example, a Freddie Mac 30-year balloon may have a renegotiation period of 5 or 7 years. In effect the mortgage is for a long-term loan under short-term conditions. The **balloon** – the repayment at maturity – is the original principal amount less the amounts of principal repaid at the various renegotiation dates.

Brady Bond

 A **Brady Bond** is usually a Eurobond or domestic bond issued by the government of a developing country to refinance its existing debt to foreign commercial banks.

In the early 1980s a number of developing countries were unable to meet their debt obligations. This situation had arisen because commodity prices had fallen and market conditions were operating against these developing economies. In order to resolve the debt crisis for these countries a number of solutions were implemented but the most successful was that proposed in 1989 by **Nicholas Brady** a former US Treasury Secretary.

In essence Brady bonds are securities which restructure the debt of a country by exchanging commercial loans for new bonds. Typically these new bonds include some kind of collateral involving US Treasury Bond zero-coupon strips or other highly rated securities are denominated in US dollars and have maturities up to 30 years. These securities are placed in a trust in order to guarantee the principal repayment and some of the interest payments.

In 1990 Mexico was the first country to issue Brady bonds, converting $48.1 billion of its debt to foreign banks into discount and par bonds in exchange for the loans. By 1996 some 13 different countries from Asia, Africa, Eastern Europe and Latin America had issued approximately $190 billion worth of Brady bonds.

There are a number of different types of Brady bonds which have been issued since their introduction in 1981. The types commonly issued are:

- **Par bonds**. In this case bank debt is exchanged at 100% of face value – par – for fixed rate bonds such that the rate is below market interest rates. The bonds are collateralised using US 30-year zero-coupon T-Bonds.

- **Discount bonds**. These bonds are collateralised also using US 30-year zero-coupon T-Bonds but the bank debt is exchanged for floating rate bonds which are issued at a discount.

- **New Money Bonds** and **Debt Conversion Bonds**. New Money Bonds are usually uncollateralised, short-term floating rate bonds which provide additional funds for the issuing country. For every currency unit of money invested in New Money Bonds, creditor banks are allowed to exchange existing loans for Debt Conversion Bonds at an agreed ratio.

- **Front Loaded Interest Reduction Bonds (FLIRBs)**. In this case bank debt is exchanged for medium term bonds which have coupons which are below the market rates at issue but which increase or step-up for an agreed initial period. Thereafter the coupon is set at a floating rate.

- **Interest Arrears Capitalisation** or **C-Bonds**. This type of Brady bond has been issued by the governments of Brazil, Argentina and Ecuador where an agreed portion of the interest rate to be paid is capitalised which therefore reduces the up-front cash coupon payments.

Most Brady bonds are rated below investment grade even though they are usually collateralised with US Treasury zero-coupon strips. Some Brady bonds have embedded warrants whose value is linked to world prices of commodities, such as oil, in the country issuing the bonds. It is assumed that the rating is equal to the credit rating of the developing countries government securities. Brady bonds for the larger developing countries are actively traded OTC in blocks of $3 – 5 millions.

The Reuters screen below shows a real time chain of prices for the major Brady bonds being traded.

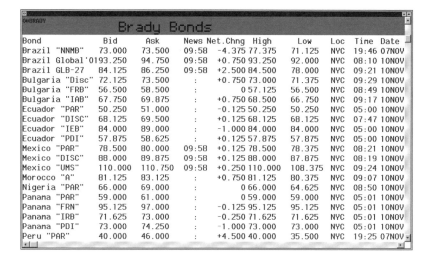

```
OWBRADY                    Brady Bonds
Bond              Bid      Ask    News Net.Chng  High     Low   Loc  Time  Date
Brazil "NNMB"   73.000   73.500   09:58 -4.375 77.375   71.125  NYC  19:46 07NOV
Brazil Global'0193.250   94.750   09:58 +0.750 93.250   92.000  NYC  08:10 10NOV
Brazil GLB-27   84.125   86.250   09:58 +2.500 84.500   78.000  NYC  09:21 10NOV
Bulgaria "Disc" 72.125   73.500     :   +0.750 73.000   71.375  NYC  09:29 10NOV
Bulgaria "FRB"  56.500   58.500     :    0     57.125   56.500  NYC  08:49 10NOV
Bulgaria "IAB"  67.750   69.875     :   +0.750 68.500   66.750  NYC  09:17 10NOV
Ecuador "PAR"   50.250   51.000     :   -0.125 50.250   50.250  NYC  05:00 10NOV
Ecuador "DISC"  68.125   69.500     :   +0.125 68.125   68.125  NYC  07:47 10NOV
Ecuador "IEB"   84.000   89.000     :   -1.000 84.000   84.000  NYC  05:00 10NOV
Ecuador "PDI"   57.875   58.625     :   +0.125 57.875   57.875  NYC  05:00 10NOV
Mexico "PAR"    78.500   80.000   09:58 +0.125 78.500   78.375  NYC  08:21 10NOV
Mexico "DISC"   88.000   89.875   09:58 +0.125 88.000   87.875  NYC  08:19 10NOV
Mexico "UMS"   110.000  110.750   09:58 +0.250 110.000 108.375  NYC  09:24 10NOV
Morocco "A"     81.125   83.125     :   +0.750 81.125   80.375  NYC  09:07 10NOV
Nigeria "PAR"   66.000   69.000     :    0     66.000   64.625  NYC  08:50 10NOV
Panana "PAR"    59.000   61.000     :    0     59.000   59.000  NYC  05:01 10NOV
Panana "FRN"    95.125   97.000     :   -0.125 95.125   95.125  NYC  05:01 10NOV
Panana "IRB"    71.625   73.000     :   -0.250 71.625   71.625  NYC  05:01 10NOV
Panana "PDI"    73.000   74.250     :   -1.000 73.000   73.000  NYC  05:01 10NOV
Peru "PAR"      40.000   46.000     :   +4.500 40.000   35.500  NYC  19:25 07NOV
```

Medium Term Note (MTN)

A **Medium Term Note (MTN)** is typically an unsecured, fixed or floating rate, non-callable debt security which is in effect a programme of bond issues for a specified aggregate amount of bonds over a specified period.

MTN programmes are a way for issuers to save both time and money. Instead of issuing a series of separate bonds a programme of issuance is registered. These programmes allow issuers to take advantage of short-term issuing opportunities, meet short-term funding needs and reduce the costs of issuance.

MTN programmes are widely used in the US markets and for Eurobonds where they are known as **Euro-MTNs (EMTNs)**.

In the US, MTNs are registered with the US Securities and Exchange Commission (SEC) and were first pioneered in 1981 when Ford Motor Credit issued bonds as part of a MTN programme using Merrill Lynch as its agent. For both MTNs and EMTNs, the program details are described in a prospectus that announces the total maximum amount for the issue together with other details of currency of denomination, coupon type, etc. In many cases, issuers offer MTNs/EMTNs continuously or at regular intervals and in smaller amounts then for conventional style bullet issues.

MTNs are typically issued for maturities ranging from 9 months to 30 years. The credit ratings of MTNs are generally the same as for other bonds issued by the organisation for similar debt. The most common structures include:

- **Fixed rate MTNs** – these are structured like a straight bond and pay a semi-annual coupon

- **Floating rate MTNs** – these usually have 3 or 6 month reset periods using LIBOR as the index. As with FRNs the spreaD over LIBOR is dependent on the credit rating of the issuer.

- **Multicurrency MTNs** – these are denominated in a non US Dollar currency but redeemed in US Dollars based on the current FX rate between the US Dollar and the denomination currency

- **Zero-coupon MTNs**

MTN programs range from $100 millions to $1 billion. The top 20 EMTN programs can be viewed on the Reuters screens below, with detail of an issue from Sweden.

```
04:07 29OCT97          LON WEBSTER MTN SERVICE  UK99999        MTNLARGE
                    TWENTY LARGEST ISSUERS BY OUTSTANDINGS
NO ISSUER                            USD EQUIVALENT NO TRANCHES   RIC
 1 KINGDOM OF SWEDEN                     37697.02      153    <MTNPROGATZ>
 2 WORLD BANK/IBRD - 1994                30634.91      162    <MTNPROGBJP>
 3 FEDERAL NATIONAL MORTGAGE ASSOCIATI   20295.61       43    <MTNPROGAOF>
 4 G.E. CAPITAL CORPORATION - 1994       19448.55      282    <MTNPROGAPO>
 5 CREDIT LOCAL                          15681.15      112    <MTNPROGAKU>
 6 MERRILL LYNCH                         15073.75      284    <MTNPROGAVW>
 7 SUDWESTDEUTSCHE LANDESBANK GIROZENT   14728.04      122    <MTNPROGBFS>
 8 BANK NEDERLANDSE GEMEENTEN NV         13254.10       67    <MTNPROGAFA>
 9 EUROPEAN BANK FOR RECONSTRUCTION AN   12859.85       80    <MTNPROGAMS>
10 BAYERISCHE VEREINSBANK                12564.25      128    <MTNPROGAGO>
11 SEK                                   12171.67      146    <MTNPROGBGJ>
12 TOYOTA MOTOR CREDIT CORPORATION       11125.97       85    <MTNPROGBHT>
13 REPUBLIC OF ARGENTINA                 10960.82       35    <MTNPROGABL>
14 RABOBANK NEDERLAND                    10135.80      103    <MTNPROGBBM>
15 FEDERAL HOME LOAN MORTGAGE CORP. (F   10058.15       39    <MTNPROGAPE>
16 HYPOBANK/BAYERNHYPO FINANCE N.V.      10012.54      163    <MTNPROGARR>
17 SOCIETE GENERALE                       9932.86      248    <MTNPROGBEW>
18 ABBEY NATIONAL                         9701.49      361    <MTNPROGAAA>
19 REPUBLIC OF FINLAND (EUROSHELF)        8824.07       33    <MTNPROGAOS>
20 RENTENBANK                             8653.69      117    <MTNPROGBBV>
HELP
```

```
04:00 29OCT97          LON WEBSTER MTN SERVICE  UK99999       MTNPROGATZ
PROGRAMME NAME  KINGDOM OF SWEDEN
ADDRESS         , Norrlandsgatan 15, S-103 74 Stockholm, Sweden

TELEPHONE
CONTACT         Maria Norstrom
SIZE (n)        USD25000        MATURITY (YRS)   1n-30
ORIGIN          SWE             LISTING          LON+
COUNTRY OF RISK SWE
SECTOR                          RATING IBCA      AA-
1ST PROSPECTUS  23 October 1992 RATING MOODY'S   Aa3
LAST PROSP      20 August 1997  RATING S&P       AA+
144A YES/NO     NO              SUB DEBT         NO
COUPON          Fxd/Flt/Zero
CURRENCIES      Any

ARRANGER        MSDW            PROGRAMME AGENT  MGTC
DEALERS         MSDW
```

MTNs/EMTNs offer issuers a number of advantages over conventional issues. These include the following:

- Issues can be priced more exactly which combined with only one set of documentation for many issues helps reduce the cost of funding

- A global program can be set up with shelf registration in the US and the possibility of issuing on the international markets in any currency

- Small amounts of debt can be issued for specific projects at short notice

MTNs/EMTNs can be created also where the issuer simultaneously transacts in the derivatives markets at the time of issuance. Instruments of this type are called **structured notes** and most commonly involve an interest rate swap or a currency swap.

Offering Circular for a Global Note Programme from Sallie Mae

What Instruments Are Used in Bond Markets?

In practice dealers, who have two functions, are appointed for programs . The first is to bid for issues and then offer the issue, the second is to offer the issuer suggestions based on their views of investors needs. The process of relaying investors needs and suggestions for future issues is sometimes known as a **reverse inquiry**. Look at the Reuters screen below to see which of the commercial banks is in the top 20 as dealers and as arrangers.

```
04:11 26NOV97            LON WEBSTER MTN SERVICE  UK99999           MTNDEALER
                  BANKS INVOLVED IN MOST PROGRAMMES - DEALERS
    ABBREV.    BANK NAME                                     TOTAL ISS.
 1  MLI        Merrill Lynch International Linited             428 387
 2  GSI        Goldnan Sachs International                     325 299
 3  MSDW       Morgan Stanley Dean Witter                      322 301
 4  LB         Lehman Brothers                                 304 274
 5  SBCW       SBC Warburg Dillon Reed                         291 264
 6  UBS        UBS Linited                                     283 256
 7  JPMSEC     JP Morgan Securities Inc                        263 250
 8  CSFB       CS First Boston Inc                             230 205
 9  SAL        Salonon Brothers International                  220 198
10  DB         Deutsche Morgan Grenfell                        215 187
11  NOM        Nonura International Linited                    184 180
12  DAI        Daiwa Europe Linited                           163 151
13  CIB        Citibank International plc                      114  95
14  IBJ        IBJ International Ltd                           104 103
15  NIK        Nikko Europe plc                                98  94
16  YAM        Yanaichi International (Europe) Limited          94  93
17  BZW        Barclays de Zoete Wedd Linited                  84  79
18  ABN        ABN-Anro Hoare Govett                           73  62
19  TMI        Tokyo-Mitsubishi International plc               61  59
20  SANWAI     Sanwa International plc                          61  58

HELP TELEPHONE 01672 518125     HELP PAGE <MTNHELP>     MAIN INDEX <MTNINDEX>
```

Who Uses These Bonds?

Asset-backed Securities

Institutions such as banks, leasing companies, finance companies, government agencies, insurance companies and building societies use these securities to remove assets from their balance sheets. The assets are converted from illiquid loans into negotiable debt.

Investors are attracted to asset-backed securities because they usually have high credit ratings, attractive coupon rates, stable cash flows, liquid markets and cover the range of maturity periods. Investors in short-term securities sometimes use them as substitutes for Money Market instruments whereas pension funds and insurance companies tend to invest in longer-term asset-backed securities.

Mortgage-backed Securities

The main issuers in the US of this type of bond are the Government National Mortgage Association (GNMA), the Federal National Mortgage Association (FNMA) and the Federal Home Loan Mortgage Corporation (FHLMC).

Investors in MBSs include commercial banks, fund managers, insurance companies and pension funds. For pass-through MBSs the investor receives a pro-rata share of cash flows from a pool of mortgage loan payments. Investors in **Interest Only** CMOs and MBSs expect prepayments to fall and remain low. This means that the mortgage holders will retain the loan for a long period of time and therefore the period of coupon payments will be extended. Investors buy **Principal Only** CMOs and MBSs when prepayments are expected to rise and continue to do so which guarantees the principal return and reduces the period of coupon payments.

REUTERS

Brady Bonds

Issuers of these bonds include the governments of countries with emerging markets such as Brazil, Argentina, Venezuela, Uruguay, Costa Rica, the Philippines, Nigeria, Bulgaria, Poland, Hungary, Ecuador etc. Below are Reuters Brady Bonds and Loan Prices pages which give an indication of the issuing governments.

```
1147          REUTER BRADY BOND AND LOAN PRICES          2LD0
SHORT NAME        R.I.C.      BID    OFFER PREV CL   NET CHNG
ARGENTINA PARS  <AR4C23=RR>   71.000  71.375  70.000  +1.000
ARGENTINA FRBS  <ARFLC05=RR>  88.125  88.625  86.875  +1.250
ARGENTINA DISC  <AR425C23=RR> 80.125  80.625  80.250  -0.125
BRAZIL DISC Z   <BRFLTD24=RR> 77.625  78.625  76.375  +1.250
BRAZIL IDUS     <BRFLA01=RR>  93.750  94.250  93.000  +0.750
BRAZIL "C"      <BR8D14=RR>   73.625  74.125  71.750  +1.875
BRAZIL PAR      <BR4D24=RR>   68.625  69.625  66.750  +1.875
MEXICO PARS     <MX625L19=RR> 80.750  81.250  79.875  +0.875
MEXICO DISC     <MXFLL19=RR>  90.625  91.250  89.750  +0.875
BRAZIL GLOBAL 01<BRGLB01=RR>  96.375  95.750  95.250  +1.125
*PLEASE SE
```

```
1147          REUTER BRADY BOND AND LOAN PRICES          2LDP
SHORT NAME        R.I.C.      BID    OFFER PREV CL   NET CHN
MOROC SERIES A  <MOFLA09=RR>  84.500  85.625  83.875  +0.625
NIGERIA PARS    <NI55K20=RR>  67.750  69.750  67.375  +0.375
VENEZ GLOBAL 27 <VZGLB27=RR>  88.125  88.625  85.500  +2.625
PHILLIP PARS    <PH425L18=RR> 85.125  85.875  84.875  +0.250
BRAZIL EI       <BRFLD06=RR>  83.250  84.000  81.750  +1.500
VENEZ PARS      <VZ675C20=RR> 86.125  86.500  84.750  +1.375
VENEZ DCBS      <VZFLL07=RR>  89.375  90.000  88.500  +0.875
VENEZ FLIRBS    <VZ6C97=RR>   87.750  88.500  87.500  +0.250
PERU PDI        <PEPDI=RR>    60.750  61.500  60.500  +0.250
VENEZ DISC      <VZDISC=RR>   87.250  88.000  87.500  -0.250
*PLEASE SEE <O#BRADY> FOR BRADYS CHAIN* SEE <FAQ/2LD0> FOR INFO
```

Although there are a wide range of investors in Brady bonds who are seeking to enhance or diversify their investments, it is worth remembering that most bonds of this type are rated below investment grade.

Medium Term Notes

Issuers of these instruments are the same as for corporate bonds and Eurobonds – corporations, banks, investment houses, sovereign states, governments and their agencies and supranationals. To see the 20 most recently notified tranches of bonds, look at the Reuters screen below.

```
04:09 26NOV97            LON WEBSTER MTN SERVICE  UK99999     MTNRECENTALL
                      TWENTY MOST RECENTLY NOTIFIED TRANCHES
ISSUER              AMOUNT      INTEREST  MAT DATE  ISSUE DATE   RIC
BANQUE GENERALE DU L ITL 20000.00  6.25%    25.01.05  25.01.99  <MTNINDIVAWN>
BANQUE GENERALE DU L ITL 20000.00  6.25%    25.07.04  25.07.98  <MTNINDIVAWN>
EIB (ESP)           ESP 3000.00   5.07%A   27.09.02  10.02.98  <MTNINDIVCQB>
COMMONWEALTH BANK OF JPY 500.00   3.8%     05.02.03  05.02.98  <MTNINDIVBXF>
KINGDOM OF SWEDEN   USD 30.40    ZeroN    02.04.01  08.01.98  <MTNINDIVHBY>
KINGDOM OF SWEDEN   USD 30.40    ZeroN    29.06.01  08.01.98  <MTNINDIVHBZ>
KINGDOM OF SWEDEN   USD 30.40    ZeroN    28.06.01  08.01.98  <MTNINDIVHBZ>
KINGDOM OF SWEDEN   USD 30.40    ZeroN    06.07.01  08.01.98  <MTNINDIVHCA>
KINGDOM OF SWEDEN   USD 30.40    ZeroN    03.07.01  08.01.98  <MTNINDIVHBZ>
KINGDOM OF SWEDEN   USD 30.40    ZeroN    05.07.01  08.01.98  <MTNINDIVHBZ>
EUROPEAN INVESTMENT SEK 500.00   6.0%     07.01.04  07.01.98  <MTNINDIVCPY>
NORDDEUTSCHE LANDESB ZAR 100.00  14.5%    05.01.01  05.01.98  <MTNINDIVF00>
MERRILL LYNCH       GBP 12.50    ZeroN    23.06.03  23.12.97  <MTNINDIVEOX>
BANQUE GENERALE DU L DEM 35.00    5.5%     23.12.03  23.12.97  <MTNINDIVAWL>
BEAR STEARNS COMPANI ITL 20000.00 ZeroN    20.06.03  22.12.97  <MTNINDIVBEP>
BANK NEDERLANDSE GEM JPY 5000.00  3.0%     22.12.09  22.12.97  <MTNINDIVASH>
HER MAJESTY IN THE R DKK 500.00   5.75%    22.12.04  22.12.97  <MTNINDIVBRF>
NIPPON OIL (U.S.A) L JPY 1500.00            22.12.00  22.12.97  <MTNINDIVFFF>
ABBEY NATIONAL      ITL 20000.00            22.12.05  22.12.97  <MTNINDIVABW>
STATE BANK OF NEW SO AUD 100.00   5.5%     22.12.00  22.12.97  <MTNINDIVGU0>

HELP TELEPHONE 01672 518125     HELP PAGE <MTNHELP>    MAIN INDEX <MTNINDEX>
```

At the outset MTNs were issued tailored for particular institutional investors, particularly in Japan. Now EMTNs are issued publicly and are now as attractive to investors as Eurobonds – in many cases investors do not distinguish between the two.

OFFERING CIRCULAR Dated February 24, 1997

CHRYSLER FINANCIAL CORPORATION
(a Michigan corporation)
U.S.$2,500,000,000
Euro Medium-Term Note Program
for the issue of Notes
with maturities of one month or longer

[body text of offering circular — illegible]

Arrangers

Lehman Brothers
Merrill Lynch International
Salomon Brothers International Limited

French Franc Arranger   Deutsche Mark Arranger

Merrill Lynch Finance SA   Salomon Brothers AG

Dealers

Lehman Brothers   Merrill Lynch Finance SA
Merrill Lynch International
                    UBS Limited

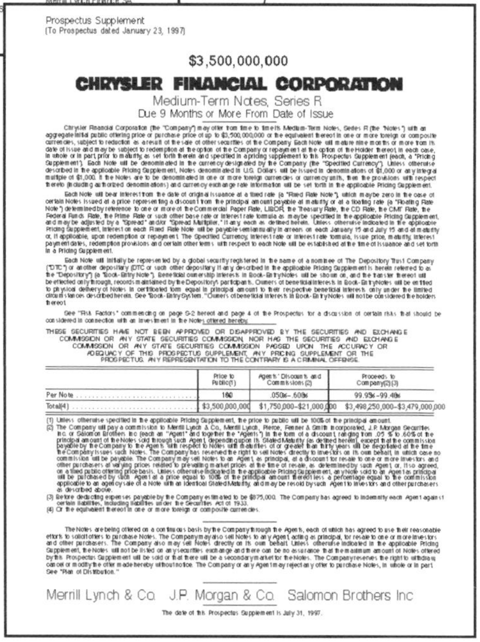

Prospectus Supplement
(To Prospectus dated January 23, 1997)

$3,500,000,000

CHRYSLER FINANCIAL CORPORATION
Medium-Term Notes, Series R
Due 9 Months or More From Date of Issue

[body text of prospectus supplement — illegible]

	Price to Public(1)	Agent's Discounts and Commission (2)	Proceeds to Company(3)(3)
Per Note	100	.050%–.500%	99.95%–99.49%
Total(4)	$3,500,000,000	$1,750,000–$21,000,000	$3,498,250,000–$3,479,000,000

Merrill Lynch & Co.   J.P. Morgan & Co.   Salomon Brothers Inc

The date of this Prospectus Supplement is July 31, 1997.

Some organisations such as the Chrysler Financial Corporation issue EMTNs and MTNs as can be seen from this Offering Circular and Prospectus

Your notes

Summary

Asset-backed Security

- An **asset-backed security** is an instrument which uses **receivables** from an underlying asset which is a non-mortgage loan

- The main types of underlying assets include student loans – **Sallie Maes**, automobile receivables – **CARS**, credit card receivables – **CARDS**, and home equity loan receivables – **HELS**

Mortgage-backed Security

- A **mortgage-backed security** is an instrument which is backed by a pool of mortgage loans made to individuals

- The three **largest issuers** of MBSs are the US agencies whose issues are known as **Ginnie Maes, Fannie Maes** and **Freddie Macs**

- A **pass-through** MBS involves the underlying mortgage payments from the pool of mortgages being directly paid to the issuer who uses them for coupon payments and principal repayments of the bond

- A **Collateralised Mortgage Obligation (CMO)** or **Real-Estate Mortgage Investment Conduit (REMIC)** is a **tranche** of bonds – the **deal** – which comprises a series of structured pass-through bonds of different maturities designed to overcome the risks of **principal repayment**

- CMOs can be structured as **Interest Only (IO)** and **Principal Only (PO)** tranches

Brady Bond

- In essence a **Brady Bond** is a security used to restructure the debt of a country by exchanging commercial loans for new bonds

- Many countries with emerging markets have **collateralised** and **uncollateralised** instruments with **fixed** or **floating rate** coupons and maturities up to 30 years

- Many of the bonds are US dollar denominated **Eurobonds** which are backed by US 30-year zero-coupon T-Bonds

- With or without collateralisation, Brady bonds are usually rated **below** investment grade but bonds issued by larger countries are actively traded OTC

Medium Term Note (MTN)

- **Medium Term Notes and Euro-Medium Term Notes** are debt securities issued under a programme which specifies the total amount of the issue over a specific maturity period

- EMTNs are very similar to **Eurobonds** being unsecured debt for **fixed** or **floating rate** bonds which are non-callable

- MTNs/EMTNs are issued through **dealers** who are appointed to issuance programmes

- MTNs/EMTNs may also be issued as **structured notes** which involves a simultaneous transaction in the derivatives market at the time of issue – typically a swap

Equity Linked Classification

There are two basic types of these **hybrid** instruments which have some features of both the bond and equity markets. In this case a bond can be a:

- **Convertible bond**

- **Bond with warrants**

Both types of bond have been available in domestic markets for some time and since the early 1970s for Eurobonds. In both cases the bonds give investors the option to convert their debt holdings into equity of the issuer. Both bonds with warrants and convertible bonds have coupon rates which are lower than for conventional bonds because they offer a greater potential for profit.

Convertible Bond

 A **Convertible** bond is usually a fixed rate debt instrument giving the holder the right, but not obligation, to exchange the bond and all the remaining coupons for a pre-determined number of ordinary shares or other debt instruments of the issuer at a pre-stated price and pre-stated date/s.

Convertible bonds have been and are currently issued by governments and corporates. There are a number of ways in which this type of bond can be issued:

- **Conversion into further debt instruments**. Although convertible bonds typically involve shares, when an issuer has no shares to convert into, such as, a government, then conversion into further government debt instruments has been used. In effect this is a way for a government to issue an interest rate option.

- **Conversion into shares of a corporation**. Usually this type of convertible bond is a corporate bond with a call option held by the investor to buy ordinary shares in the organisation as agreed in the terms for conversion set out in the bond **indenture**. Many convertible bonds also have call features with respect to the issuer which limit the share appreciation limit. There are also convertible bonds which have put options for the issuer. These options give the issuer the right, but not obligation, to convert the bond into cash, shares or other debt instruments depending on the type of put specified. In practice, puts are exercised when the organisation is not performing well and share prices are low.

- **Conversion into shares of another organisation**. These bonds are known as **exchangeable bonds** and have been issued after take-overs or issued for shares in the parent company of the issuer.

The following description of convertible bonds is concerned with bonds where the investor has a call option to convert a bond into ordinary shares of a corporation.

The right to exchange the bond into shares may extend over the whole lifetime of the bond or for only a portion of it – the indenture specifies the terms. The number of shares which will be received on conversion is determined by the **conversion ratio**. At the time of issuance the **conversion price** is set which is the price at which investors can exchange the bond for shares. The actual number of shares that are received on conversion is determined using the following equation:

$$\text{Bond conversion ratio} = \frac{\text{Principal amount of bond}}{\text{Conversion price}}$$

The amount by which the market price of a convertible bond exceeds the market price of the ordinary shares is known as the **conversion premium**. This conversion premium can be used to determine whether or not conversion of a bond is profitable at some future date. The **initial conversion premium** is calculated from the following equation:

$$\text{Initial conversion premium} = \left(\frac{\text{Conversion price}}{\text{Current ordinary share price}} - 1 \right) \times 100$$

Once the initial conversion premium has been exceeded the investor can profit by conversion and selling the shares in the markets.

Have a look at the following example to see how it works.

Example 1 – A corporate convertible bond issue
A US corporation issues a convertible bond with the following details. What is the bond conversion ratio and when can the bond be converted profitably?

Bond face value:	$1,000 par
Coupon rate :	6.00%; semi-annual
Maturity:	10 years time
Conversion period:	Until maturity
Conversion price:	$20.00
Current share price:	$16.50

The bond conversion ratio $= \dfrac{1000}{20} = 50$

This means that if an investor converts the bond, he or she would receive 50 shares.

The initial conversion ratio $= \left(\dfrac{20.00}{16.50} - 1 \right) \times 100 = 21.21\%$

This means that the issuer's ordinary shares have to appreciate by more than 21.21% before the bond can be converted by an investor profitably.

Once a convertible bond is exchanged for shares or other instruments it ceases to exist and is no longer a debt obligation of the issuer.

In the long term the potential reward for investors is that the bond can be converted into shares which can be sold at a profit in the Equity Markets. This potential for profit is reflected in the coupon which is lower than for a straight bond. Usually the coupon gives the investor a slightly higher rate of return than the historic dividends on the ordinary share price.

But why do issuers issue this type of bond? There are a number of reasons convertible bonds are issued, including:

- The cost of issuing shares is much higher than issuing debt. It is also the case that many new share issues are offered at a discount to current prices in order to attract investors.

- Interest repayments are a known cost whereas dividend payments are dependent on company profits and can fluctuate widely over time or on the company's chosen payment ratios.

- Up until conversion takes place there is no dilution of dividends and there is no decrease in the control of the organisation as there is no increase in the total number of shares.

- On conversion the equity capital of the issuer increases and its long-term debt decreases.

- If conversion does not take place, then the result is a long-term, low cost borrowing for the issuer.

For the investor the advantages of buying convertible bonds include:

- Until conversion a guaranteed fixed income is paid until maturity

- If conversion is required then the number of shares to be received is known, no brokerage charges are incurred and the timing of conversion is determined by the investor

- The bond is negotiable and so can be sold whenever required

- If the issuer goes into liquidation before conversion, then the bond holder is paid before ordinary shareholders

The Reuters screens below show the basic details for new convertible bond issues for issuers whose name begins with B. More detail is shown for the BBA issue.

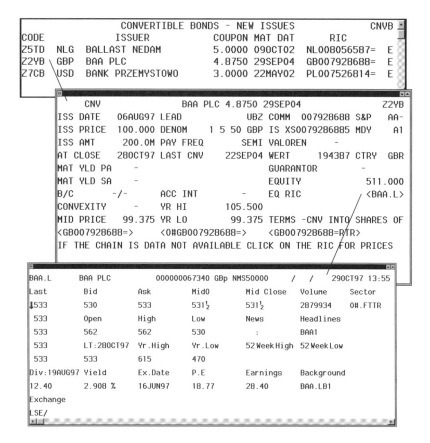

Bond with Warrants

A **Bond with Warrants** is a standard bond with coupons but has a pre-determined number of warrants attached. Each warrant gives the holder the right, but not obligation, to buy an agreed number of shares of the issuer at a specified price – the **warrant exercise price** – and at a specified future date/s. If the warrant is exercised, then **additional** payment is required to purchase the shares.

Bonds with warrants are similar to convertibles bonds for corporate shares in that they provide the investor with an option to obtain shares in the issuing organisation at a specified price. A bond with warrants is a standard corporate bond with coupons to which a specified number of warrants have been attached. However, as for convertible bonds, not all warrants are for shares. Warrants have been issued for other debt instruments and commodities such as gold. The following description covers the case of warrants for ordinary shares.

A warrant confers on the holder the right, but not obligation, to buy a specified number of ordinary shares at a specified price – the warrant exercise price. Thus, a warrant can be considered to be a long-term call option on shares sold with the bond. If the warrant is exercised, then additional funds are paid to the issuer for the shares over and above the price of the original bond.

Bonds with warrants attached can be retained as an entity and traded as **cum-warrants** and carry a higher price to reflect the greater profit potential. However, an investor also has the opportunity to detach the warrants and trade both the **ex-warrant** or **stripped** bond and the warrants separately. The remaining underlying bond and the stripped warrants are bought by different types of investors with different investment requirements. Bonds with warrants are unlike convertible bonds in that there are no call features for issuers which allow the exercise of warrants to be forced if the price of the ordinary shares exceeds a specified limit.

These Reuters screens provide a list of stories about Asian warrants, with detailed information available. This particular story is about a Bear Stearns issue, including specific detail as to the warrant prices.

```
08:36 13NOV97   INTERNATIONAL INSIDER -ASIA SERVICE-  HK27349        IIJL
---- ASIAN WARRANTS - THURSDAY - HK TEL (852) 2525-5863  -----
<IIJM> SOC GEN LAUNCHES PUTS ON THE S&P 500
<IIJN> MERRILL LYNCH LAUNCHES CALLS ON HSBC
<IIJO> MORGAN STANLEY LAUNCHES FURTHER PUTS ON S&P 500
<IIJP> * SOC GEN LAUNCHES PUTS ON HANG SENG INDEX *
<IIJQ> BEAR STEARNS CALLS ON CHINATRUST COMM BANK
<IIJR> BEAR STEARNS LAUNCHES CALLS ON SHIHLIN ELEC & ENG
*** FOR DETAILS OF THE PREVIOUS 21 ISSUES SEE PAGE <IIJK> ***

16:26 07OCT97   INTERNATIONAL INSIDER -ASIA SERVICE-  HK27349        IIJQ

   - THE BEAR STEARNS COMPANIES INC IS ISSUING 10 MILLION AMERICAN
STYLE CALL WARRANTS ON SHARES OF CHINATRUST COMMERCIAL BANK
<2815.TW>. PRICED AT TWD$3.8586 EACH, ONE WARRANT CONTROLS ONE
SHARE AT A STRIKE PRICE OF TWD43.758 (REFERENCE PRICE TWD39.78).
EXPIRY DATE IS APRIL 2, 1998. EXERCISE SETTLEMENT IN US$ CASH.
PAYMENT DATE IS OCTOBER 9. MINIMUM TRADING SIZE IS 50,000
WARRANTS.
```

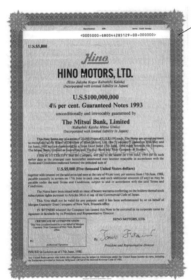

An example of a bond with an attached warrant

Equity warrants are exercised for shares at a pre-determined price that is paid on exercise. Warrants are aimed primarily at investors seeking long-term options for shares at pre-determined prices. But trading with warrants has its risks; equity warrants are speculative and volatile instruments and investors must be constantly aware of the relationship between the exercise price and the current market price of the shares.

One of the major features of equity related instruments in general is their **gearing effect**. This is the change in price of a warrant or conversion premium for a convertible compared with that of the market price of the share for which it can be exchanged. For example, the purchase price of a warrant is less than the purchase price of the underlying shares. This means that the price change in a warrant compared to that for the shares represents proportionally greater percentage profits or losses relative to the amount invested. Look at the following example to see how gearing works.

Example 2 – The gearing effect of a warrant
A warrant for XYZ shares can be bought for $7.00 and the current ordinary share price is $28.00. Suppose XYZ shares appreciate to $30.00. This rise represents an increase of 7.14% (30 – 28 ÷ 28 x 100%) in price. An increase in the underlying share price also produces an increase in the warrant price – the price rises to $9.00. The rise in warrant price represents an increase of 28.57% (9 – 7 ÷ 7 x 100%).

So the share price has increased by 7.14% producing a warrant price increase of 28.57%. In other words the share price change has produced a gearing effect of 4 times in the warrant price.

Who Uses These Bonds?

Convertible Bonds
Although governments have issued convertible bonds which can be converted into further debt instruments, most convertible bonds involve corporate equity. Corporations typically issue convertible bonds when they are seeking:

- To issue new shares at a premium – in many cases new share issues in the equity markets are at a discount in order to attract new investors

- To avoid diluting the **Earnings Per Share (EPS)** value – the greater the number of shares in an organisation the less the EPS value

What Instruments Are Used in Bond Markets?

- To avoid approaching existing shareholders

- To pay interest payments rather than share dividends – this may have tax advantages

- To issue an instrument which will attract investors in both debt and equity markets

Investors buying a bond which can be converted into a further debt instrument are in effect buying an interest rate option on a future bond issue. Investors who buy bonds with the option to convert into equity include those who prefer:

- Fixed coupon payments rather than dividend yield

- The option to convert into equity where the number of shares to be received is known and no brokerage charges are incurred on conversion

- The option to profit from equity markets at the same time as preserving the protection of the debt markets

- The higher ranking of bonds over equity if the issuer goes into liquidation

Issuers – Convertible Bonds

Advantages	Disadvantages
• Convertible bonds represent a cheaper way of issuing debt which is usually subordinated but unsecured • Equity is issued at a premium • There is no cost of carry associated with the deferred equity position • Most convertible bonds incorporate a call feature for the issuer which effectively forces conversion after specified share appreciation – often this is 130% of the conversion price	• This type of bond is not usually acceptable for swap transactions because the bond maturity date is uncertain – investors can convert within the specified conversion period • If the issuer has a high dividend yield, then the coupon rate may be too high for any significant cost

Investors – Convertible Bonds

Advantages	Disadvantages
• A convertible bond provides a coupon payment until maturity or conversion • Geared exposure to equity of issuer	• If the bond incorporates a call feature for the issuer, forced conversion can result if the share price exceeds a specified conversion price • Lack of gearing on part of issuer

REUTERS

Bonds with Warrants

Issuers in some high growth business sectors do not necessarily have a track record in issuing debt and therefore have to offer a 'sweetener' such as warrants in order to attract investors. For issuers of these bonds, providing shares in the organisation appreciate, on exercise of the warrants, the equity capital of the organisation will increase.

Investors are attracted to warrants because they have the flexibility of retaining or selling the bond, with or without the warrants. In the event of liquidation of the organisation, the investor holding the bond is ranked senior to equity holders.

Issuers – Bonds with Warrants

Advantages	Disadvantages
• Reduced coupon payments because the warrant has a value	• Warrants can only be exercised at specific dates by the investor, so if share prices increase dramatically the investor can profit – the issuer cannot force exercise of the warrant
• Cost of issuing a bond is less than issuing shares	
• As with convertible bonds, until the warrants are exercised, there are no changes in the number of shares or the capital of the organisation	• The debt element of the bond is senior if the issuer goes into liquidation
• The debt element of the bond can be used for swap transactions	

Investors – Bonds with Warrants

Advantages	Disadvantages
• Advantages of gearing	• There is an element of risk associated with warrants – share prices can rise and fall
• Bond coupon provides a cash flow similar to a fixed coupon bond	
• The issuer cannot impose any call features on warrant exercise	• The warrant element of the bond generates no income – it is a speculative instrument

What Instruments Are Used in Bond Markets?

Summary

Convertible Bond

- A **convertible bond** is usually a fixed rate debt instrument giving the holder the **option** to exchange the bond and its coupons into shares in the issuing organisation or that of another organisation or which can be exchanged for further debt instruments in the organisation

- The number of shares which can be received on exchange are specified in the bond **indentures** and is determined by the **conversion ratio** – the price of the shares is set at issuance and known as the **conversion price**

- The **initial conversion premium** is used to determine whether or not it is profitable to convert a bond

Bond with Warrants

- A **bond with warrants** is a conventional bond with coupons which has a number of warrants attached which give the holder the option of buying shares or further debt instruments in the issuing organisation or commodities

- The holder can retain and/or sell the bond with its attached warrants – **cum-warrant** – or the holder can detach the warrants and retain and/or sell the **stripped** bond – **ex-warrant** – and warrants separately

- One of the major features of warrants is their **gearing effect** – small changes in share prices can have dramatic effects on warrant prices

To test your understanding of these bonds try the following exercises. You can check your answers on page 120.

Exercise 1 – A corporate convertible bond issue

Bond face value:	$1,000 par
Coupon rate:	3.50%; semi-annual
Maturity:	5 years time
Conversion period:	Until maturity
Conversion price:	$83.330
Current share price:	$74.125

Given the details of this US convertible bond what are the following?

a) What is the initial conversion premium?

b) What is the conversion ratio?

This Reuters screen displays warrant prices.

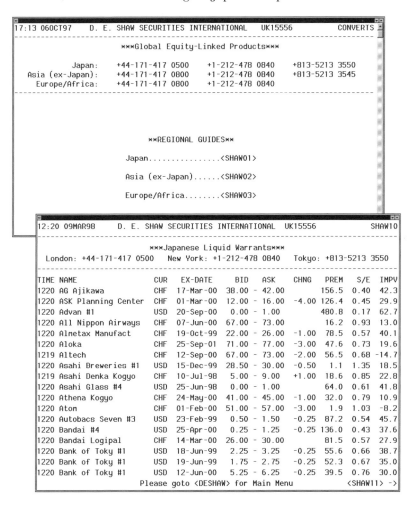

These Reuters screens give details about DE Shaw Securities offices and then, their current offerings in Japanese liquid warrants.

Exercise 2 – A bond with warrants – total issue amount $150,000,000

Bond face value:	$1,000 par
Coupon rate:	3.50%; semi-annual
Maturity:	5 years time
Conversion period:	Until maturity
Warrants:	2 warrants per bond for 5 shares each @ $93.00 per share
Current share price:	$77.00

Given the details of this bond with warrant what are the following?

a) How much additional cash will the issuer receive if all the warrants are exercised?

b) What is the initial warrant exercise premium?

Here are the answers to the examples on page 118.

Given the details of the US convertible bond:

a) *What is the initial conversion premium?*

Initial conversion premium

$$= \left(\frac{\text{Conversion price}}{\text{Current price}} - 1 \right) \times 100$$

$$= \left(\frac{83.330}{74.125} - 1 \right) \times 100 = 12.42\%$$

b) *What is the conversion ratio?*

Conversion ratio for shares

$$= \left(\frac{\text{Bond par value}}{\text{Conversion Price}} \right)$$

$$= \left(\frac{1000}{83.33} \right) = 12 \text{ shares}$$

Given the details of the bond with warrants:

a) *How much additional cash will the issuer receive if all the warrants are exercised?*

No. of bonds in issue = 150,000,000 ÷ 1000
= 150,000

On exercise additional capital raised

= No. of bonds x No. of shares x Price of shares
= 150,000 x (2 x 5) x $93.00
= $139,500,000

b) *What is the initial warrant exercise premium?*

Initial warrant exercise premium

$$= \left(\frac{\text{Conversion price}}{\text{Current price}} - 1 \right) \times 100$$

$$= \left(\frac{93.00}{77.00} - 1 \right) \times 100 = 20.78\%$$

Summary

You have now finished the third section of the book and you should have a clear understanding of the following:

- Market type

- Principal payment type

- Interest related features

- Types of borrower

- Redemption features

- Equity linked types of instruments

As you have probably realised by now, the bond markets are innovative and market participants are constantly seeking to provide new ways of financing debt or improving on existing instruments. The instruments that have been described here are not an exhaustive list and you will probably encounter variations or types not discussed. However, you should find most of the important types of bonds have been mentioned – albeit briefly.

You may find the following examples of different types of bonds interesting as you may not have the opportunity to actually see physical bonds – most are kept securely, particularly bearer bonds.

As a check on your understanding, try the Quick Quiz Questions which follow. You may also find the Overview Section to be a helpful learning tool.

A £10,000 Eurobond issued by
Credit Locale de France

A bearer bond issued in France, 1928

A non-detachable subordinated
conversion bond issued by and with
conversion rights into ordinary
shares for M.I.M. Holdings Ltd

A £10,000 FRN issued by Bradford &
Bingley Building Society – interest to
be paid quarterly

Each of these coupons was worth $3.50 when
presented at the 'Office' on the due dates for
this $100 bond

A 1000 ECU Note from the
European Investment Bank – a
supranational organisation

Quick Quiz Questions

1. Which of the following currencies of denomination dominates Eurobond issues?
   - ☐ a) Japanese Yen
   - ☐ b) US Dollar
   - ☐ c) Eurodollar
   - ☐ d) Deutschemark

2. Which of the following organisations is responsible for supervising the Eurobond market?
   - ☐ a) ISMA
   - ☐ b) FSA
   - ☐ c) CEDEL
   - ☐ d) Euroclear

3. Which of the following types of bond pays a variable rate of interest?
   - ☐ a) Straights
   - ☐ b) Vanillas
   - ☐ c) Floating Rate Notes
   - ☐ d) Perpetuals

4. Which of the following types of bond do **not** have a maturity date?
   - ☐ a) Straights
   - ☐ b) Vanillas
   - ☐ c) Floating Rate Notes
   - ☐ d) Perpetuals

5. Which of the following statements is/are true? The coupon of a straight bond –
   - ☐ a) Varies with the earnings of the issuing organisation
   - ☐ b) Depends on the price of the bond
   - ☐ c) Is usually fixed for the life of the bond
   - ☐ d) Depends on LIBOR

6. How often is the interest rate reset on a Floating Rate Note?
   - ☐ a) Once when the bond is issued
   - ☐ b) Annually
   - ☐ c) Quarterly
   - ☐ d) In line with the coupon reset reference rate

7. Which of the following types of bond allows an investor to swap it for shares in the issuing organisation?
   - ☐ a) A bond with warrants
   - ☐ b) A mortgage-backed security
   - ☐ c) A convertible bond
   - ☐ d) A zero-coupon bond

8. Which of the following types of bond gives the holder the right to buy shares in the issuing organisation at a pre-defined price?
   - ☐ a) A bond with warrants
   - ☐ b) A mortgage-backed security
   - ☐ c) A convertible bond
   - ☐ d) A zero-coupon bond

You can check your answers on page 124.

Overview

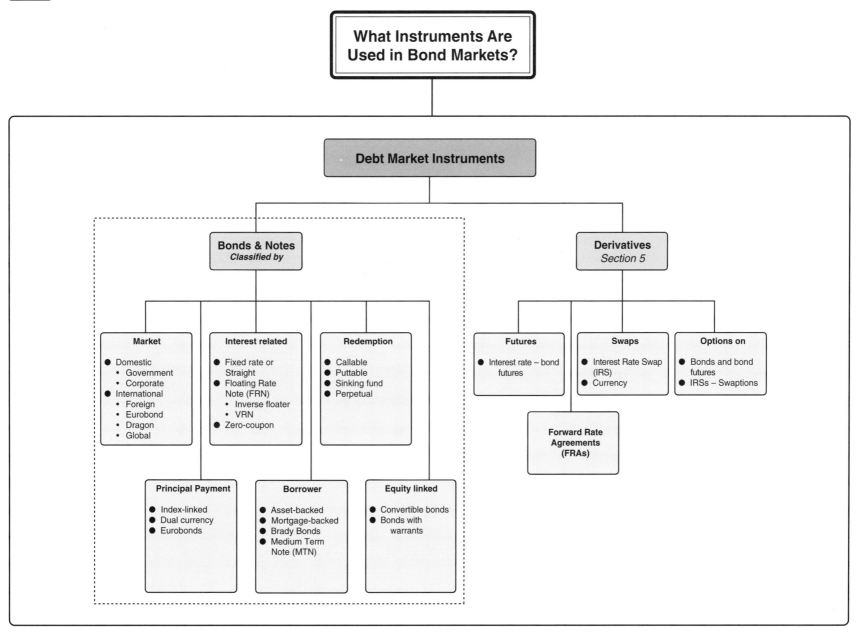

What Instruments Are Used in Bond Markets?

Quick Quiz Answers

	✓ or ✗
1. a)	☐
2. a)	☐
3. c)	☐
4. d)	☐
5. c)	☐
6. d)	☐
7. c)	☐
8. a)	☐

How well did you score? You should have scored at least 6. If you didn't you may need to revise some of the materials.

Further Resources

Books

Getting Started in Bonds
Sharon Saltzgiver Wright, John Wiley & Sons, Inc., 1999
ISBN   0 471 32377 2

A-Z of International Finance
Stephen Mahony, FT Pitman Pub., 1997
ISBN   0 273 62552 7

All About Bonds
Esme Faeber, Probus, 1993
ISBN   1 55738 437 1

The Bond Book: Everything You Need to Know About Treasuries, Municipals, Gnms, Corporates, Zeros, Funds and More
Annette Thau, Probus Publishing Company, 1994
ISBN   1 55738 809 1

The Handbook of Fixed Income Securities
Frank J. Fabozzi, Irwin Professional Press, 5th Edition, 1997
ISBN   0 786 310952

Standard & Poor's Stock and Bond Guide, 1999 (Serial)
Alan J. Miller (Introduction), McGraw Hill, 1999
ISBN   0 071 34266 4

Bond Portfolio Management
Frank J. Fabozzi, McGraw Hill, 1999
ISBN 1 883 24936 8

REUTERS

Publications

Bank of England
- Investing in Gilts: A guide for the small investor
- Gilt Repo Code of Best Practice Nov. 1995

Fidelity Investments: Special Reports
- Understanding corporate bonds
- Take a new look at US Treasury Bonds

Internet

RFT Web Site
- **http://www.wiley-rft.reuters.com**

This is the series' companion web site where additional quiz questions, updated screens and other information may be found.

Exchanges

Refer to the back of this book for a listing of worldwide stock exchange contact information and web sites.

Your notes

What Instruments Are Used in Bond Markets?

Your notes

REUTERS

This section of the book should take about 2 to 3 hours of study time. You may not take as long as this or you may take a little longer – remember your learning is individual to you.

More money has been lost reaching for a yield than at the point of a gun.

Raymond E. Devoe Jr., of the investment firm Legg Mason Wood Walker, quoted in Fortune, April 18, 1994

Introduction

Derivatives have made international headlines in recent years because of their connection with some high profile cases of spectacular losses and institutional collapses. But market players have used derivatives successfully for centuries; historically, people dealing in commodities ranging from tulip bulbs to rice used derivatives to protect their investments. Today, the daily international turnover in derivatives trading runs into billions of US dollars and has increased steadily over the last decade. But are derivatives – in today's complex, lightning speed and high volume markets – instruments that can only be traded by experienced, specialist traders, the so-called "rocket scientists?"

Although it is true that complicated mathematical models are used for pricing some derivatives, the basic concepts and principles underpinning derivatives and their trading are quite easy to grasp and understand. Indeed, derivatives are used increasingly, by various market players including governments, corporate treasurers, dealers and brokers, as well as individual investors.

The purpose of this seciton is to introduce the basic concepts and principles of derivatives and their trading by considering:

- What are and who uses derivatives?

- How do the basic derivatives instruments – futures, forwards, options and swaptions – differ from one another and when are they used?

- How are derivatives traded?

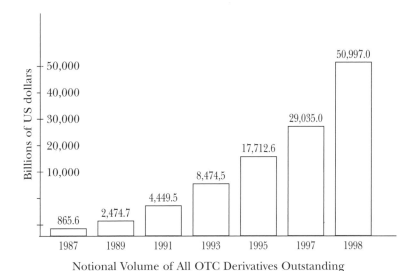

Notional Volume of All OTC Derivatives Outstanding

Source: International Swaps and Derivatives Association Market Survey 1999

What Are Derivatives?

A derivative instrument can be defined as follows:

A **Derivative** is an agreement between two counter-parties in which they agree to transfer an asset or amount of money on or before a specified future date at a specified price. A derivative's value changes with changes in one or more underlying market variables, such as interest rates or foreign exchange rates.

Originally, derivatives trading involved commodities as the underlying asset. Today, some underlying assets are still commodities but in addition, almost any other financial measure or financial instrument can be used. For example, there are derivatives based on debt instruments, interest rates, stock indices, money market instruments, currencies and even other derivative contracts. This section focuses on derivatives based on bond instruments. (For detailed information about derivatives, please refer to *An Introduction to Derivatives*, ISBN 0-471-831-76X and *An Introduction to Foreign Exchange and Money Markets*, ISBN 0-471-83174-X.)

Basic derivative instruments include **forward** contracts, **futures** contracts, **options** contracts and **swaptions**. Derivatives instruments are also sometimes called **contingent claims**, as their payout to the holder at maturity is contingent on the price or rate of the underlying asset.

Follows are the definitions of these basic instruments. The remainder of the section will cover them in depth.

A **Forward** contract is a transaction in which the buyer and seller agree upon the delivery of a specified quality and quantity of asset (usually a commodity) at a specified future date. A price may be agreed on in advance or at the time of delivery.

A **Futures Contract** is a firm contractual agremeent between a buyer and seller for a specified asset on a fixed date in the future. The contract price will vary according to the market price but it is fixed when the trade is made. The contract also has standard specifications so both parties know exactly what is being traded.

The price of a futures contract is agreed on an exchange floor in a process whereby buyers and sellers shout their orders and quotes publicly. In today's markets, it is also common for contract details to be determined electronically through an automated trading system. This means that once a contract is agreed upon everyone on the floor knows the price paid. This transparency in futures contracts prices is one of the main differences from forward contracts where prices are privately negotiated.

An **Option Contract** confers the right, but not the obligation, to **buy (call)** or **sell (put)** a specific underlying instrument or asset at a specific price – the **strick** or **exercise price** – up until or on a specific future date – the **expiry** date. The price to have this right is paid by the buyer of the option contract to the seller as a **premium**.

A **Swap Transaction** is the simultaneous buying and selling of a similar underlying asset or obligation of equivalent capital amount where the exchange of financial arrangements provides both parties to the transaction with more favourable conditions than they would otherwise expect.

One of the main reasons for using derivatives is **risk management**, that is, the user can separate and more precisely control risk by shifting it to another party, thereby creating a form of insurance. Each party involved in the contract should be able to identify all the risks involved before the contract is agreed.

To identify all the risks, the user must remember that since the derivative's value is based on an underlying price of another asset or instrument or measure, any change in the "underlying" will cause a change in the pricing of the derivative. The ability of the derivatives' users to offset their exposure to fluctuations in interest rates by assuming an opposite exposure to their existing exposure, on a loan for example, is called **hedging**.

Hedging

Hedgers seek to transfer the risk of future price or interest rate fluctuations by selling forward contracts which guarantee them a future price for their asset.

If in the future, the asset price falls, the hedger will have protected himself by having hedged – i.e., made forward sales which guaranteed the price at the sale date before the price fell. However, if the future cash price rises the hedger has lost the opportunity to make a profit, as he has already committed himself to the forward price at the outset of the hedge transaction.

Thus, hedging reduces risk but also reduces the opportunity for reward. It increases the certainty of future cash flows and allows market participants to plan into the future based on the certainty of the future cash flows guaranteed by hedging. Hedging does not increase or decrease the **expected returns** for a market participant, it simply changes the **risk profile** of those expected returns.

The underlying principle of hedging is that as price movements in the cash market move one way, the move is offset by an equal and opposite move in the price of **the hedging instrument** (almost always a **derivative instrument**).

Hedging a Long Position
If an investor holds, or intends to hold, a cash market asset, such as a treasury bill, this is said to be a **long position**. To hedge this position, he needs an offsetting **short position**. This can be achieved by selling a forward rate agreement or an interest rate futures contract in the appropriate amount to create offsetting cash flows (see next two sections for a more detailed discussion of these instruments). The profits or losses on the cash market instrument and the derivative instrument offset each other, creating an aggregate position which is unaffected by movements in interest rates. This is known as a **market neutral position**.

Hedging a Short Position
If a borrower borrows money, or intends to borrow money, in the cash market by issuing commercial paper, this is said to be a **short position**. To hedge, he needs a **long position**. This is achieved by buying an FRA or interest rate future in the appropriate amount. The offsetting cash flows create a market neutral position.

Who Uses Derivatives?

A party exposed to an unwanted risk can pass that risk on to another party willing to accept it. Originally, commodity producers used forward and futures contracts to hedge prices and reduce risk.

If, for example, a commodity producer wants to hedge her position, who takes on the other side of the contract? In many cases it could be other hedgers, for example, manufacturers, or it could be speculators. A **speculator** takes an opposite position to a hedger and takes on the exposure in the hope of profiting from price changes to her advantage.

There are also **arbitrageurs** who trade derivatives with a view to exploit any price differences within different derivatives markets or between the derivative instruments and cash or physical prices in the underlying assets.

The recent growth in swaps and OTC options instruments has been attributed to their increasing use by governments, international corporations and major institutional and financial investors. These various groups use derivatives to help achieve the following objectives.

- Lower international funding costs

- Provide better rates of exchange in international markets

- Hedge price risks

- Diversify funding and risk management

The number of different derivative instruments and volume of derivatives contracts traded are both increasing dramatically every year.

As noted earlier, with this growth has come some notable losses, though many of these situations were generally the result of management irregularities or rogue trading.

Consider this summary of derivatives characteristics when determining when their use is prudent:

- Derivatives do carry a risk – that's why they were devised. The risks associated with derivatives must be identified and managed.

- Many corporations and other organisations use derivatives successfully and benefit from their use.

- Unfortunately, there is still a lack of understanding within the markets about how to best use derivatives and by the very nature of speculation, losses can be huge. Organisations should carefully examine their risk management procedures, including the role that derivatives play.

How Are Derivatives Traded?

Traders are the market players who buy and sell derivatives contracts on behalf of their clients or on their own account in the financial and commodity markets. There are three basic ways in which trading can take place:

- On an exchange floor using open outcry

- Over-The-Counter (OTC)

- Using an electronic, automated matching system such as GLOBEX

Derivatives traders can operate across all the markets buying and selling futures, options, swaps contracts etc.

In some markets **brokers** act as intermediaries between traders and clients. Brokers do not usually trade on their own account but earn commissions on the deals that they arrange.

Traders and brokers need up-to-date financial data provided by Reuters and its competitors including:

- Information on the underlying instruments

- Technical analysis

- Prices from exchanges and contributors

- News

Open Outcry

The primary role of an exchange is to provide a safe environment for trading. Exchanges have approved members and rules governing matters such as trading behaviour and the settlement of disputes. Open outcry involves traders or brokers operating on an exchange floor where they communicate their deals by shouting at each other and using hand signals. On exchanges such as LIFFE, CME and SIMEX the floor is a very colourful, noisy place where at times the exchange activities seem to be in chaos. The floors of some of the smaller exchanges are not quite so colourful or noisy but open outcry is still used.

The SIMEX trading floor

OTC

This method originates from the days when instruments were literally bought over the counter of a bank, for example. The present day meaning describes markets which have no specific locations, have fewer rules governing trading and which may be more international in character. Trading takes place directly between dealers and principals via a telephone and computer network rather than via a highly regulated exchange floor.

Automated Matching Systems

Many exchanges use an automated matching system to extend their trading hours. The systems are either provided as a joint venture such as GLOBEX, a Reuters/MATIF/SIMEX venture, or specific to an exchange such as Automated Pit Trading (APT) on LIFFE.

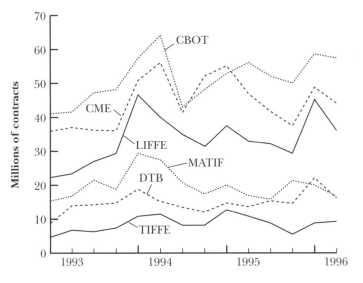

The automated matching systems operate using the same trading rules used for floor trading. They also offer the advantage of anonymity in trading and so are sometimes known as electronic brokers. There are three characteristics of an automated matching system:

- Users send their bids and offers to a central matching system

- The bids and offers are distributed to all other market participants

- The system identifies possible trades based on price, size, credit and any other rules relevant to the market

Exchange Based v OTC Trading

Although exchange based trading involves millions of contracts monthly involving the equivalent of billions of US dollars, the importance of the OTC markets is increasing as derivatives are better understood by the markets and the financial needs of market players change. By the end of 1998, according to the Bank For International Settlement (BIS), the OTC derivatives market accounted for 86% of all traded. The chart below shows the total quarterly turnover by millions of contracts for six of the major international exchanges.

Source: Bank of England Quarterly Bulletin, Novemebr 1996

Within the OTC markets, **plain vanilla** instruments for forwards, swaps and options are traded most frequently. Plain vanilla instruments have no special features and are traded to more or less standardised contract specifications and market conventions. Instruments with more specialised features are known as **exotics**.

The following tables show that currently, interest rate instruments dominate the worldwide OTC and exchange traded derivatives. The values given as outstandings are the notional or face value of OTC contracts not yet settled or completed.

Derivatives Traded USD Billion	Outstandings USD Billion	Turnover
OTC	38,304	193
OTC comprises:		
Currency swaps	8,741	4
Currency options	1,968	40
FRAs	4,588	65
Interest Rate Swaps	18,265	63
Interest Rate Options	3,548	21
Equity derivatives	805	–
Commodity derivatives	389	–
Exchange based	16,581	1136

Contract	Exchange	Average Daily Turnover USD Billions
3 Month Interest Rate		
Eurodollar	CME	337.2
Sterling	LIFFE	39.2
Euromark	LIFFE	65.1
PIBOR	MATIF	52.2
Euroyen	TIFFE	231.3
Government Bond futures		
US T-Bond	CBOT	32.4
Bund	DTB	7.5
Bund	LIFFE	19.2
Notionnel	MATIF	11.9

Although interest rate derivatives are very important worldwide as exchange based derivatives, the table below of the top ten individual contracts for April 1996 shows that bond and stock index derivatives are also important. It is also important to remember that different exchanges tend to specialise in different derivatives and are constantly introducing new products and deleting products which are not supported by the markets.

Contract	Exchange	Average Daily Turnover USD Billions
3-Month Eurodollar	CME	33,151,598
Average Interest Rate	OptionBBF	29,567,630
US T-Bonds	CBOT	29,519,887
S&P 100 Index Option	CBOE	21,419,286
Interest RateBM	&F	18,537,128
US Dollar	BM&F	16,489,524
German Government Bund	LIFFE	14,969,359
Notional Bond	MATIF	13,042,395
3-Month Euromark	LIFFE	12,930,772
IBEX 35	MEFF	10,683,428

Futures Industry Magazine June/July 1996 Vol 6, Number 6, Page 7. The magazine is produced by the Futures Industry Association (FIA).

Derivatives

The main differences mentioned so far between Exchange traded and OTC derivatives are summarised in the following table.

Exchange traded	OTC

• Derivatives available:
  • Futures
  • Options
  • Swaps
	• Derivatives available:
	  • Forwards
	  • Options

• Derivatives traded on a competitive floor, open outcry	• Derivatives traded on a private basis and individually negotiated
• Standardised and published contract specifications	• No standard specifications although plain vanilla instruments are common
• Prices are transparent and easily available	• Prices are not very visible
• Market players not known to each other	• Market players must be known toeach other
• Trading hours are published and exchange rules must be kept	• 24 hour markets which are less well regulated
• Positions can easily be traded out	• Positions are not easily closed or transferred
• Few contracts result in expiry or physical delivery	• Majority of contracts result in expiry or physical delivery
• Contracts can be traded by private investors	• Usually used by large corporations, banks etc

OTC trading by its very nature is private and contract details are not usually openly discussed. Exchange trading on the other hand is usually a very noisy, colourful, apparently chaotic affair. Traders shout at each other in open outcry and use hand signals to indicate their intentions.

In an amusing article written by Joseph Wilson entitled 'Into the Pit' he describes his first day as a member of the International Options Market (IOM), Chicago Mercantile Exchange. This short extract may give you some indication of the excitement of pit trading.

> *'My palms are sweating. My heart begins to race. The pit starts to rock back and forth as bids and offers are shouted. People are pushing and shoving each other to get good positioning. I am somewhere between total excitement and sheer panic.'*

Part of the CME trading floor

Bond Futures

Interest Rate Futures are forward transactions with standard contract sizes and maturity dates which are traded on a formal exchange.

Short-term interest rate futures contracts are almost exclusively based on Eurocurrency deposits and are cash settled based on an Exchange Delivery Settlement Price (EDSP) or the last price traded.

Long-term interest rate futures or **Bond futures** contracts are settled based on notional government bonds or notes with a coupon and maturity period specified by the exchange. The settlement price is based on the final futures contract price – the Exchange Delivery Settlement Price (EDSP).

Interest rate futures are some of the most common futures contracts traded on exchanges. Their growth stems from the mid 1970s after the breakdown of the Bretton Woods Agreement in 1973. The resulting floating exchange rates in currencies created much more volatility in interest rates and the subsequent need to hedge investments.

The Chicago Board of Trade (CBOT) introduced the first futures contracts to hedge interest rate exposure in 1975 when it introduced contracts on the US Government National Mortgage Association certificates – known as **Ginnie Maes**. These contracts are no longer traded but by 1977 CBOT had added contracts on T-Bonds and in 1982 LIFFE started trading futures contracts on 3 month sterling time deposits. The most actively traded short- and long-term contracts are for 3-month Eurodollars on the Chicago Mercantile Exchange (CME) and for US T-Bonds on the Chicago Board of Trade (CBOT).

Long-term interest rate futures or bond futures are essentially forward contracts in notional underlying fixed coupon instruments and are settled based on a **basket** of deliverable government bonds or notes. The major difference is that settlement is by physical delivery of bonds or notes with coupon rates and maturity dates stipulated by the exchange. Although some long-term futures for bonds have prices and minimum price movements quoted as hundredths of a basis point, UK Gilts and US T-Bonds are quoted as thirty-seconds of a percentage point.

An exchange traded futures contract has the following characteristics:

- A **standardised specification** in terms of unit of trading, trading cycle of contract months, delivery days, quotation, minimum price movement etc

- The **opportunity to trade** the instrument and offset the original contract with an equal and opposite trade. Very few contracts, less than 2%, reach maturity

- A **public market** in that prices for contracts are freely available. Trading takes place open outcry on an exchange floor and prices are published on exchange indicator boards, in the financial press and by providers such as Reuters.

- Once a trade has been made a **clearing house** acts as the counterparty to both sides of the trade. The contract is not directly between buyer and seller; the clearing house takes on the credit risk should a counterparty default. This is important because it means anyone can have access to the markets provided they have the required creditworthiness by the clearing house – in this way large organisations have no advantage over smaller organisations or investors.

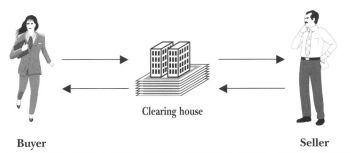

Buyer   Clearing house   Seller

Exchange Contracts

Short- and long-term interest rate futures contracts are traded on exchanges worldwide. Look at the contracts available using the Reuters screens below.

Details of some of the more important long-term contracts are summarised in the table below.

```
EXCHANGE TRADED INTEREST RATE FUTURES - REUTERS SPEED GUIDE        FUT/IR1
Detailed below are the retrieval codes for Exchange traded Interest rate Futures

=INTEREST RATE FUTURES=============== =INTEREST RATE FUTURES Cont============
AEX Guilder Bond Future........<O#EBB:>  CME (IMM) 1-nonth LIBOR.........<O#EM:>
BDP 10Yr Portuguese Govt.Bond<O#BDPOT:>  CME (IMM) 3-nonth Eurodollar....<O#ED:>
BDP Mkt Overview (Porto)........<BDP1>   CME (IMM) 90-day US T-Bill......<O#TB:>
BDP Calculated Spreads..........<BDP2>   CME (IMM) 1Yr US T-Bill.........<O#YR:>
BDP 3Mth Lisbor................<O#LBO:>  CME (IMM) Euronark..............<O#EK:>
BFOE BEF BIBOR 3nth Future.....<O#BIB:>  CME (IMM) Euroyen...............<O#EY:>
BFOE National Govt Bond........<O#BGB:>  CME (IMM) Fed Funds.............<O#FT:>
BMF Brazilian C Bond...........<O#BCB:>  CME Brady Bonds - Argentine FRB.<O#AT:>
BMF Brazilian EI Bond..........<O#BEI:>  CME Brady Bonds - Mexican Par...<O#MN:>
CBOT 30 day IR Future..........<O#FF:>   CME Brady Bonds - Brazilian C...<O#BF:>
CBOT 2-year US T-Note..........<O#TU:>   CME Brady Bonds - Brazilian EI.<O#BE:>
CBOT 5-year US T-Note..........<O#FV:>   CPSE 3nth CIBOR................<O#RDK:>
CBOT 10-year US T-Note.........<O#TY:>   CPSE Danish Govt 8% 2001.....<O#DK01T:>
CBOT 30-year US T-Bond.........<O#US:>   CPSE Danish Govt 7% 2007.....<O#DK07T:>
CBOT Long-Tern Municipal Bd....<O#MB:>   CPSE Realkredit Mtg 6% 2026....<O#RKE:>
CBOT Treasury US Spread......<O#TY-US:>  DTB Gernan Govt Bond..........<O#BDL:>
CBOT German Govt Bond..........<O#BU:>   DTB Mediun Tern Notional Bond..<O#BDM:>
Cheapest to Deliver Pages...<RTRTSYB>-9  DTB German LIBOR Future.......<O#LIB1:>
========================================================================
Futures Guide <FUTURES>      Money Guide <MONEY>        Next page <FUT/IR2>
```

```
EXCHANGE TRADED INTEREST RATE FUTURES - REUTERS SPEED GUIDE        FUT/IR2
Detailed below are the retrieval codes for Exchange Traded Interest Rate Futures

=INTEREST RATE FUTURES Cont=========== =INTEREST RATE FUTURES Cont============
DTB Schatz Short tern future..<O#SH2Z:>  LIFFE Short Sterling...........<O#FSS:>
FINEX Emerging Mkt Debt........<O#LX:>   LIFFE US T-Bond...............<O#FUS:>
Finnish Govt Benchmark Bond....<O#FBF=>  Manila Intl Futures Exch Index<MIQAA>-Z
Finnish OM HELIBOR.............<O#HEI:>  MACE Euro USD Future..........<O#UD:>
Finnish OM ROF 2001 Bond.....<O#FIO1T:>  MACE T-Bill 90 day Future......<O#XT:>
Finnish OM ROF 2006 Bond.....<O#FIO6T:>  MACE 5-year US T-Note..........<O#XV:>
HFKE HKD HIBOR Future..........<O#HIR:>  MACE 10yr T-Note Future........<O#XN:>
LIFFE 3-nonth ECU IR...........<O#FCU:>  MACE 30-year US T-Bond.........<O#XB:>
LIFFE Euro DMK 1nth............<O#FEM:>  MATIF Market Overview..........<MATIF>
LIFFE Euro DMK 3nth............<O#FED:>  MATIF 3-nonth PIBOR...........<O#PIB:>
LIFFE Euro CHF 3nth............<O#FES:>  MATIF 3-nth PIBOR Spread&Strip<O#PIB-:>
LIFFE Euro ITL 3nth............<O#FEL:>  MATIF ECU Bond................<O#PEC:>
LIFFE Euro YEN 3nth............<O#FEY:>  MATIF Notional Bond...........<O#PTB:>
LIFFE Gernan Govt Bond(BUND)..<O#FDB:>   MATIF BOBL....................<O#FBO:>
LIFFE Gernan Govt Bond(BOBL)..<O#FMB:>   MATIF OAT DEM Bund............<O#FGL:>
LIFFE Italian Govt Bond.......<O#FIB:>   MATIF OAT DEM Bund............<O#FGL:>
LIFFE Japanese Govt Bond......<O#FYB:>   MATIF BTP DEM Bund............<O#IGL:>
LIFFE Long Gilt...............<O#FLG:>   MATIF Bono DEM Bund...........<O#SGL:>
========================================================================
Futures Guide <FUTURES>     Previous Page <FUT/IR1>    Continued on <FUT/IR3>
    LOST? Selective Access?..<USER/HELP>    Reuters Phone Support..<PHONE/HELP>
```

Long-term Government Bonds	Nominal value	Maturity range years	Notional coupon, %
LIFFE			
Long Gilt (UK)	GBP 50,000	10–15	9.00
German – Bund	DEM 250,000	8.5–10	6.00
Japanese – JGB	JPY 100,000,000	7–11	6.00
Italian – BTP	ITL 200,000,000	8–10.5	12.00
CBOT			
30 year US T-Bonds	USD 100,000	At least 15	8.00
10 year US T-Notes	USD 100,000	6.5–10	8.00
DTB			
Bund	DEM 250,000	8.5–10.5	6.00
Bobl	DEM 250,000	3.5–5	6.00
Schatz	DEM 250,000	1.75–2.25	6.00
TSE			
20 year JGB	JPY 100,000,000	Benchmark	6.00
10 year JGB	JPY 100,000,000	Benchmark	6.00
5 year JGB	JPY 100,000,000	Benchmark	6.00
MATIF			
5 year OAT/BTAN	FRF 500,000	4–5.5	4.50
10 year OAT	FRF 500,000	8.5–10.5	5.50

The CBOT 30 year US T-Bond futures contract is one of the most liquid and heavily traded futures contracts worldwide. The table below indicates some of the annual volumes of bond futures traded for 1998.

	Volume in millions
CBOT	
30 year US T-Bonds	112.22
2 year US T-Notes	1.35
5 year US T-Notes	18.06
10 year US T-Notes	32.48
LIFFE	
Long gilt	16.18
Bund*	14.55
BTP*	8.21
JGB	0.69

With the advent of the Euro and EMU, the Germin Bund and Italian BTP have been replaced by the Euro Bund and Euro BTP respectively.

Typical Contract Specifications

Futures contracts specifications vary depending on the underlying notional government bond and from exchange to exchange. Exchanges publish details of their contracts in printed form, on the Internet and via information providers such as Reuters. Look at a typical bond futures contract taken from CBOT contract specifications shown opposite.

**Chicago Board of Trade
US Treasury Bond futures**

Unit of Trading	T-Bond with face value $100,000	This is the standard contract size
Delivery Months	Mar, Jun, Sept, Dec	This is the trading cycle of contract months
Delivery Day	Last business day of delivery month	This is the day the contract is settled
Deliverable grades	US T-Bonds which have a maturity of at least 15 years from the first day of delivery month, even if callable. The invoice price equals the futures settlement price times the conversion factor plus the accrued interest. The conversion factor is the price of the deliverable bond to yield 8%.	This is the type of US T-Bond that is acceptable as a deliverable bond if the contract expires
Last Trading Day	7th business day preceding last business day of month	This is the last day and time on which trading can take place
Quotation	Points and 32nds of point	The futures price is quoted according to the type of future
Tick size and value	1/32 of a point ($31.25)	This is the smallest amount a contract can change value and the 'tick' size
Trading hours	07.20 – 14.00 Chicago time	Exchange trading hours – open outcry
Project A Trading hours	14.30 – 16.60 22.30 – 06.00	Computer-based trading system hours

Look at the Reuters Futures Speed Guide and the exchange contract specifications for the LIFFE Long gilt and DTB Bund contracts.

```
LIFFE LONG GILT CONTRACT DETAILS                              LIF/FLG
Contract Details, Trading Hours, for the LIFFE LONG GILT FUTURE.


FUTURES CHAIN          -    <O#FLG:>
UNIT OF TRADING        -    GBP 50,000 nominal value notional Gilt with
                            9% coupon, 7% coupon for June 1998 delivery month
                            onwards.
DELIVERY MONTHS        -    March(H) June(M) September(U) December(Z)
DELIVERY MONTHS        -    March(H) June(M) September(U) December(Z)
DELIVERY MONTHS        -    March(H) June(M) September(U) December(Z)
DELIVERY MONTHS        -    March(H) June(M) September(U) December(Z)
TRADING MONTHS         -    3 Forward months
LAST TRADING DAY       -    2 Business days prior to the last business day in
                            the delivery month
QUOTATION              -    Per GBP 100 nominal
MIN. PRICE MOVE        -    GBP 1/32
TICK SIZE & VALUE      -    GBP 15.625

TRADING HOURS          -    08.00 - 16.15
APT TRADING            -    16.22 - 18.00

=============================================================================
Futures/Opts Guide<FUTURES> UKI Futures Guide<GB/FUTEX1> LIFFE Guide<LIF/FUTEX1>
    Lost? Selective Access...<USER/HELP>   Reuters Phone Support...<PHONE/HELP>
```

```
D.T.B. GERMAN GOVT BUND FUTURES CONTRACT                      DTB/BDL1
To access information double click in <>. For more guidance see <USER/HELP>.

CONTRACT DETAILS
FUTURES CHAIN:         <O#BDL:>
UNDERLYING:            8,5-10,5 Year Notional German Government Bond,
                       with 6% Coupon.
                       Delivery of any Bundesanleihen, with 8'5 to 10 Year remaining
CONTRACT SIZE:         DM 250,000
QUOTATION:             Per DEM 100 nominal quoted to two decimal places
MIN PRICE:             Tick Size: 0,01   Tick Value: DEM 25
DELIVERY MONTHS:       Three nearest months of the cycle, March, June, Sept, Dec
LAST TRADE DAY:        Two exchange days prior to delivery. Trading for the
                       settlement contract stops at 12:30pm Frankfurt time
SETTLEMENT:            Two day settlement through the Deutsche Kassenverein AG
DAILY SETTLEMENT
PRICE:                 Average of prices during the last minute of trading or last
                       five trades, if less than five occur in last minute
TRADING HOURS:         08:00 to 17:30 Frankfurt time.


=============================================================================
Main Guide<REUTERS>  Commodities Guide<COMMOD>  German Futures Guide<DTB/FUTEX1>
    Lost? Selective Access...<USER/HELP>  Reuter Phone Support...<PHONE/HELP>
```

What Does All This Information Mean?

Bond futures are contracts for **notional** or **fictitious** government bonds. In some cases actual government bonds with the required face value, maturity period and coupon yield do exist which can be delivered if the futures contract is not offset. However, in such cases if delivery always involved the same bond this would lead to liquidity problems in the markets. In addition, new government issues constantly vary in terms of coupon yields depending on market conditions at the time of issue. To overcome this problem exchanges and their clearing houses define a **basket of deliverable** government bonds which they will accept or deliver. Deliverable grade bonds meet a set of criteria covering their liquidity, maturity range, coupon payments etc. In most cases they are bullet bonds which are officially recognised and traded on stock exchanges such as the LSE, TSE and NYSE.

At any one time a number of government bonds are acceptable as deliverable grade and lists are published by the exchanges. It is important to remember that these lists change. Why? For example, the maturity period of a bond changes over time. This means that a bond which is of deliverable grade for one delivery month may not be acceptable for the next delivery month.

If a range of deliverable bonds are considered, then they are not all of equal value unless they all have the specified **notional yield**. This yield is selected by the exchange and is an expectation of an average value which might prevail over a long period. As you might expect this contract price is changed by exchanges as expectations change.

As government issues do not have a yield equal to the exact contract notional yield, a **price** or **conversion factor** is assigned to each deliverable bond. This price/conversion factor is based on the price that a deliverable bond would sell for at the beginning of a particular delivery month if it were to yield that specified by the bond futures contract.

If a particular deliverable bond does happen to have a coupon equal to the notional yield, then its price/conversion factor will be close to unity. The exchanges publish lists of deliverable bonds and their price/conversion factors in printed form, on the Internet and via information providers such as Reuters. For example, the Reuters screens shown here indicate the factors for deliverable grade bonds for 15-year 9% Gilt futures and 30-year 8% T-Bond futures.

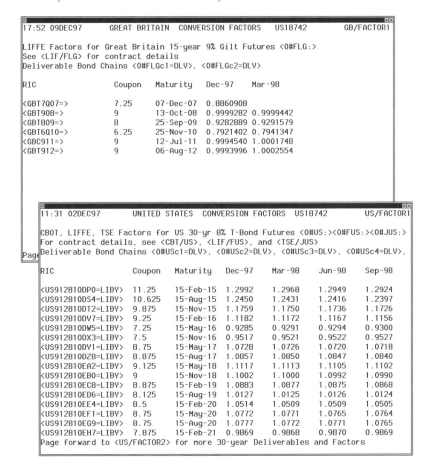

In practice, few bond futures contracts are actually delivered. However, as you will see it is important for hedging and speculating strategies that deliverable prices are known.

Typically for financial futures there are four delivery months per year – March, June, September and December. It is also possible to have maturity dates out to several years but "far month" contracts are much less liquid than the "near months". This means that it is not always possible to get prices for "far months".

The price movement of a futures contract is measured in **ticks**. The **minimum price movement** for a contract is determined by the exchange. Depending on the contract, its value is expressed in thirty-seconds of a percentage point for US T-Bonds and UK Long gilts or as hundredths of a basis point for other government bonds. A **basis point** is one hundredth of one percent, 0.01%. So one tick equals one basis point or one thirty-second.

Example
A UK Long Gilt futures quoted at 111-23 means a price of $111 \, {}^{23}/_{32}$. However there are indications that the market convention for UK Gilts and US T-Bonds may be changed in the near future to that of using basis points.

Tick values are easy to calculate for bond futures using the following equation:

$$\text{Tick value} = \text{Unit of trading} \times \frac{\text{minimum price movement}}{100}$$

Example

The tick value for the CBOT 30-year US T-Bond futures contract is calculated as follows:

$$\text{Tick value} = \text{Unit of trading} \times \frac{\text{minimum price movement}}{100}$$

$$= 100{,}000 \times \frac{1/32}{100}$$

$$= \$31.25$$

On the last day of trading, if a futures position is still open and has not been offset, the futures contract ceases to exist and the underlying bond and futures prices are the same.

The final daily futures price is often termed the **Exchange Delivery Settlement Price (EDSP)** or **settlement price** and the **invoice price** for the contract is determined using the following equation.

> **Invoice price** = $\dfrac{\text{No. of}}{\text{contracts}} \times \dfrac{\text{Futures contract}}{\text{settlement price}} \times \dfrac{\text{conversion}}{\text{factor}} + \dfrac{\text{Accrued}}{\text{Interest}}$

If it is likely that a futures contract will be allowed to expire, then for each deliverable bond a seller can calculate the return that can be earned by buying the bond and delivering it on the settlement date. The return or yield can be calculated because both the cash and agreed futures prices are known. This yield is also known as the **gross basis** and can be calculated for each bond in the basket of deliverables using the following equation:

> **Gross basis = Bond price − (Futures price x Conversion factor)**

However, the gross basis does not take into account the accrued income generated by the deliverable bond which also needs to be taken into account when calculating the return on the investment. The return on investment is better described as the **Implied Repo Rate (IRR)** and is calculated from the amount invested, amount returned and the investment period.

So, which deliverable bond is selected if a futures contract expires?

The bond with the highest, positive IRR offers the greatest profit as a percentage of the investment and is therefore the **Cheapest To Deliver (CTD)**.

Some exchanges publish yields and IRRs for deliverable bonds which indicate the CTD for the delivery month in question. The Reuters screen below shows CTD information on the current LIFFE Long gilt contracts.

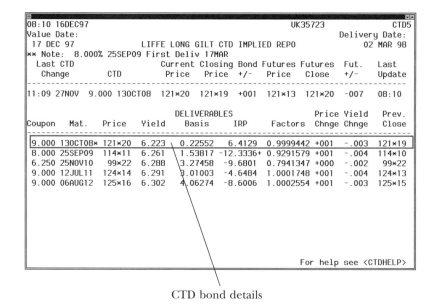

CTD bond details

Profit and Loss on a Futures Contract

This is easy to calculate using the following method:

1. Determine the number of ticks the price has moved up or down. The number of ticks is the number of one-hundredths or one thirty-seconds of the quotation price.

2. Multiply the number of ticks by the tick value and the number of contracts.

Profit/loss = Number of ticks x Tick value x Number of contracts

Example

25 June LIFFE Bund futures contracts are bought on 2nd April at 96.32. On 7th April the contracts are sold at 96.85. The tick size is 0.01 and the tick value is DEM 25. What is the profit or loss on the transaction?

$$
\begin{aligned}
\text{Profit or loss} &= (96.85 - 96.32) \times 25 \times 25 \\
&= 53 \text{ ticks} \times 25 \times 25 \\
&= \text{DEM } 33,125 \text{ profit}
\end{aligned}
$$

Typical Contract Quotations

Interest rate futures quotations are available from the financial press such as the *Financial Times* and *The Wall Street Journal* and from services such as Reuters. The information appears in formats similar to those following.

Financial press – Long-term Interest Rate futures

CBOT Treasury Bonds $100,000 points 32nds of 100%				
	Open	High	Low	Settle
Mar	112-19	112-24	110-25	110-28
Jun	112-03	112-13	110-09	110-13
Sep	111-24	111-24	109-29	109-31
Dec	110-16	110-16	109-17	109-17

Reuters 3000 Money – CBOT bond futures and Bund futures from LIFFE and DTB

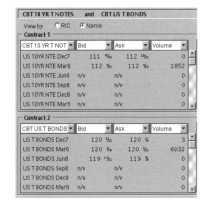

Who Uses Bond Futures?

Hedgers and Speculators

Originally futures contracts were devised so that holders of an asset could hedge or insure its price today for sometime in the future. Hedgers seek to transfer the risk of future price fluctuations by selling future contracts which guarantee them a future price for their asset. If the future cash price of their asset falls then they have protected themselves. However, if the future cash price rises then they have lost the opportunity to profit. Hedging offers some degree of certainty for future prices and therefore allows market players to fix prices, interest rate payments or receipts etc.

- **Hedgers** are typically banks, multinational organisations, governments, bond dealers and fund managers.

- **Speculator**s are market players who take on the risk of a futures contract for an appropriate price and the potential rewards.

- **Arbitrageurs** trade derivatives with a view to exploit any price differences within different derivatives markets or between the drivative instruments and cash or physical prices in the underlying assets. (Arbitrage is explained in greater detail in *An Introduction to Derivatives*, ISBN 0-471-83176-X).

The transfer of risk sought by hedgers is possible in the markets because different market players have different strategies and include:

- Hedgers with opposite risks

- Hedgers already holding positions who need to offset their positions

- Speculators with market views on likely price changes who provide the futures markets with extra liquidity

As in any futures market place for commodities, hedgers can hold **long** or **short** positions and in order to hedge their positions market players need to take an **opposite** position to the ones they hold.

It is important to understand that the principle of hedging is to maintain a neutral position. As prices in the cash market for the asset move one way, the move is compensated by an equal and opposite move in the futures' price. You can imagine the situation similar to the movement of the pans on a pair of scales.

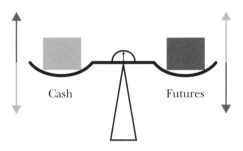

Cash   Futures

Going Short Futures
If a market player **holds**, or intends to hold, an asset in the cash market, then he has a **long** position. The opposite position in the futures markets means he must **go short** or **sell futures**.

A borrower, who intends to hold cash, needs to protect against the possibility that spot prices **fall** with a corresponding **rise** in interest rates. A **short hedge** will therefore lock in a selling price.

Going Long Futures
If a market player is short, or intends to go short, in the cash market, then the opposite position in the futures markets means he must **go long** or **buy futures**.

A lender, who intends to deposit cash, needs to protect against the possibility that spot prices **rise** with a corresponding **fall** in interest rates. A **long hedge** will therefore lock in a buying price.

Another way of considering market players using bond futures contracts is to look at whether they are **buyers** or **sellers** of the contracts.

Buyers of Bond Futures

- Agree to take delivery of the underlying instrument and therefore **go long**.

- Are **lenders** and are hedging against any **fall** in interest rates. If interest rates do fall, then any losses in buying the underlying in the future are offset by gains from the futures contracts on delivery.

The diagrams below show how the losses in the underlying instrument are offset by gains in the futures market.

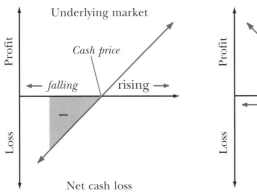

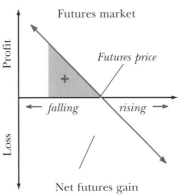

As interest rates	So futures prices
Rise	Fall
Fall	Rise

Sellers of Bond Futures

- Agree to deliver the underlying instrument and therefore **go short**.

- Are **borrowers** and are hedging against any **rise** in interest rates. If interest rates do rise, then any losses in selling the underlying in the future are offset by gains from the futures contracts on delivery.

The diagrams below show how the losses in the underlying instrument are offset by gains in the futures market.

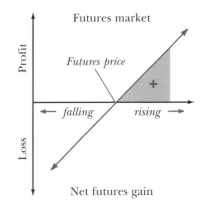

Short hedge	Long hedge
• Sell futures	• Buy futures
• Protects against **rise** in interest rates	• Protects against **fall** in interest rates
• Locks in selling price	• Locks in buying price
• Used by **borrowers**	• Used by **lenders**

Hedging and Hedge Ratio

Bond futures are widely used to hedge government bond market positions. Interest rate risk is assessed and measured using **duration** analysis and **Basis Point Value (BPV)** which deals with how bond prices change with changes in yield.

In order to hedge a position it is necessary to match the futures contracts as closely as possible with that for the underlying instrument in terms of maturity dates, amounts involved etc. In practice it is difficult to obtain the conditions for a perfect hedge!

The number of futures contracts required – the **hedge ratio** – is simply calculated from the equation:

Number of contracts required =

$$\frac{\text{Sum to be hedged}}{\text{Unit of trading}} \times \frac{\text{BPV of bond held}}{\text{BPV of CTD bond}} \times \text{Conversion factor}$$

For many simple calculations this equation reduces to an **unweighted** hedge such that:

$$\frac{\text{Number of}}{\text{contracts required}} = \frac{\text{Sum to be hedged}}{\text{Unit of trading}}$$

Some exchanges publish BPV and hedge ratio data for deliverable bonds which also indicate the CTD data in particular. The Reuters screen below shows the hedge ratios for LIFFE Long gilt contract deliverable bonds.

```
08:10 16DEC97                                        UK35723              CTD1
Value Date:                                                    Delivery Date:
 17 DEC 97                    LIFFE LONG GILT CTD HEDGE              02 MAR 98
** Note:  8.000% 25SEP09 First Deliv 17MAR
  Last CTD              Current Closing Bond Futures Futures  Fut.    Last
    Change        CTD     Price   Price  +/-   Price  Close   +/-    Update

11:09 27NOV  9.000 130CT08  121×20  121×19  +001  121×13  121×20  -007  08:10

                            DELIVERABLES               Price Yield   Prev.
Coupon   Mat.   Price  Yield  Factors      PVBP   Hedge  Chnge Chnge  Close
---------------------------------------------------------------------------
9.000 130CT08× 121×20  6.223  0.9999442  8.85080  1.00000  +001  -.003  121×19
8.000 25SEP09  114×11  6.261  0.9291579  8.99230  1.01599  +001  -.004  114×10
6.250 25NOV10   99×22  6.288  0.7941347  8.74064  0.98755  +000  -.002   99×22
9.000 12JUL11  124×14  6.291  1.0001748 10.48021  1.18410  +001  -.004  124×13
9.000 06AUG12  125×16  6.302  1.0002554 11.07038  1.25078  +001  -.003  125×15




                                              For help see <CTDHELP>
```

CTD bond details

Short Hedge – Selling Futures

A short hedge can be used by an investor needing to hedge against price falls of a bond resulting from rising interest rates. The futures contract effectively locks in the selling price of the bond for a future sale date.

Example

A portfolio manager holds £1 million of UK Long gilts with a coupon of 9.00%, maturing in 2012. It is December and a rise in interest rates is feared by the following March when the bonds are due to be sold. The manager needs to hedge this future sale position. For an unweighted hedge the:

$$\frac{\text{Number of}}{\text{contracts required}} = \frac{£1,000,000}{£50,000} = 20$$

The manager sells 20 March LIFFE Long gilts in December and it is now nearing the March delivery date and the manager offsets the position. What is the result of the manager's hedge?

Bond market	Futures market
December Gilt price = 125-6. Therefore £1 million gilts has a market value = £1,251,875	Sell 20 March contracts at 121-14. (Implied value – £1,214,375)
By March interest rates have risen *March* Gilt price = 120-22. Therefore £1 million gilts has a market value = £1,206,875	Buy 20 March contracts at 117-26 to close position. (Implied value - £1,178,125)
Loss on position By March loss = £45,000	**Gain on position** From implied values and 116 ticks x £15.625 x 20 = £36,250

This hedge is not perfect but the final loss to the manager of £8,500 is better than a potential loss of £45,000! It is important to recognise that the loss or gain on a futures position is not paid as a single instalment but as daily margin payments which are described later.

Long Hedge – Buying Futures

A long hedge is typically used by investors who plan to buy bonds in the future and are concerned that interest rates might fall causing bond prices to rise. A long hedge is often termed an **anticipatory** hedge.

Example

An investor plans to buy 50 30-year US T-Bonds with a coupon of 8.125% and maturing in 2019 for a total face value of $5 million. The current trading price of the bond is 120.00 and so the amount to be hedged is $6 million. The conversion factor for the next futures delivery month for this bond is 1.0126. The investor can use a weighted hedge. In this case the:

$$\frac{\text{Number of}}{\text{contracts required}} = \frac{\$6,000,000}{\$100,000} \times 1.0126$$

$$= 60.7 \text{ or } 61 \text{ contracts}$$

The investor buys 61 futures contracts and offsets the position shortly before the intended purchase date when 50 T-Bonds are bought in the cash markets. What is the result of the investor's hedge?

Bond market	Futures market
Now Bond price = 120-00. Therefore 50 bonds has a market value = $6,000,000	Buy 61 contracts at 119 -24 (Implied value - $7,304,750)
Prior to purchase Bond price = 124-24. Therefore 50 bonds has a market value = $6,237,500	Sell 61 contracts at 123-24 to close position. (Implied value - $7,548,750)
Loss on position By purchase date loss = $237,500	**Gain on position** From implied values = $244,000

In this case the potential cash market loss is offset by the gains of the weighted hedge in the futures market. However, small changes in prices can turn gains into losses!

Speculation

Speculators attempt to exploit price movements in the markets and thus provide additional liquidity for hedging activities. Typically speculators in bond futures have no intention of taking or making delivery of the underlying deliverable bonds. They use their market knowledge and expectations to profit. Speculators can take long or short positions depending on their market views.

Example
A trader is expecting interest rates to rise which will result in a fall in Long gilts prices and a subsequent fall in futures prices. To profit from this expectation, the trader sells 10 LIFFE Long gilt futures at 120-30.

In three days time the trader is viewing the news on his RT and is proven correct – interest rates have risen by 0.5%. The futures price has fallen to 118-30 with a resulting gain of 64 ticks.

His profit is 64 x £25.625 x 10 = £10,000

Arbitrage

There are two main forms of arbitrage employed.

- Futures – Futures Arbitrage
- Cash – Futures Arbitrage/Cash-and-carry Arbitrage

Futures – Futures arbitrage occurs when dealers attempt to profit from the change in price differential between two exchanges eg. LIFFE and NYCSCE cocoa or betewen two products, eg. Arabica and Robusta coffee.

Cash-and-carry arbitrage involves the purchase of a physical commodity against the forward sale of that commodity on the futures market. The display below illustrates examples of exchange spreads for similar products and the intermonth spreads for the same contract on the same exchange.

Interest Rate Futures in the Market Place

This section deals with a number of important matters concerning bond futures which you will need to understand.

How a Bond Futures Contract Works

When a futures contract is agreed no payment is made. Instead both parties are required to deposit a **margin** with the clearing house which acts as the counterparty to both sides. The **initial margin** is only a small percentage of the contract price and it is used to cover daily price movements of the futures' price in relation to the agreed price. Each day the futures' position is **marked-to-market** which means it is revalued at the current market price. Any profits and losses are paid over daily. By marking-to-market and settling all positions daily the clearing house effectively rewrites all futures contracts at the prevailing market price.

If the initial margin is depleted then extra margin – **variation margin** – is required. If a profit is made the account will receive it and it may be withdrawn. The system of maintaining the correct margin ensures that the loser can bear any losses and the winner is credited with gains.

Example
25 June LIFFE Bund futures contracts are bought on 2nd April at 96.32. On 7th April the contracts are sold at 96.85. The tick size is 0.01 and the tick value is DEM 25. Previously the profit was calculated as DEM 33,125. The table below shows the actual course of events.

Date	Settlement price	Previous price	Ticks	Variation margin, DEM
2.4	96.28	96.32	– 4	–2,500
3.4	96.60	96.28	32	20,000
4.4	96.82	96.60	22	13,750
5.4	95.65	96.82	– 117	– 73,125
6.4	96.26	95.65	61	38,125
7.4	96.85	96.26	59	36,875
Total	**96.85**	**96.32**	**53**	**33,125**

Dealing on margin is an example of **gearing** or **leverage**. Gearing allows investors to make a larger investment than could otherwise be afforded. Small investments are used to generate large profits, however, losses can be correspondingly large! For example, a £1000 investment in a futures contract is equivalent to buying a basic investment of £10,000 – 20,000.

As the expiry date of the contract approaches the futures price will equal the current instrument price and so the differential is not very large. This is why the vast majority, over 98%, of futures contracts are closed out before the contract reaches the agreed expiry date.

The process is illustrated as here:

On the contract date
The Seller sells a contract to the Buyer and both deposit initial margins with the clearing house.

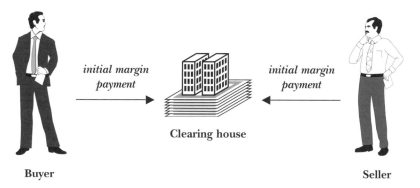

During the contract
The Seller's and the Buyer's profit and loss accounts are adjusted daily.

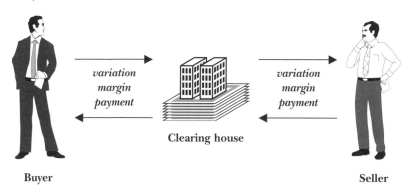

On the delivery date or contract closure
The Seller's and the Buyer's profit and loss accounts are settled for the last time.

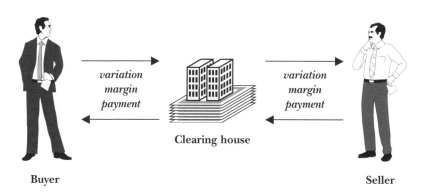

Advantages and Disadvantages of Bond Futures

The following chart summarises the advantages and disadvantages of Bond futures:

Advantages	Disadvantages
• Markets in the major contracts for, US T-Bonds, German Bunds, French OATS and UK Long gilts are large and very liquid • The use of margin payments allows highly leveraged positions • Contracts can be bought and sold without having to own the underlying asset • Most contracts are offset and only a very small percentage expire resulting in delivery	• Only a limited number of contracts available • It can be difficult to hedge positions exactly – matching exact amounts and required dates is not always easy • When hedging long-term futures, the price/yield relationship varies continuously with time and therefore the hedge ratio varies continuously • The mark-to-market settlement system can lead to large cash outflows for adverse price movements • Trading is usually concentrated in near month contracts • Liquidity can be limited for far month contracts

Trading Strategies for Bond Futures

There are a number of trading strategies that traders adopt in order to hedge positions which do not have 'perfect matches' in the futures markets. The simplest of these strategies include:

- Basis trading

- Spread trading

- Hedging portfolio duration

- Asset allocation

- Multicurrency investment using futures contracts

Basis Trading

When considering how deliverable bonds can be compared, the gross basis was described as:

$$\text{Gross basis} = \text{Bond price} - (\text{Futures price} \times \text{Conversion factor})$$

As with all financial futures, futures prices and basis are simply defined using the following equations:

$$\text{Futures price} = \text{Cash price} + \text{Net cost of carry}$$

$$\text{Basis} = \text{Cash price} - \text{Futures price}$$

If a bond futures contract is held to delivery, then the bond delivered has a known cash flow. If the cash flow generated is **greater** than the financing costs in buying the bond, then there is a net gain and the cost of carry is **positive**. If the cash flow generated is **less**, then the cost of carry is **negative**.

A simple chart of futures and cash prices shows that at maturity the two prices are equal. For a positive cost of carry or **positive basis** the CTD bond price will be **above** the futures price and vice versa for a negative basis. The chart below illustrates the situations.

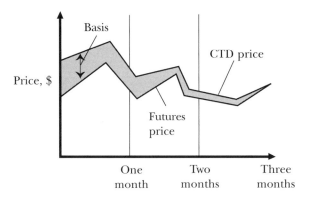

So if interest rates rise – a typical positive yield curve – the cash price of bonds fall as do the futures prices and vice versa.

Basis trading in its simplest form is where a trader takes a simultaneous position in a futures contract and in one of the bonds that comprise the basket of deliverables. The position can result in profits or losses simply from the fluctuating basis relationship between the futures and cash bond prices.

Spread Trading

There are three types of spread trading you may encounter in futures trading:

- A single contract calendar spread

- A cross market bond spread

- A yield curve spread within a single country

A single contract calendar spread

This is one of the most common types of spread trading. In this case a trader will buy and sell futures contracts **simultaneously** for the **same** country's government bonds but the contracts are for **different** delivery months. In other words a calendar spread.

Long calendar spreads involve going long – buying – the front month futures contract and going short – selling – the far month contracts. The calendar spread is calculated by subtracting the price of the far month contract from that of the front month. The spread earns profits if the price differential widens while the trade is in place – if the spread narrows then a loss will be made.

A cross market bond spread

Interest rate differentials between different countries government debt markets are important to fixed income market players. The futures markets can be used to capture changes in cross market differentials.

Within the debt markets the yields between two countries benchmark bonds can be used for comparison purposes. In particular the difference between these yields which is known as the **yield spread**.

The aim of a cross market spread trade is to capture changes in the yield spread regardless of the specific changes in the individual countries' bond yields. In the cash markets a trader will arrange to sell the benchmark bond of one country financed using a reverse repo, whilst simultaneously buying a benchmark bond in the second country financed using a standard repo.

If futures contracts in the two countries' notional bonds are used, then the exchange rate risk is reduced. The only payments required are those of initial and variation margin – the trader does not need to acquire the actual bonds. The disadvantage of using cross market bond futures is that of exposure to basis – the relationship between the yield of the benchmark bond and bond futures prices is not fixed.

A yield curve spread within a single country

The relationship between short-term interest rates and long-term government bond yields is also important in the debt markets.

Short-term and bond futures contracts can be used to take positions on the term structure of interest rates where there is a spread between the yield curves. In other words the difference or spread between short-term interest rate Eurodeposits and long-term notional government bond yields.

Hedging Portfolio Duration

As you know by now if interest rates fall then bond prices rise and vice versa. This means that portfolio managers are subject to interest rate risks and the ensuing gains/losses in their capital. Bond futures can be used by portfolio managers as a way of managing interest rate risk of their portfolio without actually altering the composition of the bonds held.

Each bond in the portfolio has a modified duration and BPV which can be calculated. These values can be used to calculate the weighted average of modified duration and BPV for the component bonds in a portfolio. This allows the manager to treat the whole portfolio as if it were a single bond having a single interest rate risk.

To alter the modified duration of a portfolio the manager could buy/sell bonds to adjust the modified duration required. Alternatively, the manager could buy or sell futures contracts to achieve the same level of interest rate risk.

The cash approach is known as bond swapping. The disadvantage in the cash markets is that of liquidity and marketability of the bonds held. In other words will the manager receive and pay fair prices for the required transactions.

Using futures means that the manager's portfolio remains intact, costs are reduced and positions can be adjusted quickly.

By **buying** bond futures contracts the duration of the portfolio is **increased**; by **selling** contracts the duration is **reduced**.

Asset allocation

With the debt markets becoming increasingly more global it is now quite common for portfolio managers and institutional investors to allocate their assets between different countries government debt instruments. For example, a manager may decide to allocate assets and therefore their interest rate risk 60% to BTPs and 40% to Bunds. Now suppose that the market expectations change and a market player wishes to reverse the risk allocation.

One method available is to use the cash markets in order to buy/sell the required bonds to redress the asset allocation. The alternative strategy is to use bond futures contracts. In this case the BTP exposure can be **reduced** by **selling** BTP futures and **buying** Bund futures to **increase** their exposure. By using bond futures the portfolio remains intact and any further adjustments required in the asset allocation can quickly be made.

Multicurrency Investing Using Futures Contracts

Asset allocation can also be performed without a market player actually holding a portfolio of cash bonds. In this case the bond futures contracts are the assets to be allocated.

A portfolio manager may have $100 million at her disposal to be divided equally between BTPs and Bunds. If the portfolio manager uses the cash markets then the funds are invested in benchmark bonds. The manager is now exposed to interest rate risks associated with the bond yields for the countries concerned together with interest rate risks associated with duration for the individual benchmark bonds. In addition there are foreign exchange risks to be considered between USD/DEM and USD/ITL.

A similar portfolio can be created using bond futures contracts where no actual bonds are held and the manager allocates the assets to be invested in futures rather than in bonds.

Bond Futures

- A Bond future is an **exchange traded forward transaction** for a notional government bond with a standard contract size, notional yield and maturity dates

- Long-term futures are settled by **physical delivery** against an **Exchange Delivery Settlement Price** of the **Cheapest To Deliver** bond in a basket of deliverable underlying government bonds or notes

- The **invoice price** is the number of contracts times the futures settlement price times the conversion price plus the accrued interest

- Hedgers who are **lenders**, **buy futures** or go long, to protect against any **fall** in interest rates

- Hedgers who are **borrowers**, **sell futures** or go short, to protect against any **rise** in interest rates

- A **Clearing house** acts as **counterparty** to both buyers and sellers of a futures contract which is marked-to-market daily

Derivatives

Forward Rate Agreements (FRAs)

> A **Forward Rate Agreement** is an agreement between two counterparties which fixes the rate of interest that will apply to a specified notional future loan or deposit commencing and maturing on specified future dates.

An FRA is essentially a promise to pay/receive a specified rate of interest in the future, regardless of what the prevailing rate of interest in the market is at that time. They are usually used by borrowers in the money markets to fix the short-term rates of interest they will pay on their short-term loans.

FRAs are **cash-settled**. This means the **buyer** will be paid in cash by the seller for any **rise** in the reference interest rate over and above the agreed contract rate. Borrowers who wish to hedge the risk of borrowing costs rising in the future therefore **buy** FRAs to hedge out this risk.

The **seller** of an FRA will be paid in cash by the buyer for any **fall** in the reference interest rate below the agreed contract rate. Lenders who wish to hedge the risk of falls in future interest rate therefore **sell**.

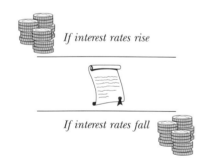

If interest rates rise

If interest rates fall

Buyer

Seller

Terms and Specifications: Forward Rate Agreements (FRAs)

FRAs have a number of features which market players need to assess before they decide on using the instrument. These features include the following:

- **Cash settlement.** As the loan/deposit is for notional funds there is no exchange of principal. Cash compensation is paid at the **beginning** of the notional loan/deposit period.

- **Flexibility.** As the loan/deposit is for notional funds there is no obligation by buyers/sellers in the markets to actually lend or deposit their funds. Market players can use other instruments which offer the best returns of their specific needs.

- **Lock-in rate.** Like forward FX contracts, if future interest rates fall the buyer will have to compensate the seller and forego any benefit from lower interest rates. Equally, if interest rates rise the seller has to compensate the buyer. FRAs effectively lock-in future interest rates for market players.

- **Low credit risk.** As there is no exchange of principal an FRA is an off-balance sheet instrument. The credit risk is low because the main risk is concerned with finding a replacement counterparty should the original party default. The risk involved is therefore on **differentials** rather than the notional amount.

- **Cancellation and assignment.** An FRA is a binding contract and cannot be cancelled or assigned to a third party without the agreement of both counterparties. As with other instruments with binding contracts, FRA positions can be closed using off-setting contracts.

REUTERS

Terms Used

There are a number of terms you need to know if you are to understand how FRAs work and are used. The table below indicates the terms and their meanings.

Term	Which means...
Contract Currency and Amount	The currency and amount of the notional loan/deposit
Trade Date	The date the deal is actually made
Fixing Date	This is **two business days before** the start of the FRA. It is the date when the LIBOR, or other, reference rate is **fixed**. The settlement amount is calculated using this rate. For domestic currency FRAs the fixing date is usually the **same** as the settlement date.
Settlement Date	This is the date when the contract period **starts** and cash compensation is paid
Maturity Date	The date the contract ends
Contract Period	This is the term of the notional loan/deposit – the period from settlement to matuirty in days
Contract Rate	The agreed forward interest rate for the contract period – the price of the FRA in % per annum

Valuing Forward Rate Agreements

FRAs are typically quoted as a two-way price with bid-offer rates, in the same way as money market deposit rates.

Prices are often quoted in standard terms, such as whole months and round numbers for notional size, although terms can be tailored to precise dates and non-standard sizes.

Standard terms are detailed in the table below:

3 month series			6 month series		
	Starts forward	Ends forward		Starts forward	Ends forward
1 x 4	4 months	4 months	1 x 7	7 months	7 months
2 x 5	5 months	5 months	2 x 8	8 months	8 months
3 x 6	6 months	6 months	3 x 9	9 months	9 months
6 x 9	9 months	9 months	6 x 12	12 months	12 months

The value of a forward rate agreement is derived from the current interest rate and the future interest rate covering the tenor of the FRA, as implied from longer-dated money market instruments or debt instruments. These interest rates can be derived using similar calculations to those used for valuing commercial paper in the previous section for this book.

There are three main instruments used to derive the prices of FRAs:
- Treasury Bills
- Interest Rate Futures
- Zero coupon bonds (similar to commercial paper but with a longer maturity)

Before we examine how to value a forward rate agreement, it is worth comparing FRAs with interest rate futures as these contracts share many features in common. For example, they are both used to fix the interes trate payable or receivable over some specific period in the future. The precise requirements of the user determine whether an FRA or interest rate future is the more appropriate contract for hedging.

Comparing FRAs with Interest Rate Futures Contracts

As interest rate futures contracts could easily be used in place of FRAs, it is useful to compare the following aspects of the instruments.

	Forward Rate Agreement	Interest Rate Futures Contract
Trading	It is an OTC contract between counterparties. In some cases the deal may be made via a broker.	Contracts are traded in pits or electronically on an exchange.
Contract Terms	Amount, period and settlement procedures are negotiated between the counterparties.	Amounts, expiry dates and settlement periods are fixed and standardised by the exchange.
Confidentiality	There are no obligations placed on the counterparties to divulge the terms of the cotnract. Different market-makers may well quote different bid/offer prices.	Deals are transacted open out cry or using electronic systems. Orders and trades are immediately visible and transparent to all market players. On an exchange there is only one market price at any one time.
Margin Payments	No margin payments are required. However, dealers will often require some form of collateral to be posted with them in order to mitigate against credit risk (see below). Settlement is in cash, and is the difference between the "forward rate" when the deal is executed and the actual rate at maturity.	Initial margin is paid as a % of the trade amount – marked-to-market. The margin payments are held by the clearing house. Variation margin is also paid to the clearing house on a daily basis depending on the market price movement.
Credit Risk	Each side is exposed to the credit risk of the counterparty, only if they are in a profitable position on the deal. This is because the contract is settled in cash with the net difference between the forward rate and actual rate at maturity being paid form one counterparty to the other. At the outset of the deal, it is not known which way the payment will be made, so both sides are taking on **potential future credit risk**.	The trading counterparty for a futures contract is the exchange clearing house. Therefore when trading interest rate futures, the credit risk is simply the credit risk of the clearing house, which is usually a very high quality counterparty.
Right of Offset	An FRA contract is binding and cannot be cancelled or assigned to a third party without the agreement of both sides.	Interest rate futures contracts can be off-set.

FRAs in the Market Place

FRA Settlement Payments

The settlement rate is usually determined two business days **before** the period of the notional loan/deposit for the specified reference rate, for example, LIBOR. It is important to note that the settlement payment is made at the **beginning** of the loan period rather than at maturity – the usual procedure for money market deposits. Therefore the settlement payment has to be discounted to its present valuea t the current market interest rate.

You will need to know two equations in order to calculate settlement payments – both equations are very similar. One caters for the situation where the settlement rate is **greater** than the contract rate so the FRA buyer compensates the seller. The other equation is for the opposite situation where the settlement rate is **less** than the contract rate so the FRA seller compensates the buyer.

Settlement rate **greater** than contract rate

$$\text{Settlement payment} = \frac{(L - R) \times D \times A}{(B \times 100) + (L \times D)} \quad ...Equation\ 13a$$

Settlement rate **less** than contract rate

$$\text{Settlement payment} = \frac{(L - R) \times D \times A}{(B \times 100) + (L \times D)} \quad ...Equation\ 13b$$

L = Settlement rate as a number **not** %
R = Contract rate as a number **not** %
B = Day basis – 360 or 365
D = Contract period in days
A = Contract amount

Example 1

It is the 10th April 1997 and the XYZ corporate treasurer foresees a forward funding requirement for 3 months (92 days) from 16th June to 15th September 1997. The treasurer thinks that there is a possible rise in interest rats and therefore wants to hedge against any interest rate rise. The treasurer buys a 2 x 5 FRA on the 10th April from OkiBank with the following terms:

FRA contract amt.	$10,000,000
Fixing date:	12th June 1997
Settlement date:	16 June 1997
Maturity date:	15th Sept. 1997
Contract rate:	6.75% pa
Year basis:	360 days

What is the settlement due if the LIBOR 3-month fixing rate is 7.25% the fixing date 10th June, and who receives payment?

Even though XYZ have bought an FRA contract they still have to raise the funds they require for 16th June to 15th September in the money markets at the increased rate of 7.25%. However, as the interest rates have risen, OkiBank have to compensate XYZ a cash sum. The settlement amount is therefore calculated using Equation 13a.

$$\text{Settlement payment} = \frac{(7.25 - 6.75) \times 92 \times 10,000,000}{(360 \times 100) + (7.25 \times 92)}$$

$$= \frac{460,000,000}{36667}$$

$$= \mathbf{\$12,545.34}$$

At this point the FRA contract ceases to exist and the XYZ corporate treasurer can now either reinvest the fRA settlement payment in the money markets or arrange a loan for $10,000,000 – 12,545.34.

In either case the XYZ loan will be based on the current LIBOR. The FRA payment acts as a subsidy bringing down the net cost of borrowing.

But what would have happened if the treasurer's fears of an interest rate rise were unfounded and on fixing LIBOR was 6.50%? This time XYZ have to compensate OkiBank. The settlement amount can be calcualted using Equation 13b.

$$\text{Settlement payment} = \frac{(6.75 - 6.50) \times 92 \times 10,000,000}{(360 \times 100) + (6.50 \times 92)}$$

$$= \frac{230,000,000}{36598}$$

$$= \$6,284.50$$

Other Risks Involved in FRAs

Apart from interest rate risk, which affects the price a final settlement value of an FRA, and credit risk, which affects the counterparties' ability to deliver the cash settlement at maturity of the FRA, there is another important risk to consider.

Basis risk is the risk that the London Interbank Offered Rate (LIBOR) which applies to the settlement value of the FRA moves away from the actual interest rate on the underlying loan that is being hedged, leaving the holder with an imperfect hedge.

The interest rates on money market instruments are all closely linked to LIBOR. However, sometimes there can be market events which can cause certain instruments to deviate from LIBOR.

In this situation, a borrower who hedges using a LIBOR-linked FRA is bound to pay the forward interest rate on the underlying loan at the FRA's maturity. If the interest rate on the underlying loan rises by more than the LIBOR rate used for settling the FRA, the borrowers profit on the FRA will be less than the loss on the underlying loan. Hence the FRA provides an imperfect hedge if the interest rate on the underlying loan is different to the interest rate to which the FRA is linked.

This risk of residual loss due to imperfect hedging is called **basis risk**.

Forward/Forward Rates

In many cases FRA **strips** of contracts are used to hedge against longer term interest rate rises. A strip is simply a number of consecutive contracts. For example, a strip of four FRA contracts, 1 x 3, 3 x 6, 6 x 9, 9 x 12 could be used to hedge for a 12 month period. However, if a strip of FRAs are used what is the effective rate FRA?

Suppose the following strip of two FRAs spans the two periods 0 to n and 0 to N. The rate of return for the time period n to N can be calcualted using an equation based on the interest rates due for the time periods.

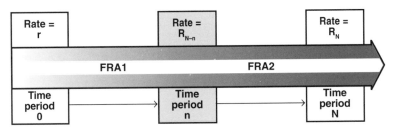

$$\binom{\text{Interest due for}}{\text{time period, N}} = \binom{\text{Interest due for}}{\text{time period, \textbf{n}}} \times \binom{\text{Interest due for}}{\text{time period, \textbf{N} - \textbf{n}}}$$

Therefore:

$$\left[1 + \left(\frac{R_N \times N}{B \times 100}\right)\right] = \left[1 + \left(\frac{r \times n}{B \times 100}\right)\right] \times \left[1 + \left(\frac{R_{N-n} \times N - n}{B \times 100}\right)\right]$$

$$R_{N-n} = \frac{\left[1 + \left(\dfrac{R_N \times N}{B \times 100}\right)\right]}{\left[1 + \left(\dfrac{R_N \times N}{B \times 100}\right)\right]} - 1 \times \frac{360 \times 100}{N}$$

$$R_{N-n} =$$

...*Equation 14*

If you need to calculate the effective annual interest rate for a strip of FRAs the following equation can be used which is based on Equation 14.

Effective annual rate, R =

$$\left[1 + \left(\frac{L_{0x3}}{4}\right)\right] \times \left[1 + \left(\frac{F_{3x6}}{4}\right)\right] \times \left[1 + \left(\frac{F_{6x9}}{4}\right)\right] \times \left[1 + \left(\frac{F_{9x12}}{4}\right)\right] - 1$$

L_{0x3} = Current LIBOR or reference rate

$F_{3x6}, F_{6x3}, F_{9x12}$ = FRA rates for periods 3 x 6, 6 x 9 and 9 x 12 respectively

...*Equation 15*

Example 2

XYZ Corporation now needs to protect interest rates for a six month period beginning in 6 months time – a 6 x 12 forward position. The XYZ corporate treasurer could use a 6 x 12 FRA. However, a strip of two 3-month FRAs, 6 x 9 and 9 x 12, offers the treasurer the flexibility of reversing the hedge at the 9 month period if necessary. The strip also provides a market limit for a 6 x 12 FRA quote.

XYZ need to borrow $5,000,000 in 6 months time for a loan period of 6 months, but the treasurer thinks interest rates will rise in this time. The treasurer investigates quotes from a numbe rof banks offering FRAs indexed on a 3-month LIBOR basis.

FRA	Bank A	Bank B
6 x 9 (91d)	6.21 – 6.15	6.23 – 6.18
9 x 12 (92 d)	6.28 – 6.22	6.30 – 6.25

The treasurer accepts the bid FRA prices from Bank A as the cheaper and buys a strip of two FRAs – 6 x 9 plus 9 x 12. This effectively locks in the interest rates for the 6-month borrowing period.

6 x 12 month exposure of $5,000,000

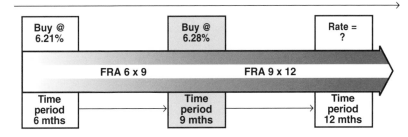

What is the effective FRA rate?

The effective FRA rate for the strip is calculated using Equation 15.

$$\left[1 + \left(\frac{R_{6x12} \times N}{B \times 100}\right)\right] = \left[1 + \left(\frac{R_{6x9} \times n}{B \times 100}\right)\right] \times \left[1 + \left(\frac{R_{9x12} \times N - n}{B \times 100}\right)\right]$$

$$= \left[1 + \left(\frac{6.21 \times 91}{360 \times 100}\right)\right] \times \left[1 + \left(\frac{6.28 \times 92}{360 \times 100}\right)\right]$$

= 1.0157 x 1.01605

= 1.03200

Therefore R_{6x12} = $(1.03200 - 1) \times \dfrac{360 \times 100}{183}$

= 6.2955 or 6.30% rounded up

The screen below displays the major currency FRAs.

Your notes

	USD	FRAs		DEM	FRAs		JPY	FRAs		GBP
1X4	5.80	5.84	16:06	3.13	3.16	14:19	0.63	0.66	15:44	6.96
2X5	5.84	5.88	16:07	3.15	3.18	14:19	0.63	0.66	15:44	7.03
3X6	5.92	5.96	15:49	3.15	3.18	14:19	0.66	0.69	15:44	7.10
4X7	5.99	6.03	16:05	3.22	3.25	15:37	0.72	0.75	15:44	7.16
5X8	6.05	6.09	16:05	3.25	3.28	15:37	0.77	0.80	15:44	7.21
6X9	6.05	6.09	16:02	3.29	3.32	15:37	0.86	0.89	15:44	7.28
7X10	6.11	6.15	16:05	3.32	3.35	15:37	0.92	0.95	15:44	7.30
8X11	6.15	6.19	15:50	3.34	3.37	14:12	0.99	1.02	15:44	7.34
9X12	6.20	6.24	15:50	3.40	3.42	15:33	1.06	1.09	15:44	7.36
12X15	6.31	6.35	15:52	3.56	3.59	15:26	1.26	1.29	15:44	7.34
15X18	6.47	6.50	15:43	3.74	3.77	15:26	1.49	1.52	06:33	7.31
18X21	6.56	6.59	15:42	4.05	4.06	15:52	1.46	1.47	12:09	7.04
21X24	6.58	6.61	16:08	4.42	4.45	21:57	1.46	1.46	21:56	7.45
1X7	5.96	5.98	16:07	3.18	3.22	14:46	0.70	0.74	09:49	7.14
2X8	5.99	6.03	16:07	3.21	3.24	14:14	0.72	0.75	15:44	7.19
3X9	6.04	6.08	16:07	3.24	3.27	15:37	0.76	0.79	15:44	7.26
4X10	6.10	6.14	16:07	3.28	3.31	14:14	0.84	0.87	15:44	7.29
5X11	6.15	6.19	16:05	3.31	3.34	14:13	0.90	0.93	15:44	7.34
6X12	6.17	6.21	15:51	3.35	3.38	14:13	0.98	1.01	15:44	7.38

Using the screen below can be useful as you can display Bid and Ask prices for a number of currencies from different contributors simultaneously. For example, you decde to look at 3 x 6 rates for DEM FRAs from 3 different contributors in order to select the best rates for you for buying and selling. You look at the rates and decide that those from HBEL are best. You now decide to check these rates and calculate the forward/forward bid and ask prices from deposit rates displayed in the lower screen.

FRMW

Currency	DEM ▼	Currency	DEM ▼	Currency	DEM ▼
Contributor	HBEL ▼	Contributor	TTKL ▼	Contributor	TRDL ▼
Term	All 3m FRAs ▼	Term	All 3m FRAs ▼	Term	All 3m FRAs ▼

FRA	Bid	Ask	Source ▼	FRA	Bid	Ask	Source ▼	FRA	Bid	Ask	Source ▼
1X4	3.13	3.16	HBEL	1X4	3.16	3.16	TTKL	1X4	3.14	3.16	TRDL
2X5	3.15	3.18	HBEL	2X5	3.15	3.18	TTKL	2X5	3.16	3.18	TRDL
3X6	3.15	3.18	HBEL	3X6	3.18	3.21	TTKL	3X6	3.19	3.21	TRDL
4X7	3.22	3.25	HBEL	4X7	3.22	3.25	TTKL	4X7	3.23	3.25	TRDL
5X8	3.25	3.28	HBEL	5X8	3.26	3.3	TTKL	5X8	3.26	3.28	TRDL
6X9	3.29	3.32	HBEL	6X9	3.29	3.32	TTKL	6X9	3.3	3.32	TRDL
7X10	3.32	3.35	HBEL	7X10	3.33	3.36	TTKL	7X10	3.33	3.35	TRDL
8X11	3.34	3.37	HBEL	8X11	3.3	3.33	TTKL	8X11	3.35	3.37	TRDL
9X12	3.39	3.42	HBEL	9X12	3.39	3.42	TTKL	9X12	3.4	3.42	TRDL
12X15	3.56	3.59	HBEL					12X15	3.56	3.58	TRDL
15X18	3.74	3.77	HBEL					15X18	n/v	n/v	TRDL
3F1	3.16	3.19	HBEL					18X21	4.04	4.05	TRDL
3F2	3.25	3.28	HBEL					21X24	n/v	n/v	TRDL

	DEM ▼	DEM ▼	DEM ▼	DEM ▼
	HBEL ▼	HBEL ▼	TTKL ▼	TTKL ▼
Period	Bid ▼	Ask ▼	Bid ▼	Ask ▼
2M	3	3.125	3	3.125
3M	3	3.125	3	3.125
6M	3.0625	3.1875	3.0625	3.1875
9M	3.125	3.25	3.125	3.25
1Y	3.125	3.25	3.1875	3.3125

From the 3-month and 6-month bid and ask deposit rates shown opposite calculate the forward/forward bid and ask rates. Assume 3-months is 90 days and 6-months is 180 days.

a) Forward/forward bid rate

b) Forward/forward ask rate

You can check your answer on the next page.

a) Forward/forward bid rate = 2.976%
Use Equation 2 – for Bid use Far depo Bid and
Near depo Ask

$$\text{Interest} = \frac{(3.0625 \times 180) - (3.125 \times 90)}{(180 - 90) \times \left[1 + \left(\dfrac{3.215 \times 90}{360 \times 100}\right)\right]}$$

$$= \frac{270.00}{90.703125}$$

a) Forward/forward bid rate = 3.349%
Use Equation 2 – for Ask use Far depo Ask and
Near depo Bid

$$\text{Interest} = \frac{(3.1875 \times 180) - (3.00 \times 90)}{(180 - 90) \times \left[1 + \left(\dfrac{3.00 \times 90}{360 \times 100}\right)\right]}$$

$$= \frac{303.75}{90.6750}$$

Your notes

Interest Rate Swap

An **Interest Rate Swap** is an agreement between counterparties in which each party agrees to make a series of payments to the other on agreed future dates until maturity of the agreement. Each party's interest payments are calculated using different formulas by applying the agreement terms to the **notional principal** amount of the swap.

If you need an overview of swap derivatives or you need to remind yourself about derivatives in general, then you may find it useful to refer to *An Introduction to Derivatives*.

IRSs are the most important of the OTC swap derivatives currently traded in the global markets. An IRS is in effect an agreement which allows both parties access to better interest rates than they would normally receive in the markets.

In other words Party A and Party B both borrow the same amount, at the best interest rates they can and then swap the interest rate payments to the benefit of both parties. The cost of borrowing for both parties is reduced without altering the underlying principal loans. The interest rates bases for the loans are therefore separated from the underlying instruments.

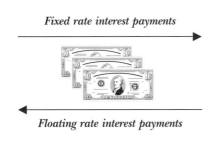

Fixed rate interest payments

Floating rate interest payments

Party A

Party B

The growth of IRSs can be traced to the early 1980s. But why have these long term OTC derivatives become so important? IRSs are characterised by the following:

- The interest amounts for both sides of the agreement are calculated from the same **notional principal** amount. This means that there is **no** physical exchange of the principal. Therefore the risk involved in the swap is reduced to that of assessing the credit risk that the other side may default on their interest rate payments.

- The two rates of interest are calculated for the **same** currency.

- The interest payments between both parties are usually netted so it is only the **difference** in payments which is paid to one side or the other. It is for this reason that IRSs are sometimes known as **contracts for difference**.

The OTC nature of IRSs means that their terms and conditions can be very flexible. However, in practice, most agreements are for **plain vanilla – fixed-for-floating –** swaps. One side pays a fixed rate whilst the other pays a floating rate – the situation illustrated in the original diagram opposite.

Floating-for-floating swaps are available but terms and conditions involved with these can be quite complex.

Although OTC agreements are customised for individual customer requirements, both the British Bankers Association (BBA) and the International Swaps and Derivatives Association (ISDA) issue standard terms and conditions relating to a range of swap derivatives. Once an agreement is made, most confirmation notes include the relevant information. For example, a plain vanilla IRS confirmation note typically includes:

- **Effective date**
  This is the date of the swap when interest on both sides starts to accrue. For plain vanilla swaps this date is taken as spot and LIBOR is fixed on the trade date. These are the same conventions as used for Money Market deposits.

- **Termination date**
  This is the end date of the contract – the date of the final difference in interest payments.

- **Notional amount**
  This is the amount used for interest rate calculations on both sides.

- **Fixed rate payor/receiver**
  As it could be misleading to refer to buying or selling swaps, it is usual to refer to the party who pays or receives the fixed rate.

- **Floating rate payor/receiver**
  If the fixed rate receiver has been specified, then by implication this side must be also the floating rate payer and vice versa. In many cases swap traders only specify what is happening on the fixed side.

- **Interest rate calculations**
  This includes all the necessary details relating to:
  - Reference interest rate, for example, LIBOR
  - Payment periods and dates
  - Day count conventions

- **Arrangement fees**

Confirmation

Date: July 1, 1997
To: OkiBank
Attention: Swaps Group Leader
From: MegaBank

We are pleased to confirm our mutually binding agreement to enter into a Rate Swap Transaction with you in accordance with our telephone conversation with Mr. Deal on July 1, 1997, pursuant to the Master Interest Rate Exchange Agreement between us dated as of July 1, 1997.

OkiBank Rate Swap Transaction Reference Number 00000

Effective Date: July 1, 1997
Termination Date: July 1, 2002

Notional Amount $50,000,000

Fixed Rate Payor: OkiBank
Floating Rate Payor: MegaBank

MegaBank Calculation Periods for Payments:
  First period: Effective Date to but excluding January 5, 1998.
  Last period and End Dates: Each July 1 and January 1 after the first Period End Date, subject to the Modified Following Banking Day convention, and finally the Termination Date.

OkiBank Calculation Periods for Payments:
  First period: Effective Date to but excluding July 1, 1998.
  Last period and End Dates: Each July 1 after the first Period End Date, subject to the Modified Following Banking Day convention, and finally the Termination Date.

Payment Dates: Each party date on its own Period End Dates
Fixed Rate: x percent per annum
                 Fixed Rate Day Count Fraction: 30/360

Floating Rate Option: LIBOR
                 Designated maturity: six months
                 Floating Rate Day Count Fraction: Actual/360
                 Reset Dates: First day of each MegaBank Calculation Period

Office or branch through which we are acting: Principal Office in New York
Office or branch through which you are acting: Principal Office in New York

Arrangement Fee: None

Documentation: The Master Interest Rate Exchange dated as a July 1, 1997 between OkiBank and MegaBank as modified by this confirmation.

Please confirm to us that the terms set forth herein accurately reflect our Rate Swap Transaction with you by signing a copy of this Confirmation and sending it back promptly by hand or by facsimile transmission. Please notify us immediately if you believe there is an error in this Confirmation.

                                              Confirmed:

MegaBank   OkiBank

By   By

Title: Title:

An example of a typical fixed/floating swap confirmation note based on Satyajit Das, Swaps, IFR 1987

IRSs are the most important of the swap derivatives both in terms of the face value of OTC contracts not yet settled – the notional outstanding values, and in terms of the average daily turnover. The following statistics are taken from the *BIS Report May 1999: Central Bank Survey of Foreign Exchange and Derivatives Market Activity.*

Derivative	Outstanding notional USD billion	Average daily turnover USD billion
Interest Rate Swap	32,942	155
Currency swap	2,324	10

The 1997 data from the *ISDA Summary of OTC Derivatives Market Data* confirm the dominance of the IRS markets as the chart below shows.

The ISDA data as of 1997 year end also shows that IRSs involving the USD dominate the markets. The chart below indicates the top five currencies by percentage market share based on the USD equivalent of notional principal outstanding.

Currency	% Market	USD billion equivalent
USD	**30.40**	**5,827.5**
JPY	23.17	4,441.8
DEM	12.97	2,486.2
FRF	8.14	1,560.9
GBP	7.13	1,367.1
Other	18.19	3,487.3
Total	100.00	**19.170.8**

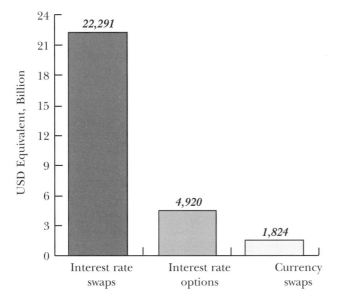

Notional principal outstandings

Source: ISDA

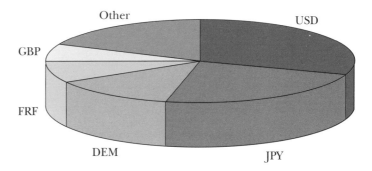

Source: ISDA

Who Uses IRSs?

Banks and Corporations

The ISDA data below shows that the market players using IRSs the most are banks and multinational corporations.

Market player	% of users based on year end outstandings
Corporations	24
Banks	53
Institutional investors	7
Government	9
Other	7
Total	100

IRSs are used increasingly by these market players for two main reasons:

- To hedge exposure on interest rates

- To speculate in the swaps markets in order to make a profit from offsetting fixed/floating rate transactions

IRSs also offer the following benefits to corporations and banks:

- Counterparties are able to convert underlying interest rates from fixed to floating and vice versa over a long term period

- Usually there are cost savings to both sides

- IRSs provide access to markets not normally available to the market players, for example, for reasons relating to credit rating

It is this access to different markets which in effect provides credit arbitrage in the markets. The difference in organisations' credit ratings can result in considerable differences in yield gaps on fixed rate debt such as bonds and floating rates paid on loans. Many bond issues are swap driven because issuers can take advantage of IRSs to swap the interest payments on the funds raised into a different rate basis. Often these transactions also involve a currency swap which effectively converts a domestic loan into one for a foreign currency.

Organisations with **good** credit ratings usually find it easier to borrow at **fixed** rates, whilst those with **lower** ratings tend to get their best terms on a **floating** rate basis.

Have a look at the following example to see how a plain vanilla IRS works between the XYZ and AYZ Corporations. The original lenders of the loans on both sides need not even know that the counterparties have entered into a swap agreement.

Example – a plain vanilla IRS
Consider the following situation:

XYZ is a multinational corporation with a credit rating of AAA. XYZ needs to borrow $50 million for 5 years. XYZ can borrow at a low fixed rate but would prefer to take advantage of a floating rate basis loan. XYZ would like to take advantage of floating rates in order to maximise any interest rate gaps.

AYZ is a corporation with a lower credit rating of BBB who also need to raise $50 million for 5 years. Because of AYZ's lower credit rating borrowing on a floating rate basis or issuing a bond with a high value coupon is easier than obtaining a fixed rate loan. AYZ would prefer a fixed rate loan in order to predict future interest rate payments.

The chart below summarises both corporation's position.

Rates	XYZ can borrow	AYZ can borrow
Fixed @	10.00%	12.00%
Floating @	LIBOR	LIBOR + 1%
Required basis	**Fixed**	**Floating**

In order to obtain the type of loan both corporations require they enter into a swap agreement. Both corporations need to assess the risks involved if the other side defaults on payments – if this does happen then the party who does not receive an interest payment still has to pay the interest due on the underlying loan.

This is how the IRS works...

❶ XYZ borrows at a fixed rate of 10%

❷ AYZ borrows at a floating rate of LIBOR + 1%

❸ XYZ and AYZ enter into an IRS agreement for a notional principal amount of $50 million with interest payments to be exchanged for a 5 year period where:

- XYZ make **floating rate** payments of LIBOR + 1% to AYZ
- AYZ make **fixed rate** payments of 11.75% to XYZ
- AYZ pays this higher fixed rate to XYZ to compensate this corporation as it has the higher credit rating

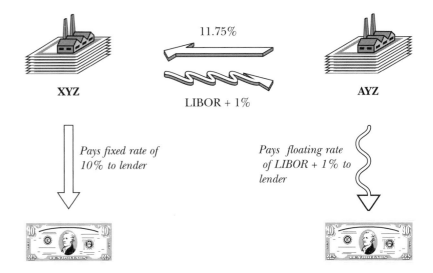

XYZ — 11.75% — LIBOR + 1% — AYZ

Pays fixed rate of 10% to lender

Pays floating rate of LIBOR + 1% to lender

The chart below shows how both sides benefit from the swap.

	XYZ	AYZ
Pays out	LIBOR + 1% + 10%	11.75% + LIBOR + 1%
Receives in	11.75%	LIBOR + 1%
Payments =	LIBOR + 0.75%	11.75%
Without swap	LIBOR	12.00%
Savings	**0.75%**	**0.25%**

Another way of considering the swap is as follows:

- Without the swap both XYZ and AYZ pay a total of 12.00% + LIBOR in interest rate charges

- With the swap both parties pay a total of 11.00% + LIBOR (10.00% + LIBOR + 1%) in charges

Thus using the swap there is a net saving of 1.00% which in this case is split 0.75%/0.25% in favour of XYZ which is the organisation with the better credit rating.

Originally swaps were arranged directly between counterparties with banks merely acting as agents for both sides. Now many banks act as **intermediaries** and make a two-way market in swaps by taking one side of the transaction.

Market Makers

Most IRS agreements now involve a market maker and two separate clients who wish to enter a swap, but not necessarily with each other. For example, it may be that the perceived credit risks involved in a direct swap agreement are not acceptable to one or both parties. By acting as a two-way market maker a bank acts as an intermediary creating a double swap in which both parties are effectively guaranteed interest payments will take place.

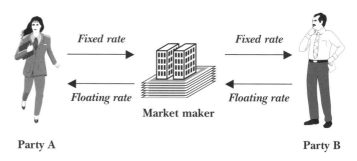

Party A   *Fixed rate*   **Market maker**   *Fixed rate*   *Party B*

Floating rate   *Floating rate*

Of course, the market maker does not enter into these swaps for no reward. The intermediary is paid a fee which is either based on the principal notional amount involved, a spread between the two-way prices quoted for swap repayments – the **swap rate**, or both.

In the US and to a lesser extent in the UK, swap rates are quoted over the yield on a Treasury note with comparable maturity.

For example, a market maker may quote **'70/75 over'** for a swap based on a 5-year T-Bond which has a yield of 8.00%. This means the market maker pays (bids) at a rate of 8.70% and receives (ask) at a rate of 8.75%.

Look at the following example to see how a double swap works.

Example – a double swap

Consider the following situation:

A US swap market maker, BigBank, is quoting a fixed rate of 70/75 based on a 5-year T-bond which has a yield of 8.0% against a floating rate of LIBOR flat.

XYZ is a money market fund which has invested in floating rate assets which are yielding, on average, LIBOR + 0.2%. XYZ believe that LIBOR will fall so they would prefer fixed rate interest payments. XYZ enters into a swap with BigBank to receive a fixed rate of 8.70% against paying a floating rate of LIBOR.

AYZ is a corporation that can either borrow at a fixed rate of 10% or issue a Floating Rate Note (FRN) with a floating rate repayment of LIBOR + 1%. AYZ would also prefer fixed rate interest payments for their loan. AYZ also enters into an IRS with BigBank but AYZ pay 8.75% against receiving LIBOR.

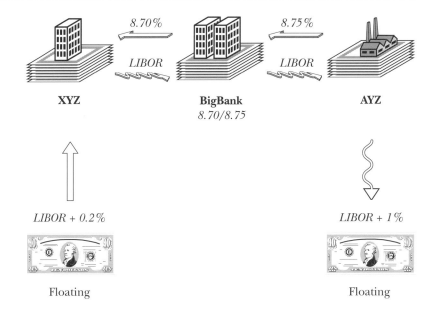

The chart below shows how both XYZ and AYZ effectively turn their interest rate payments/receipts into fixed rates and the savings AYZ makes.

	XYZ	**AYZ**
Pays out	LIBOR	LIBOR + 1% + 8.75%
Receives in	LIBOR + 0.2% + 8.70%	LIBOR
Payments =	8.90%	9.75%
Without swap	–	10.00%
Savings	–	**0.25%**
Loan basis	**Fixed**	**Fixed**

The convention of quoting a swap rate as described separates the credit risk element from the general interest rate in the market. However not all currencies have well developed government Treasury instruments across a range of maturity dates. In these cases swap dealers will quote **all-in** prices as a total rate.

Are IRSs as simple as has been described? Well, in principle the answer is yes, but in practice there are a number of issues to be reconciled if you are trying to compare swap rates. In other words are you comparing like-with-like?

Differences between swap rates can arise based on the following:

- Quotation terms for fixed and floating rates

- The underlying instruments used to calculate swap rates

- The frequency of interest rate payments

- Day count bases used to calculate interest rate payments

These issues are all discussed in the next section.

If you were asked to explain the mechanics of an IRS to a colleague would you be able to do it?

Your notes

IRSs in the Market Place

This section deals with a number of important matters concerning IRSs which you will need to understand:

- Swap differences
- Swap spreads
- Swap valuations
- Swap structures

Swap Differences

The four main types of difference were mentioned at the end of the last section.

Quotation Terms

Within the US markets in particular there are a number of different ways interest payments can be calculated for fixed and floating rates together with a number of different ways payment schedules can be stipulated. Different swaps may use a combination of any of the following terms

Terms	Fixed Rate	Floating Rate
Rate quotation	• Absolute level • Spread over Treasury instrument	• Any LIBOR • Prime rate • CD, CP or T-Bill
Payment schedule	• Quarterly • Semi-annually • Annually	• Periodic • Irregular
Basis	• Eurobond • T-Bond • Money Market Instrument	• Bond • Money Market Instrument

Underlying Instruments

The instruments used to calculate swap rates for different currencies vary. For example, USD swaps are usually quoted as a spread over the appropriate Treasury instrument which have semi-annual coupons; DEM swaps are quoted on an annual Eurobond basis.

The chart below indicates the various instruments used for the major currencies together with the Day count method used for the interest payment calculations.

Currency	Quoted as...	Coupon	Day Count
USD	Spread over T-Bond	Semi-annual	Actl/Actl
DEM	Fixed Eurobond	Annual	30/360
CHF	Fixed Eurobond	Annual	30/360
FRF	Fixed Eurobond	Annual	30/360
GBP	Spread over Gilt	Semi-annual	Actl/365
JPY	Fixed Government Bond	Semi-annual	Actl/365

Frequency of Interest Payments

In order to compare swap rates fairly you may need to convert annual payments into semi-annual or vice versa.

The chart below indicates the equations to use to convert yields or swap rates as appropriate.

From ➡	To ➡	Use ➡
Semi-annual	Annual	$R_A = \left[\left(1 + \dfrac{R_S}{2}\right)^2\right] - 1$
Annual	Semi-annual	$R_S = 2 \times \left[\sqrt{(1 + R_A)} - 1\right]$ R_A = Annual rate % ÷ 100 R_S = Semi-annual rate % ÷ 100

Day Count Bases

You may also need to convert swap rates depending on the day count basis used to calculate interest payments in order to compare like-with-like or value swaps.

The chart below gives the various methods of converting different day counts.

From ➡	To ➡	Use ➡
30/360 or Actual/365	Actual/360	$\text{Yield} \times \dfrac{360}{365}$
Actual/360	30/360 or Actual/365	$\text{Yield} \times \dfrac{365}{360}$
Actual/365	30/360	No adjustment
30/360	Actual/365	No adjustment

Swap Spreads

Interest rate trends cause variations in swap spreads over the yield curves for Government benchmark instruments.

When interest rates are expected to **fall** there are many fixed rate investors wanting to swap into paying **floating** and receiving **fixed**, so spreads **narrow**.

When interest rates are expected to **rise** there are plenty of borrowers (issuers) wanting to swap into **fixed** but not many willing to receive it, so spreads **widen**.

Another factor affecting swap spreads is credit risk. In a swap the market player and the market maker take on each other's risk. If either party fails to honour payment commitments, then the other party has an unwanted interest rate exposure.

For IRSs the net difference in fixed/floating payments is made, so the risk of loss is based to some extent on an estimate of the **volatility** of the future floating rate basis, for example, LIBOR.

Swap Valuation

Consider a plain vanilla IRS in which XYZ Corporation borrow $100 million for 5 years at a floating rate but enter into an IRS agreement with AYZ Bank to make **fixed** rate payments at 9.00% every 6 months. In return the swap dealer, AYZ, will pay a floating rate of LIBOR every 6 months.

9.00% Fixed

LIBOR Floating
Both payments are
made every 6 months

XYZ   XYZ

The spot rate for the transaction is 1st June so the first payment is due on 1st December. The amount of interest due on the 1st December is already known on the 1st June. How can this be the case? The answer is that LIBOR for the first payment is fixed on the 1st June as the floating rate **to be paid in 6 months time**. In a similar manner the 1st December LIBOR fixing determines the rate to be paid for the second payment on the following 1st June and so on until the final payment in 5 years.

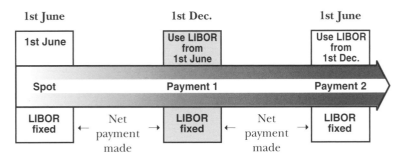

The interest payments are netted between XYZ and AYZ based on the following calculation:

$$\text{LIBOR} - 9 \times \$100 \text{ million} \times \frac{\text{No. of days in 6 month period}}{360 \times 100}$$

Depending on the value, either XYZ or AYZ receive the net payment.

At the start of the plain vanilla swap the derivative has no value to either party. The interest rates that have been agreed for both sides are determined so that the present value – the value the swap will have at a future date – of the fixed side equals the present value of the floating side taking into account the conditions of the agreement.

If the terms of the agreement remain constant then neither side gain or lose at the expense of the other.

However, suppose interest rates rise and LIBOR increases. In this case XYZ will gain at the expense of AYZ because XYZ pays a fixed rate and receives a floating rate which has just increased. So the swap now has a **positive** value to XYZ which can be considered to be an **asset**. The actual value of the asset can be calculated from the difference in present values. Unfortunately in the case of AYZ the swap has a **negative** value and is considered to be a **liability**.

There are two basic ways that swaps can be valued:

- Pricing from the swap curve

- Pricing from the spot curve

Using the spot curve method produces a more accurate figure than the swap curve method, but the calculations involved can be quite complex. Both methods of pricing involve calculations for bonds which are dealt with in more detail in the *Bond valuation* section of this workbook. Read on...

Pricing from the Swap Curve

Yield curves are an essential part of valuing future cash flows and calculating forward interest rates. Plain vanilla swap rates are priced from benchmark bond yield prices as has already been mentioned. The benchmark Yield To Maturity (YTM) curves are used for pricing over a range of maturities as shown in the Reuters screen below.

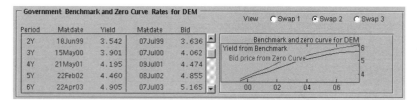

In terms of valuing a fixed-for-floating swap the transaction can be thought of as a series of **coupon payments** from an imaginary **straight bond** on the **fixed side** netted against a series of payments from an imaginary or **synthetic Floating Rate Note (FRN)** on the **floating side**.

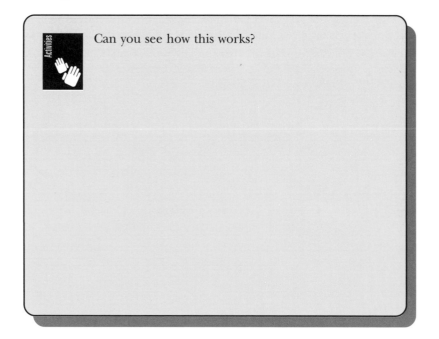

Can you see how this works?

Example – Fixed side – Straight bond: Floating side – FRN

Suppose a plain vanilla swap has been arranged between XYZ Corporation and AYZ Bank for a $100 million notional principal amount for a 3 year period. On the fixed side the payments are 9.30% on an annual basis; on the floating side the payments are 12 months LIBOR.

The cash flows over the 3 year period would look something like those shown in the chart below.

Payments equivalent to coupons from a straight bond

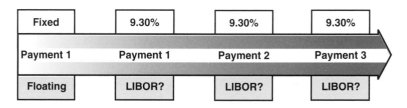

Payments equivalent to those from a Floating Rate Note

A plain vanilla swap can therefore be valued as follows:

Notional straight bond present value	–	Notional floating instrument present value

XYZ and AYZ enter into the swap on the stated conditions. On the spot date LIBOR is fixed at 7.50% for the first payment. As has been mentioned the swap has no value at the start of the agreement. On the first payment date the 3 year swap rate is now quoted at 9.00% on the fixed side and 12 months LIBOR is fixed at 7.79%. What is the value of the swap now? Is the swap an asset or a liability to the receiver of the fixed side?

What is the value now of the swap that matures in the future? The present value of the fixed side can be calculated using the general straight bond valuation equation. For a bond with an annual coupon this is Equation 1.

$$\text{Present Value (PV)} = \frac{C}{1+R} + \frac{C}{(1+R)^2} + ... + \frac{(C+100)}{(1+R)^n}$$

Where: C = Coupon rate
R = Discount or swap rate as a decimal
n = Number of years to maturity

...Equation 1

In this example then: C = 9.30%; R = 0.090; n = 3

$$PV = \frac{9.30}{1.09} + \frac{9.30}{(1.09)^2} + \frac{109.30}{(1.09)^3}$$

$$= \$100.7594 \text{ million}$$

The present value for the floating side can be calculated using the more direct relationship between the present and future value of an instrument, Equation 2.

$$PV = \frac{\text{Future Value}}{(1+R)}$$

$$= \frac{\text{Principal } + \text{ Interest due}}{(1+R)}$$

Where: R =   Discount or LIBOR rate
as a decimal   *...Equation 2*

In this example then: Principal = 100 million; Interest = 7.50; R = 0.0779. Because the floating rate is based on Actual/360 the values used need to be adjusted to a 365 day year.

$$PV = \frac{\left[100 + \left(7.50 \times \frac{365}{360} \right) \right]}{1 + \left(0.0779 \times \frac{365}{360} \right)}$$

$$= \$99.7257 \text{ million}$$

The net value of the swap is therefore $1.03 million in favour of the fixed side. This is because the swap rate quoted by the bank at the end of the first payment is less than the coupon rate of 9.30% on the position. The floating side has lost value because LIBOR has increased.

Treating the value of a swap as the difference between a straight bond and a floating rate instrument gives rise to market makers hedging or **warehousing** a swap position by temporarily buying or selling the underlying bond.

The payer of the fixed side **buys** the underlying which can then be sold to offset the position if the swap rates fall.

The receiver of the fixed side **sells** the underlying to offset any losses if swap rates rise.

The calculations here are quite complicated and time consuming to perform. In practice, traders will often use a graphical representation to assess the relationship of the swap with a benchmark instrument of the same maturity. The graphical representation used is the **spot curve** or **zero coupon yield curve**.

Pricing from the Spot Curve

The Yield To Maturity (YTM) curve is simply a graph of YTM values of bonds against maturity period. Unfortunately this is a simplistic view of yields and it is better to use a graph of **spot rate** against maturity period. The spot rate is a measure of the YTM on an instrument at any moment in time which takes into account a variety of market factors. A graph of spot rate against maturity is known as a spot curve. It is also known as a zero coupon yield curve because the spot rate for an instrument is equivalent to the yield on an instrument which has no coupon repayment – zero coupon. This means that spot rates for a series of instruments with zero coupons for a range of maturity periods can be compared directly.

The curves represent the perceived relationship between the return on an instrument and its maturity – usually measured in years. Depending on the shape of the curve it is described as either:

- Positive

- Negative or inverse

Positive Yield Curve

In this case the shorter term interest rates are **lower** than the longer term rates. This is usually the case – the longer the period of the investment the higher the yield paid. If an interest rate rise is expected, then investors will move their assets into long term instruments which produces a fall in short term rates and an increase in long term rates.

Negative or Inverse Curve

When short term rates fall investors move their investments into longer term instruments to lock in a higher rate of return. This increase in supply of long term funds causes the long term rates to fall.

The shapes of 'theoretical' yield curves are shown below – in practice they may not appear so clear.

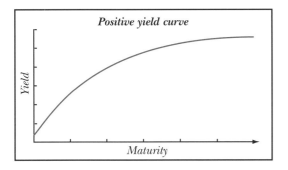

Positive yield curve

Yield / Maturity

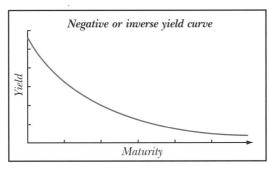

Negative or inverse yield curve

Yield / Maturity

Yield curves are used to identify anomalies between instruments of similar credit standing, for example, an IRS and a T-Bond of similar maturity.

The following chart may help in assessing the value of an instrument when compared to its spot curve.

Instrument Curve	Instrument Value
Above spot	Cheap
Below spot	Expensive

How does the spot curve help in pricing a swap? A more accurate way of considering an IRS is to consider the instrument as a series of fixed cash flows on one side combined with a series of notional floating cash flows on the other which are considered as a **strip of FRAs or futures contracts**.

In other words the spot curve rates are used to calculate, in advance, the net settlement amount of each future interest payment date.

The swap rate is effectively an average rate for a strip of FRAs or futures contracts.

The calculations are quite complex and in the previous example if the swap were valued using this more accurate method, then the net value in favour of the fixed side is $1.043 million.

Swap Structures

Plain vanilla swaps usually have very narrow spreads – typically only 5 to 10 basis points. This means that the profit margins for dealers are small. In order to widen their profit margins and to cater for more complicated client requirements, dealers can structure more complex IRSs based on the following basic types:

- **Plain vanilla swap**

- **Forward start swap**
  This is a fixed-for-floating IRS in which the accrual date of the swap for the first interest period starts sometime after the spot date. This type of swap can still be considered as a strip of FRAs on the floating side except the near FRAs have been removed. Forward start swaps are often used to hedge against forward interest rate movements.

- **Swaption**
  This is similar to a forward start swap to which has been added the option whether or not to start the swap on the accrual date. Hence the name is derived from the fact it is an **option on a swap**. One counterparty buys the option, whilst the other writes or sells the option.

  If you need to know more about the basics of options then you may need to refer to *An Introduction to Derivatives*. Swaptions are also dealt with in more detail in this book.

There are many types of structured swaps available now – some of the more common types are briefly discussed next.

Accreters, Amortisers and Rollercoasters
These are all IRSs which involve variable notional principal amounts in the agreement.

Accreting and amortising swaps consist of strips of swaps with different start or end dates.

- **Accreting swaps** have notional amounts that **increase** in steps over the life of the swap

- **Amortising swaps** have notional amounts that **decrease** in steps over the life of the swap

These types of swaps are used in real estate markets where developers seek to lock in the interest cost of future floating rate borrowings which either diminish or expand over time. The following charts illustrate these swaps.

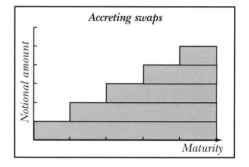

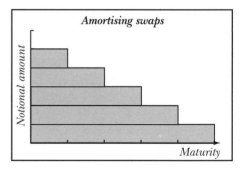

A **rollercoaster** swap is simply a combination of one or more accreting and amortising swaps and is illustrated in the chart below.

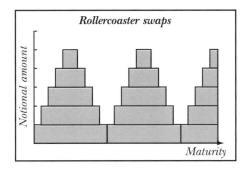

Rollercoaster swaps

Notional amount / Maturity

Basis Swaps

Whereas most IRS are plain vanilla swaps, basis swaps cater for floating interest payments on both sides. The interest rates for both floating sides are calculated on **different** bases. Typical basis swaps include the following:

- USD prime rate against LIBOR

- 12 month LIBOR against 6 month LIBOR

- LIBOR against US Commercial Paper (CP) rates

In all other respects basis swaps are used, priced etc in the same way as described previously.

One important variation is the **cross-currency basis swap** in which floating rates in different currencies are exchanged, for example, USD LIBOR against DEM LIBOR.

Why is this type of basis swap important? If a plain vanilla swap is arranged in one currency and combined with a cross-currency basis swap, then the result is a **Currency swap**.

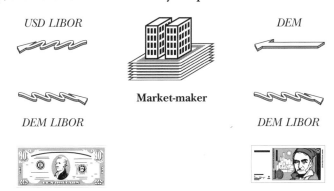

USD LIBOR / DEM / Market-maker / DEM LIBOR / DEM LIBOR

Interest Rate Swap (IRS)

- An IRS is an exchange or **swap of interest rate payments** calculated according to different formulas on the **same notional principal amount**

- **No exchange of principal occurs during a swap** – no funds are lent or borrowed between the counterparties as part of the swap

- Interest rate payments are usually netted and only the **difference** is paid to one party or the other

- **Any underlying loan or deposit is not affected by the swap** – the swap is a separate transaction

Derivatives

These Reuters screens show the **Speed Guide** for **Currency and Interest Rate Swaps,** the IRS rates for the major currencies, the US IRS rates against 3-Month LIBOR, as well as the Intercapital Brokers Ltd IRS rates for various currencies.

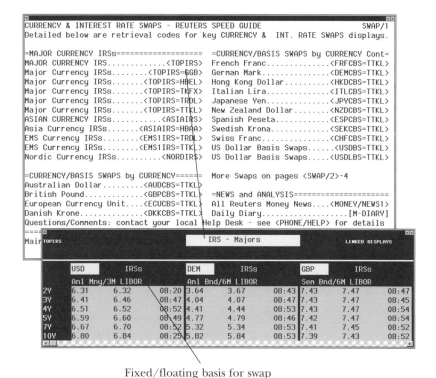

Fixed/floating basis for swap

```
CURRENCY & INTEREST RATE SWAPS - REUTERS SPEED GUIDE          SWAP/1
Detailed below are retrieval codes for key CURRENCY &  INT. RATE SWAPS displays.

=MAJOR CURRENCY IRSs==================  =CURRENCY/BASIS SWAPS by CURRENCY Cont=
MAJOR CURRENCY IRS.............<TOPIRS>  French Franc.............<FRFCBS=TTKL>
Major Currency IRSs........<TOPIRS=GGB>  German Mark..............<DEMCBS=TTKL>
Major Currency IRSs.......<TOPIRS=HBEL>  Hong Kong Dollar.........<HKDCBS=TTKL>
Major Currency IRSs.......<TOPIRS=TKFX>  Italian Lira.............<ITLCBS=TTKL>
Major Currency IRSs.......<TOPIRS=TRDL>  Japanese Yen.............<JPYCBS=TTKL>
Major Currency IRSs.......<TOPIRS=TTKL>  New Zealand Dollar.......<NZDCBS=TTKL>
ASIAN CURRENCY IRSs..........<ASIAIRS>   Spanish Peseta...........<ESPCBS=TTKL>
Asia Currency IRSs.......<ASIAIRS=HBAA>  Swedish Krona............<SEKCBS=TTKL>
EMS Currency IRSs........<EMS1IRS=TRDL>  Swiss Franc..............<CHFCBS=TTKL>
EMS Currency IRSs........<EMS1IRS=TTKL>  US Dollar Basis Swaps.....<USDBS=TTKL>
Nordic Currency IRSs..........<NORDIRS>  US Dollar Basis Swaps....<USDLBS=TTKL>

=CURRENCY/BASIS SWAPS by CURRENCY=====   More Swaps on pages <SWAP/2>-4
Australian Dollar.........<AUDCBS=TTKL>
British Pound............<GBPCBS=TTKL>   =NEWS and ANALYSIS====================
European Currency Unit....<ECUCBS=TTKL>  All Reuters Money News....<MONEY/NEWS1>
Danish Krone.............<DKKCBS=TTKL>   Daily Diary.................[M-DIARY]
Questions/Comments: contact your Help Desk - see <PHONE/HELP> for details
Main
```

```
11:02 09MAR98        INTEREST RATE SWAPS        US18742        RTRSWP1

MATY      PRICE        YIELD     YLD MID   SPREAD    SA 30/360       ANN A/360
2YR   99.28-29 +01  5.567-550   5.559     32/31   5.879 - 5.869   5.884 - 5.874
3YR   99.15-16 +01  5.572-560   5.566     38/36   5.946 - 5.926   5.952 - 5.931
4YR                    ***      5.597     39/37   5.987 - 5.967   5.993 - 5.973
5YR   99.14-15 +03  5.631-623   5.627     40/39   6.027 - 6.017   6.034 - 6.024
6YR                             5.636     43/41   6.066 - 6.046   6.074 - 6.053
7YR ***   INTERPOLATED   ***    5.646     45/43   6.096 - 6.076   6.104 - 6.084
8YR       YIELD ***      ***    5.655     46/44   6.115 - 6.095   6.123 - 6.103
9YR                      ***    5.665     47/45   6.135 - 6.115   6.144 - 6.123
10YR  98.21-23 +10  5.678-670   5.674     49/47   6.164 - 6.144   6.173 - 6.153
11YR  \                         5.674     53/49   6.204 - 6.164   6.214 - 6.173
12YR   \ SPREAD TO               5.674     54/52   6.214 - 6.194   6.224 - 6.204
13YR    \10-YEAR NOTE            5.674     57/54   6.244 - 6.214   6.255 - 6.224
14YR   /                        5.674     59/57   6.264 - 6.244   6.275 - 6.255
15YR  /                         5.674     61/59   6.284 - 6.264   6.295 - 6.275
20YR /                          5.674     69/67   6.364 - 6.344   6.377 - 6.356
30YR 101.30-31 +16  5.984-982   5.983     40/37   6.383 - 6.353   6.396 - 6.365

                       3M LIBOR 6M LIBOR
                        5.68750  5.71875
           U.S. Interest Rate Swaps quoted against 3-month libor.
                       ** SEE <RTRSWP2> **
```

```
1604 INTERCAPITAL BROKERS LTD     * INDEX PAGE ICAK *        ICAP
        --- YEN ---        ------ USD -------      ------CAD------
1 YR     0.71-0.68                 5.81-5.78              5.29-5.25
2 YRS    0.82-0.79    32-30        5.88-5.85    30-26     5.29-5.25
3 YRS    1.03-1.00    38-36        5.95-5.92    30-26     5.39-5.35
4 YRS    1.27-1.24    39-37        5.99-5.96    28-24     5.47-5.43
5 YRS    1.49-1.46    40-38        6.03-6.00    25-21     5.54-5.50
6 YRS    1.69-1.66    42-40        6.07-6.04    25-21     5.65-5.61
7 YRS    1.86-1.83    44-42        6.11-6.08    26-22     5.65-5.61
8 YRS    2.01-1.98    46-44        6.15-6.12    26-22     5.77-5.73
9 YRS    2.13-2.10    47-45        6.18-6.15    26-22     5.82-5.78
10 YRS   2.24-2.21    48-46        6.20-6.17    26-22     5.82-5.78
12 YRS   2.43-2.38    54-52        6.26-6.23    00-       5.94-5.90
```

Enter details in these fields

Fixed/floating terms

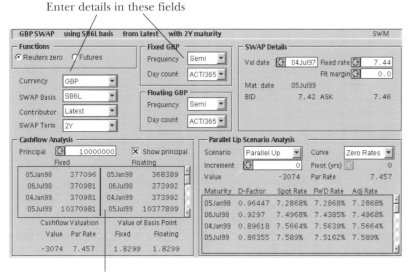

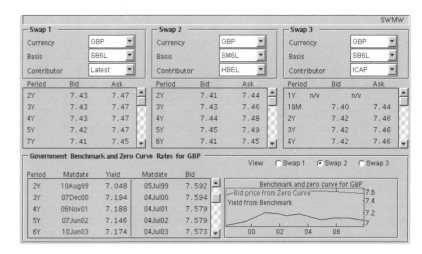

Fixed/floating cash flows

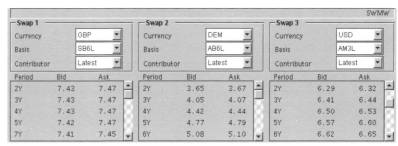

Currency Swap

A **Currency Swap** is an agreement between counterparties in which one party makes payments in one currency and the other party makes payments in a different currency on agreed future dates until maturity of the agreement.

If you need an overview of swap derivatives or you need to remind yourself about derivatives in general, then you may find it useful to refer to *An Introduction to Derivatives*.

A currency swap is a long term OTC derivative instrument which is characterised by the following:

- There is an **exchange of principal**, usually at the beginning and at maturity of the agreement. These exchanges are usually made at the spot rate prevailing at the start of the contract.

- The exchange of interest rate payments is made in full and in **two different currencies**.

In effect, a currency swap is an OTC method by which Party A can swap a loan in one currency, for example Deutschemarks, into one denominated in a different currency, for example US dollars, simultaneously with Party B who has the opposite loan requirements.

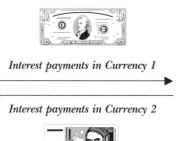

Interest payments in Currency 1

Interest payments in Currency 2

In its simplest form a currency swap is a simultaneous agreement for a **spot transaction** followed by a **series of long term forward currency transactions**. There are normally three steps comprising a currency swap:

❶ Spot exchange of principal
The exchange of principal takes place at the start of the agreement, usually at an agreed exchange rate of **spot**.

❷ Exchange of interest rate payments
During the agreement period a series of interest payments are exchanged at agreed forward dates. In the case of a fixed-to-fixed swap, both sides swap fixed interest rates based on the principal amounts and at fixed rates agreed for the contract.

❸ Re-exchange of principal
On maturity of the agreement, the principal amounts are re-exchanged at the original spot rate. Even though years may have passed and the spot rate changed dramatically, the principal amounts involved have not changed so the original spot rate is used as neither side is disadvantaged.

A currency swap and a FX swap are two different instruments. Could you explain to a colleague the difference between the two instruments?

In a FX swap, the interest rate differential between the two currencies is taken into account in the forward points for the forward delivery date. For a currency swap the interest rate differential is paid during the life of the swap at each payment date. This means that the principal amounts can be swapped at the original spot rate at both the beginning and end of the OTC agreement.

Within the global markets currency swaps are second in importance to IRSs in terms of the face value of OTC contracts not yet settled – the notional outstanding values, and in terms of the average daily turnover. The following statistics are taken from the *BIS Report May 1999: Central Bank Survey of Foreign Exchange and Derivatives Market Activity.*

Derivative	Outstanding notional USD billion*	Average daily turnover USD billion*
Currency swap	2,324	10
Interest Rate Swap	32,942	155

* as of end-June 1998

The data from the *ISDA Summary of OTC Derivative Market Data* for the year 1997 confirm the dominance of the IRS markets as the chart below shows.

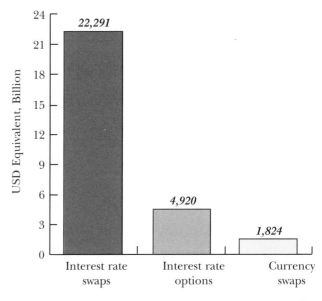

Notional principal outstandings

Source: ISDA

The ISDA data also shows that currency swaps are dominated by the USD on one side of the swap. The data also indicates that the most important currency pair involved in a currency swap is USD/JPY.

In practice, the most common type of currency swap used is a **fixed-for-floating** where one side pays fixed rate interest payments and the other side's payments are based on a floating rate. This is a similar situation to that found for interest rate swaps (IRSs) and you may find it useful to consider currency swaps as just a variation of an IRS.

You may find it useful to review IRSs before moving on.

Who Uses Currency Swaps?

Banks and Corporations

The ISDA data below shows that the market players using currency swaps the most are banks and multinational corporations.

Market player	% of users based on year end outstandings
Corporations	**32**
Banks	**37**
Institutional investors	6
Government	21
Other	4
Total	100

The main reason that currency swaps are used is because they offer market players the flexibility of privately negotiated OTC agreements. Both parties must know each other in order to assess the credit and other risks associated with the derivatives.

Currency swaps also offer the following benefits to corporations and banks. Currency swaps are used:

- To hedge FX risk over a medium to long term

- To save costs – a single OTC agreement costs less than arranging a series of forward FX transactions

- To gain access to foreign capital markets in order to obtain non-domestic funds at lower rates than could normally be expected and without any FX exposure

- To take advantage of both party's favourable market conditions in their respective currencies

Example – a plain vanilla currency swap

Consider the following situation:

XYZ is a Japanese multinational corporation that needs to borrow $100 million for 5 years. XYZ can borrow JPY in the domestic market at a fixed rate of 3.25% but USD would cost LIBOR + 0.25%.

The current spot rate is USD/JPY 110.00.

XYZ issue a Euroyen bond to raise 11 billion yen which pays a coupon of 3.25%. The value of the Euroyen bond is equivalent to a US dollar principal amount of $100 million. XYZ would prefer to raise a US dollar loan on a floating basis in order to take advantage of any interest rate fluctuations.

AYZ is a US bank requires the equivalent of $100 million in yen for 5 years in order to finance its operations in Japan. AYZ would prefer a fixed rate loan in order to predict future interest rate payments. In the domestic US market, AYZ can borrow at a floating rate of LIBOR but to raise yen would cost 3.5% on a fixed basis.

Both AYZ and XYZ are of equal credit rating and agree upon a currency swap to take advantage of both sides' favourable borrowing rates in their own markets.

In general terms, could you explain to a colleague what will happen in the currency swap?

The chart below summarises both organisations' positions.

Rates	XYZ can borrow	AYZ can borrow
Fixed JPY @	3.25%	3.50%
Floating USD @	LIBOR + 0.25%	LIBOR
Required basis	**Fixed**	**Floating**

In order to obtain the type of loan both organisations require they enter into a swap agreement. Both organisations need to assess the risks involved if the other side defaults on payments – if this does happen then the party who does not receive an interest payment still has to pay the interest due on the underlying loan.

This is how the currency swap works...

① Exchange of principal

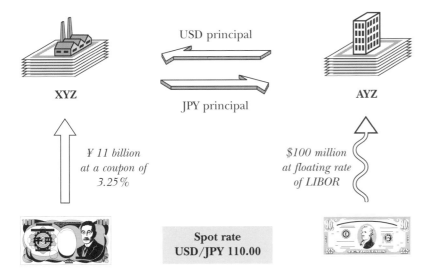

XYZ

USD principal

JPY principal

AYZ

¥ 11 billion
at a coupon of
3.25%

$100 million
at floating rate
of LIBOR

**Spot rate
USD/JPY 110.00**

② Exchange of interest payments
Every six months there is an exchange of interest payments.
- XYZ make **floating rate** payments of US LIBOR to AYZ
- AYZ make **fixed rate** payments of JPY 3.25% to XYZ

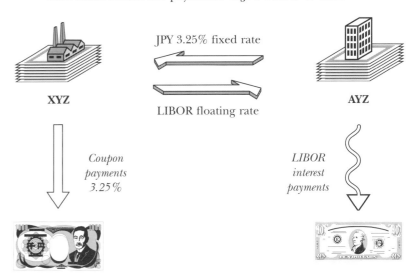

XYZ

JPY 3.25% fixed rate

LIBOR floating rate

AYZ

*Coupon
payments
3.25%*

*LIBOR
interest
payments*

	XYZ	AYZ
Pays out	LIBOR + 3.25%	3.25% + LIBOR
Receives in	3.25%	LIBOR
Payments =	LIBOR	3.25%
Without swap	LIBOR + 0.25%	3.50%
Savings	**0.25%**	**0.25%**

The chart below shows how both sides benefit from the swap.

Both XYZ and AYZ make the same savings as both are of equal credit ratings. If there had been a difference in ratings then the proportions of total savings would have been biased to the organisation with the better credit rating as in the case of IRSs.

❸ Re-exchange of principal – 5 years later

Because the principal loans are repaid at the same amounts borrowed 5 years previously, the original spot rate is used for the re-exchange of principal amounts.

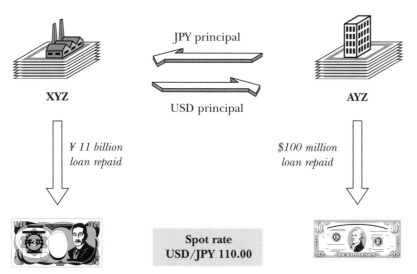

XYZ

JPY principal

USD principal

AYZ

¥ 11 billion
loan repaid

$100 million
loan repaid

Spot rate
USD/JPY 110.00

Market Makers

As with IRSs a currency swap does not have to take place directly between both parties. Most currency swap agreements now involve a market maker and two separate clients who wish to enter a swap, but not necessarily with each other. For example, it may be that the perceived credit risks involved in a direct swap agreement are not acceptable to one or both parties. By acting as a two-way market maker a bank acts as an intermediary creating a double swap in which both parties are effectively guaranteed interest payments will take place.

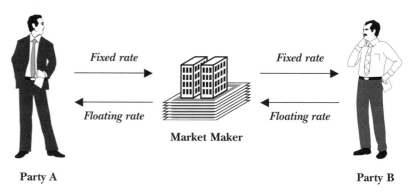

Party A

Fixed rate

Floating rate

Market Maker

Fixed rate

Floating rate

Party B

Of course, the market maker does not enter into these swaps for no reward. The intermediary is paid a fee which is either based on the principal notional amount involved, a spread between the two-way prices quoted for swap repayments – the **swap rate**, or both.

It is unlikely that the market maker has the underlying assets to match the exchange of principal amounts. As a result the bank usually matches a currency swap with an offsetting contract with another counterparty to manage the interest rate and FX exposures.

If the offsetting contract conditions match those of the original contract exactly, then the risks have been removed. However, there are still credit risks to be considered for both counterparties in the offsetting contracts.

Banks quote swap rates at the current spot rates against USD 6-month LIBOR. You will see prices quoted as **Bid** and **Ask** for a range of currencies. For example, you may see bank quotes similar to those for GBP shown in the chart below.

Maturity	Bid	Ask
2Y	6.71	6.75
3Y	7.17	7.21
4Y	7.48	7.52
5Y	7.68	7.72
7Y	7.96	8.00
10Y	8.26	8.30

But what do these rates mean? For example, for a 4-year period the bank is willing to enter into a swap at the current spot rate on the following terms:

- The bank **receives** the fixed **ask** price of 7.52% on GBP and **pays** a floating 6-month LIBOR on USD

- The bank **pays** the fixed **bid** price of 7.48% on GBP and **receives** a floating 6-month LIBOR on USD

By matching two offsetting currency swaps, the market maker effectively is at the centre of a **double swap**.

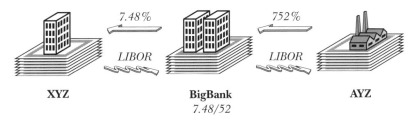

7.48%		752%
LIBOR		LIBOR
XYZ	**BigBank** 7.48/52	**AYZ**

In the US and to a lesser extent in the UK, swap rates are quoted over the yield on a Treasury note with comparable maturity.

For example, a market maker may quote **"70/75 over"** for a swap based on a 5-year T-Bond which has a yield of 8.00%. This means the market maker pays at a rate of 8.70% and receives at a rate of 8.75%

The convention of quoting a swap rate as described separates the credit risk element from the general interest rate in the market. However not all currencies have well developed government Treasury instruments across a range of maturity dates. In these cases swap dealers will quote **all-in** prices as a total rate.

Are currency swaps as simple as has been described? Well, in principle the answer is yes, but in practice there are a number of issues to be reconciled if you are trying to compare swap rates. In other words are you comparing like-with-like?

Differences between swap rates can arise based on the following:

- Quotation terms for fixed and floating rates

- The underlying instruments used to calculate swap rates

- The frequency of interest rate payments

- Day count bases used to calculate interest rate payments

These issues are all discussed in the next section.

If you were asked to explain the mechanics of a currency swap to a colleague would you be able to do it?

Currency Swaps in the Market Place

This section deals with a number of important matters concerning currency swaps which you will need to understand:

- Swap differences

- Swap spreads

- Swap valuations

Swap Differences

The four main types of difference were mentioned at the end of the last section.

Quotation Terms

Within the US markets in particular there are a number of different ways interest payments can be calculated for fixed and floating rates together with a number of different ways payment schedules can be stipulated. Different swaps may use a combination of any of the following terms

Terms	Fixed rate	Floating rate
Rate quotation	• Absolute level • Spread over Treasury instrument	• Any LIBOR • Prime rate • CD, CP or T-Bill
Payment schedule	• Quarterly • Semi-annually • Annually	• Periodic • Irregular
Basis	• Eurobond • T-Bond • Money Market Instrument	• Bond • Money Market Instrument

Underlying Instruments

The instruments used to calculate swap rates for different currencies vary. For example, USD swaps are usually quoted as a spread over the appropriate Treasury instrument which have semi-annual coupons; DM swaps are quoted on an annual Eurobond basis.

The chart below indicates the various instruments used for the major currencies together with the day count method used for the interest payment calculations.

Currency	Quoted as...	Coupon	Day count
USD	Spread over T-Bond	Semi-annual	Actual/Actual
DM	Fixed Eurobond	Annual	30/360
CHF	Fixed Eurobond	Annual	30/360
FRF	Fixed Eurobond	Annual	30/360
GBP	Spread over Gilt	Semi-annual	Actual/365
JPY	Fixed Government Bond	Semi-annual	Actual/365

Frequency of interest payments

In order to compare swap rates fairly you may need to convert annual payments into semi-annual or vice versa.

The chart below indicates the equations to use to convert yields or swap rates as appropriate.

From ➡	To ➡	Use ➡
Semi-annual	Annual	$R_A = \left[\left(1 + \dfrac{R_S}{2} \right)^2 \right] - 1$
Annual	Semi-annual	$R_S = 2 \times \left[\sqrt{(1 + R_A)} - 1 \right]$ R_A = Annual rate % ÷ 100 R_S = Semi-annual rate % ÷ 100

Day Count Bases

You may also need to convert swap rates depending on the day count basis used to calculate interest payments in order to compare like-with-like or value swaps.

The chart below gives the various methods of converting different day counts.

From ➡	To ➡	Use ➡
30/360 or Actual/365	Actual/360	Yield x $\dfrac{360}{365}$
Actual/360	30/360 or Actual/365	Yield x $\dfrac{365}{360}$
Actual/365	30/360	No adjustment
30/360	Actual/365	No adjustment

Swap Spreads

Interest rate trends cause variations in swap spreads over the yield curves for Government benchmark instruments.

When interest rates are expected to **fall** there are many fixed rate issuers wanting to swap into paying **floating** and receiving **fixed**, so spreads **narrow**.

When interest rates are expected to **rise** there are plenty of borrowers wanting to swap into **fixed** but not many willing to receive it, so spreads **widen**.

Another factor affecting swap spreads is credit risk. In a swap the market player and the market maker take on each other's risk. If either party fails to honour payment commitments, then the other party has an unwanted interest rate exposure.

For Currency swaps fixed and floating payments are made, so the risk of loss has to take into account an estimate of the **volatility** of the future floating rate basis, for example, LIBOR.

Derivatives

Swap Pricing

Swap rates are determined as a way of indicating the value now of a swap that matures in the future. In other words you need to calculate the present value for the swap sides – fixed or floating – in order to be able to set the swap rates.

Consider a fixed-for-floating currency swap in which XYZ Corporation and AYZ Bank enter into a 5-year agreement to swap $100 million for 170 million DEM at a spot rate of USD/DEM = 1.7000. Every 6 months XYZ pay AYZ a fixed rate of 6.00% DEM and in return AYZ pays US LIBOR on the floating side to XYZ.

6.00% DEM Fixed

US LIBOR Floating

XYZ

AYZ

Both payments are made every 6 months

The spot rate for the transaction is 1st June so the first payment is due on 1st December. The amount of interest due on the 1st December is already known on the 1st June. How can this be the case? The answer is that LIBOR for the first payment is fixed on the 1st June as the floating rate **to be paid in 6 months time**. In a similar manner the 1st December LIBOR fixing determines the rate to be paid for the second payment on the following 1st June and so on until the final payment in 5 years.

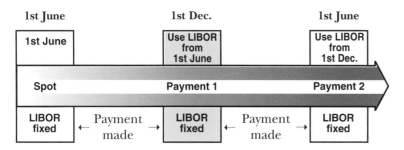

In terms of pricing this fixed-for-floating swap the transaction can be thought of as a series of **coupon payments** from an imaginary **straight bond** on the **fixed side** against a series of payments from an imaginary or **synthetic Floating Rate Note (FRN)** on the **floating side**.

Payments equivalent to coupons from a straight bond

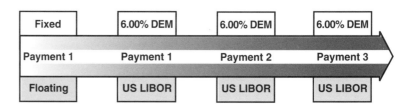

Payments equivalent to those from a Floating Rate Note

The present value of the fixed side can be calculated using the general straight bond valuation equation. For a bond with a face value of $100 and with an annual coupon this is Equation 1.

$$\text{Present Value (PV)} = \frac{C}{1 + R} + \frac{C}{(1 + R)^2} + ...+ \frac{(C + 100)}{(1 + R)^n}$$

Where: C = Coupon rate
R = Discount or swap rate as a decimal
n = Number of years to maturity

...Equation 1

REUTERS

The present value for the floating side can be calculated using the more direct relationship between the present and future value of an instrument, Equation 2.

$$PV = \frac{\textbf{Future Value}}{(1 + R)}$$

$$= \frac{\textbf{Principal} + \textbf{Interest due}}{(1 + R)}$$

Where: R =   Discount or LIBOR rate
         as a decimal   *...Equation 2*

Pricing from the Spot Curve

The Yield To Maturity (YTM) curve is simply a graph of YTM values of bonds against maturity period. Unfortunately this is a simplistic view of yields and it is better to use a graph of **spot rate** against maturity period. The spot rate is a measure of the YTM on an instrument at any moment in time which takes into account a variety of market factors. A graph of spot rate against maturity is known as a spot curve. It is also known as a zero coupon yield curve because the spot rate for an instrument is equivalent to the yield on an instrument which has no coupon repayment – zero coupon. This means that spot rates for a series of instruments with zero coupons for a range of maturity periods can be compared directly.

The curves represent the perceived relationship between the return on an instrument and its maturity – usually measured in years. Depending on the shape of the curve it is described as either:

- Positive

- Negative or inverse

Positive yield curve

In this case the shorter term interest rates are **lower** than the longer term rates. This is usually the case – the longer the period of the investment the higher the yield paid. If an interest rate rise is expected, then investors will move their assets into long term instruments which produces a fall in short term rates and an increase in long term rates.

Negative or inverse curve

When short term rates fall investors move their investments into longer term instruments to lock in a higher rate of return. This increase in supply of long term funds causes the long term rates to fall.

Derivatives

The shapes of 'theoretical' yield curves are shown below – in practice they may not appear so clear.

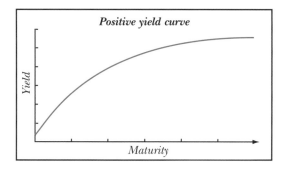

Positive yield curve

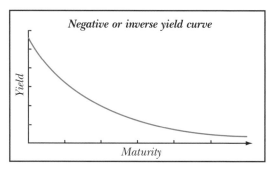

Negative or inverse yield curve

Yield curves are used to identify anomalies between instruments of similar credit standing, for example, an IRS and a T-bond of similar maturity.

The following chart may help in assessing the value of an instrument when compared to its spot curve.

Instrument curve	Instrument value
Above spot	Cheap
Below spot	Expensive

So how are swap prices determined? The following example is simple and outlines the process for a currency swap for a one year maturity.

Example – Fixed-for-floating Currency swap rates
AYZ is a bank deciding on the rates for a one year currency swap in which it will pay fixed and receive 6 month LIBOR. The floating rates are already known from the LIBOR curve but how much should the bank charge on the fixed side?

The profitability of the swap is zero if the net present value of the two 6 month floating rate payments equals the interest payments on the fixed side. This is the **break-even** price.

At the start of the swap the first LIBOR is known and is equal to 9.00%. The second 6 month LIBOR can be implied from the LIBOR yield curve.

LIBOR yield curve		
6 month	12 month	18 month
9.00%	9.50%	10.00%

The return on investing $1 at LIBOR 9.00% for 6 months is $0.045. So after 6 months the $1 invested is worth $1.045. 12 month LIBOR is 9.50%. What rate of interest is therefore required for the second 6 month LIBOR payment to turn $1.045 into $1.095?

This can be calculated using Equation 2.

$$PV = \frac{Future\ Value}{(1 + R)}$$

$$1.045 = \frac{1.095}{(1 + R)}$$

$$R = \left(\frac{1.095}{1.045}\right) - 1$$

$$= 0.04785$$

So the rate for the 6 month period is 2 x 0.04785 = 9.57%. This rate is the expected 6 month rate in 6 months time implied from the yield curve. In other words $1.045 invested at 9.57% for 6 months would yield $1.095.

So the two **floating rates** for the two payments are 9.00% and 9.57%.

These floating rates can now be used to calculate the fixed rate by equating them with a break-even value.

To do this the interest flows are discounted to the present value. Suppose the notional principal of the swap is $100. Using Equation 1 the present value of the first floating payment can be calculated using the 6 month LIBOR yield curve.

$$PV = \frac{C}{1 + R}$$

For first payment:

$$PV = \frac{4.50}{(1 + 0.090) \times 6/12}$$

$$= \$4.3062$$

For second payment:

$$PV = \frac{4.785}{(1 + 0.095) \times 12/12}$$

$$= \$4.3699$$

Therefore total interest = 4.3062 + 4.3699 = $8.6761

Equation 1 can be used again to calculate the fixed rate for the present value cash flow which has just been calculated. If C is the fixed rate, then ...

$$PV = \underbrace{\frac{C/2}{1 + R}}_{\substack{\textit{First 6 month} \\ \textit{payment}}} + \underbrace{\frac{C/2}{1 + R}}_{\substack{\textit{Second 6} \\ \textit{month payment}}}$$

$$8.6761 = \frac{C/2}{1 + 0.09/2} + \frac{C/2}{1 + 0.095}$$

$$8.6761 = \frac{C}{2} \left(\frac{1}{1 + 0.09/2} + \frac{1}{1 + 0.095} \right)$$

$$8.6761 = \frac{C}{2} \left(0.9569 + 0.9132 \right)$$

$$C = 2 \times \left(\frac{8.6761}{1.8701} \right)$$

$$C = 9.28\%$$

This means that a fixed rate of 9.28% equals the return on the floating rates of 9.00% and 9.57% for the two 6 month periods.

The value calculated is the break-even rate. In order to ensure profitability the bank's swap rate would be **lower** than this.

Using this method to price the swap depends on the rate that is discounted to calculate cash flows. This example used the spot rate for zero coupon yields but a forward rate could have been used for forward/forward rates for the period between the first and second fixed coupon dates.

Currency Swap

- A currency swap usually involves an **exchange of currencies** between counterparties at the outset of the agreement and at its maturity. If no exchange takes place at the outset, then there must be an exchange at maturity. **Because exchange of principal takes place there is an additional credit risk attached to the transaction.**

- **Interest payments between the counterparties are usually paid in full**

- Interest payments on the two currencies can be calculated on a **fixed** or **floating basis for both currencies**, or **payments for one currency can be on a fixed basis and floating for the other**

Your notes

These Reuters screens show the Speed Guide for Currency and
Interest Rate Swaps, the rates from Tullets, as well as the fixed/
floating basis for each currency.

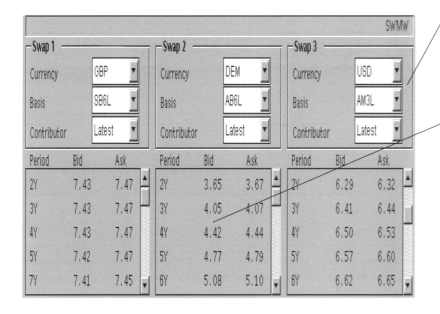

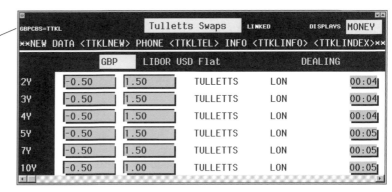

Interest Rate Option

Definitions

An **Interest Rate Option** is an agreement by which the buyer of the option pays the seller a **premium** for the **right**, but not the obligation –

to buy	a **call** option
or sell	a **put** option
a specific quantity	contract amount
of a specific instrument	the underlying instrument a Treasury security, the YTM of a Treasury security or a **bond futures** contract
on or by a set date	the expiry date depends on the style of the option – **American** or **European**
at an agreed price	**Strike price** for the underlying security, the YTM of a Treasury security or a **bond futures** contract

If you need an overview of options or you need to remind yourself about derivatives in general, then you may find it useful to refer to *An Introduction to Derivatives*.

The relationship between the rights and obligations for the different types of options is summarised in the following diagram – you may find it useful to refer to when considering some of the examples which follow.

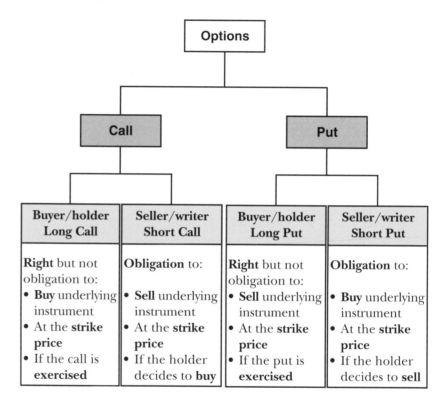

Buyer/holder Long Call	Seller/writer Short Call	Buyer/holder Long Put	Seller/writer Short Put
Right but not obligation to: • **Buy** underlying instrument • At the **strike price** • If the call is **exercised**	**Obligation** to: • **Sell** underlying instrument • At the **strike price** • If the holder decides to **buy**	**Right** but not obligation to: • **Sell** underlying instrument • At the **strike price** • If the put is **exercised**	**Obligation** to: • **Buy** underlying instrument • At the **strike price** • If the holder decides to **sell**

Interest rate options are financial derivatives first introduced in the 1980s to hedge interest rate exposure. Interest rate options can be written on bonds and bond futures. Options written on bonds are both OTC and exchange traded and are usually cash settled even though the underlying instruments are physical bonds. The exchange traded options settled for cash are for contracts on the Chicago Board Options Exchange (CBOE) and are quoted on the yield to maturity for the latest US T-bond, T-note and T-bill auctions.

Options on bond futures are exchange traded and settled using the same conditions as for the underlying government bond futures contracts.

The diagram below indicates the availability of options on bonds and bond futures.

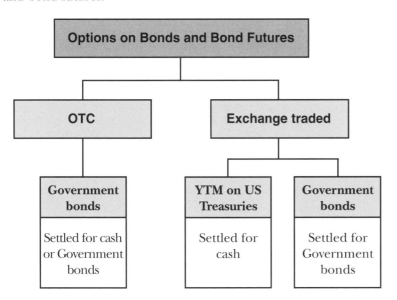

Options on Bonds

OTC contracts

Option contracts written on underlying cash debt instruments are also known as **options on physicals**. Although CBOE used to trade such contracts on US T-Bonds these are now discontinued but Interest rate options on US Treasuries are available which are explained later.

OTC options are written for most major government securities and bonds issued by their agencies. A Treasury option gives the buyer the right, but not obligation to buy or sell a specified amount of bonds or notes for a pre-determined price. If the option is exercised, then the seller of the option is obliged to deliver the specified instrument – physical delivery. However, most OTC transactions are **cash settled** based on the difference between the option strike price and the cash market price on the settlement date. Options on physicals provide a way of hedging against adverse interest rate movements for a particular instrument whilst being able to take advantage of any favourable interest rate movements. Other more unusual OTC options involve yield curves or yield spreads between instruments such as US Treasuries and mortgage-backed assets.

There are a number of disadvantages with trading OTC options on bonds which have helped to establish the exchange traded contracts on bonds and bond futures. These disadvantages include the following:

- An option on an underlying cash market bond requires accrued interest to be taken into account at settlement which is not the case for a bond futures contract.

- There may be liquidity problems in the underlying cash market and a bond required for delivery may not be available or it may be very expensive to obtain. Bond futures markets are more liquid and futures prices are always quoted.

Exchange traded Contracts

Interest rate options are available on CBOE which are based on 10 times the value of the following:

- YTM of the most recently auctioned 30 -year US T-Bond

- YTM of the most recently auctioned 10 -year US T-Note

- YTM of the most recently auctioned 5 -year US T-Note

- Discount rate of the most recently auctioned 13 -week US T-Bill

For example, a YTM of 6.50% on the current 30-year US T-Bond places the underlying value of the interest rate option on this bond at 65.00. If the YTM of the next auctioned issue rises to 6.75%, then the underlying option value rises to 67.50.

These exchange traded options offer market players a way of managing the interest rate risk on their investments and have the following characteristics:

- **Cash settled**. There is no need for buyers or sellers to hold the bonds. The cash settlement is the difference between the **strike price** – the underlying option value – and the **exercise-settlement price** or **spot yield** multiplied by the contract **multiplier** – $100. The spot yield is the YTM on the most recently issued instrument as reported by the Federal Reserve Bank of New York.

- **European style exercise**. The holder of the option can only exercise the right to buy or sell at expiration. This eliminates the risk of early settlement and simplifies investment decisions.

Exchange Traded Options on Bond Futures

The underlying instruments for interest rate options on an exchange are notional government bonds. Exchange traded options are standardised in terms of :

- Underlying instrument and its trading amount

- Strike prices – in general exchanges try to have a range of In-The-Money, At-The-Money and Out-of-The-Money strike prices

- Expiry dates

- Style – most exchange options on bond futures are American

- Premium quotations – these are percentage rates expressed in basis points or fractions

- Margin payments are required to be paid to the Clearing house

In effect, interest rate options on futures give the buyer or the seller of the instrument the right to lend or borrow money. The following chart indicates these rights from the buyer's perspective – sellers would have the opposite views.

Exchange Contracts

Options on bonds and bond futures are available on a number of exchanges worldwide. The chart below indicates a selection of the contracts available.

Long-term Government Bonds	Nominal value	Maturity range years	Notional coupon, %
LIFFE			
Long Gilt (UK)	GBP 50,000	10–15	9.00
German – Bund	DEM 250,000	8.5–10	6.00
Italian – BTP	ITL 200,000,000	8–10.5	12.00
CBOT			
30 year US T-Bonds	USD 100,000	At least 15	8.00
10 year US T-Notes	USD 100,000	6.5–10	8.00
DTB			
Bund	DEM 250,000	8.5–10.5	6.00
Bobl	DEM 250,000	3.5–5	6.00
CBOE			
30 year US T-Bonds	YTM of most recent auction issue		
10 year US T-Notes	YTM of most recent auction issue		
5 year US T-Notes	YTM of most recent auction issue		

Your notes

Typical Contract Specifications

Options contracts details vary from type to type and from exchange
to exchange but the following examples taken from a LIFFE contract
and a CBOT contract are typical specifications.

Option on German Government Bond (Bund) future	
Underlying contract	One German Bund futures contract – DEM 250,000
Premium quotations	Multiples of 0.01 (0.01%)
Minimum Price Fluctuation (Tick)	0.01 (DEM 25)
Contract expiry	March, June, September, December
Exercise procedure	American

Options on US Treasury Bond futures	
Underlying contract	One US Treasury Bond futures contract – $100,000
Premium quotations	Multiples of 1/64th of a point
Minimum Price Fluctuation (Tick)	1/64 ($15.625)
Contract expiry	March, June, September, December
Exercise procedure	American

This is the standard contract size.

Quotes as either basis points or fractions of rate

This is the smallest amount a contract can change value and the 'tick' size.

Option contracts are referred to by the trading cycle of the futures contract months.

This means that contract can be exercised on or before expiry date – American

Who Uses Options on Bonds and Bond Futures?

Buyers/Sellers

Interest rate options are used to manage interest rate risks. Investors who are concerned about rising interest rates have a choice of options that they may trade. Buying a put option offers the possibility to profit from lower bond prices at expiry – the put is the right to sell the bonds which would be at a higher price than the cash markets. Alternatively selling a call option offers the possibility of earning a premium.

When interest rates are expected to fall, investors might buy call options to profit from higher bond prices or sell puts to earn a premium.

As with options in general the risk to the buyer is limited to the premium cost whereas the risk to the seller can be unlimited. The examples of trading strategies given later may help to clarify buying and selling puts and calls.

OTC Contracts

Options on physical bonds are of particular interest to market players who need to hedge the interest rate risk linked to a particular instrument. For example, a future fixed rate loan may be linked to the spread over a specific 10-year US T-Note yield.

Exchange traded Contracts

The chart below indicates the buyers and sellers of options and the rights to the respective underlying instruments if the options are exercised. The underlying instrument has been taken as a bond futures contract but for the CBOE options the underlying is more like interest rates used for cash settled short-term interest rate options on Eurocurrencies. The second chart describes the same information as given above but in a slightly different way and describes the way market players might use the different types of options.

Option on futures contract	Buyer/holder has right to:	On exercise Seller/ writer has obligation to:
Call	**Buy** a futures contract **Go long**	**Sell** a futures contract **Go short**
Put	**Sell** a futures contract **Go short**	**Buy** a futures contract **Go long**

Option type:	On exercise:	Use
Long put	**Right** to **sell** a futures	Protect against **rising** interest rates/**falling** bond prices for issuers and borrowers
Short put	**Obligation** to **buy** a futures	As for long call but the expectation is that prices will remain stable/rise slightly
Long call	**Right** to **buy** a futures	Protect against **falling** interest rates/**rising** bond prices for investors and lenders
Short call	**Obligation** to **sell** a futures	As for long call but the expectation is that prices will remain stable/fall slightly

It is important to remember that options are traded independently and separately from the underlying instruments. Long puts and long calls are used as hedges whereas short puts and short calls are more speculative in their use. It is also important to remember that when dealing with bond futures the underlying instrument is notional and that there is a basket of deliverable grade bonds and conversion factors which have to be taken into account if delivery occurs.

Another way of looking at the use of interest rate options on futures is summarised in the chart below:

Market player who is a ...	wants to...
buyer of a **Call – Long call**	guarantee a **maximum** price for buying bonds – a **cap** or **ceiling**
buyer of a **Put – Long put**	guarantee a **minimum** price for selling bonds – a **floor**

Your notes

Options on Bonds and Bond Futures in the Market Place

This section deals with typical contract quotations, how options are traded and how premiums are calculated for interest rate options which are based on:

- Exchange traded bond futures

- Exchange traded contracts based on the YTM value for most recent auctioned US Treasury security

Typical Exchange traded Bond Futures Quotations

Interest rate option quotations are available from the financial press such as the *Financial Times* and *The Wall Street Journal* and from products such as Reuters Money 3000. The information appears in a similar style to that in the following examples.

Financial press – Option on long-term Interest Rate futures contract

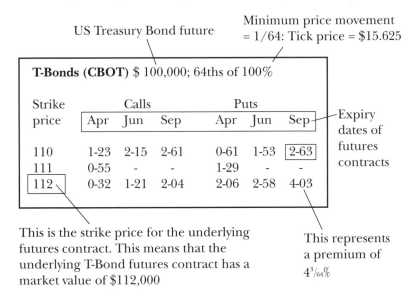

US Treasury Bond future

Minimum price movement = 1/64: Tick price = $15.625

T-Bonds (CBOT) $ 100,000; 64ths of 100%

Strike price	Calls			Puts		
	Apr	Jun	Sep	Apr	Jun	Sep
110	1-23	2-15	2-61	0-61	1-53	2-63
111	0-55	-	-	1-29	-	-
112	0-32	1-21	2-04	2-06	2-58	4-03

Expiry dates of futures contracts

This is the strike price for the underlying futures contract. This means that the underlying T-Bond futures contract has a market value of $112,000

This represents a premium of $4^{3}/_{64}\%$

The information in the chart allows you to calculate the premium cost of any option which is quoted.

Example

Suppose a portfolio manager needs to hedge the price of US T-Bonds for sale in September. To hedge the price of the bond against an adverse changes in interest rates the manager decides to use an option. He will need to buy a September Put option at a strike price which depends on his view of the markets and the current cash market price - he decides on a strike price of 110.

Buying a Sep Put option gives him the right, but not obligation, to sell the underlying futures contract on or before the September expiry date at a strike price of 110. But how much will the manager have to pay the seller for this right?

Contract premium price

This is calculated using the following simple equation:

$$\text{Premium cost} = \text{Number of ticks} \times \text{Tick size}$$

The premium cost for a **Sep110 Put** which gives you the right to sell US Treasury Bond futures at the strike price at any time to expiry is quoted at $2^{63}/_{64}\%$ in the chart opposite. So the premium cost is therefore:

$$= \text{Number of ticks} \times \$15.625$$

$$= \frac{2^{63}/_{64}}{^{1}/_{64}} \times \$15.625$$

$$= 191 \times \$15.625 = \$2984.38$$

The following is a section of a Reuters screen showing bid/ask prices for US T-Bond futures call and put options on CBOT.

CBT TREAS BOND JUN7

View by: ○ RIC ● Name

Contract: CBT US T BONDS

Expiry: US T BONDS Jun7

Option Series

Call Options	Close	OInt
US Jun7 98.0 C	$9\ \frac{11}{32}$	100
US Jun7 100.0 C	$7\ \frac{11}{32}$	44
US Jun7 102.0 C	$5\ \frac{3}{8}$	612
US Jun7 103.0 C	n/v	0
US Jun7 104.0 C	$3\ \frac{35}{64}$	200

Put Options	Close	OInt
US Jun7 110.0 P	$2\ \frac{61}{64}$	28101
US Jun7 111.0 P	$2\ \frac{17}{64}$	1350
US Jun7 112.0 P	$4\ \frac{45}{64}$	20749
US Jun7 113.0 P	$3\ \frac{35}{64}$	500
US Jun7 114.0 P	$6\ \frac{21}{32}$	6531

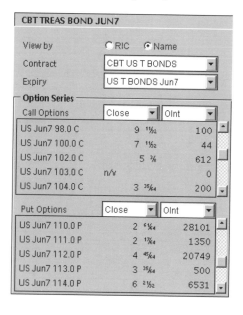

Exchange traded Options on Bonds Quotations

The Reuters screens below show options on bonds quotations from exchanges such as CBOE using the **Exchange Traded Interest Rate Options Speed Guide**. The Reuters screen is a chain of prices for the CBOE 30-year US T-Bond yields.

```
EXCHANGE TRADED INTEREST RATE OPTIONS - REUTERS SPEED GUIDE               OPT/IR1
Detailed below are the retrieval codes for Exchange Traded Interest Rate Options

=INTEREST RATE OPTIONS=================  =RULES TO CREATE FUTURES & OPTIONS=====
CBOE 13 Week Treasury Yld....<0#IRX*.W>  How to create an Option......<RULES1>-7
CBOE 5 Year Treasury Yld.....<0#FVX*.W>
CBOE 10 Year Treasury Yld....<0#TNX*.W>
CBOE 30 Year Treasury Yld....<0#TYX*.W>
AEX NED Option 7.5% 93-23....<0#NLL*.E>
AEX NED Option 6% 96-06......<0#NLX*.E>
IOM 1 Year Mid Curve RIC Root........EG
IOM 2 Year Mid Curve RIC Root........EH
ME Can Bnd 9.5% 2001.........<0#OBA*.M>  =RELATED GUIDES========================
ME Can Govt Bnd 9.5% 2011....<0#OBK*.M>  Broker Index...................<BROKER>
ME Can Govt Bnd 9.75% 2021...<0#OBY*.M>  Specialist Data Guide.........<SPECIAL>
MATIF Traded Interest Rate Options.....  Cross Market Package.......<CROSS/MKT1>
..........................<MAT/OPTEX1>
                                         =NEWS and ANALYSIS====================
                                         All Reuters Money News....<MONEY/NEWS1>
                                         Daily Diary...................[M-DIARY]

Questions/Comments: Contact your local Help Desk - see <PHONE/HELP> for details
================================================================================
Main Guide<REUTERS>    Exchange Traded IR Futures<FUT/IR1>    Money Guide<MONEY>
  Lost?Selective Access?...<USER/HELP>    Reuters Phone Support...<PHONE/HELP>
```

30 Y TSY YLD NDX WCB/ USD .TYX WCB/ LT↓59.80 14:01 H59.82 L59.71

Strike	Mth	Calls	Bid	Ask	Volume	Time	Puts	Bid	Ask	Volume	Time
55	DEC7		$4\frac{3}{4}$	5		14:50			0\01		18:30
57.5	DEC7		$2\frac{1}{4}$	2\07		14:42			0\01		19:36
60	DEC7		$0\frac{1}{8}$	$0\frac{1}{4}$		17:35		0\05	0\07		13:32
62.5	DEC7			0\01		18:44	↓$2\frac{5}{8}$	2\09	$2\frac{3}{4}$	75	13:51
65	DEC7			0\01		15:28		5	$5\frac{1}{4}$		15:52
67.5	DEC7			0\01		13:44		$7\frac{1}{2}$	$7\frac{3}{4}$		16:40
70	DEC7			0\01		20:14		10	$10\frac{1}{4}$		13:26
72.5	DEC7			0\01		18:09		$12\frac{1}{2}$	$12\frac{3}{4}$		18:26
75	DEC7			0\01		12:32		15	$15\frac{1}{4}$		14:10
77.5	DEC7			0\01		17:46		$17\frac{1}{2}$	$17\frac{3}{4}$		17:01
80	DEC7			0\01		18:39		20	$20\frac{1}{4}$		:
85	DEC7			0\01		17:11		25	$25\frac{1}{4}$		15:35
57.5	JAN8		$2\frac{1}{2}$	2\11		19:51		0\03	0\05		:
60	JAN8	↑1	0\15	1\01	10	13:42		1	$1\frac{1}{8}$		14:18
62.5	JAN8		0\03	0\05		20:33		2\11	$2\frac{7}{8}$		15:43
65	JAN8			$0\frac{1}{8}$		13:27		5	$5\frac{1}{4}$		:
67.5	JAN8			0\01		16:40		$7\frac{3}{8}$	$7\frac{5}{8}$		:
70	JAN8			0\01		:		$9\frac{7}{8}$	$10\frac{1}{8}$		:
72.5	JAN8			0\01		:		$12\frac{3}{8}$	$12\frac{5}{8}$		:
57.5	FEB8		3	$3\frac{1}{4}$		19:14		$0\frac{5}{8}$	$0\frac{3}{4}$		:
60	FEB8		1\09	1\11		18:48		$1\frac{5}{8}$	$1\frac{3}{4}$		20:00
62.5	FEB8		$0\frac{5}{8}$	$0\frac{3}{4}$		15:40		$3\frac{1}{8}$	$3\frac{3}{8}$		:
65	FEB8		0\03	0\05		:		$5\frac{1}{8}$	$5\frac{3}{8}$		:

In order to profit from these European style options then there must be a move in the anticipated direction of the interest rate or bond yield. It is important to remember the inverse relationship between interest rates and bond yields. The following example may help you to understand the use of options on bonds.

Example

A portfolio manager expects US T-Bond yields to rise by the time the next bond auction takes place. The current 3-month T-Bond option has a Yield-To-Maturity (YTM) of 8.00% and an At-The-Money (ATM) call option has a premium of $2.00. The manager buys 5 call options which means that in order to profit the YTM of the next T-Bond issue must have a yield of more than $8.00 + 0.20 = 8.20\%$.

The cost of the trade = Premium x No. of contracts x Multiplier

      = $2.00 x 5 x $100

      = $1,000

The yield rises, as expected, to 8.50% and the manager exercises the option. He receives the cash difference between the strike price and the exercise-settlement price. His profit is this value less the premium paid.

Exercise-settlement price	=	85.00
Strike price	=	80.00
Cash received	=	Difference x Contracts x Multiplier
	=	5.00 x 5 x 100
	=	$2,500
Less premium	=	$1,000
Total profits	=	**$1,500**

How an Exchange traded Interest Rate Option Contract Works

Exchange traded interest rate options on bonds and bond futures are traded in a similar way to exchange traded futures contracts in that margin payments are required by the Clearing house. Initial margin is payable by the appropriate party at the time of the trade.

The price of an option is marked-to-market every day that the option is open and the resulting profits/losses are credited/debited to both counterparty margin accounts.

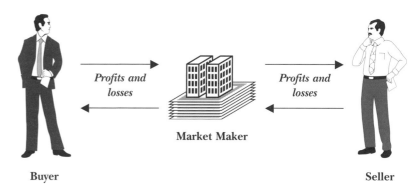

For an interest rate option on a bond, if the contract is allowed to expire, then expiry takes place on the date specified by the exchange and is **cash** settled.

For options on bond futures, if the contract is allowed to expire, then expiry takes place at the same date as the underlying notional bond futures contract. In such cases the bond actually delivered will be determined by the current basket of deliverable grade bonds and will probably be the **Cheapest To Deliver (CTD)**.

The settlement price is calculated simply from the difference between the Exchange Delivery Settlement Price (EDSP) and the strike price using the following equation:

Settlement price = (EDSP – Strike price in ticks) x Tick value

Derivatives

A simple way of calculating the option profit/loss is to use the following equation:

$$\text{Profit/loss} = (\text{EDSP} - \text{Strike price} - \text{Premium in ticks}) \times \text{Tick value} \times \text{Number of contracts}$$

Example

A long call option can be used to hedge falling interest rates/rising bond prices. An investor who has decided to buy long-term UK gilts in the future needs to hedge rising interest rates and so buys 10 LIFFE Long gilt call options on the underlying notional government bond futures at a strike of 119. The current futures price is 121-12. The premium for this In-The-Money (ITM) option is 3-48.

The futures price rises to 123-16 when the investor offsets his position. What is the profit or loss on his position?

Difference in settlement and strike prices
$$= 123\text{-}16 - 119$$
$$= 4\text{-}16 = 4 \times 64 + 16$$
$$= 272 \text{ ticks}$$

Premium paid
$$= 3 \text{-} 48 = 3 \times 64 + 48$$
$$= 240 \text{ ticks}$$

Profit on position
$$= (272 - 240) \times £7.8125 \times 10$$
$$= £2,500$$

If an option on a bond futures contract is allowed to expire, then the underlying contract is either delivered or received. As the underlying is a notional bond the actual strike price of the option has to be adjusted for the specific deliverable grade bond involved. For example, the strike price must be multiplied by CTD bond conversion factor.

Trading Strategies for Options

There are many strategies available in the options markets – some are quite complex and have colourful names.

The various strategies are usually represented diagrammatically as **break-even graphs** which show the potential for making a profit. The diagrams use the break-even point as the basis for the diagram where

$$\textbf{Break-even point} = \textbf{Strike price} \pm \textbf{premium}$$

The most basic buy/sell strategies for puts and calls are illustrated using profit/loss charts in the following examples. You may find it useful to refer to option strategies in general by referring to *An Introduction to Derivatives*.

Depending on whether the market player is a buyer or seller of a call or put, gains or losses either have ceiling values or are limitless.

Buying a Call option – Long Call

A trader in an investment bank is planning on buying long-term government bonds in the future but her expectations are that interest rates will fall by the time the bonds are required. The trader needs to protect against increased bond prices whilst retaining the possibility of prices actually falling.

By buying call options the trader can hedge her anticipated future bond purchase. The call options effectively place a ceiling on the investment bank's purchase price for the bonds but still allows the holder to take advantage if prices fall.

If prices do go up as anticipated and the trader has to pay more for the bonds in the cash market, then the effective loss is offset by the gains on the call option. The result is that the trader locks in a maximum future purchase price for the bonds.

However, if bond prices fall in the future the trader can take advantage of lower cash prices and there is an effective net gain. The size of this gain is dependent on the value of the premium paid which can be regarded as insurance.

It is now December and the trader decides to protect her intended February UK long gilt bond purchase by buying Call options on LIFFE Long gilt futures contracts having a strike price of 121. She buys 121Feb Calls with a premium of 1-20.

At expiry the profit/loss chart for the Long Call looks like this:

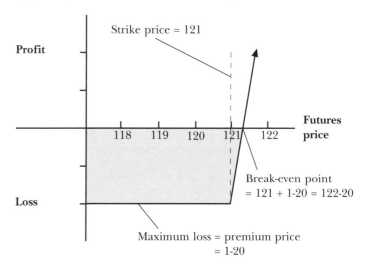

Market price	Outcome
> 122-20	Profit increases as futures prices rise (bond prices rise) and are unlimited
122-20	Break-even point
121 – 122-20	Loss which increases as futures price falls (bond prices fall)
< 121	Loss is limited to a maximum of the premium price

Buying a Put option – Long Put

A portfolio manager, who has invested heavily in 10-year US Treasury T-Notes, anticipates that interest rates will rise in the next few months resulting in a lowering of bond prices and the value of his portfolio. He would like to protect the current market value of the portfolio whilst retaining the opportunity to profit if bond prices rise instead of fall.

By purchasing put options the manager can establish a floor level price for the bonds he holds the level of which is determined by the strike price of the options bought. The higher the strike price the higher the floor level and option premium.

If interest rates rise with the corresponding fall in bond prices, then the gains from the put option offset the decrease in the market value of the bonds below the floor level which has been established.

Buying puts does not preclude profits if bond prices actually increase. In this case the option is allowed to expire and the bonds sold or held at the market price and the profit is the difference less the premium which once again has acted as insurance.

It is now December and the manager decides to protect his investment in T-Notes by buying Put options on 10-year US T-Note futures contracts having a strike price of 108. He buys 108Feb Calls with a premium of 2-16.

At expiry the profit/loss chart for the Long Put looks like this:

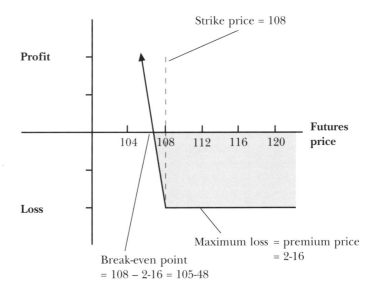

Market price	Outcome
> 108	Maximum loss is equal to the premium
108 – 105-48	Loss decreases as future prices fall (bond prices fall)
105-48	Break-even point
< 105-48	Profit increases as future prices fall (bond prices fall) and is unlimited

Selling a Call option – Short Call

A portfolio manager expects relatively stable interest rates and bond prices for the foreseeable future. The expectation is that interest rates will remain steady or fall slightly. The manager is keen to increase the current return on her investment and decides to write call options on government bond futures. The premium received from writing call options can increase the return on investment. The strategy employed here as a call writer is to limit the opportunity to benefit from an increase in prices by establishing a **maximum** or **ceiling** for the potential value of the bonds held. If the bonds rise above this ceiling price then there is the potential for loss.

The option strike price is the major decision the manager has to make. Once this has been made then the premium can be determined. OTM calls provide less premium and are less likely to be exercised. ATM calls provide more premium but the writer needs to be reasonably sure that the options are unlikely to be exercised.

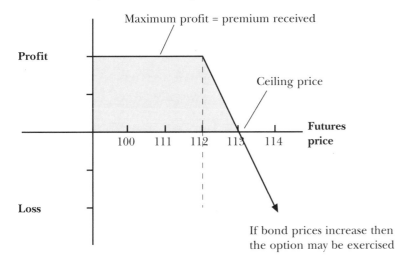

At expiry the profit/loss chart for the Short Call looks like this:

Selling a Put option – Short Put

This is more or less the same scenario as for a Short Call except that this time the portfolio manager believes that interest rates will remain steady or rise slightly. The manager plans to add bonds to his existing portfolio and would like to pay less than the market price when the bonds are required. The manager decides to write put options on government bond futures which effectively establishes a **minimum** or **floor** price for the future purchase of the required bonds.

At expiry the profit/loss chart for the Short Put looks like this:

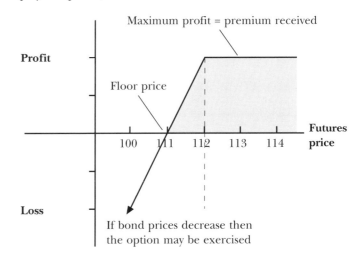

Options on Interest Rate Futures

- **Exchange traded options on bonds** are available on the **YTM** of the most recently auctioned US Treasury securities – these options are European style and on exercise the contracts are **cash settled**.

- **OTC options on bonds** are available for many government bonds and those of their agencies which on exercise are **cash settled** or settled by **physical delivery**

- Exchange traded options on bond futures are available on a wide range of notional government bonds which on exercise are settled by **physical delivery of bonds** from a basket of deliverable grade bonds – usually the **Cheapest To Deliver (CTD)** bond

- For options on bond futures the **buyer** or **holder** of a **call/put** has the **right** to **buy/sell** the **underlying futures** contract if the option is exercised

- For options on bond futures the **seller** or **writer** of a **call/put** has the **obligation** to **sell/buy** the **underlying futures contract** if the option is exercised

- Most options on bond futures traded on exchanges are **American style** – exchange traded options on bonds are **European** style

- Premium quotations are as a basis point percentage or a fractional percentage value of the underlying contract

Your notes

These Reuters screens display the **MATIF Options Contracts Speed Guide** and the floor prices on the current **notional** futures contract.

These Reuters screens show the premium prices for interest rate options. In the screens shown here, call and put premiums are displayed for various strike prices for the underlying US T-Bond and German Bunds futures contracts on a variety of exchanges.

```
MATIF OPTIONS CONTRACTS - SPEED GUIDE            <FRANCE>      MAT/OPTEX1
To access information double-click in <>. For more information see <USER/HELP>.

Listed Contracts=====Chains=========First Mth======Volatility==Contract Details
Bobl             : See below...... <O#OBLc1>...... <O#.OBL+>....... <MAT/OBL1>
5 YR Gvt Bond    : See below...... <O#OY5c1>...... <O#.YR5+>....... <MAT/YR52>
Notional Bond    : See below...... <O#ONNc1>...... <O#.PTB+>....... <MAT/PTB2>
Pibor 3-month    : See below...... <O#OPIc1>...... <O#.PIB+>....... <MAT/PIB2>
Pibor 3M Mid-curve : See below.... <O#OPMc1>...... <O#.OPM+>....... <MAT/PIB3>
Sugar            : <MAT/OPTEX3>... <O#OSUc1>...... <O#.OSU+>....... <MAT/PSA2>
Forex            : <MAT/OPTEX3>

Stats /Vol.Tot:    <O#.AD.MATIF>.. <.AD.MATOPT>................. <FR/STATS6>

By months...======================Composite=========Globex=========Floor====
MAR 98 - Pibor 3M................. <O#OPIBH8+>..... <O#1PIBH8+>.... <O#2PIBH8+>
       - Pibor 3M Mid-Curve....... <O#OPMH8+>...... <O#1OPMH8+>.... <O#2OPMH8+>

APR 98 - Pibor 3M................. <O#PIBJ8+>...... <O#1PIBJ8+>.... <O#2PIBJ8+>
       - Notional................. <O#PTBJ8+>...... <O#1PTBJ8+>.... <O#2PTBJ8+>
       - 5 Year................... <O#YR5J8+>...... <O#1YR5J8+>.... <O#2YR5J8+>
================================================================================
French Options<FR/OPTEX1>    Matif Futures<MAT/FUTEX1>    Next Months<MAT/OPTEX2>
  Lost? Selective Access<USER/HELP>    Reuter Phone Support<PHONE/HELP>
```

```
NOTIONNEL  JUN8  MAT/    FRF    2PTBM8×MAT/   LT↑103.43   15:31 H103.43 L102.95
Strike Mth    Calls  Bid    Ask   Volume Time  Puts   Bid    Ask   Volume Time
97.5   APR8                                  :                          :
98     APR8                                  :                          :
98.5   APR8                                  :                          :
99     APR8                                  :                          :
99.5   APR8                                  :                          :
100    APR8                                  :                          :
100.5  APR8                                  :                          :
101    APR8                                  :     0.01   0.04          :
101.5  APR8                                  :   ↓0.04            1300 13:37
102    APR8                                  :   ↓0.06   0.04   0.07   2186 15:20
102.5  APR8 ↑0.92                  75 09:56↓0.12  0.10   0.13    605 15:01
103    APR8 ↑0.57  0.59   0.62    150 10:38↓0.27  0.24   0.26    170 14:19
103.5  APR8 ↑0.34  0.31   0.33   3206 15:09↓0.41  0.44   0.47     10 15:05
104    APR8 ↑0.16  0.14   0.16   2852 15:04                      :
104.5  APR8 ↑0.06  0.05   0.07    900 15:09                      :
105    APR8 ↓0.03  0.01   0.03    250 15:03                      :
105.5  APR8                                  :                          :
106    APR8                                  :                          :
106.5  APR8                                  :                          :
107    APR8                                  :                          :
107.5  APR8                                  :                          :
108    APR8                                  :                          :
```

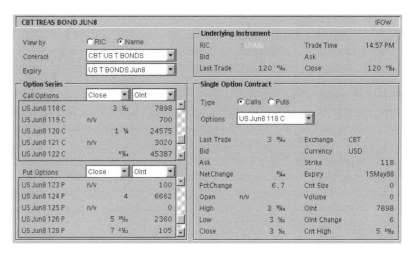

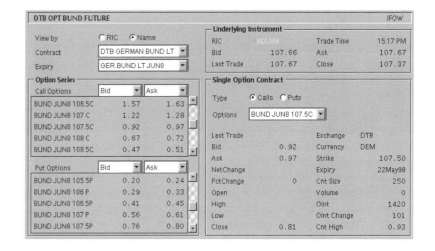

These Reuters screens show the **Interest Rate History** page, and the **Future Option Model** page.

The **Interest Rate History** page displays the deposit rates you select for up to three currencies simultaneously – you can choose any combination of currencies and deposit periods as required. The **Future Option Model** page can be useful if you need to know the option delta values and whether an option premium is In-The-Money (ITM), At-The-Money (ATM) or Out-of-The-Money (OTM).

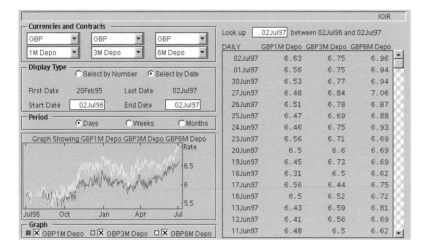

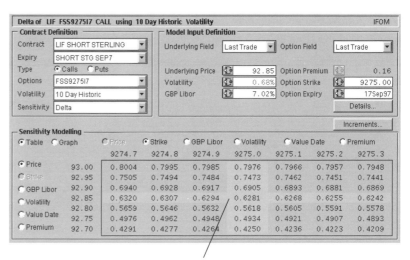

Here you can see that the call for this 9275 strike for the September contract which has an underlying value of 92.85 has a delta value of 0.6281 which means it is ITM

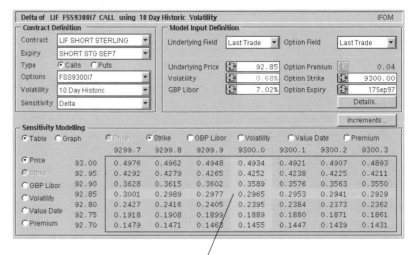

Here you can see that the call for this 9300 strike for the September contract which has an underlying value of 92.85 has a delta value of 0.2965 which means it is OTM

Swaption

A **Swaption** is a financial derivative which grants the right, but not the obligation, to buy or sell an Interest Rate Swap (IRS) on agreed terms of interest rate, maturity, fixed or floating rate payer, on or by an agreed date. In return for this right the buyer of a swaption pays the seller a premium.

If you need an overview of options and swaps derivatives or you need to remind yourself about the types of derivatives available, then you may find it useful to refer to *An Introduction to Derivatives*.

Swaptions are OTC contracts used by market players who seek the advantages of an IRS but who also would like to benefit from any favourable interest rate movements.

Swaptions, in common with other options, use the terms call and put. However, their meanings are not quite as obvious as before. The meanings and uses of swaptions calls and puts are described in the chart below.

Call Swaption	Put Swaption
• Also called a **Payer** or **Right-to-pay** Swaption	• Also called a **Receiver** or **Right-to-receive** Swaption
• The buyer has the right to **pay the fixed side to** and receive the floating side from the holder of the underlying IRS	• The buyer has the right to **receive the fixed side from** and pay the floating side to the holder of the underlying IRS
• The buyer is hedging against **falling** interest rates	• The buyer is hedging against **rising** interest rates

Who Uses Swaptions?

Banks and Corporations

Swaptions are used by the same market players who use IRSs – banks and multinational corporations.

Swaptions are used increasingly by these market players for two main reasons:

- To hedge exposure on interest rates

- To speculate in the swaps markets in order to make a profit from offsetting fixed/floating rate transactions

Swaptions offer similar benefits to corporations and banks as IRSs:

- Counterparties are able to convert underlying interest rates from fixed to floating and vice versa over a long term period

- Usually there are cost savings to both sides

- IRSs provide access to markets not normally available to the market players, for example, for reasons relating to credit rating

Swaptions in the Market Place

This section deals with examples of how call and put swaptions work in the market place.

Call Swaptions

Example

XYZ Corporation decides to hedge against falling interest rates using a **1 plus 4 Call Swaption**. This means they **buy** an instrument which grants the right to exercise the option in one year for an underlying 4 year **Fixed pay/Floating receive** (Current interest rate/LIBOR) IRS for a Swaption rate of Fixed pay/Floating receive, 6.5%/LIBOR.

This means that if XYZ, the Swaption holder, exercises their right in a year, they will pay the **IRS holder** a fixed rate and receive LIBOR, and at the same time receive 6.5% fixed interest from the **option seller** and pay LIBOR.

To justify exercising the swaption, the interest rates of the underlying instrument must be **less** than the Swaption rates.

At expiration the current rate for a 4 year Fixed pay/Floating receive IRS is 6.0%/LIBOR. XYZ exercise their right on the Swaption and make a net gain of 0.5% in interest rate payments, so hedging against falling interest rates.

The process is illustrated in the chart opposite.

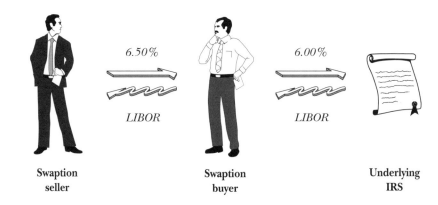

Payments	XYZ receive	XYZ pay	Net % position
Fixed	6.50%	6.00%	+ 0.50
Floating	LIBOR	LIBOR	Cancel out

Put Swaptions

Example

XYZ Corporation needs to hedge against rising interest rates using a **1 plus 4 Put Swaption**. This means they **buy** an instrument which grants the right to exercise the option in one year for an underlying 4 year **Fixed receive/Floating pay** (Current interest rate/LIBOR) IRS for a Swaption rate of Fixed receive/Floating pay, 6.5%/LIBOR.

This means that if XYZ, the Swaption holder, exercises their right in a year, they will pay the **IRS holder** LIBOR and receive a fixed rate, and at the same time receive LIBOR from the **option seller** and pay a fixed rate of 6.5%.

To justify exercising the swaption, the interest rates of the underlying instrument must be **greater** than the Swaption rates.

At expiration the current rate for a 4 year Fixed receive/Floating pay IRS is 7.0%/LIBOR. XYZ exercise their right on the Swaption and make a net gain of 0.5% in interest rate payments, so hedging against rising interest rates.

These Reuters screens show the **Speed Guide** for swaptions; as with other OTC option prices the bid and ask quotes from the various contributors are as volatilities. Also shown is swaption volatilities for the USD from the **Tokyo Forex Co Ltd**.

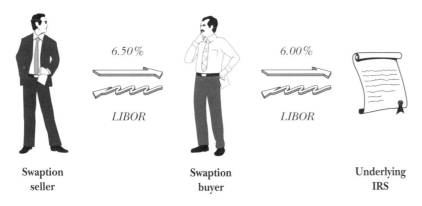

Swaption seller — 6.50% LIBOR → Swaption buyer — 6.00% LIBOR → Underlying IRS

Payments	XYZ receive	XYZ pay	Net % position
Fixed	6.50%	6.00%	+ 0.50
Floating	LIBOR	LIBOR	Cancel out

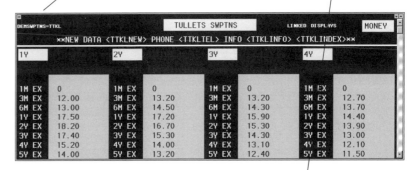

Derivatives

 Summary

You have now finished the fourth section of the book and you should have a clear understanding of derivatives based on bond instruments. You should also understand that derivatives allow market players to manage risk, but at the same time, entail risk and thus require market players to employ prudent management. Ultimately, though some of the formulas and modeling behind derivatives is very complex, use of derivatives need not be limited only to specialised traders when prudence is exercised.

You have reviewed these basic concepts:

- What are and who uses derivatives?

- How do the basic instruments – futures, forwards, options and swaptions – differ from one another and when are they used?

- How are derivatives traded?

As a check on your understanding, try the Quick Quiz Questions on the next page. You may also find the Overview Section to be a helpful learning tool.

Your notes

Quick Quiz Questions

1. What will the invoice amount be for the following 12.00% bond deliverable against a T-Bond futures contract where the settlement price is 99-16? The contract size is $100,000 and the conversion factor is 1.215.
   - ☐ a) $99,500.00 + accrued interest
   - ☐ b) $100,000.00 + accrued interest
   - ☐ c) $120,892.50 + accrued interest
   - ☐ d) $121,500.00 + accrued interest

2. If you place an order for a futures contract, when will you be required to pay an initial margin?
   - ☐ a) At expiry of the contract
   - ☐ b) Only if you buy a contract
   - ☐ c) At the time of trading the contract
   - ☐ d) Only if you sell a contract

3. When trading in futures, credit risk lies with which of the following?
   - ☐ a) The exchange Clearing house
   - ☐ b) The broker who takes your order
   - ☐ c) The counterparty with whom the trade is made
   - ☐ d) The pit trader placing your order

4. Consider the following CBOT T-Note futures prices.
   Mar 109-15   Jun 108-29   Dec 108-09
   Which one of the following statements is true?
   - ☐ a) The USD yield curve is inverted
   - ☐ b) The USD yield curve is positive
   - ☐ c) A weak USD on foreign exchanges is expected
   - ☐ d) None of the above

5. A portfolio manager holds US T-Bonds with a face value of $1 million. The current cash market price is 120-00. The manager predicts that interest rates will rise in the near future. The manager wants to protect her portfolio so sells 10 CBOT Futures contracts at 112-04. The tick size of the contract is one thirty-second of a point and the tick value is $31.25.

   a) If the manager is correct and interest rates rise and the contracts are closed by buying at 101-24, how much profit does the manager make?

   b) If the trader is wrong, interest rates fall and the contracts are closed at 115-17, what is the manager's loss?

Answer a)

Answer b)

Quick Quiz Questions

6. In an IRS, the principal amounts involved are usually:
   - ☐ a) Exchanged at the end date
   - ☐ b) Exchanged at the start date
   - ☐ c) Not exchanged
   - ☐ d) Exchanged at an interim date

7. In an IRS, interest payments are exchanged:
   - ☐ a) On a net basis at the end of each interest period
   - ☐ b) On a gross basis at the end of each interest period
   - ☐ c) At the start of each interest period, as with a FRA
   - ☐ d) On a cumulative basis at maturity

8. A client asks you to quote for a 2 year GBP IRS. You quote 7.39–7.439. The client deals at 7.39. What have you done?
   - ☐ a) Agreed to receive fixed/pay floating
   - ☐ b) Transacted a basis swap
   - ☐ c) Agreed to pay fixed/receive floating
   - ☐ d) Transacted a fixed/fixed swap

9. A borrower pays LIBOR + for floating USD. He decides to fix his interest repayments using an IRS. He receives a quote of 6.75–80 using the same interest basis and decides to fix. What will be the net cost of his borrowing?
   - ☐ a) 6.750%
   - ☐ b) 6.800%
   - ☐ c) 7.375%
   - ☐ d) 7.425%

Using the chart of premium prices for options on CBOT US T-Notes answer the following:

T-Notes (CBOT) $ 100,000; pts and 64ths of 100%						
Strike	Calls			Puts		
price	Apr	Jun	Sep	Apr	Jun	Sep
108	0-39	1-11	1-33	0-52	1-26	2-16
109	0-16	0-48	1-08	1-29	1-61	2-53
110	0-05	0-29	0-52	2-19	2-41	3.32

Tick size for this contract is one sixty-fourth and the tick value is $15.625

10. Why are the Calls with higher strikes cheaper than those with lower strikes, and why are the Puts with higher strikes more expensive than those with lower strikes?

    Answer:

Quick Quiz Questions

11. At what price would the buyer of a 108Jun Put break even at expiry?

    Answer:

12. What is the premium cost for a 109Jun Call?

    Answer:

13. You buy an option on LIFFE which can be exercised at any time. Which of the following describes this type of option?
    - ☐ a)   European
    - ☐ b)   American
    - ☐ c)   Asian
    - ☐ d)   Average

You can check your answers on page 221.

Overview

What Are Derivatives?

A derivative instrument can be defined as follows:

 A **Derivative** is an agreement between two counterparties in which they agree to transfer an asset or amount of money on or before a specified future date at a specified price. A derivative's value changes with changes in one or more underlying market variables, such as interest rates or foreign exchange rates.

Types of Derivatives
- Interest Rate Futures
- Interest Rate Swaps (IRS)
- Currency Swaps
- Interest Rate Options
- Swaptions

Derivatives

Interest Rate Futures

 Interest Rate Futures are forward transactions with standard contract sizes and maturity dates which are traded on a formal exchange.

Short-term interest rate futures contracts are almost exclusively based on Eurocurrency deposits and are cash settled based on an Exchange Delivery Settlement Price (EDSP) or the last price traded.

Long-term interest rate futures or **Bond futures** contracts are settled based on notional government bonds or notes with a coupon and maturity period specified by the exchange. The settlement price is based on the final futures contract price – the Exchange Delivery Settlement Price (EDSP).

- Who Uses Interest Rate Futures?
  - Hedgers
  - Speculators
  - Arbitrageurs
- Trading Strategies
  - Basis trading
  - Spread trading
  - Hedging portfolio duration
  - Asset allocation
  - Multicurrency investment using future contracts

Currency Swaps

 A **Currency Swap** is an agreement between counterparties in which one party makes payments in one currency and the other party makes payments in a different currency on agreed future dates until maturity of the agreement.

- Three Steps
  - Spot exchange of principal
  - Exchange of interest rate payments
  - Re-exchange of principal
- Who Uses Currency Swaps?
  - Banks
  - Corporations

Interest Rate Swaps (IRS)

 An **Interest Rate Swap** is an agreement between counterparties in which each party agrees to make a series of payments to the other on agreed future dates until maturity of the agreement. Each party's interest payments are calculated using different formulas by applying the agreement terms to the **notional principal** amount of the swap.

- Who Uses Interest Rate Swaps?
  - Banks
  - Corporations
- Swap Structures
  - Plain vanilla swap
  - Forward start swap
  - Swaption

Interest Rate Option

 An **Interest Rate Option** is an agreement by which the buyer of the option pays the seller a **premium** for the **right**, but not the obligation –

to buy	a **call** option
or sell	a **put** option
a specific quantity	contract amount
of a specific instrument	the underlying instrument a Treasury security, the YTM of a Treasury security or a **bond futures** contract
on or by a set date	the expiry date depends on the style of the option – **American** or **European**
at an agreed price	**Strike price** for the underlying security, the YTM of a Treasury security or a **bond futures** contract

Interest Rate Option

Options

Call	Put

Buyer/holder Long Call	Seller/writer Short Call	Buyer/holder Long Put	Seller/writer Short Put
Right but not obligation to: • **Buy** underlying instrument • At the **strike price** • If the call is **exercised**	**Obligation** to: • **Sell** underlying instrument • At the **strike price** • If the holder decides to **buy**	**Right** but not obligation to: • **Sell** underlying instrument • At the **strike price** • If the put is **exercised**	**Obligation** to: • **Buy** underlying instrument • At the **strike price** • If the holder decides to **sell**

Options on Bonds and Bond Futures

OTC	Exchange traded

Government bonds	YTM on US Treasuries	Government bonds
Settled for cash or Government bonds	Settled for cash	Settled for Government bonds

Swaptions

 A **Swaption** is a financial derivative which grants the right, but not the obligation, to buy or sell an Interest Rate Swap (IRS) on agreed terms of interest rate, maturity, fixed or floating rate payer, on or by an agreed date. In return for this right the buyer of a swaption pays the seller a premium.

- Who Uses Swaptions?
  - Banks
  - Corporations

Call Swaption	Put Swaption
• Also called a **Payer** or **Right-to-pay** Swaption	• Also called a **Receiver** or **Right-to-receive** Swaption
• The buyer has the right to **pay the fixed side to** and receive the floating side from the holder of the underlying IRS	• The buyer has the right to **receive the fixed side from** and pay the floating side to the holder of the underlying IRS
• The buyer is hedging against **falling** interest rates	• The buyer is hedging against **rising** interest rates

Quick Quiz Answers

		✓ or ✗
1.	c)	☐
2.	c)	☐
3.	a)	☐
4.	b)	☐

5. a) $103,750.00 ☐
   Contract moves $112\,^4/_{32} - 101\,^{24}/_{32} \div\,^1/_{32} = 332$ ticks
   Therefore profit $= 332\;$ x $\;31.25\;$ x $10 = \$103,750.00$

   b) $34,062.50 ☐
   Contract moves $115\,^{17}/_{32} - 112\,^4/_{32} \div\,^1/_{32} = 109$ ticks
   Therefore loss $= 109\;$ x $\;31.25\;$ x $10 = \$34,062.50$

6. c) ☐

7. a) ☐

8. c) ☐

9. d) ☐

10. The higher the strike the lower the Call prices ☐
    because they are further Out-of-The-Money.
    The higher the Put prices because they are further
    In-The-Money.

		✓ or ✗

11. Put break even = Strike – Premium ☐
                    = 108-00 – 1-26
                    = 106-38

12. Premium is 0-48, $^{48}/_{64}$, the tick size for this contract is ☐
    $^1/_{64}$ and the tick value is $15.625
    Premium cost = 48 x $15.625
                  = $750

13. b.

How well did you score? You should have managed to get most
of these questions correct. If you didn't, revise the materials
again.

Further Resources

Books

All About Bond Funds: A Complete Guide for Today's Investors
Werner Renberg, John Wiley & Sons, Inc., 1995
ISBN   0 471 31195 2

New Financial Instruments
Julian Walmsley, John Wiley & Sons, Inc., 2nd Edition 1998
ISBN   0 471 12136 3

Derivatives: The Theory and Practice of Financial Engineering
Paul Wilmott, John Wiley & Sons, Inc., 1998
ISBN   0 471 98389 6

Bonds and Bond Derivatives
Miles Livingston, Blackwell Press, 1998
ISBN   0 631 20756 2

Derivatives: A Comprehensive Resource for Options, Futures,
Interest Rate Swaps and Mortage Securities
Fred D. Arditti, Harvard Business School Press, 1996
ISBN   0 875 84560 6

Bond Markets, Analysis and Strategies
Frank J. Fabozzi, Prentice Hall International, 3rd Edition 1996
ISBN   0 13 520370 8

Investments
William F. Sharpe, Gordon J. Alexander & Jeffrey V. Bailey, Prentice
Hall, 5th Edition 1995
ISBN   0 131 83344 8

Options, Futures, and other Derivatives
John C. Hull, Prentice Hall International, 3rd Edition 1997
ISBN   0 132 64367 7

Financial Derivatives
David Winstone, Chapman & Hall, 1st Edition 1995
ISBN   0 412 62770 1

Publications

Chicago Mercantile Exchange
- An Introduction to Futures and Options: Interest Rates

Swiss Bank Corporation
- Financial Futures and Options
- Options: The fundamentals
ISBN   0 964 11120 9

Chicago Board of Trade
- Financial Instruments Guide
- An Introduction to Options on Financial Futures
- Trading in Futures
- Proj A Annual Volumes (1994 – current)

London International Financial Futures and Options Exchange (LIFFE)
- Government Bond Futures
- Options: a guide to trading strategies
- Annual Volumes

Bank of England
- Gilts and the Gilt Market Review 1996/1997
- The Official Gilts Strips facility Oct. 1997

Fannie Mae
- Mortage-backed Securities

Federal Reserve Bank of Philadelphia
- Inflation-Indexed Bonds: How do they work?

The International Swaps and Derivatives Association (ISDA)
- Summary of Market Survey Statistics: 1997

The Bank for International Settlements (the BIS)
- Central Bank Survey of Foreign Exchange and Derivatives Market Activity 1998

Internet

RFT Web Site

• http://www.wiley-rft.reuters.com

This is the series' companion web site where additional quiz questions, updated screens and other information may be found.

ISMA

• http://www.ISMA.org

The International Securities Market Association (ISMA) is the self-regulatory organisation and trade association for the international securities market.

ISDA

• http://www.isda.org

The International Swaps and Derivatives Association (ISDA) is the global trade association representing leading participants in the privately negotiated derivatives industry, a business which includes interest rate, currency, commodity and equity swaps, as well as related products such as caps, collars, floors and swaptions.

BIS

• http://www.bis.org

The Bank for International Settlements (the BIS) is owned and controlled by central banks and it provides a number of highly-specialised services to central banks and, through them, to the international financial system more generally. The Monetary and Economic Department of the BIS conducts research, particularly into monetary and financial questions, collects and publishes data on international banking and financial market developments, and runs an intra-central bank economic database to which contributing central banks have automated access.

British Bankers Association

• http://www.bba.org.uk

British Bankers' Association (BBA) is the principal representative body for banks active in the UK, with over 300 member banks from more than 60 countries.

Bank of England

• http://www.bankofengland.co.uk

The Bank of England is the central bank of the United Kingdom.

Fannie Mae

• http://www.fanniemae.com

Brady Net

• http://www.bradynet.com

Exchanges

Refer to the back of this book for a listing of worldwide stock exchange contact information and web sites.

Your notes

This section of the book should take about 2 hours of study time. You may not take as long as this or you may take a little longer – remember your learning is individual to you.

Just imagine that a bond is a slice of cake, and you didn't bake the cake, but every time you hand somebody a slice of the cake a tiny little bit comes off, like a bittle crumb, and you can keep that.

Mrs Sherman McCoy, wife of a bond trader, explaining to their daughter what daddy does for a living, in Tom Wolfe, Bonfire of the Vanities (Farrar Straus & Givoux, 1987)

Equation 1

$$\text{Return} = (\text{Selling price} - \text{Buying price})$$

Equation 2

$$\text{Rate of return} = \frac{(\text{Selling price} - 1)}{\text{Buying price}} \times 100\%$$

Equation 3

$$\text{Annualised rate of return as \%} = \frac{\text{Rate of return as \%}}{\text{Investment period in years}}$$

Equation 4

$$FV = PV \times [1 + (R \times n)]$$

Equation 5

$$FV = PV \times \left(1 + \frac{R}{t}\right)^{nt}$$

Equation 6

$$R = t \times \left[\left(\frac{FV}{PV}\right)^{\frac{1}{nt}} - 1\right]$$

Equation 7

$$PV = \frac{FV}{\left(1 + \dfrac{R}{t}\right)^{nt}}$$

Equation 8

$$PV_{Total} = \sum_{i=1}^{N} \frac{FV_i}{\left(1 + \dfrac{R}{t}\right)^{nt}}$$

Equation 9

$$PV_{Total} = \frac{C/t}{(1 + R/t)} + \frac{C/t}{(1 + R/t)^2} + \ldots + \frac{P + C/t}{(1 + R/t)^N}$$

Equation 10

$$PV_{Total} = \frac{C/t}{(1 + R/t)^a} + \frac{C/t}{(1 + R/t)^{a+1}} + \ldots + \frac{P + C/t}{(1 + R/t)^{a+n}}$$

Equation 11

$$\text{Accrued interest} = \text{Principal} \times \frac{R}{t} \times \frac{D}{B}$$

Equation 12

$$\text{Market Value (MV)} = \text{Principal Value (P)} + \text{Accrued Interest (A)}$$

Equation 13

$$\text{Current yield} = \frac{\text{Coupon rate}}{\text{Clean price}} \times 100$$

Equation 14

$$ACY = \text{Current yield} + \frac{(100 - \text{Clean price})}{\text{Years to maturity}}$$

Bond Valuation and Bond Yields

Equation 15

$$R_A = \left[\left(1 + \frac{R_S}{2}\right)^2\right] - 1$$

Equation 16

$$R_S = 2 \times \left[\sqrt{(1 + R_A)} - 1\right]$$

Equation 17

$$D = \left[a \times \frac{C_{(a)}}{DP}\right] + \left[(a + 1) \times \frac{C_{(a+1)}}{DP}\right] + ... + \left[(a + n) \times \frac{C_{(a+n)}}{DP}\right]$$

Equation 18

$$\text{Modified duration} = \frac{\text{Macaulay duration in years}}{\left(1 + \frac{R}{t}\right)}$$

Equation 19

$$BPV = \frac{\text{Modified duration}\%}{100} \times \frac{\text{Dirty price}}{100}$$

Equation 20

$$DP \% \text{ change} = -\left[\text{Modified duration} \times \Delta YTM\right]$$

$$+ \left[\text{Convexity} \times \frac{(\Delta YTM)^2}{2}\right]$$

Your notes

REUTERS

Introduction

You have now reviewed the variety of bond and derivative instruments used in the market place. To effectively use these instruments, market players must employ bond valuation techniques and various yield calculations and risk analysis. This section will provide you with all of the requisite information and tools you need to value bonds. Laid out on the previous pages for your easy reference are the equations used throughout this section. The explanations and examples of how to use each equation are in the text. You may find it useful to photocopy the equations to have for your ready reference.

This section will include coverage of:

- The basic characteristics of bonds, including the concepts of market and credit risk

- The basics of bond valuation, including examples using all the equations you will need to calculate bond values

- Bond yields, including yield conventions, conversions and curves, for straightforward bullet bonds as well as for some of the more complicated bonds

- Risk and yield analysis, in particular, the concepts of duration, basis point value and convexity

Bond Characteristics

The Price of a Bond

The price or valuation of a bond in the markets is influenced by a number of factors including:

- The value of a government bond of similar maturity

- The bond coupon rate and frequency

- The maturity of the bond – the longer the period the riskier the investment

- The credit rating of the issuer

- The type of bond – straight, callable, puttable, sinking fund, index-linked, zero-coupon etc

- Whether the bond is registered or in bearer form – bearer bonds often have tax advantages

- The liquidity of the bond – the number of market-makers, the cost of transactions, market volatility etc

- The taxation situation of the bond – is the income taxed at source, at what rate and when?

As you can see, several of the factors influencing bond prices, as with financial instruments in general, involve elements of risk.

Bond Valuation and Bond Yields

The following model encompasses four basic types of risk and places their level of importance as concentric rings with the most important at the centre.

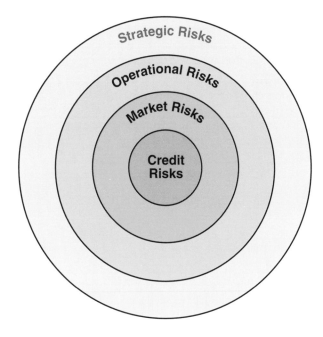

Each type of risk –

- **Credit**

- **Market**

- **Operational**

- **Strategic**

is now considered briefly.

Credit Risk

 Credit Risk is the risk that a counterparty will fail to honour its agreed obligations.

In other words the risk of default or delay in payments of coupons and/or the principal of the bond. Different rating agencies use different combinations of letters (uppercase and lowercase) and numbers to represent their rating order. (This is covered in detail in Section 6.)

Market Risk

 Market Risk results as a change in the value of a bond caused by any movements in the level or volatility of the current market yields or cost of money.

Within this type of risk there is the specific risk associated with liquidity. The **liquidity risk** is an assessment of the risk involved in trading an instrument quickly and in quantity without affecting its price significantly.

Credit and market risks are the two most important types of risk involved when considering trading bonds.

Operational risk covers matters such as:

- **Settlement** or **Herstatt risk** which arise from timing differences which may arise between receiving and delivering assets

- **Legal risk** which is concerned with contract enforcement

Strategic risk arises from the way in which trading is carried out by market players operating for their institutions.

REUTERS

Bond values incorporate an element of risk premium to reflect a particular bond's credit and liquidity risks which can be assessed from credit ratings, market activity etc. However, the assessment of market risk is different and involves the concepts of duration and convexity as a way of managing risk in bond trading – these concepts are discussed later in this section under the heading of *Bond Risk and Yield Analysis.*

The Reuters screen below describes a bond issued by the African Development Bank.

Your notes

Market conventions
This information can be used for yield and price calculations

Payments
This information can be used to assess **market risk**

Issue information
This information can be used to assess **liquidity risk**

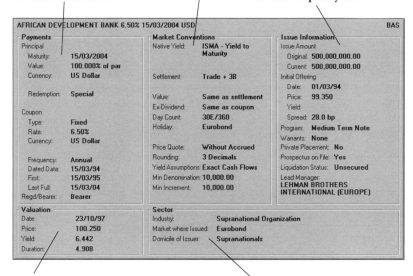

Valuation
The current bond value in price and yield terms.
Duration provides a measure of bond price risk.

Sector
Information on the issuer and the type of bond market

Other Bond Characteristics

At the time of issue the price of a bond is fixed according to the current market conditions. This price is dependent on a number of factors which are described later. Before looking at these factors you need to know the main characteristics of a bond and how they interrelate. The following characteristics are described, and where appropriate they are illustrated with examples:

- Principal and par
- Maturity
- Coupon
- Accrued interest

Principal and Par

The **Principal** is the **Face Amount** of a bond bought by an investor. Many bonds have a face value of $1000 but values of $5000 and $10,000 are also quite common.

The term **par** refers to **100%** of the face value. It is important to understand this term as the price of a bond is quoted as a **percentage of par**.

Example
If a $1000 bond is at par (100% of face value) then it is quoted at **100**.

If it is quoted at 98.5, it is priced at 98.5% of par which is $985. This bond is said to be trading at a **discount to par**.

If it is quoted at 102, it is priced at 102% of par which is $1020. This bond is said to be trading at a **premium to par**.

Why is par quoted as a percentage? Quoting as a percentage overcomes the problem of quoting more than one price for the various face values of a bond.

Maturity

The **Maturity** of a bond is the length of time elapsing between the issue date and when the bond is due for repayment, that is, when the final interest payment and the principal are returned to the investor. This process is known as **redemption**.

Most bonds have a known or specified maturity date; those without are called **perpetuals** or **irredeemables**.

The longer the life of a bond, the greater the perceived investment risk. This is because a bond with a long life, for example 30 years, is more susceptible to interest rate changes than shorter-term instruments. The longer the maturity of a bond the more volatile its price could be. Investors will normally require a higher return from a long-term bond to compensate for this volatility.

Not all bonds follow the normal pattern of maturity. Some bonds have **call privileges** which allow the issuer to redeem the bond before the scheduled maturity date. Other bonds have **sinking fund provisions** in which a prearranged portion of the debt is repaid prior to maturity.

Coupon

A **Coupon** is the periodic interest payment during the lifetime of a bond. In the normal situation the coupon is fixed for the life of the bond and is referred to as a **fixed income security**.

Payment of coupons can be quarterly, semi-annual or annual. The coupon is quoted as a percentage of par – the face value of the bond.

The reason these documents are called coupons is that many bonds are **bearer instruments** with the required number of coupons physically attached. In order to receive the interest payment each coupon must be detached from the bond and presented to the paying agent. It is assumed that bearer instruments belong to the person who holds them. Today, many bonds are registered in the holder's name and have no physical coupons. Instead, the holder receives automatic payment from the issuer which is a more convenient and secure method.

As has been mentioned the frequency of coupon payment varies. The common methods are:

- Annually for Eurobonds regardless of their currency

- Semi-annually in the UK and US government markets

Example
The owner of a $1000 Eurobond paying a 10% interest rate will receive $100 once a year. However if this was a $1000 US Treasury Bond paying the same interest rate, the owner would receive $50 every six months.

It is important to remember that not all bonds pay a coupon, for example, **zero coupon bonds**.

Example
A typical price of a 10 year zero coupon bond might be $20. On maturity the investor receives the par value – $100. The difference of $80 compensates the investor for the lack of coupons over the life of the bond.

Floating Rate Notes have a coupon that is reset at intervals, usually between 3 and 6 months, in relation to a benchmark such as LIBOR (London InterBank Offered Rate).

Example
A FRN may have a coupon of 10 **basis points** (bp) above LIBOR. As 100 bp = 1%, this bond would have a coupon of 0.1% above the prevailing LIBOR rate.

For a bond of a given rating the higher the coupon in relation to current interest rates, the more valuable it is and the higher its price.

Example
In year 1, an investor buys Bond X, a $1000 bond maturing in 20 years with a 10% coupon. In year 2, interest rates have gone down and the investor buys Bond Y with the same principal and maturity but with a coupon of 6%. What are the relative values of the bonds?

Bond X   Value = $1000 × 10% × 20 years = $2000

Bond Y   Value = $1000 × 6% × 20 years = $1200

This means at maturity Bond X is worth $800 more than Bond Y and it would therefore trade at a premium.

However if the interest rates had risen in year 2 to 13% rather than falling, then Bond Y would be worth $600 more than Bond X.

Accrued Interest

If a bond is sold before a coupon payment date then the coupon is lost to the seller. However, the buyer has to compensate the seller in proportion to the amount of time the bond has been held since the last coupon was paid. The amount of interest that has gathered since the last payment date is known as the **Accrued Interest**.

The value of accrued interest depends on calculating the fraction of the coupon period that has elapsed. This fraction is normally expressed in days divided by the number of days in the year:

- 365 for UK Gilts

- 360 for Eurobonds

Example

A $5m Eurobond with a 7% coupon paid on March 1st is sold on March 15th. How much accrued interest is the original owner entitled to?

> Accrued interest = Coupon as decimal ×
> fraction of year × face value

In this case accrued interest $= \dfrac{7}{100} \times \dfrac{14}{360} \times 5{,}000{,}000$

$= \$13611.11$

There are two further terms you need to know when dealing with accrued interest:

- **Clean price**. The price of a bond **without** the accrued interest. This is also called the **flat price**.

- **Dirty price**. The price of the bond **plus** the accrued interest. This is the invoice price and is also known as the **gross price**.

So the interest that accrues on a bond depends on the coupon rate, time passed since the last coupon payment and amount of the loan. This provides the starting point for the basic concepts of bond valuation.

Your notes

Bond Valuation

As stated, this section introduces and illustrates the basic concepts of bond valuation using simple examples and cash flow diagrams. In most cases the concepts involve calculations and each new formula introduced is numbered. You will also find a list of these formulae at the beginning of this section which you may find useful to photocopy in order to refer to, particularly as you progress through the section and for the Quick Quiz Questions. This section covers the following aspects of bond valuation:

- Rate of return

- Simple and compound interest

- Equivalent interest rates

- Present Value

- Day count method

- Accrued interest

- The concept of yield

- Bond prices

Before moving on use the space opposite to answer a few simple questions about investments – no answers are given because the following text covers everything you will need to know.

1. Would you rather receive $1000 today or $1000 in a year's time? Give the reason for your answer.

2. Do you know what the difference is between simple and compound interest? If you do, give a simple explanation.

3. Do you know why you would buy a bond which has a lower coupon than current interest rates? If you do, give a simple explanation.

Answer 1

Answer 2

Answer 3

Bond Valuation and Bond Yields

Rate of Return

Within the financial markets the **time value of money** is important. This means that the **Present Value (PV)** of money is worth **more** than its **Future Value (FV)**. For example, if you have savings of $1000 today – the present time – you have the opportunity to invest your savings and earn interest. But, if you are promised and receive a $1000 at a future date, that is all you will have.

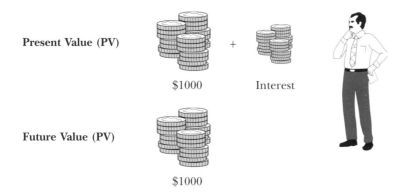

Present Value (PV)   +

$1000   Interest

Future Value (PV)

$1000

Obviously investors are interested in the future value of their investments and need some kind of indication to guide their investment decisions. The simplest guide is **return**. In effect, the return on an investment is the difference between the cost of buying and selling any financial instrument. An investor hopes that the selling price will be greater than the buying price but there is always an element of risk.

$$\text{Return} = (\text{Selling price} - \text{Buying price})$$

... Equation 1

Any calculation of return using Equation 1 gives no indication of performance. In other words how well is the instrument performing compared with other instruments? How attractive an investment is it?

To help overcome this difficulty, a return can be expressed as a **rate of return** which is a function of the buying price expressed as a **percentage** as shown in Equation 2.

$$\text{Rate of return} = \frac{\text{Return}}{\text{Buying price}} \times 100$$

$$= \left[\frac{(\text{Selling price} - 1)}{\text{Buying price}} \right] \times 100$$

... Equation 2

The rate of return provides some guide for the investor if returns are compared for **similar** maturity periods. But what if the maturity periods are different? For example, is a 10% rate of return over one month a better deal than an 8% rate over one year?

This problem is resolved using **annualised** rates of return which express any rate of return as a percentage for a **one year period** – as defined in Equation 3.

$$\text{Annualised rate of return as \%} = \frac{\text{Rate of return as \%}}{\text{Investment period in years}}$$

... Equation 3

The interest payments for bonds is stated as an annualised rate of return or coupon rate for the maturity of the bond. This means that the bond's future value can be calculated.

The greater the annualised rate of return and maturity period, the greater the future value and therefore the greater the return on the investment.

Simple and Compound Interest

In their most basic form, annualised rates of return are expressed as **simple interest rates**. Simple interest rates assume interest is paid at maturity regardless of maturity period. The Future Value (FV) of an investment with simple interest for a known Present Value (PV), Coupon rate (R) as a decimal and a maturity period in years expressed as n can be calculated using Equation 4.

$$FV = PV \times [1 + (R \times n)]$$

... Equation 4

The factor $[1 + (R \times n)]$ is sometimes known as the **future value factor**.

Example 1
What is the FV of a $10,000 bond with a simple interest rate of 6.375% with a maturity period of 18 months?

Using Equation 4:

$$FV = 10,000 \times [1 + (0.06375 \times 1.5)]$$

$$FV = \$10,956.25$$

The simple interest is therefore $956.25. The cash flow diagram opposite illustrates the situation.

In general it is important to remember the following:

- For a **given maturity period**, the **higher** the coupon rate, the **greater** the FV

- For a **given coupon rate**, the **longer** the maturity period, the **greater** the FV

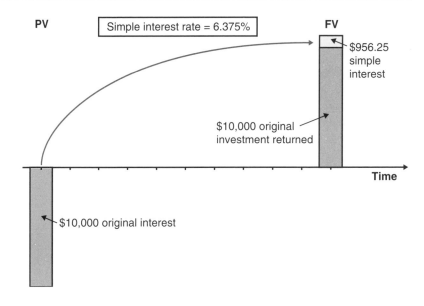

In practice, most bonds do not pay simple interest at maturity. Bonds pay interest at the end of an accrual period which is typically:

- Annually

- Semi-annually

- Quarterly

This means that interest may be earned on interest – in other words **compounded**.

Example 2

What is the FV of a $10,000 bond with a simple interest rate of 6.375% if the coupon payments are semi-annual? This means that interest earned after 6 and 12 months can be re-invested. For simplicity it is assumed that the re-investment rate is the same as for the bond – 6.375%.

Using Equation 4:

$$FV = 10,000 \times [1 + (0.06375 \times 0.5)] \dots ①$$

$$FV = \$10,318.75$$

The FV after 6 months now becomes the PV for the second investment period.

So at the end of the second 6 month period:

$$FV = 10,318.75 \times [1 + (0.06375 \times 0.5)] \dots ②$$

However, substituting ① in ② :

$$FV = 10,000 \times [1 + (0.06375 \times 0.5)] \times [1 + (0.06375 \times 0.5)]$$

$$FV = 10,000 \times [1 + (0.06375 \times 0.5)]^2$$

$$FV = \$10,647.66$$

By re-investing the interest from the first 6 month period an extra $10.16 has been earned over two simple interest payments of $318.75 x 2 = $637.50.

Following a similar logic, at the end of the third 6 month period:

$$FV = 10,000 \times [1 + (0.06375 \times 0.5)]^3$$

$$FV = \$10,987.05$$

The following cash flow chart may help you to understand the process.

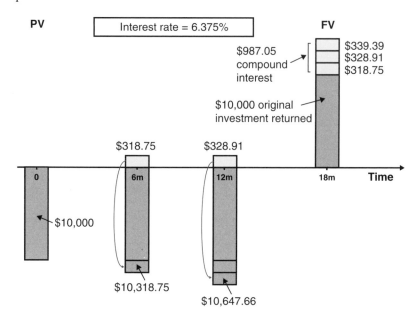

So by compounding the interest $987.05 of interest has been earned compared with the simple interest of $956.25 earned in Example 1.

The FV equation for compound interest can be generalised as Equation 5.

$$FV = PV \times \left(1 + \frac{R}{t}\right)^{nt}$$

... Equation 5

R = annualised coupon rate as a decimal
t = Number of coupons per year
n = Number of years to maturity
nt = Number of **coupon periods**

As you will see in the following sections it is useful to rearrange Equation 5 in terms of R and PV respectively.

$$R = t \times \left[\left(\frac{FV}{PV} \right)^{\frac{1}{nt}} - 1 \right]$$

... *Equation 6*

$$PV = \frac{FV}{\left(1 + \frac{R}{t} \right)^{nt}}$$

... *Equation 7*

Equivalent Interest Rates

In order to help investors to compare instruments on a direct basis accurately, **equivalent interest rates** can be used. These convert an original compound rate into another using a different convention. The following examples illustrate the use of equivalent interest rates.

Example 3 – To convert compound interest into simple interest
The FV of a $10,000 bond with an interest rate of 6.375% compounded was calculated as $10,987.05 in the previous example. What is the equivalent interest rate for the maturity period of 18 months?

By rearranging Equation 4:

$$R = \frac{\left(\frac{FV}{PV} - 1 \right)}{n}$$

$$R = \frac{\left(\frac{10,987.05}{10,000} - 1 \right)}{1.5}$$

$$R = 0.0658$$
$$= 6.58\%$$

This means that a bond with a maturity of 18 months paying semi-annual coupons with a rate of 6.375% is equivalent to a bond of the same maturity period having a simple interest rate of 6.58%

Bond Valuation and Bond Yields

Example 4 – To convert an annual compound rate to a semi-annual rate
This is a particularly important conversion as many government bonds pay semi-annual coupons whereas many corporate bonds and Eurobonds have annual payments. You are offered two bonds both having a face value of $1 million and a maturity period of five years. Which offers the best investment opportunity?

Bond	Interest rate, %	Coupon payment
A is a US T-Bond	7.00	Semi-annual
B is a Eurobond	7.05	Annual

To decide which is the better investment:
i) First calculate the FV for the Eurobond using Equation 5.

$$FV = 1,000,000 \times \left(1 + \frac{0.0705}{1}\right)$$
$$= \$1,405,831.79$$

ii) Using Equation 6 calculate the equivalent compound rate for the Eurobond.

$$R = 2 \times \left[\left(\frac{1,405,831.79}{1,000,000}\right)^{\frac{1}{5 \times 2}} - 1\right]$$

$$R = 2 \times (1.03465 - 1)$$

$$= 0.06930 = 6.93\%$$

As you can see the T-Bond with a 7.00% rate is a better investment in terms of return than the Eurobond – this simple example highlights the importance of equivalent interest rates.

Your notes

Present Value

As you have seen the Present Value (PV) of a bond is **not** always equal to its par or face value. A bond can trade at a **premium** or at a **discount**. The PV reflects how the fixed coupon instrument compares with current market interest rates and the frequency of coupon repayments.

In the simplest case for an instrument with compound interest, the PV is the amount that would need to be invested today to provide a FV of cash flows to be received for the required coupon frequency rate and maturity period. The following example illustrates a simple future cash flow payment.

Example 5

What is the PV of a bond having a single FV payment of $1.5 million in 2 years at an annualised interest rate of 6.75%?

The PV can be calculated using Equation 4 and rearranging:

$$PV \ = \ \frac{FV}{\Big(1 \ + \ (R \times n)\Big)}$$

$$= \ \frac{1,500,000}{\Big(1 + (0.0675 \times 2)\Big)}$$

$$= \ \$1,321,585.90$$

So approximately $1.32 million needs to be invested today for a single future payment of $1.5 million in 2 years time if invested at 6.75%.

The process is illustrated in the cash flow chart opposite.

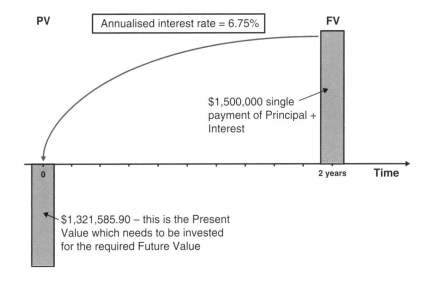

In general it is important to remember the following:

- For a **given investment period** and **FV**:
  A **higher** rate of interest requires a **lower** PV
  A **lower** rate of interest requires a **higher** PV

- For a **given interest rate** and **FV**:
  A **longer** maturity period requires a **lower** PV
  A **shorter** maturity period requires a **higher** PV

The process of determining the PV of a FV is often referred to as **discounting a future cash flow**.

As for the interest calculations discussed so far, most bonds do not have a single FV payment but consist of a stream of coupon payments over the defined investment or maturity period. In other words there is a cash flow stream which you have seen illustrated in diagrams previously.

In principle the process of calculating the PV for a stream of cash flows is the same as for the simple case, except the PV calculation is required for **each** cash flow in the stream. In order to make these calculations the coupon frequency and the maturity period must be known.

The PV of a cash stream is the sum of each discounted PV in the stream. The process is shown in the diagram here:

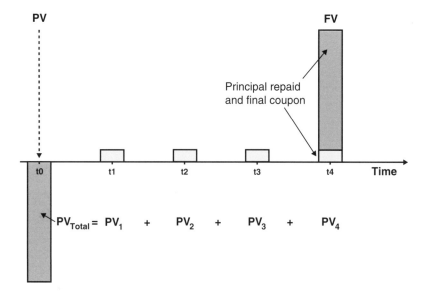

Mathematically, the PV for the general calculation of a bond with a series of cash flows is given by Equation 8.

$$PV_{Total} = \sum_{i=1}^{N} \frac{FV_i}{\left(1 + \dfrac{R}{t}\right)^{nt}}$$

... *Equation 8*

i = The ith cash flow – a number from 1 onwards
n = Number of years to maturity
N = Number of cash flows in stream
t = Number of coupons per year

In practice it may be easier to use the following Equation 9:

$$PV_{Total} = \frac{C/t}{(1 + R/t)} + \frac{C/t}{(1 + R/t)^2} + \ldots + \frac{P + C/t}{(1 + R/t)^N}$$

... *Equation 9*

P = Principal
C = Coupon rate as a %
R = Rate of return as a decimal
t = Number of coupons per year

Day Count Method

In all the examples used so far the assumption has been made that bonds are bought or sold for settlement dates which coincide with coupon dates. The maturity date of a bond is the final date on which the principal and any final interest payment is made. Coupon payment dates are fixed on an annual, semi-annual or quarterly date according to the maturity date specified at issue.

As it is not usually the case that a trade is settled exactly on a coupon date, a **value date** – the date at which the bond is valued – must be set for which the PV can be calculated for a future cash flow.

Once the maturity and value dates are known, the difference between them determines the exact investment period. The method of determining the length of time between the dates is known as the **day count** or **day basis**. It will probably come as no surprise to learn that there are a number of different methods by which days are counted in different bond markets and for different instruments. This period is also used to calculate the **accrued interest** for the bond. The chart opposite indicates the day count/day basis conventions most commonly used in the bond markets.

Example 6
A bond with a semi-annual coupon has payment dates of 7th April and 7th October each year. As an investor you buy this bond which is due for settlement on 15th October. Assuming the year is not a leap year, calculate the fraction of the coupon period remaining for the following day count methods. The answers are given on the next page.

a) Actual/Actual

b) 30/360

Convention	Explanation	Market
Actual/ Actual	Actual number of days in the investment period over the actual number of days in a year – 366 for a leap year	US T-Bonds
Actual/ 365	Actual number of days in the investment period over 365 days for a year – regardless of whether or not a leap year	UK gilts
30/360	Assumes that every calendar month has 30 days and 360 days for a year regardless of actual number of days in both. If D1 = 31, set D1 = 30. If D1 = 30 and D2 = 31, set D2 = 30.	US Corporate bonds
30E/360	This is almost the same as the 30/360 count except it does **not** include an end-month rule. If D1 = 31, set D1 = 30. If D2 = 31, set D2 = 30. Occasionally this shows **1 day less** than 30/360.	Eurobonds

Example 6 – Answers

a) **Actl/Actl**

Number of days left in October	= 31 – 15	= 16
Number of days November to 7th April	= 30+31+31+28+31+7	
	= 158	
Total number of days to next coupon date	= 158 + 16	= **174**
Total number of days in 6 month period	= 174 + 8	= **182**
Fraction of coupon period remaining	= **174/182**	
	= **0.9560**	

b) **30/360**

Number of days left in October	= 30 – 15	= 15
Number of days November to 7th April	= (5 x 30)+7	
	= 157	
Total number of days to next coupon date	= 157 + 15	= **172**
Total number of days in 6 month period	= 6 x 30	= **180**
Fraction of coupon period remaining	= **172/180**	
	= **0.9555**	

As you can see there is a small difference between the fractions of coupon periods remaining. As you will see in the next section, it is important to know which day count basis is being used or should be used as it affects PV calculations and amounts of interest due.

The **general bond pricing formula** can be derived from Equation 9 and takes into account the fractional coupon period. This important equation is Equation 10.

$$PV_{Total} = \frac{C/t}{(1 + R/t)^{a}} + \frac{C/t}{(1 + R/t)^{a+1}} + \ldots + \frac{P + C/t}{(1 + R/t)^{a+n}}$$

... Equation 10

P	=	Principal
C	=	Coupon rate as a %
R	=	Rate of return as a decimal
t	=	Number of coupons per year
a	=	Fractional coupon period
n	=	Number of whole coupons remaining to maturity

Accrued Interest

If an investor buys a bond and the value date coincides with its coupon date, then the time to the next interest payment is one full period.

However, as has been mentioned, most bonds in the secondary markets have value dates such that bonds are traded between coupon dates. In these cases it would be unfair if the buyer received all the interest due for the coupon period. The seller is compensated therefore for any interest due which has accumulated since the last coupon payment – this is known as accrued interest.

Accrued interest can be calculated using Equation 11.

$$\text{Accrued interest} = \text{Principal} \times \frac{R}{t} \times \frac{D}{B}$$

... Equation 11

R = Coupon rate as a decimal
t = Number of coupons per year
D = Number of days in coupon period
B = Number of days in basis for coupon

Example 7

A US Corporate bond has a face value of $1 million and a 6.00% coupon paid semi-annually on 15th February and 15th August. An investor buys the bond with a value date of 20th August. The day count method for this bond is 30/360. What is the accrued interest for which the buyer has to compensate the seller?

Using the 30/360 day count, the number of days of accumulated interest is 20 – 15 = 5. The number of days in the coupon period is 6 x 30 = 180.

Therefore:

$$\text{Accrued interest} = 1,000,000 \times \frac{0.06}{2} \times \frac{5}{180}$$

$$= \$833.33$$

This example illustrates how accrued interest depends on the day count method but also how accrued interest is important in the calculation of the market value of a bond.

Accrued interest for a bond can be seen on the Reuters **Bond Calculator** page below.

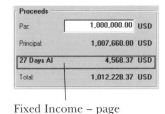

These screens are for the same US T-Bond taken on the same day

Fixed Income – page

Page for a specific market maker

The Concept of Yield

A bond is an IOU and as such an investor is lending money to an issuer. The important terms and conditions for the loan are detailed in the bond's **indenture**. For example, terms such as total principal of the issue, maturity date, coupon dates etc. It is important to remember that the coupon rate specified is the **annualised interest rate** to be paid.

Once all the details are known, the future cash flow is known over the maturity period. However, as you have already seen the market price of a bond is not always its issue price and market interest rates for money will almost certainly differ from the coupon rate.

In order to be able to compare the relative attractiveness of bonds, investors need to compare **annualised rates of return**. The term used to describe such an annualised rate of return for a bond traded in the secondary market is its **yield** or **Yield To Maturity (YTM)**.

The **Yield** or **YTM** is the annualised interest rate that makes the Present Value (PV) of a bond's future cash flows equal to its **market value**.

Yield is most often encountered in two ways:

- To calculate the PV of a bond when the yield is known

- To calculate a yield when the PV of a bond is known

Example 8

A bond with a par value of 100 and a 6.00% semi-annual coupon has payment dates of 7th April and 7th October each year. As an investor you buy this bond which is due for settlement on 15th October and there are 18 months to maturity. The day count method for the bond is Actl/Actl and the fractional coupon period has already been calculated as 0.956 in Example 6.

At the time of buying the bond the current fixed income interest rate or yield for the maturity period is 7.00%. What is the PV or market value of the bond? In other words how much should the investor expect to pay for the bond?

The method of calculation involves Equation 10 and assumes that the 6 monthly coupons are re-invested at an annual rate of 7.00%.

The cash flows are discounted as follows:

Coupon date	Interest period	Payment	PV	
7th April	0.956	3.00	$\dfrac{3.00}{(1+0.035)^{0.956}}$	= 2.90
7th October	1.956	3.00	$\dfrac{3.00}{(1+0.035)^{1.956}}$	= 2.81
7th April	2.956	103.00	$\dfrac{103.00}{(1+0.035)^{2.956}}$	= 93.04
			PV_{Total}	= 98.75

This means that the PV of the bond is 98.75. In other words a $1000 par bond would cost $987.50 today. In effect this means that the 6.00% coupon plus the capital gain on the investment at maturity equals a total return of 7.00%.

This method of calculating PV assumes that the coupon re-investment rate is the same for all cash flows which may not be the case. As you will appreciate PV calculations involving variable re-investment rates can get quite complicated.

Market players often refer to the total PV, which includes accrued interest, of a bond's future cash flows as its **market value**.

As you have seen the accrued interest is **independent** of market factors such as yield – it is only dependent on the coupon rate and the investment period.

Market players therefore prefer to separate a market value into its two components as given in Equation 12.

Market Value (MV) = Principal Value (P) + Accrued Interest (A)

... Equation 12

Therefore:

$$MV = P + A$$

$$P = MV - A$$

It is important to recognise that the principal value is **not** the same as the face value or principal of a bond. It is the portion of a bond's market value which is sensitive to market factors such as interest rates.

Bond Prices

As a bond approaches a coupon payment the holder expects to receive interest and the PV of the bond increases. However, if an investor buys a bond but does **not** have the right to receive the next dividend, for example, a UK gilt, the bond is said to go **ex-dividend**. In such circumstances the buyer has to be compensated by adjusting the bond price. After the ex-dividend date, which is prior to the coupon date by a specified number of days, the bond is said to trade **flat**.

A bond price is also affected by its face value. In order to standardise prices and overcome technical fluctuations which arise from coupon payments, the markets use the following prices.

- **Dirty price**. This is the full market value of a bond **including** accrued interest expressed as a percentage of the face value. This is the simplest way of expressing a bond price but is less commonly used because accrued interest can be calculated separately and is independent of market factors.

- **Clean price**. This is the full market value which has been **"cleansed"** of the accrued interest expressed as a percentage of face value. This is usually the price quoted by market makers.

The following chart summarises the terms used for trading bonds with relation to their face value.

Market price	= 100	less than 100	more than 100
Bond price	Par	Discount	Premium

Example 9

The method of calculating the PV of the bond used in Example 8 was for its clean price as the accrued interest for the period 7th to 15th October – 8 days – were excluded from the PV calculation.

The accrued interest for these 8 days is:

$$\text{Accrued interest} \quad = \quad 3.00 \ \text{x} \ \frac{8}{182}$$

$$= \quad 0.131868 \text{ or } \$0.13 \text{ per } \$100 \text{ face value}$$

Therefore the bond's clean price = 98.75
and the bond's dirty price   = 98.75 + 0.13 = 98.88

It is worth remembering that, at present, both US and UK government bond markets usually quote prices on a clean basis to the nearest one thirty-second of face value not as a decimal. Market makers and dealers quote two-way prices in the secondary markets. For example, a UK gilt price may be quoted as:

99 - 22 / -24

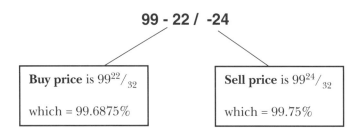

Buy price is $99^{22}/_{32}$	**Sell price** is $99^{24}/_{32}$
which = 99.6875%	which = 99.75%

Sometimes fractional prices are quoted in terms of sixty-fourths, for example, **99 - 28+**. This means:

$$99^{28}/_{32} \ + \ ^1/_{64} \ = \ 99^{57}/_{64}$$

The following relationships are important in the bond markets, particularly in understanding the inherent risk in trading:

- The **higher** the market value of a bond, the **lower** its PV and therefore the **lower** its clean price

- When interest rates **rise**, PV and bond prices **fall**

- When interest rates **fall**, PV and bond prices **rise**

Bond Yields

The Relationship Between Bond Price and Yield

The yield or **Yield-To-Maturity (YTM)** of a bond is the annualised rate of return comprising an amount determined by the markets – the **market value** – and an amount determined by the bond – the **accrued interest**.

Yield-To-Maturity (YTM) is the uniform discount rate at which the present value of a bond's future cash flows equals the bond's **dirty price**.

As you have seen there is an **inverse** relationship between bond prices, their PVs and interest rates – as one rises the other falls. There is also an **inverse relationship between bond price and yield** – as prices rise, yields fall and vice versa. In effect the price of a bond in the secondary market depends on the market rate of return on new debt at the time of the trade.

At the time of issue most bonds are issued with a coupon rate close to the market return for instruments of comparable maturity and risk. This usually means that bonds are issued at or near par.

Once traded in the secondary market the bond yield will fluctuate depending on market conditions. One simple measure of yield is **current yield** which is useful for comparing bonds in a similar way to which dividend yields are used to compare equities. Current yield can be calculated using Equation 13.

$$\text{Current yield} = \frac{\text{Coupon rate}}{\text{Clean price}} \times 100$$

$$\dots \textit{Equation 13}$$

Example 10

The bond used in Example 9 had a clean price of 98.75 and a coupon rate of 6.00%. What is its current yield?

$$\text{Current yield} = \frac{6.00}{98.75} \times 100$$

$$= 6.08\%$$

Current yield provides a simple way of comparing bonds but it ignores the fact that a bond may have been bought at a premium or a discount. At maturity the original bond price can represent a gain or loss on the face value. The **Adjusted Current Yield (ACY)** takes this situation into account using Equation 14.

$$\textbf{ACY} = \textbf{Current yield} + \frac{(\textbf{100 - Clean price})}{\textbf{Years to maturity}}$$

$$\dots \textit{Equation 14}$$

Example 11

The bond used in Example 10 had a clean price of 98.75, a current yield of 6.08% and a maturity period of 18 months. What is the bond's ACY?

$$\text{ACY} = 6.08 + \frac{(100 - 98.75)}{1.5}$$

$$= 6.91\%$$

Bond Valuation and Bond Yields

ACY is a simple calculation and is used in some markets such as Japanese bonds where this type of yield is known as **Japanese simple yield**.

The Reuters screen below displays details of domestic Japanese corporate bonds which use this type of yield. In this screen you can see details of a domestic bond from **Hino Motors Ltd**.

Yield convention

HINO MOTORS LTD 3.45% 11/18/1999 JPY		BAS
Payments	**Market Conventions**	**Issue Information**
Principal	Native Yield: Japanese - Simple Yield	Issue Amount
Maturity: 11/18/1999		Original: 15,000,000,000.00
Value: 100.000% of par		Current: 15,000,000,000.00
Currency: Japanese Yen	Settlement: Trade + 7B	Initial Offering
		Date: 11/18/93
Redemption: Bullet	Value: Same as settlement	Price: 100.0000000
	Ex-Dividend: Same as coupon	Yield: 3.450
Coupon	Day Count: Actual/365	Spread:
Type: Fixed	Holiday: Japan	Program: N/A
Rate: 3.45%		Warrants: None
Currency: Japanese Yen	Price Quote: Without Accrued	Private Placement: No
	Rounding: 7 Decimals	Prospectus on File: No
Frequency: Semi-annual	Yield Assumptions: Exact Cash Flows	Liquidation Status: Unsecured
Dated Date: 11/18/93	Min Denomination: 1,000,000.00	Lead Manager:
First: 5/18/94	Min Increment: 1,000,000.00	
Last Full: 11/18/99		
Regd/Bearer: Both		
Valuation	**Sector**	
Date: 12/10/97	Industry: Automobiles	
Price: 104.3332028	Market where Issued: Japan	
Yield: 1.138	Domicile of Issuer: Japan	
Duration: 1.855		

Domestic bond

However, ACY is still limited as it does not take into account the timing of a bond's cash flows.

As you have seen the Yield To Maturity is the annualised rate of return of a bond held to maturity. However, this does not take into account a bond's future cash flows which assumes that the coupons are re-invested at the same rate of return.

The YTM can be calculated using Equation 10.

$$PV_{Total} = \frac{C/t}{(1 + R/t)^a} + \frac{C/t}{(1 + R/t)^{a+1}} + \ldots + \frac{P + C/t}{(1 + R/t)^{a+n}}$$

... Equation 10

In this case the PV value – the dirty price – is known and the value for R – in this case the YTM – is determined by trial-and -error or more often using a calculator or computer.

It is worth remembering that YTM is a theoretical measure of return based on a constant re-investment rate for coupon payments. However, in practice this situation is unlikely; the price of 1 year money is unlikely to be the same for 2, 5 and 10 year money.

When pricing a bond varying re-investment rates could be used in Equation 10 or cash flows could be calculated at different rates. Both of these calculations are performed for analysing yields.

YTM is a useful means by which investors can compare returns implied in different bond prices or for determining fair prices for bonds with comparable returns.

Yield Conventions

Not all bond markets use the same conventions for expressing yield. You will probably encounter all of the following conventions at some time.

- **Current yield**

- **Adjusted Current Yield** or **Japanese Simple Yield**

- **YTM** or **ISMA YTM**. The ISMA YTM specifies the ISMA yield as the discount rate that makes the sum of PVs of all assumed future cash flows equal to the price of the bond plus accrued interest – the dirty price. This definition is identical to that previously described for YTM in Equation 10. You can display information on yield using the **Help** facility in Reuters 3000 Fixed Income.

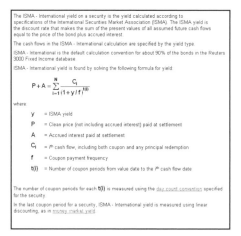

The ISMA - International yield on a security is the yield calculated according to specifications of the International Securities Market Association (ISMA). The ISMA yield is the discount rate that makes the sum of the present values of all assumed future cash flows equal to the price of the bond plus accrued interest.

The cash flows in the ISMA - International calculation are specified by the yield type.

ISMA - International is the default calculation convention for about 90% of the bonds in the Reuters 3000 Fixed Income database.

ISMA - International yield is found by solving the following formula for yield:

$$P + A = \sum_{i=1}^{N} \frac{C_i}{(1 + y/f)^{t(i)}}$$

where:

y = ISMA yield
P = Clean price (not including accrued interest) paid at settlement
A = Accrued interest paid at settlement
C_i = i^{th} cash flow, including both coupon and any principal redemption
f = Coupon payment frequency
$t(i)$ = Number of coupon periods from value date to the ith cash flow date

The number of coupon periods for each $t(i)$ is measured using the day count convention specified for the security.

In the last coupon period for a security, ISMA - International yield is measured using linear discounting, as in money market yield.

- **Greenwell-Montagu (weekend) Yield**. This method of calculating yield is similar to that used for ISMA YTM but takes into account the possibility that a coupon date falls on a holiday or weekend. In such circumstances the interest is not paid until the next business day but the investor is **not** compensated for this payment delay. This means that the yield is slightly reduced compared with the ISMA YTM. UK gilts use this type of yield.

The Reuters screens below display the type of yield used for the bond in the **market conventions** panel.

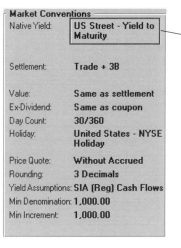

The **US Street** yield is the ISMA International yield with the day count 30/360 and coupon frequency as semi-annual

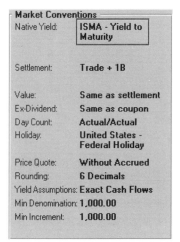

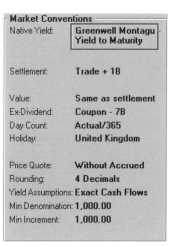

Yield Conversions

In the previous section, under *Equivalent Interest Rates*, the importance of converting annual rates into semi-annual rates was discussed in order to compare bonds on an equal standing.

A similar situation exists when comparing YTMs for annual and semi-annual coupon paying bonds. It is usual to quote a semi-annual YTM for a semi-annual bond and annual YTM for an annual bond. However, this is not always the case – Italian government bonds pay semi-annual coupons but market-makers often quote yields on these bonds on an annual basis.

There are two equations you need to know for the required conversions – Equations 15 and 16.

$$R_A = \left[\left(1 + \frac{R_S}{2}\right)^2\right] - 1$$

... Equation 15

$$R_S = 2 \times \left[\sqrt{(1 + R_A)} - 1\right]$$

... Equation 16

R_A = Annual YTM as a decimal
R_S = Semi-annual YTM as a decimal

You may find the chart below useful in calculations.

From ➡	To ➡	Use ➡
Semi-annual	Annual	$R_A = \left[\left(1 + \frac{R_S}{2}\right)^2\right] - 1$
Annual	Semi-annual	$R_S = 2 \times \left[\sqrt{(1 + R_A)} - 1\right]$

Example 12

A US Corporate bond pays an annual coupon and has a yield quoted at 6.75%. An investor needs to compare the YTM of this bond with that of a US T-Bond which has semi-annual coupons paying the same rate. What is the equivalent annual YTM for the semi-annual US T-Bonds?

Using Equation 15:

$$R_A = \left[\left(1 + \frac{0.0675}{2}\right)^2\right] - 1$$

$$R_A = 0.06864 = 6.86\%$$

The difference between these YTMs is 6.86 – 6.75 = 0.11% which is significant in investment terms.

Most market players would express this difference as a **yield spread** between the two bonds described in terms of **basis points**.

1 Basis Point (bp) = One hundredth of one percent

= 0.01 x 0.01 = 0.0001

In the example above, the spread is 11bp–11/100ths of a percentage point.

Yield Curves

One of the major market factors in valuing a bond is to compare its value with that of a **benchmark** bond of a similar maturity. Benchmark instruments are normally government securities because they are usually considered to be free of credit risk and usually government bond markets are large and liquid.

In order to compare bond yields over a whole range of maturities a **yield curve** of benchmark instruments is constructed. This plot displays graphically the relationship between interest rates for government securities at different maturities having the same credit risk and is often called the **term structure of interest rates**.

In practice the interest rate on these benchmark instruments is the YTM and so yields are plotted against maturities. A line of best fit is drawn through the points producing a number of possible shapes which are illustrated here.

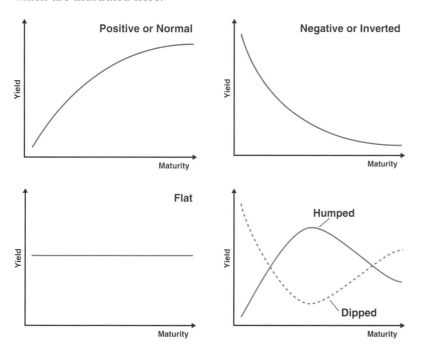

Most yield curves are positive or normal and show that as maturity increases so does the yield. The result on bond values is that they normally follow the same pattern thus keeping the risk/reward ratio constant.

Yield curves represent market expectations about future interest rates, government policy, liquidity of markets etc and there are a number of economic theories concerning yield curves which will not be discussed here.

Yield curves provide investors with a simple way of determining investment strategies.

If investors expect interest rates to rise in the next 12 months, then they will look for higher rates for long-term securities to compensate for losing the opportunity to invest at higher rates in the near future.

If, on the other hand, investors believe that interest rates will fall in the near future, then they will lock-in long-term loans and benefit as rates fall.

Unless the yield curve for benchmark government securities is flat, which is most uncommon, then yields for different maturities are different. In calculating YTMs for bonds the assumption was made that coupon payments were re-invested at the same rate as the coupon. This obviously is not the case. Is there a better way of plotting yield curves to overcome this problem?

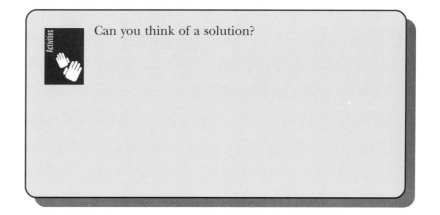

Can you think of a solution?

The solution is to use **zero-coupon** bonds. These bonds pay no coupons over their lifetimes and as such are sold at a deep discount. However, as you are probably aware it is possible to **strip** bonds into their component bond and coupon payments thus generating a series of zero-coupon bonds.

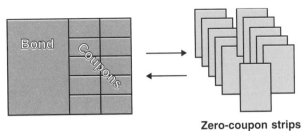

Zero-coupon strips

Zero-coupon government bonds are not necessarily issued. However, for many bonds strips are permitted but not necessarily for the whole maturity range. Zero-coupon yields are also known as **spot yields** which are YTMs for securities which pay no coupons during their lives.

To overcome the shortcomings of ordinary yield curves a **theoretical zero-coupon yield curve** or **theoretical spot rate curve** is constructed for the term structure of interest rates for the required range of government securities. The Reuters screens below display both benchmark yield and zero-coupon yield curves.

30 year US T-Bond   10 year UK gilt

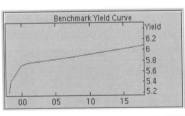

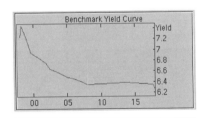

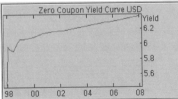

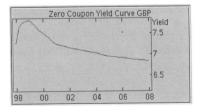

Total Return Analysis

In the section on *Bond Characteristics* the annualised rate of return was described as one of the factors investors consider in deciding on the attractiveness of a particular bond as an investment. Calculations involving YTM produce **expected** measures of return whereas the **actual** rate of return is often termed the **total rate of return**.

Components of Total Return

There are a number of components including the following:

- **Holding period**
  Implicit in the calculations for FV discussed so far has been the assumption that the bond is held to maturity. For many investors this is an unlikely event. For such market players YTM is merely a way of selecting the most attractive bond for investment and the actual return will depend on the length of time the bond is held.

- **Market value**
  The actual return received for a bond is clearly influenced by the value at which the bond is sold at the end of the holding period.

- **Re-investment rate**
  It should be clear by now from the discussion on YTM and yield curves that coupon payments will not be re-invested during the lifetime of the bond at the same rate. The fluctuation in these rates can affect dramatically the actual rate of return.

Total Return Measures

There are two measures which are commonly used:

- **Historical total return**
  This measures the performance of a bond over an historical period during which the bond was actually held using actual re-investment income and capital gains to calculate an annualised rate of return. Historical total return can be calculated using Equation 4 or 5 as follows:

$$FV = PV \times [1 + (R \times n)]$$

... Equation 4

$$FV = PV \times \left(1 + \frac{R}{t}\right)^{nt}$$

... Equation 5

PV = Total money spent – price + accrued interest on settlement date

FV = Total money received on sale of bond

nt = Number of coupon periods is calculated from the holding period – the actual number of days the bond is held

R = Interest rate which is the **historical total return**

- **Horizon total return**
  This measures the performance of a bond to a future date which uses assumptions for re-investment rates and capital gains based on the markets to calculate an annualised rate of return. The calculation is the same as for historical total return except the re-investment rates and market rates are assumed instead of actual. Calculations of horizon total return or **horizon analysis** are carried out by investors who wish to incorporate their views/expectations over near-term time horizons to gauge the performance of a particular bond.

Yields for Complicated Bonds

So far all of the examples used to illustrate cash flows have been for straight bonds with bullet repayments of principal at maturity. Although many new issues are straights, as you are probably aware by now, there are many different ways in which bonds can be issued. This section describes briefly some of the more common types of complicated bonds and how their yields are affected. The bonds covered here are:

- Callable bonds

- Puttable bonds

- Sinking fund bonds

- Index-linked/inflation-indexed bonds

- Convertible bonds

- Bonds with warrants

Callable Bonds

In this case the issuer can redeem the bond before the maturity date specified at issue. However, most bonds of this type have a **call protection period** which is the period from issuance to the first date on which the issuer can exercise the right to redeem the bond.

There are two ways in which callable bonds can be exercised – **American** or **European** style. In the case of American style, once the call protection period has ended the issuer can exercise the bond at any time. European style callable bonds can only be exercised on specific dates. The chart below illustrates the difference between the styles.

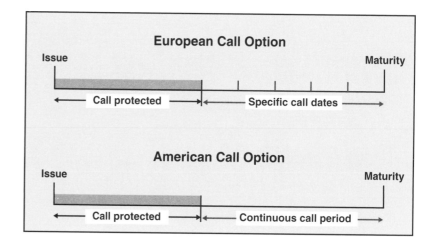

Yield to Call

As there is some uncertainty concerning the eventual redemption date of a callable bond it is termed **call risk**. Market players try to take into account the effect of early redemption if a call is exercised in **yield to call** calculations. The yield to call can be calculated when the first **call date** and **call price** are used instead of the **maturity date** and **par redemption price**. A callable bond can also have a **yield to worst** which is the lowest of yields calculated to each call date and maturity. Issuers generally retire debt early when it is financially advantageous. In other words when it is cheaper to retire old debt and issue new debt at a lower coupon.

Using the **Bond Calculator** page under the Risk/Return tab in Reuters 3000 Fixed Income it is possible to calculate Yield to Call (YTC) and Yield to Worst (YTW) values in the **Additional Yields** panel. The Reuters displays here are for a callable bond issued by **Tenet Healthcare Corporation** and providing Yield to Call (YTC) and Yield to Worst (YTW) values.

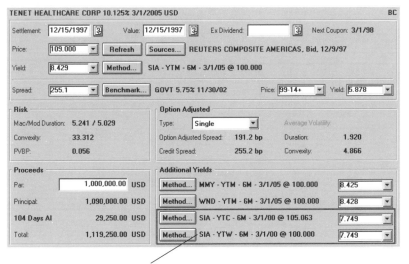

Yield to Call and
Yield to Worst values

Puttable Bonds

Puttable bonds give the investor the right, but not the obligation, to redeem the bond at a specific price on a specific date before scheduled maturity.

Yield to Put

The **yield to put** can be calculated when the first **put date** and **put price** are used instead of the **maturity date** and **par redemption price**. When a puttable bond is trading above par, then it is in the interests of investors to hold the bonds until maturity. If the bonds are trading below par, then investors would be wise to calculate the yield to put and assess their position. A puttable bond can also have a **yield to worst** which is the highest of yields calculated to each put date and maturity.

The Reuters displays here are for a puttable bond issued by **Coca-Cola Enterprises Inc**. and provide Yield to Put (YTP) values.

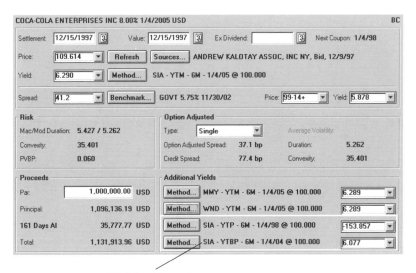

Yield to Put values

Sinking Fund Bonds

Investors buying sinking fund bonds face two uncertainties:

- The amount of any future cash flow

- The length of time of any future cash flow

Yield to Average Life

One method of calculating the yield on a bond involving a series of principal repayments is to use the yield to average life. The method involves determining the average life of a bond by weighting the time to each future principal date by the amount paid on that date. The results are summed and the sum is divided by the total principal amount paid. In other words the method converts a sinking fund bond into a straight bond.

The Reuters displays here are for a sinking fund bond issued by **Rohm & Haas Co** and provide the Yield to Average Life (YTAL) value.

Yield to Average Life (YTAL) value

Index-linked/Inflation-indexed Bonds

The coupon rates for this type of bond are periodically reset based on the percentages change in an inflation index between coupon reset dates. In addition, most types of index-linked bonds also adjust the principal at redemption for inflation, although not necessarily.

In order to curb the effect of potential volatility in index rates, many index-linked bonds have **ceilings** or **caps** and **floor** values which prevent the index rate moving too high or too low.

The real YTM is calculated by adjusting each cash flow for inflation. A service such as Reuters allows the user to calculate yields for different scenarios for changes in the index being used. In these Reuters screens, the bond is a UK index-linked gilt and the detail shows yields for different scenarios for changes in the index being used.

The RPI value is indicated here

This Reuters service allows the user to calculate yields for different scenarios by changing conditions here

Floating Rate Notes

One disadvantage of fixed rate coupon payments is that as interest rates rise then the value of bonds fall – this inverse relationship has been discussed previously.

A Floating Rate Note (FRN) has a coupon which changes periodically based on a fixed spread – positive or negative – linked to a reference rate which is often LIBOR or US T-Bills but can be a commodity index such as for oil. Often there is a cap/floor placed on this reference rate.

Since the coupon reset adjusts the cash flow stream to be in line with current interest rate levels, FRNs typically trade at or near to par on reset dates. Institutional investors use FRNs as hedges against rising rates.

Inverse floating rate issues have coupons that change in the opposite direction to the reference index. In bullish markets when interest rates are falling, the coupon on an inverse floater rises; in a bearish market when interest rates are rising, inverse floater coupons fall. Inverse floaters are used by market players to speculate on interest rates.

FRN YTM

A bond which has a coupon rate which is reset periodically means that the interest rate is only known with certainty during the current coupon period.

The value of the remaining future coupons has to be estimated before a YTM can be calculated. By 'guessing' and substituting in the formula for yield a value is obtained which in essence converts the FRN into a straight bond. Such estimated YTMs for FRNs can be highly subjective and uncertain.

Convertible Bonds

Most convertible bonds are corporate bonds which allow the holder to convert the bond into equity at some point. However, some government convertible bonds allow conversion into further debt instruments.

For the more usual case of conversion into equity, if the bond is held the investor receives coupon and principal payments as with a conventional straight bond. In such circumstances it is possible to calculate the total PV of the cash flows as in the general case. The PV calculated thus is termed the convertible bond's **investment value**.

If the conversion feature of a convertible bond is considered worthless, then the investment value is the **minimum** value of the bond.

If an investor converts a bond, then the loan is exchanged for equity – shares in the issuing organisation. The bond issue indenture states the terms for conversion either as a **conversion ratio** or as a **conversion price**. The conversion ratio fixes the number of shares the bond can be converted into, therefore the price per share may vary. By fixing the conversion price per share the conversion ratio may vary on conversion.

If the current market price of shares in the organisation are known then the bond can be valued on the basis of the current value of the number of shares which would be received on conversion. This is known as the bond's **parity price**.

> **Parity price = Conversion ratio x Current share price**

Once calculated market players can compare the parity price with the bond's market value.

The price of a convertible bond in the secondary market therefore depends on the bond's investment value, its parity price and the market's perception about the future of the issuing organisation.

Bonds with Warrants

This type of bond is usually a corporate bond which permits the bond holder to buy shares in the issuing organisation by exercising a long-term call option – a **warrant**. The warrant gives the holder the right, but not the obligation to buy shares. A warrant involves new equity capital for the issuer and is therefore different from a convertible bond which involves an exchange of debt for equity.

The shares acquired on exercise of a warrant are usually that of the issuing organisation and therefore dilute the share value of existing shares. It is important to recognise that although warrants are long-term call options they are not the same as exchange **traded options** in shares which involve options on **existing** shares in the organisation.

The value of a bond with warrants comprises two elements:

- The fixed income value of the bond which can be as for a conventional bond

- The equity value derived from the value of the warrant

Warrants are valued using two measures – **premium** and **gearing**.

The warrant **premium** is the extent to which the cost of acquiring a share through exercise of the warrant exceeds the share's current market price.

The premium can be calculated using the following equation:

$$\text{Premium} = \left(\frac{\text{Exercise price} + \text{Per share price of warrant}}{\text{Current share market price}} - 1 \right) \times 100$$

Because a warrant is the right to buy shares, the warrant price will always be less than the market price of the underlying shares – otherwise there would be no attraction in buying the warrant. So what attracts an investor to buying warrants?

Warrant **gearing** expresses how many warrants may be bought for the current market price of a **single** share. The gearing can be calculated using the following equation:

$$\text{Gearing} = \frac{\text{Current share price}}{\text{Current warrant price}}$$

The gearing value indicates how much leverage is provided by the warrant – the percentage profit or loss relative to the investment is greater for the warrant than the underlying shares by a factor equal to the gearing.

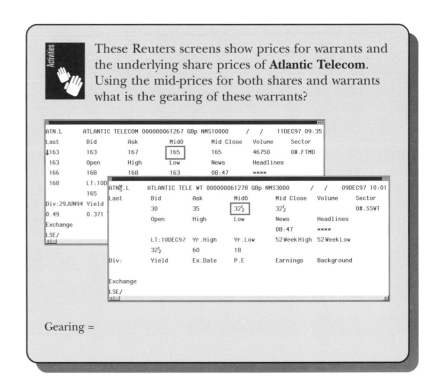

These Reuters screens show prices for warrants and the underlying share prices of **Atlantic Telecom**. Using the mid-prices for both shares and warrants what is the gearing of these warrants?

Gearing =

Bond Risk and Yield Analysis

By now you should have an understanding of yield, its calculation and its use. At the beginning of this section under *Bond Characteristics*, risk was discussed and in particular risks associated with credit, liquidity and markets.

The yield on a bond contains an element of risk premium to reflect the **credit** and **liquidity** risks associated with the bond. However, in order to fully manage interest rate risks and market exposure, **market risk** needs to be assessed thoroughly and separately.

There are a number of measures dependent on yield which are used by market players to assess market risk including:

- Duration

- Basis Point Value (BPV)

- Convexity

Before moving on to discuss these measures, it is worth reviewing some of the fundamental concepts covered so far concerning the relationships between bonds and their yields. Try the activity opposite; you can check your answers on the next page.

There are a number of relationships between bond characteristics and yield. Write down any you can think of here.

You can check your answer on the next page.

Bond Valuation and Bond Yields

The relationships between bond characteristics and yield are often described as the **Laws of Fixed Income** and cover the following:

1. There is an **inverse** relationship between bond prices and their yields:

   As a bond price **falls** its yield **rises**
   As a bond price **rises** its yield **falls**

2. The **longer** a bond's maturity period, other factors being equal, the **more sensitive** its price for a given change in yield.

3. The **lower** a bond coupon rate, the **more sensitive** the investment will be to a given change in yield.

Your answer to the activity should have covered these relationships and you should make sure you understand them before moving on.

In the discussion on bond yields the attractiveness of a bond for an investor was often mentioned. Now consider the situation where an investor is offered two bonds which have **different coupon rates** for the same remaining maturity period but with the **same yield**. Which bond should the investor buy? The answer starts with duration.

Duration

The concept of duration was developed by Frederick R. Macaulay in the 1930s to help solve the problem of which bond to buy if both have the same yield.

Duration or **Macaulay Duration** is a way of comparing interest rate or market risk between two bonds with different coupon rates and different **original** maturities. Duration is a measure of the **weighted average life** of a bond which takes into account the size and the timing of each cash flow. In effect it is a weighted average of the PVs of all cash flows.

The weight given to each time period is the PV of the cash flow paid at that time as a proportion of the dirty price of the bond.

Mathematically, duration can be calculated using Equation 17.

$$D = \left[a \times \frac{C_{(a)}}{DP}\right] + \left[(a+1) \times \frac{C_{(a+1)}}{DP}\right] + ... + \left[(a+n) \times \frac{C_{(a+n)}}{DP}\right]$$

... Equation 17

D = Duration
C = PV of cash flow for time period.
$C_{(a+n)}$ includes the final coupon and principal repayment
a = Fractional period to next coupon
n = Number of whole coupon periods to maturity
DP = Dirty price of bond

The weighted PV values for each period can be represented graphically where the duration point, **D**, is the **balance point**. In other words D represents the point at which all the weighted coupon payments on the left **exactly** balance the principal and weighted coupon payments to the right.

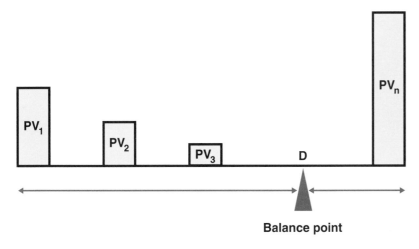

Balance point

So how does calculating or visualising duration help with deciding which bond to buy in the original question? Duration is calculated in **years** and as such has two main uses:

1. The **higher** the duration on an instrument, the **higher** its market risk

2. Duration can be used to assess the market risk of an entire portfolio of instruments such as bonds and money market instruments simply by combining the individual durations

There are a number of factors which affect duration including the following:

- The duration of an instrument which does **not** pay a coupon from issue or during its remaining maturity period, for example, a zero-coupon bond, is **equal** to its maturity term.

- The duration of a conventional bond is always **less** than its maturity period. For example, a 10 year bond paying a 10.00% coupon has an approximate duration of 7 years.

- The **higher** the coupon rate the **lower** the duration, therefore the less risky the bond and vice versa.

- The duration of a bond **moves** over time – as the bond approaches maturity the balance point shifts.

- The **higher** the yield on a bond, the **lower** the duration and vice versa. This is because at higher yields the future cash flows are discounted proportionately more heavily than nearer cash flows. This means the balance point moves to the left. Conversely, when yields fall the balance point moves to the right.

Bond Valuation and Bond Yields

Modified Duration

Duration allows a market player to rank bonds in terms of their market risk but as has just been mentioned yield changes affect duration. Market players need a way of assessing market risk which takes into account the sensitivity of bond prices for a given change in yields. This measure is called **Modified Duration**.

 Modified Duration is the percentage change in a bond's dirty price for a 1% change in yield.

Modified duration can be calculated simply using Equation 18.

$$\text{Modified duration} = \frac{\text{Macaulay duration in years}}{\left(1 + \dfrac{R}{t}\right)}$$

... *Equation 18*

R = YTM of bond as a decimal
t = Number of coupons per year

Example 13
A bond with an annual coupon has a yield of 10.00% and a Macaulay duration of 2.50 years. What is the bond's modified duration?

Using Equation 18:

$$\text{Modified duration} = \frac{2.50}{(1 + 0.10)} = 2.27\%$$

What this means is that if the bond yield moves from 10.00% to 11.00%, then the value of the bond is **reduced** by 2.27%.

Modified duration can be translated into cash terms simply from the dirty price of a bond.

Example 14
Suppose the yield for the bond in the previous example does change to 11.00% and the current dirty price of the bond is 120.00. If your current holding of these bonds is $100 million, what is your approximate loss?

$$\text{Price change} = \frac{120}{100} \times 2.27 = 2.724\%$$

The approximate loss on your holding is therefore $2,700,000.

Basis Point Value

Macaulay duration is dependent on yield and modified duration is based on a 1% change in yield. In terms of basis points, a 1% change is 100bp, which is a very large change in markets. It is much more likely that changes will be smaller and therefore market players need a finer measure to assess risk. This measure is known as **Basis Point Value (BPV)** and can be calculated using Equation 19.

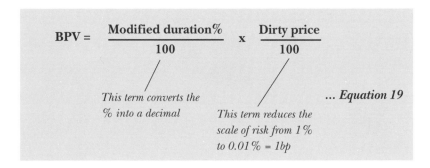

$$BPV = \frac{\text{Modified duration\%}}{100} \times \frac{\text{Dirty price}}{100}$$

This term converts the % into a decimal

This term reduces the scale of risk from 1% to 0.01% = 1bp

... *Equation 19*

Example 15

For the bond used in the previous example with a modified duration of 2.27% and dirty price of 120.00 the BPV is calculated using Equation 19:

$$BPV = \frac{2.27}{100} \times \frac{120}{100} = 0.02724$$

This means that for every basis point change in yield there is a profit or loss of 2.724 cents per $100 face value of bond held.

Because the BPV values are very small they are sometimes scaled by a factor of 100. However, it is important to recognise that this is not the same as suggesting a 1% change in yield even though numerically it is identical – it is just a way of being able to manage numbers with large numbers of decimal places.

Duration, modified duration, BPV and convexity values for a bond can be seen using the Reuters screen below for government bonds.

	Selected Bond	Benchmark
RIC	JP11970067=	JP6MT=RR
Clean Price	103.030	0.400
Accrued Interest	0.634	0.000
Dirty Price	103.664	0.400
Yld to Maturity	2.26588	
Duration	8.64298	
Modified Duration	8.54616	
Basis Point Value	0.08859	
Convexity	83.24385	
Spread	n/v	

$$BPV = \frac{8.54616}{100} \times \frac{103.664}{100} = 0.088593$$

Convexity

By now you should be aware that as yields rise both the Macaulay and modified durations fall and vice versa. As a measure of fluctuations in duration, BPV introduces risk assessment in terms of basis point changes in yields.

At this point it is worth recalling the first law of fixed income.

Can you remember it?

This law describes the inverse relationship between bond price and yield. For a conventional bond a chart of the price/yield relationship is a **convex** curve – it bows in – as illustrated in the chart below.

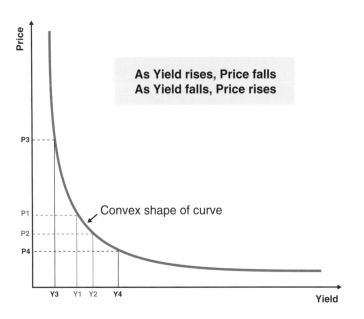

As Yield rises, Price falls
As Yield falls, Price rises

Convex shape of curve

If you look closely at this chart for small changes in yield, Y1 fi Y2, the relative increase/decrease in price, P1 fi P2, is similar to that for the yield change. However, for larger changes in yield, Y3 fi Y4, the price changes, P3 fi P4, are **not** in proportion to the yield changes.

The shape of the curve is used to explain these price/yield relationships and is termed **convexity**.

Convexivity explains why modified duration may not give an exact change in a bond's dirty price for a 1% change in yield. Precise calculations of convexivity are complex but to simplify matters convexivity is often defined as follows.

> **Convexivity** is the change in modified duration for a 1% change in yield.

In practice market players can use Equation 20 to calculate the percentage change in the dirty price of a bond.

$$DP \% \text{ change} = -\left[\text{Modified duration x } \Delta YTM\right]$$
$$+ \left[\text{Convexivity x } \frac{(\Delta YTM)^2}{2}\right]$$

... *Equation 20*

DP   =   Dirty price of bond
ΔYTM   =   Change in yield in basis points

Example 16

For the bond used in the previous example with a modified duration of 2.27% the yield rises by 50 bp and the convexity is calculated as 0.05%. What is the loss on your bond now?

Using Equation 20:

$$\text{Change in dirty price as a \%} = -\left[2.27 \times 0.5\right] + \left[0.05 \times \frac{(0.5)^2}{2}\right]$$

$$= -1.13500 + 0.00625$$

$$= -1.12875\%$$

The convexity adjustments to modified duration tend to be very small but for a large holding of say $100 million, the loss is significant.

By looking at the price/yield curve you can see that as yields rise, the loss on a bond becomes less and less whereas as yields fall the gains on a bond become more and more. The charts opposite illustrate both situations. The Reuters page below displays yield, duration, BPV and convexity values simultaneously for a number of government bonds.

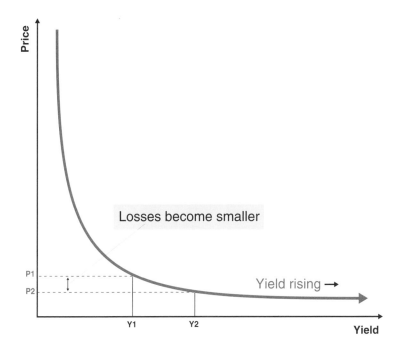

Gilts-Medium	Maturity	Yield	Duration	ModDur	BPV	Convex
TREASY 11.5% 04	19Mar04	8.654	4.646	4.453	0.052	26.055
FUND 3.5% 04	14Jul04	5.484	5.805	5.650	0.051	37.558
CONV 9.5% 04	25Oct04	6.694	5.276	5.105	0.060	33.137
CONV 9.5% 01	12Jul01	6.420	3.039	2.944	0.034	11.132
TREASY 6.75% 04	26Nov04	6.649	5.653	5.471	0.056	36.704
TREASY 8.5% 05	07Dec05	6.600	6.079	5.885	0.066	43.710
CONV 9.5% 05	18Apr05	6.668	5.546	5.367	0.064	36.861
TREASY 12.5% 05	21Nov05	7.813	5.559	5.350	0.069	37.918
TREASY 7.75% 06	08Sep06	6.592	6.485	6.278	0.069	50.608
TREASY 7.5% 06	07Dec06	6.555	6.776	6.561	0.070	54.312
TREASY 8% 06	05Oct06	7.325	6.464	6.236	0.067	50.198
TREASY 7.25% 07	07Dec07	6.490	7.359	7.128	0.076	64.640
TREASY 8.5% 07	16Jul07	6.567	6.753	6.538	0.077	56.565
TREASY 11.75% 07	22Jan07	8.511	5.931	5.689	0.072	44.972
TREASY 9% 08	13Oct08	6.450	7.406	7.175	0.088	68.270
TREASY 13.5% 08	26Mar08	8.466	6.345	6.088	0.084	52.169

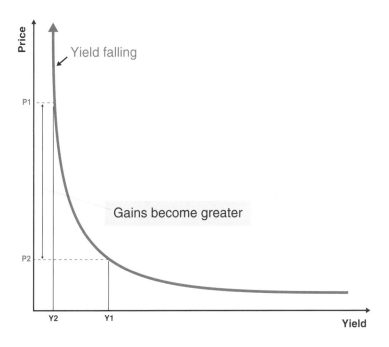

Bond Valuation and Bond Yields

Summary

You have now finished the fifth section of the book and you should have a clear understanding of the following:-

- The basic characteristics of bonds, including the concepts of market and credit risk

- The basics of bond valuation, including all the equations you will need to calculate bond values

- Bond yields, including yield conventions, conversions and curves, for straightforward bullet bonds as well as for some of the more complicated bonds

- Risk and yield analysis, in particular, the concepts of duration, basis point value and convexity

As a chcek on your understanding, try the Quick Quiz Questions on the next page. You may also find the Overview section to be a helpful learning tool.

Your notes

Quick Quiz Questions

1. A $1000 Eurobond with a coupon of 8.25% is trading at 102.25 and interest rates are falling. What will happen to the bond price? Will it –
   - ☐ a) Rise
   - ☐ b) Fall
   - ☐ c) Stay the same

2. Which of the following prices is correct for a bond with a face value of $5000 and a par price of 97.80?
   - ☐ a) $4800
   - ☐ b) $4890
   - ☐ c) $5000
   - ☐ d) $5110

3. What is the clean price of a bond?
   - ☐ a) The price of a bond excluding accrued interest
   - ☐ b) The accrued interest paid on a bond
   - ☐ c) The price of a bond including accrued interest
   - ☐ d) The same as the gross price of a bond

4. What is a basis point?
   - ☐ a) 0.001%
   - ☐ b) 0.01%
   - ☐ c) 0.1%
   - ☐ d) 1.0%

5. What is the present value of $10,000 to be paid in 18 months and discounted at a quarterly compounded rate of 8.75%?
   - ☐ a) $8,781.69
   - ☐ b) $8,782.40
   - ☐ c) $9,125.00
   - ☐ d) $11,386.40

6. What is the market value of a $10,000,000 bond whose full price is 99–13+?
   - ☐ a) $942,187.50
   - ☐ b) $9,913,500.00
   - ☐ c) $9,942,187.50
   - ☐ d) $99,135,000.00

7. What is the interest payable after one year for a bond with a coupon of 6.00%, face value $5000 on an Actual/Actual basis? Calculate the compounded interest for interest paid on the following:

   a) Annually

   b) Semi-annually

   c) Quarterly

Quick Quiz Questions

8. What is the PV of a $1000 bond payable in 2 years time when discounted at 7.00%?

   a) Annually compounded

   b) Semi-annually compounded

9. For settlement 18th April 1998, you buy a 7.50% US corporate bond maturing 18th October 1999 with a yield of 7.00%. Coupons are paid semi-annually and the day count basis is 30/360.

   a) What is the dirty price of the bond?

   b) What is the clean price of the bond?

   c) What is the settlement amount for a $15 million deal?

10. Which of the following best describes the term yield?
    - [ ] a) The coupon rate payable on a bond
    - [ ] b) The redemption value of a bond
    - [ ] c) The measure of the return on an investment
    - [ ] d) The current interest rate

11. A $1,000,000 bullet bond paying 6.00% semi-annual coupons matures after a full coupon period on 29th October 1998 and is being settled on 15th November 1998. What cash flows are projected for this bond on the value date?
    - [ ] a) $30,000 coupon payment on 29th April + $1,030,000 coupon and principal payment on 29th October 1998
    - [ ] b) A final payment of $1,060,000
    - [ ] c) $30,000 coupon on 15th May + $1,030,000 coupon and principal on 29th October 1998
    - [ ] d) $530,000 on 29th April + $530,000 on 29th October 1998

12. Which of the following statements about fixed-coupon bullet bonds is true?
    - [ ] a) As price increases, the coupon rate decreases
    - [ ] b) As yield increases, the coupon increases
    - [ ] c) As maturity increases, yield increases
    - [ ] d) As yield increases, price decreases

13. Yield to Worst for a callable bond is calculated to which of the following?
    - [ ] a) The next call date
    - [ ] b) The call date that produces the lowest yield
    - [ ] c) The last call date
    - [ ] d) The call date that produces the lowest price

Quick Quiz Questions

14. If the conversion ratio of a 6.00% convertible bond is given as 18.75 shares per $1000 face value and the market value of the bond and underlying stock is 102.50% of par and $44 respectively, what is the conversion premium ratio?
    - ☐ a) 0.239%
    - ☐ b) 0.242%
    - ☐ c) 23.9%
    - ☐ d) 24.2%

15. Which statement about bond total return is false?
    - ☐ a) As the reinvestment rate increases, total return increases
    - ☐ b) The shorter the holding period, the more pronounced the effect the sale price has on the total return
    - ☐ c) Holding period return is expressed as an annualised rate
    - ☐ d) Total return can be calculated for both historical and horizon time periods

16. Which of the following is true for a puttable bond?
    - ☐ a) Investors can purchase more bonds before maturity
    - ☐ b) Issuers can buy back bonds from investors before maturity
    - ☐ c) Investors can sell bonds back to issuers before maturity
    - ☐ d) Issuers can change the coupon rate of the bond

17. For settlement 20th April 1998 you buy a 6.00% US T-Bond maturing 19th October 2001 at a clean price of 102-08 and a YTM of 7.00%. You sell the bond on 21st May 1998 at a price of 102-16. In the current coupon period there are 182 days.

    a) What is the dirty price on 20th April to 2 decimal figures?

    b) What is the dirty price on 20th May to 2 decimal figures?

    c) What was the holding period yield achieved?

    d) Why was the holding period yield higher than the bond's YTM?

Quick Quiz Questions

18. Using the information from the Reuters page for this
    particular Japanese government bond on the TSE:

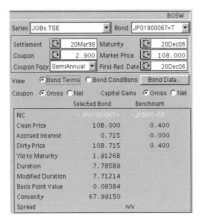

a) What is the bond's current yield?

b) What is the bond's ACY?

c) What is the bond's YTM?

You can check your answers on page 274.

Overview

```
                    ┌─────────────────────────────────────┐
                    │  Bond Valuation and Bond Yields      │
                    └─────────────────────────────────────┘
```

Bond Characteristics

- Price
- Credit and Market Risk
- Maturing, Coupon and Accrued Interest

Bond Yields

- The Relations Between Bond Price and Yield
- Definition for YTM
- Yield Conventions
  - Current Yield
  - Adjusted Current Yield or Japanese Simpel Yield
  - YTM or ISMA YTM
  - Greenwell-Montage (Weekend) Yield
- Yield Conversions
- Total Return Analysis
- Yields for Complicated Bonds

Bond Risk and Yield Analysis

- Duration
- Basic Poitn Value (BPV)
- Convexity

Bond Valuation

- Rate of Return
- Simple and Compound Interest
- Equivalent Interest Rates
- Present Value
- Day Count Method
- Accrued Interest
- The Concept of Yield
- Bond Prices

Quick Quiz Answers

	✓ or ✗

1. a) ☐

2. b) ☐

3. a) ☐

4. b) ☐

5. b) Use Equation 7 ☐

6. c) $9,942,187.50 ☐
   $99 + {}^{13}/_{32} + {}^{1}/_{64} \% \times 10,000,000$
   $= 0.99421875 \times 10,000,000 = \$9,942187.50$

7. Use Equation 5

$$FV = PV \times \left(1 + \frac{R}{t}\right)^{nt}$$

PV = 5000 and R = 0.06

a) $FV = 5000 \times (1 + 0.06) = \$5,300$
   Interest $= \$300.00$ ☐

b) $FV = 5000 \times \left(1 + \frac{0.06}{2}\right)^{2}$

   $= 5000 \times 1.0609$
   $= \$5,304.50$
   Interest $= \$304.50$ ☐

c) $FV = 5000 \times \left(1 + \frac{0.06}{4}\right)^{4}$

   $= 5000 \times 1.0614$
   $= \$5,306.82$
   Interest $= \$306.82$ ☐

	✓ or ✗

8. Use Equation 7 $\quad PV = \dfrac{FV}{\left(1 + \dfrac{R}{t}\right)^{nt}}$

   FV = 7000 and R = 0.07

   a) $PV = 1000 \div (1 + 0.07)^{2} = 1000/1.1449$
      $PV = \$873.44$ ☐

   b) $PV = 1000 \div \left(1 + \dfrac{0.07}{2}\right)^{4} = 1000/1.1475$

      $PV = \$871.46$ ☐

9. Use Equation 10

$$PV_{Total} = \frac{C/t}{(1 + R/t)^{a}} + \frac{C/t}{(1 + R/t)^{a+1}} + \ldots + \frac{P + C/t}{(1 + R/t)^{a+n}}$$

   C = 7.5, R = 0.07, t = 2, a = 1

   a) $Dirty\ Price = \dfrac{3.75}{1.035} + \dfrac{3.75}{(1.035)^{2}} + \dfrac{103.75}{(1.035)^{3}}$

      $= 3.623 + 3.501 = 93.577 = 100.70$ ☐

   b) Use Equation 11
      Accrued interest $= 0.075/2 \times 180/360 \times 100$
      $= 1.875$ ☐

   c) Clean price $= 100.70 - 1.875 = 98.825$ ☐

   d) Settlement $=$ Clean price + Accrued Interest
      $=$ Dirty price $\times$ 5,000,000
      $= \$5,035,000$ ☐

Quick Quiz Answers

✓ or ✗   ✓ or ✗

10.c) ☐

11.a) ☐

12.d) ☐

13.b) ☐

14.d) ☐

15.c) ☐

16.c) ☐

17.a) Clean price   =   102.00 + 8/32   =   102.25

Accrued interest   = $\dfrac{1}{182}$ x $\dfrac{0.06}{2}$ x 100 = 0.016

Dirty price   =   102.25 + 0.016 =   102.27   ☐

b) Clean price   =   102.00 + 16/32=   102.50

Accrued interest   = $\dfrac{32}{182}$ x $\dfrac{0.06}{2}$ x 100 = 0.527

Dirty price   =   102.50 + 0.527 =   103.03   ☐

c) Holding period yield

$$= \left(\frac{103.03 - 102.27}{102.27}\right) \text{ x } \frac{365}{31} \text{ x } 100$$

$$= \; 0.76 \,/\, 0.00743 \;=\; 8.75\% \qquad ☐$$

d) The holding period yield is higher than the YTM because the bond is not held to maturity and the return includes the gain on capital.   ☐

19.a) Use Equation 13

Current yield   = $\dfrac{2.90 \text{ x } 100}{108.00}$ = 2.6852%   ☐

b) Use Equation 14

ACY   = $2.6852 + \left(\dfrac{100 - 108}{8.83}\right)$ =   1.7792   ☐

c) From BOSW screen

YTM   =   1.91268   ☐

This shows how YTM and ACY differ at low yield values.

How well did you score? You should have managed to get most of these questions correct. If you didn't, revise the materials again.

Further Resources

Books

Trading and Investing in Bond Options: Risk Management , Arbitrage, and Value Investing
Anthony M. Wong and Robert High, John Wiley & Sons, Inc., 1991
ISBN   0 471 52560 X

Managing Credit Risk: The Next Great Financial Challenge
John B. Caouette, Edward I. Altman and Paul Narayanan, John Wiley & Sons, Inc., 1998
ISBN   0 471 11189 9

Pricing Convertible Bonds
Kevin B. Connolly, John Wiley & Sons, Inc., 1999
ISBN   0 471 97872 8

Money Market and Bond Calculations
Marcia Stigum and Franklin L. Robinson, Irwin Professional Press, 1996
ISBN   1 556 23476 7

Bond Markets: Structures and Yield Calculations
Patrick J. Brown and Patrick J. Ryan, AMACOM, 1998
ISBN   0 814 40473 1

High Yield Bonds: Market Structure, Portfolio Management, and Credit Risk Modelling
Thedore M. Barnhill, William F. Maxwell and Mark R. Shenkman (Ed.), McGraw Hill, 1999
ISBN   0 070 06786 4

Yield Curve Analysis: The Fundamentals of Risk and Return
Livingston G. Douglas, New York Institute of Finance, 1988
ISBN   0 139 72456 7

Mastering Financial Calculations
Robert Steiner, Financial Times Management 1998
ISBN   0 273 62587 X

Publications

Internet

RFT Web Site
* **http://www.wiley-rft.reuters.com**
This is the series' companion web site where additional quiz questions, updated screens and other information may be found.

ISMA
* **http://www.ISMA.org**
The International Securities Market Association (ISMA) is the self-regulatory organisation and trade association for the international securities market.

Exchanges

Refer to the back of this book for a listing of worldwide stock exchange contact information and web sites.

This section of the book should take about 60 minutes of study time. You may not take as long as this or you may take a little longer – remember your learning is individual to you.

Dealers told us that they love their work. 'There's the thrill, the risk, who can make the most money. It's an ego trip, it's legalised gambling. It's exciting, your adrenalin surges, and you get immediate results. There's a good working environment, and a juvenile sense of fun. There's no in tray or out tray.'

'The Stress Factor', .R, March/April 1994

Introduction

By now you are probably aware that the trading of bonds involves three groups of market players:

- Issuers

- Investors

- Intermediaries

You should also be aware that the most active trading of bonds takes place in the secondary markets. The various methods used to issue government securities into the primary markets were discussed briefly in *Section 2*. But how are corporate bonds issued in the primary markets and what factors are involved in an issue?

Trading in the bond markets is mainly OTC, so how does trading actually take place and how are trading practices regulated? This section is concerned with:

- Players in the primary markets – issuers, how a corporate organisations

- Players in the secondary markets – intermediaries, investors, how bonds are traded and how trading is regulated

Select a market player from each of the issuers, investors and intermediaries groups and describe briefly their roles in trading bonds.

Issuers in the Primary Markets

> An **Issuer** is the borrower of funds responsible for ensuring that interest and principal payments are made to bond holders usually via a paying agent.

The types of issuers and their reasons for borrowing in the bond markets have been discussed in previous sections. The following descriptions of issuers are summaries to help you understand more about the "mechanics" of trading. Issuers in the primary markets fall broadly into one of four categories:

- Governments and sovereign organisations

- Supranationals

- Corporates

- Banks and other financial institutions

The following diagram indicates the relative importance of these market players according to their percentage of new issues in the international markets in 1996. As you can see, banks and corporates had by far the largest share of the new issue market in the international markets for foreign bonds and Eurobonds.

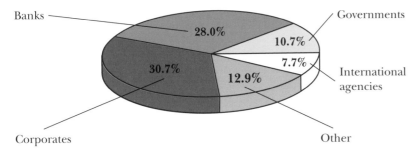

Source: Bank of England Quarterly Bulletin May 1997

Governments and Sovereign Organisations

Central government debt instruments usually form the largest proportion of the particular country's domestic market. The instruments nearly always have the highest credit rating of that country and are used as benchmarks against which other domestic bonds are priced.

Government bond markets are also the most liquid of the domestic markets. However, many governments now issue Eurobonds in the international markets.

Government agencies and organisations created or sponsored by central governments but operating more as corporations also fall into this category. For example, the US Federal National Mortgage Association (FannieMae) and the Australian Industrial Development Corporation.

Sovereigns include states, provinces and municipalities, which may be countries or local/regional governments within a country, for example, the Kingdom of Sweden, the Province of British Columbia, Canada and the City of Kobe, Japan.

Supranationals

These are organisations that raise capital for economic growth in developing countries and that have a high credit rating. Supranationals include:

- International Bank for Reconstruction and Development – the "World Bank"

- European Investment Bank

- African Development Bank

- Asian Development Bank

- Council of Europe

Corporates

Multinational corporations use the debt markets for many reasons to fund their activities. Credit ratings vary from issuer to issuer and can rank as high as governments to below investment grade – **junk bonds**.

Banks and Other Financial Institutions

These organisations use the bond markets to raise capital to fund their activities just like corporations. In some markets such as Eurobonds, banks and financial institutions form a significant percentage of the issuers.

Credit Rating and Agencies

One of the major considerations in pricing a new issue is the creditworthiness of the organisation issuing the bond. In other words, investors have to assess the risks that the issuer may default on interest payments or principal repayment. Credit ratings are carried out by agencies and include an evaluation of an issuer's credit history and capability to repay its obligations.

As you have seen, governments have the highest credit rating in their country because, in theory, governments can always raise taxes to meet their obligations.

Corporate bonds range from ratings equivalent to governments down to junk bonds. But who determines these ratings and what do the ratings mean?

 Activities

Write down the names of any credit rating agencies you know here.

There are a number of credit rating agencies, some of which are specific to particular types of bond markets. Some of the more well-known agencies include:

- **Moody's Investor Services** which has been rating bonds since 1909 when it first issued bond ratings as part of Moody's Analyses of Railroad Investments. By 1924 Moody's ratings covered nearly 100% of the US bond market

- **Standard & Poor's Corporation**, which started rating bonds in 1940

- **Duff & Phelps**

- **Fitch**

- **Mikuni**

The most widely recognised of the agencies are Moody's and Standard & Poor's. The rating structures for both organisations are shown in the table opposite. Moody's uses numbers to rate between Aaa and C, whereas Standard & Poor's uses a system of plus and minus from AAA to C. Some rating agencies also have D grades to indicate the issuer is in default.

Bonds that are classified as **speculative grades**, that is, **non-investment grades**, are commonly known as **junk** bonds. In many cases junk bonds have high yields in order to attract investors.

Investment grades	Moody's Highest → Lowest	Standard & Poor's Highest → Lowest
Highest quality	Aaa, Aaa1, Aaa2, Aaa3	AAA, AAA−, AA+
Excellent	Aa, Aa1, Aa2, Aa3	AA, AA−, A+
Good	A, A1, A2, A3	A, A−, BBB+
Medium	Baa, Baa1, Baa2, Baa3	BBB, BBB−, BB+
Speculative grade		
Questionable	Ba, Ba1, Ba2, Ba3	BB, BB−, B+
Poor	B, B1, B2, B3	B, B−, CCC+
Very poor	Caa, Caa1, Caa2, Caa3	CCC, CCC−, CC+
Extremely poor	Ca, Ca1, Ca2, Ca3	CC, CC−, C+
Lowest	C	C

The ratings determined by the agencies are an opinion of the issuer's ability to repay debt which is dependent not only on the credit risk of the issuer but also on the type of debt instrument.

This opinion is based on a number of criteria including:

- Geographical location of the issuer. Even a top quality issuer will be considered a less safe risk if they are based in an unstable political climate.

- Type of business

- Future prospects for the issuer's industry

- Ranking of the organisation within their market place

- Management of the organisation

- Profit and loss accounts

- Liquidity and cash flow

- Future plans of the organisation

- Type of instrument

The credit rating given by an agency is therefore an indication of the financial strength or risk of default of an issuer. It plays an important part in determining the coupon the issuer will have to pay. So, for example, a ten-year security issued by the US government will have a higher credit rating and therefore a lower rate of interest than a similar issue from JP Morgan. The higher the issuer's credit risk the more it must pay in interest to attract investors.

"Government-guaranteed" is usually the highest rating with an implied rating better than Moody's Aaa. Some governments, however, due to their financial situation or political instability, are rated lower.

If an organisation's credit rating changes, then the price of all the issuer's outstanding debt is affected.

The rating agencies charge fees for their bond ratings based on the size of the issue and the amount of analysis required.

The costs of rating to an organisation are usually recouped in the savings from lower yields of a proposed issue. In many cases the underwriters are involved with presentations to the credit rating agencies on behalf of the issuers.

The rating agencies review their ratings regularly by requesting updated information from issuers. They also offer a service to organisations wishing to improve their ratings.

The Reuters screens below show historical data for KMart Corporation.

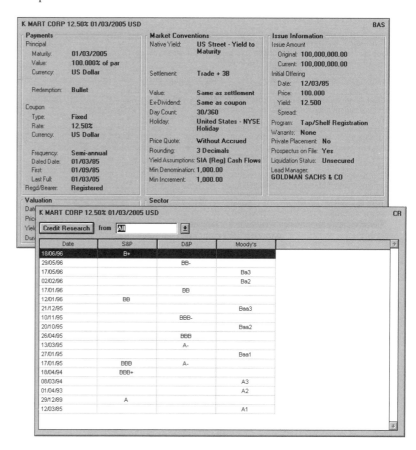

The Reuters' Bond Rating Speed Guide provides a listing of global ratings services. From the speed guide, note various services' recent ratings.

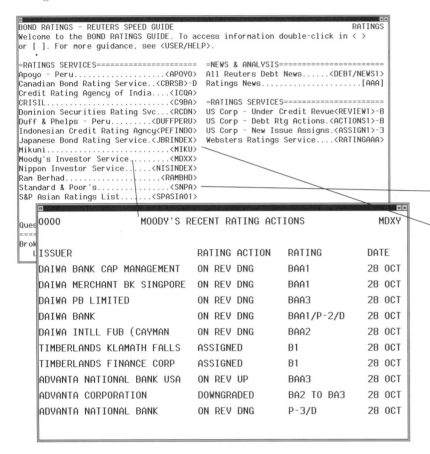

```
BOND RATINGS - REUTERS SPEED GUIDE                           RATINGS
Welcome to the BOND RATINGS GUIDE. To access information double-click in < >
or [ ]. For more guidance, see <USER/HELP>.

=RATINGS SERVICES====================  =NEWS & ANALYSIS======================
Apoyo - Peru...................<APOYO>  All Reuters Debt News......<DEBT/NEWS1>
Canadian Bond Rating Service..<CBRSB>-D  Ratings News......................[AAA]
Credit Rating Agency of India....<ICQA>
CRISIL..........................<C9BA>  =RATINGS SERVICES=====================
Doninion Securities Rating Svc...<RCDN>  US Corp - Under Credit Revue<REVIEW1>-B
Duff & Phelps - Peru........<DUFFPERU>  US Corp - Debt Rtg Actions.<ACTIONS1>-B
Indonesian Credit Rating Agncy<PEFINDO>  US Corp - New Issue Assigns.<ASSIGN1>-3
Japanese Bond Rating Service.<JBRINDEX>  Websters Ratings Service....<RATINGAAA>
Mikuni.........................<MIKU>
Moody's Investor Service........<MDXX>
Nippon Investor Service......<NISINDEX>
Ran Berhad..................<RAMBHD>
Standard & Poor's.............<SNPA>
S&P Asian Ratings List....|...<SPASIA01>

Ques
====
Brok
```

```
0000       STANDARD + POORS - LATEST RATING ACTIONS           SNPB
FOR MORE INFORMATION -CALL THE LONDON RATINGS DESK 0171 826 3540
NAME                    TYPE     RTG     TO       FROM    DATE
BANK OF MELBOURNE LTD   L/TERM           AA-      A-      OCT 20
BANK OF MELBOURNE LTD   S/TERM           A-1+     A-2     OCT 20
WESTPAC BANKING CORP    L/TERM   AA-     AFFIRMED         OCT 20
WESTPAC BANKING CORP    S/TERM   A-1+    AFFIRMED         OCT 20
SECURA N.V.             CPA      A-      ASSIGNED         OCT 20
B.A.T. INDUSTRIES PLC   L/TERM           A-       A+      OCT 20
B.A.T. INDUSTRIES PLC   S/TERM           A-2      A-1     OCT 20
(REMAINS ON CREDITWATCH
NEGATIVE)
```

```
0000          MOODY'S RECENT RATING ACTIONS            MDXY

ISSUER                  RATING ACTION    RATING       DATE
DAIWA BANK CAP MANAGEMENT   ON REV DNG   BAA1         28 OCT
DAIWA MERCHANT BK SINGPORE  ON REV DNG   BAA1         28 OCT
DAIWA PB LIMITED            ON REV DNG   BAA3         28 OCT
DAIWA BANK                  ON REV DNG   BAA1/P-2/D   28 OCT
DAIWA INTLL FUB (CAYMAN     ON REV DNG   BAA2         28 OCT
TIMBERLANDS KLAMATH FALLS   ASSIGNED     B1           28 OCT
TIMBERLANDS FINANCE CORP    ASSIGNED     B1           28 OCT
ADVANTA NATIONAL BANK USA   ON REV UP    BAA3         28 OCT
ADVANTA CORPORATION         DOWNGRADED   BA2 TO BA3   28 OCT
ADVANTA NATIONAL BANK       ON REV DNG   P-3/D        28 OCT
```

```
MIKUNI ASSIGNS PRELIMINARY BOND CREDIT RATINGS            MIKU
    TOKYO, OCT 24 (REUTER) - MIKUNI AND CO LTD SAID ON FRIDAY
IT HAD ASSIGNED THE FOLLOWING PRELIMINARY RATINGS TO PLANNED
BOND ISSUES:
    -BBB-
    SUMITOMO ELECTRIC IND LTD <5802.T>,
    10 BILLION YEN UNSECURED DUE 2005.
    10 BILLION YEN UNSECURED DUE 2009.
    KASAI KOGYO CO LTD <7256.T>, 35 MILLION SWISS FRANCS UNSECUR
ED DUE 2001, PRIVATE PLACEMENT, GUARANTEED BY ASAHI BANK.


24-OCT-0120. STK135 T0643500
                                                         MORE
```

Issuing A Bond in the Primary Market

The primary market is concerned with bond issues and as such, the amounts of money are often so large — running into even billions of dollars — that no single organisation could possibly raise the loan by itself. If it did it would likely overstretch its finances and overexpose itself to risk. The solution is for organisations responsible for issuing debt to form groups or **syndicates**, sharing the risk and splitting the loan into more manageable amounts. Thus, a new issue may involve many people and can be quite complex in its operation.

You may have seen announcements such as the one opposite in the financial press. They are known as **tombstones**. All the members of the syndicate are listed on the tombstone. The most important members, known as the **Lead Managers**, are shown first in larger, bolder type than the **Co-Managers**, shown beneath.

This announcement appears as a matter of record only

Bank of Greece

(Incorporated with limited liability into the Hellenic Republic)

FRF 1,000,000,000

$7^1/_2$ per cent. Bonds due 1998

Issue price: 99.355 per cent.

Banque Nationale de Paris   **Crédit Lyonnais**

Caisse des Dépôts et Consignations   J.P. Morgan & Cie S.A.

Paribas Capital Markets   Banque S.G. Warburg   Société Générale

The syndicate comprises two Lead Managers and 5 Co-Managers who are issuing a loan of FF 1 billion on behalf of the Bank of Greece

In order to understand who is involved in the issue of a bond, you can now follow a fictitious step-by-step bond issue that identifies all the key players and their roles. This is the scenario:

> British Airways (BA) is planning a five-year program to re-equip its ageing fleet of Boeing 747s and they have come to the Eurobond market to raise $440m to finance their first year's purchases.

There are five basic steps involved in the issue. Each of the steps are described here as self-contained scenarios for clarity, but of course in practice matters are not quite as simple. The five steps are:

> Step 1 – Appoint a Lead Manager and Agree on Fees
> Step 2 – Determine the Deal Structure and Pricing
> Step 3 – Form an Underwriting Syndicate
> Step 4 – Set Up the Administration of the Bonds
> Step 5 – Primary Trading

Step 1 – Appoint a Lead Manager and Agree on Fees

The first step is that BA must appoint an issuing house to handle the issue for them. BA will need to ensure that whoever they choose are of a sufficient stature and reputation in the markets to be able to manage the issue successfully. BA must also expect to pay fees for the services they receive. These fees are usually determined according to the maturity of the bonds and the currency sector.

Which issuing house should BA choose? BA may well look at the "league tables" to help – over 50% of all primary issues go to the top ten names. As you might expect, there is intense competition to be in the top ten, which as of 1996, are:

> 1. Merrill Lynch
> 2. Morgan Stanley
> 3. SBC Warburg
> 4. Goldman Sachs
> 5. JP Morgan
> 6. Credit Suisse First Boston
> 7. Deutsche Morgan Grenfell
> 8. Lehman Bros.
> 9. Nomura Securities
> 10. Union Bank of Switzerland

Top 10 league table for international bonds – 1996

BA may also take into account an issuing house's experience, relationships with other key players and the strength of the sales team. BA decided to approach Nomura to handle the issue. Nomura now becomes the **lead manager** for the issue. Nomura will want to appoint one or more **co-lead managers** if the issue is to take place in a number of countries, or if they plan to **swap** currencies or interest rate structures following the issue. In this case, BA and Nomura agree to appoint two co-lead managers, one to handle the US side of the issue and the other to manage the currency swaps.

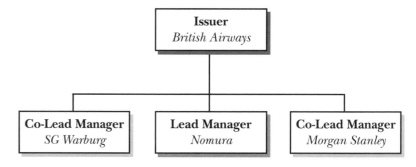

Nomura, as lead manager, keeps the best job for itself, which is known as 'running the books'. As b**ook runner**, they will make all the necessary arrangements for the issue, for example:

- Sending out invitations to subscribe

- Allotting tranches of bonds

- Making all the necessary press announcements

- Coordinating operations

So far, BA seems to be well on its way to its bond issue but did they have to appoint an investment bank as their lead manager? The answer is no. Large corporations and banks may lead manage their own issues. Although rare, this is happening increasingly as the market grows in size and users gain experience.

Step 2 – Determine the Deal Structure and Pricing

At the same time that Nomura is arranging its underwriting syndicate, it must also ensure that the issue will trade and that the fees, issue details and price are fixed. Whether or not the syndicate makes money depends on their sales ability and how well the issue has been priced. Nomura's fees are based on the issue size, maturity, class of issuer and market conditions – in most cases the longer the maturity the higher the fees. These fees would be split into management and underwriting.

This fee guarantees the $440m issue and is paid to the underwriting and selling groups according to their level of commitment or risk.

A **fixed price re-offer** is when the underwriters have bought the total issue and fix the price and **coupon** at the launch. In this case the fees are a lot lower than normal. Most new issues today are in the form of fixed price re-offer deals. It is very unusual for a new issue to be offered with only an indicated price and coupon. In the case of a fixed price re-offer, the underwriting group hopes that interest rates do not move against them before the selling group have sold the bonds. There are ways they can protect themselves, hedging their position by buying instruments which offer forward cover.

Once the coupon, maturity details etc have been agreed upon, then the bond may be given a **rating**. The price of the bond and its saleability in the market are closely tied to this rating.

Historically it was usual for companies to be given ratings, such as AAA from Standard and Poor's or Aaa from Moody's. Because the financial instruments developed for the Eurobond market are so varied and diverse, it is now usual to rate the specific issue rather than the issuing organisation. The rating thus takes into account the risk associated with the particular instrument being issued, as well as the issuing organisation.

Step 3 – Form An Underwriting Syndicate

The lead and co-lead managers decide to split the issue between them so the lead manager is responsible for $240m, and the co-lead managers for $100m each. The lead manager appoints a number of other banks as **co-managers** in order to dilute the risk exposure – the co-lead managers do the same. Each co-manager agrees to underwrite a $10m slice. The group outlined here forms what is known as the **underwriting group** or **syndicate**. The structure now looks like this:

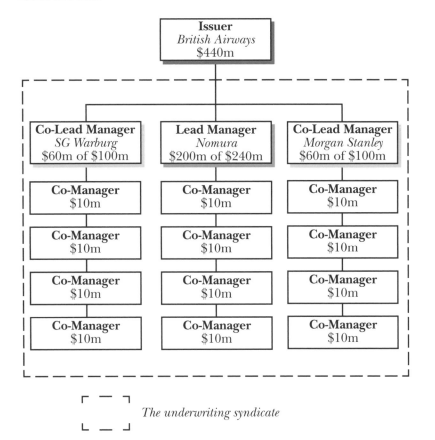

The underwriting syndicate

 Underwriting is a way of guaranteeing that the issuer gets its funds. In the unlikely event that they are unable to sell the whole of an issue, the underwriters of an issue undertake to provide the issuer with the necessary funds. It may be that after an issue is announced interest rates rise, making the bond less attractive to investors. At this stage the bond's coupon is fixed, so the underwriters are forced to sell the issue at a lower price than they had expected.

The story does not always end here. For very large deals the banks in the underwriting syndicate may also invite other banks to join them to enlarge the selling group. These banks are only sellers and not underwriters and therefore do not receive a fee – only a commission on what they sell. So the selling group looks like this:

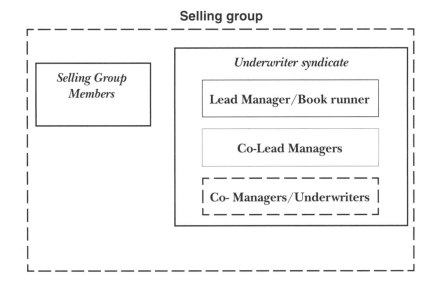

The underwriting group takes the issue onto its books and assumes liability for it. The issue, and therefore the risk, is distributed among the group.

Distribution is typically in these proportions:

Lead Managers	50% or more
Co-Lead Managers	20–30% in total
Co-Managers	10–15% in total
Selling Group	The remainder: 5–10%

The underwriting commitment means that the issuer, BA, receives $440m, less Nomura's fees, on an agreed date.

So Nomura has now fixed all the details and the issue price, but it is not yet ready for the market

Step 4 – Set Up the Administration of the Bonds

As you can probably imagine, the issuing of a bond requires a large amount of documentation and information for all the key players, potential investors etc. As lead manager, Nomura will need to employ solicitors to review and approve all the documentation for issue.

The lead manager is responsible for drafting and circulating documentation including the following:

- **An invitation to underwrite**, which is sent to potential co-managers. It contains brief details about the issue.

- A **prospectus** or **offering circular** which contains a more complete description of the issue and financial information relating to the borrower.

- **Agreement documents** between the lead manager and other groups, for example, a selling group agreement.

Auditors or accountants will also be involved to supply the relevant financial information and produce an audit report for inclusion in the prospectus.

Nomura has now completed all that is necessary and the bond is ready for launch. So how does Nomura launch the issue?

Step 5 – Primary Trading

On finalising the new BA bond issue, Nomura feeds the details to Reuters and other vendors for display. Once the details have been announced it is usual for a **grey market** to be activated. This "if, as and when issued" market allows banks not invited into the underwriting syndicate to start "dealing". It is also an opportunity for potential investors to check the deal.

In order to ensure that Nomura does not have an inventory of underwritten bonds, it ensures that the terms are realistic. Nomura also has a strong investor base of names to attract to the investment.

Although the competition among Eurobond issuing houses is intense and borrowers can "shop" for the best terms and lowest fees, the introduction of the re-offered price ensures that bonds are distributed at a price controlled by the lead manager, protecting investors and borrower.

Originally there may have been a **signing ceremony** between Nomura and BA once the final terms had been agreed. However, in a fixed price re-offer the signing of the issue agreement can take place at any time, before or after the selling period.

Nomura places a **tombstone** notice in the financial press. This sets out the particulars of the issue and lists the main parties in the issue – the issuer, lead manager, co-lead managers and, if any, auditors or accountants. The tombstone for this issue might look something like the one opposite.

During the selling period the lead manager obviously tries to keep the issue at or near to the issue price in order to gain the most from the fees. However, activity on the grey market can affect the bond pricing adversely and the lead manager may be forced to buy loose bonds in order to stabilise the price. There are various ways in which the lead manager can reduce losses incurred if this happens but these are strictly controlled by the International Securities Market Association (ISMA).

In this scenario Nomura successfully brings the new BA issue to the market and there is a celebratory lunch following a signing ceremony.

This announcement appears as a matter of record only

British Airways
$440,000,000
5 per cent. Bonds due 2003

Lead Manager

Nomura

Co-Lead Managers

SG Warburg   Morgan Stanley

Co-Managers

You have now completed the overview of the players in the primary market and their roles. To check your understanding and to bring what you have learned to life, try the exercise below.

Below is the International Insider Screen Service and a page with details of a new issue.

```
09:04 26MAY98    INTERNATIONAL INSIDER SCREEN SERVICE  UK31060        IIIA
-----------  SCREEN INSIDER - TUESDAY ------ +44 171 353 7311
<IIIB> ABN AMRO FORMS GROUP FOR ONTARIO STERLING STRAIGHT
<IIIC> ** CSFB LAUNCHES SWISS RE FINANCE EXCHANGE INTO ING **
<IIID> MUNICH HYPO SET AT FPR 99.31 - FTT 11:15 FFURT *
<IIIE> ** DAIWA LAUNCHES 1-YEAR DOLLAR FRN FOR GECC **
<IIIF> PAINEWEBBER FORMS GROUP FOR DSL DRACHMA DEAL
<IIIG> SBCWDR FORMS GROUP FOR AUSTRIA DM BUNDESANLEIHE
<IIIH> ** SWEDBANK LAUNCHES SKR STRAIGHT FOR KOMMUNINVEST **
<IIII> ** WESTLB JUMBO PFANDBRIEF INCREASED TO DM 2.5BN *
<IIIJ> DRESDNER BANK FLUX GROUP // ALCATEL-ALSTHOLM EQTY-LNKD
<IIIK> NOMURA LAUNCHES SFR CV FOR NISSEI ASB MACHINE CO
<IIIL> ** BERLIN-HANNOVERSCHE INC PRICED: 98.09, 97.91RE **
---------------------------------------- FAX +44 171 583 1895
FOR ASIAN NEWS SEE <IIJA>, BONDWATCH <WATCH01>, EM <EMMA01>
```

Imagine you are a dealer in the new issues department of Morgan Guaranty. You want to see if there are any new issues which might be of interest to your clients. Look at the International Insider Screen Service to the right, a useful new issue news service. You will see listed a number of headlines relating to current new issues, with the page number of the relevant detail pages on the left. Below the screen is the page of an issue you think looks interesting. Write down your answers to the questions.

Who is the issuer?

What is the size of the issue, and in what currency?

When is the maturity date?

Is the bond a straight, FRN, convertible, or another type?

What is the coupon?

What is the issue price?

What is its rating?

Who is the Lead Manager?

Who are the Co-Lead Managers?

Who are the Co-Managers?

Intermediaries Involved in the Primary Markets

The role of intermediaries is to bring together issuers and investors. As has been described previously, most governments use a system of **primary dealers** and brokers to issue their bonds in their domestic markets. These primary dealers have different names in different domestic markets and their roles may also differ slightly. To help understand the roles of these intermediaries in the primary market, the systems used in the UK and US are described in a little more detail here.

UK Gilts Issue

Within the UK Gilts market, **Gilt Edged Market Makers (GEMMs)** provide a continuous market and effective two-way prices for the whole range of government securities. GEMMs agree to quote in all market conditions and thus provide liquidity to the market.

GEMMs have access to **InterDealer Brokers (IDBs)** in order to trade with other Market makers on a no-names basis. IDBs do not take positions and earn commission on the transactions they arrange between GEMMs.

The GEMMs and IDBs are members of the LSE and are regulated by the rules of the exchange in their activities as broker dealers or agency brokers – these functions are described later.

The diagram below shows the relationships of the intermediaries with the Bank of England, among themselves and with investors.

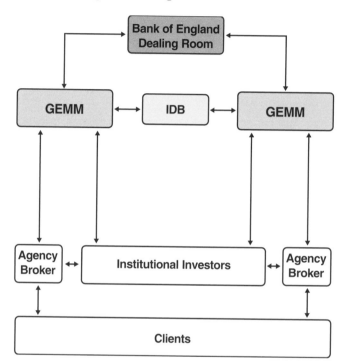

US Treasuries

Primary dealers in the US are banks and securities broker-dealers that trade in US government securities with the Federal Reserve Bank of New York who operates on behalf of the Federal Reserve.

Primary dealers who are banks are subject to supervision by the US federal bank system. Institutions who are broker-dealers must be registered with the US Securities and Exchange Commission (SEC).

Primary dealers have to bid in the competitive auction system and are required to make a market. All market information must be reported to the Fed. The operation of this system provides liquidity to the market.

These is also a system of IDBs in the US who operate in much the same way as in the UK market.

Players in the Secondary Markets

Once a new issue has been placed or sold in the primary market it can be traded in the secondary market. Some secondary markets are **illiquid**, that is there is little secondary trading. For example, Eurobonds are or can become illiquid – many of them are held to maturity.

Even though many eurobonds are illiquid, the secondary eurobond market is very large – in the week to July 1, 1999 turnover in the Eurobond and related markets was $1.336 trillion. The secondary market in government bonds, such as US Treasury Notes, Bills and Bonds is also very large.

So who are the players in the secondary market? There are six types of people you will encounter, each with a different role:

- Market Makers
- Agency or Retail Brokers
- InterDealer Brokers (IDBs)
- Dealers or Traders
- Sales People
- Financial Analysts and Economistsa

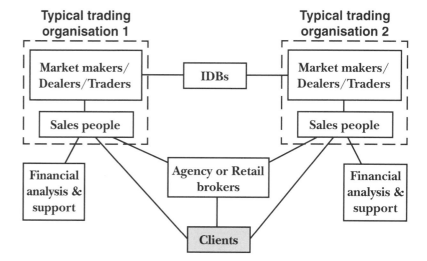

Market Makers

These are profit-seeking players and their role is to set the price at which instruments will be traded. The market makers are committed to quote both bid and offer prices even if there are no investors wishing to trade. They make their profit on the difference or **spread** between the prices at which they buy and sell the instruments. Each day they report to the **International Securities Market Association (ISMA)** the Eurobond issues for which they are prepared to trade. This information is quoted in the *Financial Times.*

Market makers act as principals, who use their own capital to buy, sell and hold instruments, trading for their own account. Within the secondary market the greatest volume of trading takes place among the market makers.

Agency or Retail Brokers

These act as agents who buy and sell on behalf of an investor. They help preserve the anonymity of the investors and issuers. They do not hold a position but earn their income from the commission they charge.

InterDealer Brokers

IDBs operate in a different way to that of brokers. Their role is to bring market makers together in order to preserve anonymity and market efficiency. They do not take positions themselves but earn a small commission for their services.

Dealers or Traders

These act as principals, taking instruments onto the trading organisation's books, hoping to make a profit on their resale.

Sales People

Sales people are the interface between the client, or the investor, and the dealers. Their job is to provide their clients with information about the market, relay prices and pass on orders to the traders to transact. They also try to sell the bank's position, such as its underwriting commitments.

Financial Analysts and Economists

These are responsible for the compilation and examination of the detailed information in the market place. The information from these analysts is condensed into a set of forecasts which are used as guidelines for investment to support sales people.

Within the secondary market the key players buy and sell instruments mostly OTC. Although much relevant information is displayed on screens from Reuters and other services, the rates quoted are only indicators. Market prices can change very quickly and so telephone trading is used for firm rates to be quoted and accepted.

In order to take advantage of the markets there are two simple techniques which are used:

Go long – In this case the instruments are bought in the hope that their prices will rise and they can be sold when the price has peaked.

Go short – In this case the instruments, prices are expected to fall so they are sold in the hope that they can be bought back after the price has fallen.

Of course the situation in practice is more complex than described here. If you would like to keep up to date with news on Eurobonds try this.

In effect all these people form part of the group described as intermediaries and are banks or broker-dealers who are vital in the operation of the secondary markets. These intermediaries bring together issuers and investors by:

- Providing advice to their clients on corporate finance, mergers and acquisitions

- Participating in the new issue process

- Placing new issues with investors through their sales system

- Acting as market makers in the secondary markets

- Acting as IDBs – the broker's broker

- Acting as an agency or retail broker

To gain a better idea of how the players in this market operate, look at the following pages describing a typical morning's events. Reuters screens are provided to illustrate the information that market players need for their daily decision-making. Once you have completed this, look at the *Diary of a Salesperson,* which describes in more detail how the players relate to each other and the pace of market activity. The notes accompanying the diary entries will also give you a feel for some of the jargon salespeople use, which will be useful for you to understand.

The diary is in the left column, and the notes concerning relevant jargon and other points are in the right column.

As you will see, sales people are in many ways the lynch pin of the secondary market – they are in contact with all the others involved in the sale of a bond.

Your notes

Market Makers/Traders/Dealers

Activity

1. At the beginning of the day the first thing Market makers/Dealers/Traders will want to know is what events have taken place overnight. The screens they will use will depend on the currencies they trade in. Suppose they need to know about US dollars, sterling and economic indicators... ➡

For news on US dollars they would look at currency news update page like this.

```
08:46  26 May  RTRS-Dollar/yen, mark/yen testing new highs in Europe
   0830 GMT - Dlr/yen ticks to fresh peak, highest since Aug 1991, mark/yen at over
five-year high in morning Europe, testing cap at 78.00. U.S. Treasury's Rubin
reported comments tolerating yen decline and no BOJ intervention behind latest
yen fall. Mkt shrugs off Japan's MOF warning of unfavourable effects of weak
yen. U.S. April home sales, May consumer confidence 1400 GMT.

For full London dollar report in English click [USD/L-LEN]
   0830 GMT - Dlr/yen ticks to fresh peak, highest since Aug 1991, mark/yen at over
five-year high in morning Europe, testing cap at 78.00. U.S. Treasury's Rubin
reported comments tolerating yen decline and no BOJ intervention behind latest
yen fall. Mkt shrugs off Japan's MOF warning of unfavourable effects of weak
yen. U.S. April home sales, May consumer confidence 1400 GMT.
For full London dollar report in English click [USD/L-LEN]

For related news, double click on one of the following codes:
[M] [T] [MF] [D] [E] [FRX] [US] [LEN] [RTRS] [USD/]

Tuesday, 26 May 1998 08:46:49
RTRS [nFLLF5Q3AD]
```

For news on sterling they would pull up screens focussing on sterling news.

```
08:27  26 May  RTRS-Sterling eases from session peaks against mark
   0820 GMT - Stg/mark eases from session peaks, needs to sustain gains above
2.8770 to keep upside in focus. Cable steady.
  * Stg/mark at 2.8788/98 vs Tuesday's high of 2.8823 and 2.8745/50 late in Europe
on Monday. Cable at $1.6292/02 vs $1.6275/85 yesterday.
  * No major UK economic reports or events scheduled for Tuesday.
  * Britain's Barclays Bank forecasts UK rates to fall to 5.5 pct by end of 1999 and
expects growth to slow to 1.5 pct next year, expects stg to fall back too.
  * September short-sterling futures contract down two basis points at 92.63,
giving implied rate of 7.37 pct.
  * Stg/yen firm amid broad-based yen weakness, at 224.21/52 vs 223.08/18 late in
Europe on Monday. Dlr/yen hit highest in nearly seven years on Tuesday,
reaching 137.73.
  * BoE's stg trade-weighted index at 102.9 vs Fri close of 102.5 and about 5.5 pct
below its April peaks.
((Swaha Pattanaik, London newsroom +44 171 542 6384

For related news,
[M] [T] [UKI] [IRL]
[GBPX1=] [RTAW

For related price
<GBPX1=> <RTA

Tuesday, 26 May
RTRS [nFLLF5Q3
```

For news on economic indicators, the Reuters consensus of Key Economic Indicators page is very useful.

```
06:50  26 May  RTRS-TABLE-Reuters consensus of key economic indicators
GMT--DAY------KEY INDICATOR--------F/CAST-----RANGE----PRVS
0645 Tue   FRA. CONSUMER SPEND   APR   N/F PCT      N/A    -0.1
0645 Tue   FRA. CONSUMER PRICES APR  +0.3 PCT      N/A    +0.3
0645 Tue   FRA. CPI FINAL (Y/Y) APR  +1.0 PCT      N/A    +1.0
0645 Tue   FRA. HOUSING STARTS NAPR   N/F PCT      N/A     9.3
1230 Tue   CAN. INDUSTRIAL PRICEAPR  +0.03 PCT     N/A    -1.0
1230 Tue   CAN. RAW MATERIALS    APR  +1.3 PCT      N/A    -2.7
1400 Tue   U.S. EXIST HOME SALESAPR  4.72 MLN      N/A     4.89
1400 Tue   U.S. CONSUMER CONF    MAY  134.7         N/A   136.7
N/A  Tu-Th W.G. CST OF LVNG (PRVMAY  +1.1 PCT   1.1/1.1   +1.3
0645 Wed   FRA. TRADE BAL. (FF.)MAR   N/F BLN      N/A   +13.9
2350 Wed   JPN. INDUST PROD PRELAPR   N/F PCT      N/A    -2.3
2350 Wed   JPN. INDUST PREL (NSAAPR   N/F PCT      N/A    -5.1
2350 Wed   JPN. RETAIL SLS (PRELAPR   N/F PCT      N/A   -13.8
0500 Thu   JPN. LEADING IND     MAR   N/F PCT      N/A    22.2
0500 Thu   JPN. COINCIDENT IND  MAR   N/F PCT      N/A    25.0
1230 Thu   U.S. JOBLESS CLMS   23-Ma +311K         N/A   +313K
1230 Thu   U.S. REAL GDP (prel) Q1   +4.4 PCT      N/A    +4.2
1230 Thu   U.S. IMPLICIT DEFLATOQ1   +0.9 PCT      N/A    +0.9
1230 Thu   U.S. PRICE INDEX      Q1   +0.9 PCT      N/A    +0.9
1230 Thu   CAN. AVG WKLY ERNS   MAR   +2.2 PCT      N/A    +2.2
1400 Thu   U.S. DURABLE GDS ORDSAPR   +0.8 PCT      N/A    +0.5
1400 Thu   U.S. EX DEFENCE      APR   N/F PCT      N/A    +0.8
1400 Thu   U.S. HELP WANTED INDXAPR   N/F          N/A     92
2030 Thu   U.S. M1              18-Ma N/F BLN      N/A   -17.8
```

Market Makers/Traders/Dealers

Activity

1. (cont.) The Market Makers/Traders/Dealers may also want to find out about sterling new issues...➡

For news on sterling new issues they would look at the page with sterling news updates.

```
07:20  26 May  RTRS-UK gilts gain in early trade, outclass Bunds
  0719 GMT - UK gilts push ahead slightly from opening levels, trade seen
subdued. Spread to Bunds dips below 100, short end inches up.
⋈ June 10-yr futures up 0.33 at 108.86 after 108.71 open.
⋈ June sht stg up 0.01 at 92.50, Sept up 0.20 at 92.63.
  LONDON, May 26 (Reuters) - British gilts pushed ahead in early trade on
Tuesday, after a public holiday in London on Monday, managing to outperform
Bunds on the way.
  Traders expected a subdued start to the week, with little for the market to get
its teeth into before Thursday's Confederation of British Industry monthly trends
survey.
  "We've got a fairly quiet week in prospect," said one senior gilts trader. "I've got
107.50 as a good buying level and 109.25 as a good selling level – so I wouldn't
expect to find too many aggressive buyers at the moment but I'm not sure it's
ready to sell yet."
  The June 10-year contract built on opening gains in early trade. By 0725 GMT it
was up 0.37 at 108.91 after opening at 108.71. The September contract was up
0.43 at 109.20.
  Analysts at HSBC Markets said they favoured the shorter or intermediate
sector of the gilt curve, around five years.
  They noted that the potentially tricky part of the month when the consumer side
economic numbers are published had passed. "Gilts now face the trade and
industrial reports which are, if anything, likely to provide a further fillip to interest
rate sentiment," they said.
  HSBC said the 10-year sector of the curve looked relatively expensive,
suggesting investors should consider shortening trades out of 10s into fives.
```

2. As Market Makers/Traders/Dealers trade in markets other than debt they will need to find out what has been happening in the currency markets and what has been happening to interest rates. To do this they would look at... ➡

For Currency and interest rate news, these pages are useful.

```
EFX=                   Latest Spots
RIC          Bid/Ask   Contributor   Loc Srce Deal   Time  High     Low
DEM=   ↓  1.7655/60    CHASE         LON CHFX CHFX   09:00 1.7687   1.7625
JPY=   ↓  137.57/7.67  BARCLAYS      GFX BGFX        08:59 137.73   137.04
GBP=   ↑  1.6308/13    ULSTER BANK   DUB UBFX UIBI   09:00 1.6310   1.6288
CHF=   ↓  1.4699/09    SBC WARBURG   ZUR SBZX SBZX   09:00 1.4740   1.4708
FRF=   ↓  5.9211/31    SAN PAOLO     PAR      SPSP   09:00 5.9304   5.9110
NLG=   ↓  1.9900/05    ING BANK      AMS INGX INGX   09:00 1.9930   1.9862
ITL=   ↓  1740.50/2.00 BARCLAYS      LON BAXX BBIL   09:00 1743.90  1736.00
BEF=   ↓  36.420/460   BARCLAYS      LON BAXX BBLD   08:57 36.472   36.360
ECU=   ↑  1.1142/47    BCI           MIL BCIX BCIY   08:59 1.1170   1.1134
XAU=   ↓  298.80/9.20  J ARON        LON JAUK JAUK   08:40 299.65   298.80
XAG=   ↑  5.28/5.31    UBS           ZRH UBZB UBCH   08:46 5.31     5.28
IEP=   ↓  1.4240/60    ULSTER BANK   DUB UBFY UIBI   09:00 1.4280   1.4244
AUD=   ↓  0.6235/45    BARCLAYS      GFX BGFX        08:57 0.6268   0.6233
CAD=   ↓  1.4510/15    ROYAL BK CAN  LON RBCL RBCL   08:58 1.4514   1.4495
ATS=   ↓  12.4240/90   BKS           KLU BKSB BKSK   09:00 12.4440  12.4004
ESP=   ↑  150.03/0.08  BC ATLANTICO  MAD ATLX ATLY   08:57 150.24   149.73
SEK=   ↓  7.7048/98    SE BANKEN     STO SEBI SEBI   09:00 7.7142   7.6910
NOK=   ↑  7.4510/13    CHASE         LON CHEQ CHNO   09:00 7.4625   7.4380
DKK=   ↑  6.7243/83    SE BANKEN     SIN SEBX SEBS   09:01 6.7339   6.7133
FIM=
PTE=
GRD=
RUB=
TRL=
```

```
GBPX=                 GBP X-RATES CALC
RIC         Bid      Ask      Srce Time     RIC         Bid      Ask      Srce Time
GBP=        1.6308   1.6318   BGFX 09:01
GBPDEM=R    2.8795   2.8805        09:01    AUDGBP=R    0.3822   0.3831        08:58
GBPJPY=R    224.36   224.48        08:59    GBPCAD=R    2.3663   2.3678        09:00
GBPCHF=R    2.3971   2.3995        09:00    NZDGBP=R    0.3281   0.3289        08:58
GBPFRF=R    9.6561   9.6624        09:00    GBPHKD=R    12.6283  12.6377       08:58
GBPNLG=R    3.2450   3.2468        09:01    GBPSGD=R    2.6955   2.6988        08:59
GBPBEF=R    59.394   59.477        09:00    GBPMYR=R    6.2323   6.3666        08:58
GBPITL=R    2838.41  2841.72       09:00    GBPECU=R    1.4630   1.4641        09:00
GBPDKK=R    10.9660  10.9759       09:01    GBPATS=R    20.2594  20.2738       09:01
GBPFIM=R    8.747    8.758         09:01    GBPESP=R    244.67   244.83        09:00
GBPNOK=R    12.1511  12.1553       09:00    GBPZAR=R    8.3597   8.3697        08:58
GBPSEK=R    12.5650  12.5770       09:00    IEPGBP=R    0.8728   0.8745        09:01
XAUGBP=R    183.13   183.49        09:01    XAGGBP=R    3.2361   3.2565        09:01
GBPPTE=R    294.8976 295.1185      09:00
```

3. The next thing to be done is to re-price the books and update screens. Updating can be carried out either:

   • Manually
   • From a Reuters page
   • From another trader's books

Market Makers/Traders/Dealers

Activity

4. In the normal course of events the next thing to happen would be a check on prices from different brokers – see what the opposition is up to! ➤

Information on different brokers can be viewed on broker pages.

*It is likely that the code for particular information will be well known and entered directly, for example, **CFIGBX**.*

5. As for item 2. because Market Makers/Traders/Dealers trade in markets other than debt they will need to find out what has been happening in the futures and options markets. In particular they will be interested in market trends... ➤

For this information they would use the suite of pages starting with the index page.

6. The Market Makers/Traders/Dealers will need to compare world yields for bonds. They may also need LIFFE Gilts Cheapest to Deliver futures information... ➤

For this information they would use pages such as the world yields and LIFFE CTD page.

7. Finally, the Market Makers/Traders/Dealers can carry out a Rich/Cheap analysis. This identifies bonds which are over/under performing and therefore which should be bought or sold ... ➤

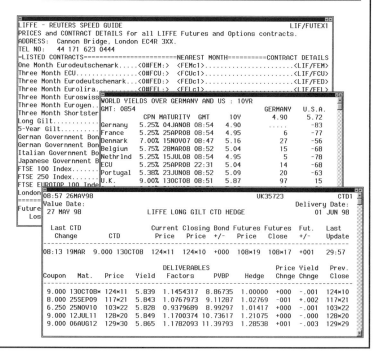

Agency or Retail brokers/IDBs/Financial Analysts and Economists

Activity

Agency or Retail Brokers

First thing each day these brokers need to look at the overnight news. They need to know what's moving and follow the trends in the market. These brokers do not take positions in the market – they flourish on turnover, so they have to be on the ball... ➨

There are a number of pages of interest to these brokers such as these, which are all concerend with new issues.

```
08:57  RTRS-Österreich bringt eine Mrd DM 10J-Anleihe
08:57  RTRS-WESTLB ADDS 500 MLN MARKS TO 4.75 PCT DEC 2006 BOND, TO BE PRICED +8.5 BP -
       LEADS
08:55  RTRS-GECC SETS $300 MLN ONE-YEAR FRN, 3ML -12.5 BP, AT 100.04 -DAIWA
08:48  RTRS-Kommuninvest sets 1.0 bln SEK May 2005 bond
08:46  RTRS-KOMMUNINVEST SETS 1.0 BLN SEK MAY 2005 MUNICIPAL FUNGIBLE BOND -
       SWEDBANK
08:43  Russia Tatarstan sees S&P rating,bond licence soon
08:39  RTRS-Kommuninvest utökar femårigt lån - FSPA<FSPAa.ST>
08:38  Lowest Russian repo rate at auction 48.61 pct
08:35  JI
08:34  S   08:57  RTRS-Österreich bringt eine Mrd DM 10J-Anleihe
08:33  R   08:57  RTRS-WESTLB ADDS 500 MLN MARKS TO 4.75 PCT DEC 2006 BOND, TO BE PRICED +8.5 BP -
       M           LEADS
08:33  JI  08:55  RTRS-GECC SETS $300 MLN ONE-YEAR FRN, 3ML -12.5 BP, AT 100.04 -DAIWA
08:33  JI  08:48  RTRS-Kommuninvest sets 1.0 bln SEK May 2005 bond
08:32  JI  08:46  RTRS-KOMMUNINVEST SETS 1.0 BLN SEK MAY 2005 MUNICIPAL FUNGIBLE BOND -
08:26  R           SWEDBANK
           08:43  Russia Tatarstan sees S&P rating,bond licence soon
           08:21  RTRS-Austria sets 1.0 bln mark 10-year bond, +6 b.p.
           08:18  RTRS-AUSTRIA SETS 1.0 BLN MARK 10-YEAR BOND TO BE PRICED +6 BP-LEAD
           08:06  RTRS-Berlin Hannover Hypo adds 500 mln marks to bond,
           08:05  RTRS-DSL <SLRGg.D> sets 10 bln drachma three-year bond
           08:02  RTRS-BERLIN HANNOVER HYPO ADDS 500 MLN DEM TO 4.5 PCT JUN 2005 BOND, TBP +9 BP -
```

```
09:04 26MAY98    INTERNATIONAL INSIDER SCREEN SERVICE   UK31060           IIIA
----------- SCREEN INSIDER - TUESDAY ------ +44 171 353 7311
<IIIB> ABN AMRO FORMS GROUP FOR ONTARIO STERLING STRAIGHT
<IIIC> ** CSFB LAUNCHES SWISS RE FINANCE EXCHANGE INTO ING **
<IIID> MUNICH HYPO SET AT FPR 99.31 - FTT 11:15 FFURT *
<IIIE> ** DAIWA LAUNCHES 1-YEAR DOLLAR FRN FOR GECC **
<IIIF> PAINEWEBBER FORMS GROUP FOR DSL DRACHMA DEAL
<IIIG> SBCWDR FORMS GROUP FOR AUSTRIA DM BUNDESANLEIHE
<IIIH> ** SWEDBANK LAUNCHES SKR STRAIGHT FOR KOMMUNINVEST **
<IIII> ** WESTLB JUMBO PFANDBRIEF INCREASED TO DM 2.5BN *
<IIIJ> DRESDNER BANK FLUX GROUP // ALCATEL-ALSTHOLM EQTY-LNKD
<IIIK> NOMURA LAUNCHES SFR CV FOR NISSEI ASB MACHINE CO
<IIIL> ** BERLIN-HANNOVERSCHE INC PRICED: 98.09, 97.91RE **
                                           ---- FAX +44 171 583 1895
FOR ASIAN NEWS SEE <IIJA>, BONDWATCH <WATCH01>, EM <EMMA01>
```

IDBs

The IDBs are interested in the current prices of new issues because they have the highest turnover of the secondary market players. Their profit depends on the spread of this turnover... ➨

The IDBs use the same pages as the agency brokers.

Financial Analysts and Economists

These experts use data of the historic performance between markets for forecasting purposes... ➨

They too use the new issue pages.

```
02:06 26MAY98   Eurobonds : New Issues                CA01952        NEWEUROS
    Issuer        Coupon   Mat Dat  Cur  War  Reuter ID Code  Z Code

MEDIQ            11.0000   01JUN08  USD       <Z91W=>          <Z91W>
LB RHEINLAND-PFZ  6.0300   11DEC00  GBP       <DE008740895=>   <Z93K>
DEPFA AG            -      12JUN02  GRD       <DE008770727=>   <Z93L>
SEK                 -      12JUN08  ESP       <Z93M=>          <Z93M>
SUNTORY           2.0000   10JUN08  JPY       <JP008768641=>   <Z930>
SUDWEST LB        8.2500   05JUN01  GRD       <DE008765197=>   <Z93F>
SEARS CREDIT      6.0000   15AUG05  USD       <Z93H=>          <Z93H>
BAY VEREINSBANK   8.0000   19JUN01  NZD       <DE008762325=>   <Z91M>
SCHIG             5.1250   18JUN10  FRF       <AT008764042=>   <Z91P>
BANK AUSTRIA      9.5500   29MAY00  HKD       <Z91S=>          <Z91S>
JUMBO ASSET FIN   2.0300   28MAY03  JPY       <KY008680400=>   <Z92F>
BANK NEDERL GEM   8.2500   04JUN01  GRD       <NL008765286=>   <ZBZW>
NATL AUST BANK      -      18JUN01  XEU       <AU008763712=>   <Z91Q>
ECCO              5.2500   18JUN08  DEM       <US008763089=>   <Z91O>
ITALY             6.0000   29MAY08  USD       <IT008762988=>   <Z92E>
NORD LANDESBK     2.5000   30JUN01  ESP       <Z91N=>          <Z91N>
ROYAL BK OF CAN     -      02JUN03  GBP       <CA008762210=>   <Z91U>
JUMBO ASSET FIN   4.0000   28MAY03  JPY       <Z92G=>          <Z92G>
FED HOME LOAN     5.6250   02JUN00  USD       <US008768579=>   <Z91V>
ECCO              5.5000   18JUN08  DEM       <US008763143=>   <Z91R>
For more information, see the following:
<BONDS> <EUROBONDS> <NEWGOVS> Page Forward: <NEWEUROT> 1st Page: <NEWEUROS>
```

Sales People

Activity

1. At the beginning of the day the first thing sales people will want to know is the overnight news and relationships between markets. They will want to know both current and projected interest rates. The pages they will use will depend on the currencies they trade in. Suppose they need to know about sterling... ➡

For general details on deposits they would use this index page, and then select, for example, GBPF = for information on the sterling markets.

2. They will also need to find out what has been happening in the currency markets and what has been happening to interest rates. To do this they would look at... ➡

For currency and interest rate news, pages such as these are useful.

```
DEPOSITS - REUTERS SPEED GUIDE                                      DEPO/1
Detailed below are retrieval codes for key DEPOSIT displays.

=DEPOSITS MAJORS=====================   =DEPOSITS BY CURRENCY Cont=============
Major Deposits...................<DM=>   German Mark Deposits...........<DEMF=>
Asia Deposits....................<DA=>   German Mark Domestic Deposits..<DEDEPO>
                                         Greek Drachna Deposits.........<GRDF=>
=DEPOSITS by CURRENCY=================    Hong Kong Dollar Deposits......<HKDF=>
Australian Dollar Deposits......<AUDF=>  Hungarian Forint Deposits......<HUFF=>
Austrian Schilling Deposits.....<ATSF=>  Indian Rupee Deposits..........<INRF=>
Belgian Franc Deposits..........<BEFF=>  Irish Punt Deposits............<IEPF=>
British Pound Deposits..........<GBPF=>  Italian Lira Deposits..........<ITLF=>
Canadian Dollar Deposits........<CADF=>  Japanese Yen Deposits..........<JPYF=>
Czech Koruna Deposits...........<CZKF=>  Kuwaiti Dinar Deposits.........<KWDF=>
Danish Krone Deposits...........<DKKF=>  Latvian Lat Deposits...........<LVLF=>
Dutch Guilder Deposits..........<NLGF=>
Estonian Kroon Deposits.........<EEKF=>  More currencies on page <DEPO/2>
Eurodeposits - Netherlands.<EURODEP=NL>
ECU Dep
Finnish  GBPF=              GBP Deps & Fwds
French   RIC       Bid     Ask     Srce Time    RIC        Bid     Ask    Srce Time
Questio  GBP=     1.6310  1.6320  SCXX 09:09
         GBPOND=   7.25    7.37   DRPP 08:53   GBPON=    -0.81   -0.78   DDBZ 09:00
Main In  GBPTND=   7.31    7.43   KRB3 07:35   GBPTN=    -0.83   -0.80   DDBZ 09:00
    Los  GBPSWD=   7.25    7.37   DRPP 08:53   GBPSN=    -0.84   -0.79   CLUK 08:39
         GBP1MD=   7.40    7.50   MPSX 08:52   GBPSW=    -5.65   -5.55   DDBZ 09:00
         GBP2MD=   7.40    7.46   NMRM    :    GBP1M=   -26.8   -24.7    SWEG 08:39
         GBP3MD=   7.40    7.53   GIBX 07:02   GBP2M=    -49     -47     NWNB 08:58
         GBP6MD=   7.43    7.53   MPSX 08:52   GBP3M=    -72.0   -69.0   SWEG 08:39
         GBP9MD=   7.37    7.50   RABQ    :    GBP6M=   -135.0  -134.0   AAFW 09:07
         GBP1YD=   7.34    7.46   DRPP 08:15   GBP9M=   -186    -183     DDBZ 09:02
                                              GBP1Y=   -239    -229     UBZF 09:05
                                              GBP2Y=   -357    -325     BBOR 09:07
```

3. Next the sales people will need information on yields... ➡

Yields for the major currencies are found on the World Yield Index. The world yields over Germany and US where the yields are annualised for comparison.

```
WORLD YIELDS OVER GERMANY AND US : 10YR
GMT: 0854                                          GERMANY    U.S.A.
           CPN MATURITY  GMT      10Y              4.90      5.72
Germany   5.25% 04JAN08 08:54    4.90              ....      -83
France    5.25% 25APR08 08:54    4.95               6        -77
Dennark   7.00% 15NOV07 08:47    5.16              27        -56
Belgium   5.75% 28MAR08 08:52    5.04              15        -68
Nethrlnd  5.25% 15JUL08 08:54    4.95               5        -78
ECU       5.25% 25APR08 22:31    5.04              14        -68
Portugal  5.38% 23JUN08 08:52    5.09              20        -63
U.K.      9.00% 13OCT08 08:51    5.87              97         15
Spain     6.00% 31JAN08 08:54    5.08              19        -64
Italy     6.00% 01NOV07 08:55    5.17              27        -56
Sweden    6.50% 05MAY08 08:15    5.12              23        -60
Austria   5.00% 15JAN08 08:53    4.99              10        -73
Swtzrlnd  4.25% 08JAN08 08:52    3.06            -184       -266
Finland   6.00% 25APR08 08:32    5.02              12        -70
Norway    6.75% 15JAN07 08:49    5.50              60        -22
N.Zealand 7.00% 15JUL09 06:03    6.64             174         92
Australia 8.75% 15AUG08 08:38    5.65              75         -7
Japan     1.90% 20MAR08 08:22    1.54            -336       -418
Canada    6.00% 01JUN08 08:25    5.45              55        -27
U.S.A.    5.63% 15MAY08 18:07    5.72              82        ....
          Note: All yields annualized for conparison
```

4. Once the yields have been looked at it may be necessary to use an analytic service such as RT Graphics... ➡

RT Graphics provides a core set of analysis functions for all financial markets.

Sales People

Activity

5. Next they will probably want to look at benchmarks. Depending on the currencies they are interested in they can use the Treasury index page. Suppose they are interested in Japanese government bonds... ➡

From the TREASURY page they would go to the Japanese Government Bonds Benchmark – OTC. The TREASURY page can be used to access information on benchmarks for all countries.

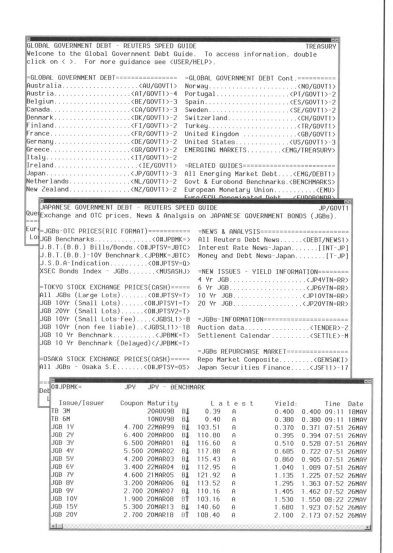

6. They will also need to look at the new issues pages... ➡

NEWEUROS and IIIA are the pages they use.

7. Once all this has been done they can then catch up with reading quotes and information from other sources. The sales people are now ready to start with their telephone calls – unless they have been interrupted already!

Diary

7:45 *Just come out of the morning meeting armed with run-downs of what happened in New York and Tokyo overnight, and what the economist forecasts for today's US figures due out at 1:30. We've also got the traders' "shopping list", bonds they particularly want us to try and sell or buy for them today. Some hope on that Toyota DEM issue - the trader has had that on his books for about ten days now without a glimmer of interest from the clients. He'll have to cut it out soon and take his losses. Oh well, time to start the morning round of calls.*

8:30 *Taken an overnight order from a Far East customer who thinks the market is going to rally after the figure so has left an order to sell US Treasuries into the strength.*

9:15 *I've now finished ringing round all my major accounts to give them the daily run-down and see if they have got anything special to do. I've been asked for a few price levels but no-one has actually traded*
so far, they seem to be waiting for something.

9:30 *A big Middle Eastern customer has just rung up for a price on a French name US dollar straight and would you believe it the trader was in the loo! The supranational name trader gave me a price but it wasn't very aggressive because he doesn't know how French AAs trade over Treasuries and so just compared it to how his book trades.*

Anyway, the customer traded away from me so I missed out on that one. At least he phoned.

Notes

The morning meeting is held by most trading houses everyday and is an opportunity for traders and sales to get together and pass on information about what has happened overnight in the other centres, and to let each other know what they think is going to happen that day and any particular situations they may have.

Traders will generally be given a maximum amount of time they are allowed to hold any position on their books. They must work with a short term investment horizon and will have to take their losses by selling back into the market if they are unable to sell their stock to customers.

This is an order that can be executed any time before the following morning without further reference to the client giving the order.

Asking for a price level is asking for information on where the market has been trading, but not for a dealing price. If a customer asks for a price level and then wants to deal there is no obligation on the trader to deal at the price previously given. If there is intent to deal the customer must ask for a price.

Traders will normally trade a certain type of bond, either a certain type of name or a certain type of maturity. They will then know how their bonds will trade compared to the benchmark market (the treasury bond market), but this knowledge may not directly translate to another sector of the market. This is why it is difficult for traders to swap books as they may be unaware of the peculiarities of each other's markets.

Traded away: Dealt with another house.

Diary

9:45   *Just heard a rumour that there could be a new jumbo deal coming out from Italy in fixed-rate dollars. I'm hearing 2 or 3 billion dollars and five years maturity, priced at about T+35.*

     I had better mention it to the Syndicate desk and see what they have got to say about it.

9:50   *The ECU trader has just been on the voice-box with a really good offer in ECU 10 million EIB. This sounds ideal for one of my Central Bank accounts so I had better rush straight off and show it to them.*

10:00   *The Central Bank is interested in the EIB but needs to sell some World Bank before they have room to take it. I've told the trader what price they are looking for, which, as usual, is in the middle of his bid-offer spread, so he isn't willing to buy it outright, but I've got an order for fifteen minutes firm, and then subject after that, to see if we can find another customer willing to take them.*

     The trader is willing to pass it through for a couple of ticks.

10:05   *Another salesman has got a buyer for the World Bank ECU so I've been able to do the switch out of World Bank into EIB. Incidentally the Syndicate desk weren't too happy when I mentioned the Italy to them but I haven't had a chance to talk about it because I was caught up with this trade, so I'll give them a call back now and find out what's going on..*

Notes

Jumbo: A large deal, greater than USD 1 billion.

T+35 means the yield on this issue is expected to be the yield on the equivalent benchmark, in this case the 5 year Treasury Bond, plus an additional 35 basis points. For example, if the 5 year Treasury was yielding 7.00%, this deal would yield 7.35%.

The Syndicate desk are the people who create the new issues.

A firm order is one that can be executed without further reference for a given period of time.

A subject order is one that can only be executed with reference to the customer. Not a firm commitment to buy or sell.

The trader is willing to buy the bonds from one customer and sell it to another for only a couple of basis points difference in price. This deal is not intended to be very profitable but will enable the trader to make money on another trade. Also this deal will be a risk-free trade, matching up a buyer and a seller.

A switch is selling one security and buying another in its place.

The reason the Syndicate desk may not have been happy about this is because they could be afraid that all their potential investors will choose to buy the Italy deal rather than another deal that they themselves are pricing and will bring to the market.

Diary

10:15   Now I know why they weren't too happy! It seems they are working on a sovereign deal themselves and are worried this Italy will steal their thunder. I've got to ring round the customers and find out what their reaction to a 7 year, top-quality sovereign would be. We always do this to test the market's appetite and help with pricing the deal.

11:00   I've had a few customers selling out fixed rate dollar paper and making room for the new issues they think are on their way. It seems as though the Italy is definite, the rumour has even been mentioned on the screens. I don't think Syndicate are happy bunnies!

11:05   The Italy has just been announced and it looks rather tight to me. Not T+35 but T+30. Anyway we are Co-Manager in the deal and have got 20 million to go at the fixed price re-offer. I might ring up that Middle East customer who sold the French paper this morning and see if he was clearing out ready to buy this one.

11:30   The market seems really bullish because this Italy is selling like hot-cakes. I managed to do five million with the Middle Eastern and we quickly sold out of our commitment. Syndicate are trying to get hold of the Lead Manager to see if we can have our commitment increased and in the meantime the new issues trader is trying to buy paper in the market. I'm going to ring up a few of the small Italian banks who are Co-Managers to see if I can get any paper from them.

11:40   I've just found out our deal is going to be launched this afternoon. The issuer is the UK so it should go really well. I'm a bit worried about the timing, though, because if the market does go up after the figures it could look a bit cheap, but maybe I'm just a pessimist.

12:00   Lunch

Notes

A paper is a general term for securities, commercial paper, money market instruments etc.

A tight deal has a narrow spread to Treasuries and is therefore offering a low yield to investors.

The fixed price re-offer is the fixed price at which every member of the syndicate group must offer their underwriting commitment to their customers, and no cheaper.

A bullish market is one in which prices are rising and yields are falling.

Diary

13:20 *Had to make sure I was back in time for the figures today. We are waiting for unemployment figures and the market expects unemployment to have risen which will be good for the market. At the moment, with just ten minutes to go, the markets are all very quiet. I'm about to ring up my biggest customer so that I have them on the line when the figure comes out and they can hear what our economist has got to say about it.*

13:35 *The figure has just come out and unemployment has actually risen slightly more than we expected it to, so this should be really good for the market. My customer immediately asked for an offer in the long bond and bought ten million for a quick punt.*

The long bond trader has just shouted out that he is paying 6 ticks higher for them now so I'll see if the customer wants to take their profit.

13:40 *The economist says the figure was higher than expected on a technical readjustment so he expects the market to come back again. I told this to my customer who sold back his 10 million long bonds – at a profit of 8 ticks! Not a bad ten minutes work for him. I must check where the order from this morning was filled so I can send a message to them confirming the trade and telling them what happened post-figure.*

13:50 *The market seems to have eased off, but only slightly. The market is still very bullish. We've just been called to a quick meeting about this UK which is going to be announced in ten minutes.*

14:00 *The UK has just come out and we are all up to our eyeballs ringing round letting the customers know the terms and conditions. Syndicate are on the phone to the news services so it will be on the screen in a few minutes, but in the meantime it's best to let people know it's out, that we're the Lead Manager, and to offer paper at the fixed price re-offer. It does look quite cheap yield-wise, especially since the yields*

Notes

The markets will always become very quiet immediately before major economic figures are announced as traders and investors wait to see what the figures have to say about the state of the underlying economy. If unemployment rises, this means the economy is slowing and so the Fed may lower the interest rates to stimulate the markets. If interest rates fall, then bond prices rise.

The long bond is the thirty year US Treasury.

A quick punt is a short term investment made purely in anticipation of a price rise.

The price of the bond has risen by six minimum price movements. In this instance for the long bond this means 6/32nds.

To come back again: to fall back in price.

Diary

have come down this afternoon, but the spread over Treasuries is quite good at T+5. I'm going to suggest to people that maybe they want to take profit on the Italy from this morning and buy this instead. This would not be a classic switch as they will pay up in price and give up in yield, but on the other hand the UK is a better credit, has tremendous rarity value and is likely to go up in price when the syndicate is broken.

Ultimately the whole deal is likely to be well placed so I don't think they are likely to lose out on this one.

14:20   *This deal seems to be going really well, the phones haven't stopped ringing. We're also getting a lot of interest from the off-shore US accounts, and I think it should go well in Tokyo.*

I've been in touch with a few of the representative offices here of the Japanese regional banks who might be interested out of their Tokyo offices, and if I make the effort to ensure they are kept in touch they will probably come back to us if they have interest.

15:00   *We have already broken the syndicate on the UK and it is free to trade away from the re-offer price. This is a good indication of how well the deal has been received. The market is very strong this afternoon. Secondary market prices have gone up, on average, by about $1/_4$ - $1/_2$%, which is a pretty big movement. I think we are bound to see a bit of profit-taking before the end of the day.*

Notes

When the syndicate is broken the deal will be free to trade at any price determined by the market.

The deal is likely to be placed with investors rather than being left on the inventory of dealers.

A new US dollar eurobond deal cannot normally be sold in the primary market to US investors, as the intention is to sell the deal internationally. However many US customers have off-shore accounts, such as in Bermuda, through which they will book their trades in new issues.

Representative offices are not allowed to deal for their own account but are only representing the head office, and can therefore only act on their instructions.

Diary

15:30 *I've just been asked by a customer whether it's true that the UK might be increased in size, and I've had a big row with the Syndicate desk. If we are the Lead Manager on the deal I think we salespeople ought to be told things like that before our customers ask us something we know nothing about. Apparently it is just a rumour, but there is a chance it will be increased because of the terrific demand.*

15:50 *The UK has just been increased by another USD500 million. It shouldn't really have too much impact on the price because it was expected, and the market has really calmed down now. I think the traders have had a pretty good day, but they are a bit long on paper now with customers doing a bit of profit-taking, so we are doing a quick run round showing out a few special offers to see if we can help flatten their books for them.*

16:20 *Time to add my bit to the daily summary which goes across to the New York office, and is then passed on to the Far East. It is mainly for the traders to put down their positions and what they are trying to do with them, but the salespeople will also mention any situations we have got going on, such as customers potentially buying or selling anything or any information we have picked up from London offices which might be useful for people talking to the New York or Tokyo offices of the same firm. It is also helpful for them just to have a rundown of what our customers have been doing and looking at.*

16:45 *This has been a busy day, I wish they were all like this. It makes a big difference when you have a good product to show people, and also the mood of the market was helpful as everyone was keen to get involved. We sold a lot of paper today and the good thing is that there still seems to be more appetite out there, so as long as nothing goes wrong overnight I think we can expect a good day tomorrow.*

17:00 *Time to go home.*

Notes

To go long on paper means that they have bought a lot of debt from their customers and need to resell it.

Flatten their books: to reduce the positions on the traders' books.

How Bonds Are Traded

Bonds may be issued in a number of ways – different markets have their own conventions. The main methods used are:

- **Registered**
  This is where the current owner is recorded in a register retained by the issuer or the issuer's agent. As ownership changes the register is altered accordingly.

- **Bearer bonds**
  In this case the owner is anonymous in that no investor's name is recorded on the bond – whoever "bears" the bond owns it. In some cases bearer bonds are also registered.

- **Book-entry**
  These instruments do not have a physical certificate but are registered electronically with **custodian banks**.

It is worth remembering that bonds mainly trade OTC but some exchange trading of listed bonds also takes place. The regulation of each of these markets differs considerably and investors should be aware of the appropriate trading procedures.

Some markets for bonds are extremely liquid, for example, trading in US government securities. Trading in some Eurobonds can be illiquid as the instruments have been targeted at a small group of investors as a long-term investment. An indication of the relative liquidity for any particular bond can be gained from the **difference between the bid and ask prices** for the bond – this is termed the **spread**. The smaller the spread the greater the liquidity; the wider the spread the more illiquid the bond.

In the case of Eurobonds, which are usually bearer bonds, there is a risk of loss or theft of the bonds to consider. Most Eurobonds are not kept by the investors but are held in safe custody on their behalf by one of the clearing houses. The two largest international clearing houses are **Euroclear** based in Brussels and **Cedel** in Luxembourg.

The Euroclear System was created in 1968 and is owned by the participants of the Belgian co-operative corporation – Euroclear Clearance System Société Coopérative. The Euroclear System is run under contract from Brussels by the Morgan Guaranty Trust Company of New York.

Cedel was originally created in 1970 by 66 world financial institutions as a clearing organisation to minimise risks in the Eurobond markets. The group headquarters is in Luxembourg and there are offices in Dubai, Hong Kong, London, New York and Tokyo.

Both clearing houses offer similar services, which broadly cover the following:

- **Clearance**
  This provides buyers and sellers with an efficient and economic means of settling transactions. It covers issues in the primary as well as transactions in the secondary markets. This facilitates swift and efficient settlement and helps to protect the anonymity of investors. These clearing houses will also arrange for the physical delivery of the bond certificates if this is required.

- **Custody**
  This is a safe-keeping facility for securities based on a worldwide network of major banks acting as depositories.

- **Securities Lending and Borrowing**
  This allows participants to lend securities and increase the yield on them. It allows participants to borrow securities in order to settle transactions and so contributes to the overall liquidity of the market.

- **Money Transfer and Banking**
  The purpose of this facility is to provide long- or short-term borrowing for participants.

Investors in Bond Markets

Although some bond issues are designed to attract individual investors, by far the largest group of investors are financial institutions and corporations.

There are a number of broad categories of large investors who have funds available from a variety of sources. There are four important categories which are discussed briefly here:

- Performance Funds

- Pension Funds, Life Assurance and Insurance Companies

- Central Banks

- Corporate Investors

Performance Funds

These are funds such as unit and investment trusts which have been established to achieve returns for a given level of risk. The funds have no liabilities to meet and are often designed to cater for specific purposes.

Pension Funds, Life Assurance and Insurance Companies

These are funds that are designed to meet a set of liabilities. Typically pensions and life insurance policies provide lump sum payments after a specified period.

Pension funds for large public and private organisations may have their own registered company in their own right. Other company schemes may use the services of a specialist fund management company.

Many pension funds are not allowed to trade OTC derivatives and therefore tend to buy the more complex bonds such as convertibles and bonds with warrants.

In order to meet claims for insurance policies on vehicles and property which are short-term contracts, most general insurance companies invest in instruments with shorter maturities which can readily be converted into cash.

Central Banks

Most government central banks hold large amounts of bonds. These comprise the following:

- New government issues which can be used for monetary policy control

- Foreign government or highly rated corporate bonds which can be used to control government FX reserves

Corporate Investors

Most large corporations use the bond markets to invest surplus cash and finance schemes such as pensions.

Many commercial banks are significant investors in the bond markets using bonds to finance their activities. FRNs are bought by many banks to fill gaps in their borrowing and lending requirements.

Regulation of Markets

There are a number of organisations involved with regulating the markets all of which are concerned basically with ensuring the following:

- Maintenance of high ethical and professional standards among all market participants who deal with each other and individual investors

- Fair treatment for all investors

- Prevention of fraud and dishonest practices

There are two major groups of regulatory bodies which operate in the domestic markets and the international markets

Each of these groups and some of the individual organisations are considered briefly here.

Domestic Regulatory Bodies

In most countries the government has a range of bodies to regulate the markets. Central banks such as the Fed and the Bank of England have certain direct responsibilities for regulating the primary market whereas regulations governing secondary market activities are the responsibility of a variety of government agencies. For example, in the US the **Securities and Exchange Commission (SEC)** and in the UK the **Financial Services Authority (FSA)** oversee the activities of organisations dealing with investments and the protection of investors.

In addition exchanges are self-regulating and have their own rules and regulations for members. For example, stock exchanges such as the LSE and NYSE are self-regulating. Also in the US the **National Association of Securities Dealers (NASD)** is a self-regulating body, reporting to the SEC, which oversees trading on **NASDAQ** – the automated quote market.

International Regulatory Bodies

Although most of the rules of these organisations cannot be legally enforced these self-regulatory bodies provide recommendations to ensure ethical and standardised trading practices in the international bond markets.

The two main organisations are:

- The International Primary Market Association (IPMA)

- The International Securities Markets Association (ISMA)

International Primary Market Association (IPMA)

This organisation has a framework of standards and documentation within which issuing houses in the Eurobond markets are expected to operate. IPMA members are obliged to report any deviations from these standards to each other.

International Securities Markets Association (ISMA)

For an international market such as the Eurobond market an international regulatory body is required. The **International Securities Markets Association** (**ISMA**, formally AIBD), based in Zurich acts as the regulatory body for the international securities market. ISMA sets a framework of rules and regulations in which its members operate.

In order to help regulate the market, ISMA has set up a **Transaction Exchange System (TRAX)**. This is a real-time on-line facility for the comparison and confirmation of transactions between dealers. The system provides the means by which users can see whether their trades will be settled or what details are required for settlement.

The system is constantly updated throughout the day and both parties to a transaction are expected to input details within 30 minutes of the deal. If the details match, the trade is good and it can only be cancelled if both parties consent. If the details do not match then the transaction may be cancelled.

ISMA also keeps a register of **lost and stolen** bonds. You may remember that Eurobonds are normally issued as **bearer bonds** which means that possession is sufficient to prove ownership. A lost or stolen bond may represent a substantial amount of money, so ISMA publish a list of these bonds. Once a bond has been relocated and reported to ISMA the stop payment is released.

Summary

You have now finished the last section of this book and you should have a clear understanding of trading in the debt markets including:

- Players in the primary markets – issuers, how a corporate bond is issued and the importance of the credit rating of organisations

- Players in the secondary markets – intermediaries, investors, how bonds are traded and how trading is regulated

As a check on your understanding, try the Quick Quiz Questions on the next page. You may also find the Overview section to be a useful study tool.

Quick Quiz Questions

1. An InterDealer Broker's main function is:
   - ☐ a) To act anonymously as an intermediary between market makers providing liquidity to the market
   - ☐ b) To buy and sell on behalf of clients
   - ☐ c) To make a continuous two-way price even if a counterparty does not exist
   - ☐ d) To act as a principal trading on his own account

2. Which of the following market players is **not** involved in the secondary bond markets?
   - ☐ a) Traders
   - ☐ b) Brokers
   - ☐ c) Pension fund managers
   - ☐ d) Underwriters

3. Who sets the bid and offer prices in the secondary bond markets?
   - ☐ a) Sales people
   - ☐ b) Market makers
   - ☐ c) Brokers
   - ☐ d) Dealers

4. Who is responsible for appointing syndicate members when a new bond is issued?
   - ☐ a) Lead Manager
   - ☐ b) Co-Manager
   - ☐ c) Underwriter
   - ☐ d) Market maker

5. Who shares the risk of a new issue with the lead manager?
   - ☐ a) Co-Managers
   - ☐ b) Book runners
   - ☐ c) Syndicate
   - ☐ d) Market makers

6. What is the name of the process whereby an issuer is guaranteed to raise funds, whether or not the new issue sells?

7. There is always a difference between the buying and selling prices of a debt instrument in the secondary market. What is this difference called?

8. Where does most secondary market trading take place?

You can check your answers on page 314.

Overview

Issuers

An **Issuer** is the borrower of funds responsible for ensuring that interest and principal payments are made to bond holders usually via a paying agent.

- **Governments & sovereign organisations**
- **Supranationals**
- **Corporates**
- **Banks and other financial institutions**

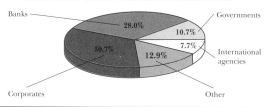

Banks 28.0%
Governments 10.7%
International agencies 7.7%
Other 12.9%
Corporates 30.7%

Credit Rating and Agencies

Investment grades	Moody's Highest → Lowest	Standard & Poor's Highest → Lowest
Highest quality	Aaa, Aaa1, Aaa2, Aaa3	AAA, AAA−, AA+
Excellent	Aa, Aa1, Aa2, Aa3	AA, AA−, A+
Good	A, A1, A2, A3	A, A−, BBB+
Medium	Baa, Baa1, Baa2, Baa3	BBB, BBB−, BB+
Speculative grade		
Questionable	Ba, Ba1, Ba2, Ba3	BB, BB−, B+
Poor	B, B1, B2, B3	B, B−, CCC+
Very poor	Caa, Caa1, Caa2, Caa3	CCC, CCC−, CC+
Extremely poor	Ca, Ca1, Ca2, Ca3	CC, CC−, C+
Lowest	C	C

Issuing a Bond in the Primary Market

Step 1 – Appoint a lead manager and agree on fees
Step 2 – Determine the deal structure and pricing
Step 3 – Form an underwriting syndicate
Step 4 – Set up the administration of the bonds
Step 5 – Primary trading

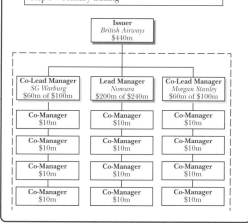

Issuer
British Airways
$440m

Co-Lead Manager
SG Warburg
$60m of $100m

Lead Manager
Nomura
$200m of $240m

Co-Lead Manager
Morgan Stanley
$60m of $100m

Co-Manager $10m (×12)

Intermediaries

- **UK Gilts issue**
  - Gilt Edged Market Makers (GEMMs)
  - InterDealer Brokers (IDBs)
- **US Treasuries**
  - Primary Dealers

Trading in Bond Markets

Players in the Secondary Markets

Typical trading organisation 1
Market makers/ Dealers/Traders
IDBs
Typical trading organisation 2
Market makers/ Dealers/Traders
Sales people
Financial analysis & support
Agency or Retail brokers
Clients

Regulation of Markets

- **Domestic US markets**
  - SEC
  - NASD
  - Stock exchanges
- **Domestic UK markets**
  - FSA
  - LSE
- **International**
  - IPMA
  - ISMA

How Bonds Are Traded

- Registered
- Bearer
- Book-entry
  - CEDEL
  - Euroclear

Investors in Bond Markets

- Performance funds
- Pension funds
- Assurance/Insurance organisations
- Central banks
- Corporate investors

Quick Quiz Answers

	✓ or ✗
1. a)	☐
2. d)	☐
3. b)	☐
4. a)	☐
5. c)	☐
6. The process is known as **underwriting**.	☐
7. The difference is known as the **spread**.	☐
8. Most trading is carried out **OTC**.	☐

How well did you score? You should have scored at least 7. If you didn't you may need to revise some of the materials.

Further Resources

Books

Forbes Guide to the Markets: Becoming a Savvy Investor
Marc M. Groz, John Wiley & Sons, Inc., 1999
ISBN   0 471 24658 1

Fixed Income Arbitrage: Analytical Techniques and Strategies
M. Anthony Wong and Robert High, John Wiley & Sons, Inc., 1993
ISBN   0 471 55552 5

Charlie D: the Story of the Legendary Bond Trader
William D. Falloon, John Wiley & Sons, Inc., 1997
ISBN   0 471 15672 8

The Bond Market: Trading and Risk Management
Christina I. Ray, Irwin Professional Press, 1992
ISBN   1 556 23289 6

Liar's Poker
Michael Lewis, Coronet Books, 1989
ISBN   0 430 53469 9

Winner Takes All: A Brutally Honest and Irreverent Look at the Motivations and Methods of Top Traders
William R. Gallacher, Irwin Professional Press, 1997
ISBN   0 786 31191 6

The Guide to Investing in Bonds
David Logan Scott, Globe Pequot Pr, 1997
ISBN   0 762 700602

Publications

Bank of England
- The Gilt-Edged Market: The Bank of England's relationship with the Gilt-Edged Market-Makers and Inter-Dealer Brokers
  June 1997

New York Stock Exchange
- Guidelines to investors

Videos
- Bonfire of the Vanities
- Capital City
- Wall Street – Michael Douglas as Gordon Gecko
- The Eurobond Market: An overview

Internet

RFT Web Site
- http://www.wiley-rft.reuters.com

This is the series' companion web site where additional quiz questions, updated screens and other information may be found.

ISMA
- http://www.ISMA.org

The International Securities Market Association (ISMA) is the self-regulatory organisation and trade association for the international securities market.

Asian Development Bank
- http://www.adb.org

The Asian Development Bank is a multilateral development finance institution, founded in 1966.

The Word Bank
- http://www.worldbank.org

The World Bank offers loans, advice, and an array of customized resources to more than 100 developing countries and countries in transition.

African Development Bank
- http://www.afdb.org

The African Development Bank Group is a multinational development bank supported by 77 nations (member countries) from Africa, North and South America, Europe and Asia. Headquartered in Abidjan, Cote d' Ivoire, the Bank Group consists of three institutions: The African Development Bank [ADB], The African Development Fund [ADF], The Nigeria Trust Fund [NTF].

European Investment Bank
- http://www.eib.org/

The EIB is the European Union's long-term lending institution. It was created in 1958 as an autonomous body set up to finance capital investment furthering European integration by promoting EU economic policies.

Council of Europe
- http://www.coe.fr/index.asp

The Council of Europe is an international organisation based in the French city of Strasbourg. Its main role is to strengthen democracy, human rights and the rule of law throughout its member states.

Exchanges

Refer to the back of this book for a listing of worldwide stock exchange contact information and web sites.

Your notes

Glossary of Bond Related Terms

compiled from the London Stock Exchange's on-line glossary

Entries in this glossary are compiled from the London Stock Exchange's (LSE) on-line glossary as well as definitions found in this book. The full version of the LSE's glossary can be found on the internet at the URL address, http://www.londonstockex.co.uk/about/about.asp. The Publisher will not be responsible for any inaccuracies found in the glossary below. Queries and reproduction requests should be addressed via the on-line contact form available on the LSE web site (see above URL).

A

Arbitrageur
Derivatives traders who want to exploit any price differences within different derivatives markets or between the derivatives instruments and cash or physical prices in the underlying assets.

Asset-backed Security
Part of a group of fixed income debt instruments whose coupon payments are governed by the cash flow generated by an underlying asset. By convention an asset-backed security is backed by non-mortgage assets.

B

BANS (Bons du Tresor a Taux Fixe et a Interet Annual)
Issued by the French government as fixed-rate, medium-term, coupon-bearing, 2–5 year instruments. Coupons are paid annually and the principal is repaid in bullet form.

Bear
An investor who sells a security in the hope of buying it back at a lower price, as he thinks the market will go down. A bear market is a falling market in which bears would prosper.

Bank for International Settlements (BIS)
A central banking institution that provides specialised services to central banks around the world.

Bid Price
The buying price for securities in the market.

Bobls (Bundesobligationen)
Medium-term bonds issued by the German government.

Bond
A bond is an agreement in which an issuer is required to repay to the investor the amount borrowed plus interest over a specified period of time. A bond is in effect an IOU which can be bought and sold.

Bond Futures
Long-term interest rate futures contracts with settlement based on notional government bonds or notes with a coupon and maturity period specified by the exchange. The settlement price is based on the final futures contract price – the Exchange Delivery Settlement Price (EDSP).

Bond Markets
Deal in financial instruments such as notes (one to ten year maturities) and bonds (ten to thirty year maturities) that represent loans to large organisations investors believe will be able to honour their obligations to repay the loan and interest payments due. Also may be referred to as the debt market.

Bond with Warrants
A standard bond with coupons but has a pre-determined number of warrants attached. Each warrant gives the holder the right, but not the obligation, to buy an agreed number of shares of the issuer at a specified price – the warrant exercise price – and at a specified future date/s. If the warrant is exercised, then additional payment is required to purchase the shares.

Brady Bonds
Usually a Eurobond or domestic bond issued by the government of a developing country to refinance its existing debt to foreign commercial banks.

Broker/Dealer
An exchange member firm, which provides advice and dealing services to the public and can deal on its own account.

Glossary of Bond Related Terms

Bull
An investor who buys a security in the hope of selling it at a higher price, as he thinks the market will go up. A bull market is a rising market in which bulls would prosper.

Bullet Bond (also called a Fixed Rate, Plain Vanilla or Straight Bond)
Has no special features and pays a fixed rate of interest to investors throughout its maturity period. The bond has a final maturity date when the final interest payment is made and the principal of the loan is repaid.

Bunds (Bundesanleihen)
Bonds issued by the German government with usual maturities of 10 years, but ranging from 6–30 years.

C

Callable Bond
A callable bond gives the issuer the right or option, but not the obligation, to redeem a bond at agreed specific prices and dates before the scheduled maturity date.

Capital Markets
The financial markets where money is raised and traded, comprising three key areas, the money markets (short-term, one year and under, borrowings); debt markets (characterised by instruments paying interest, with maturities of one to 30 years; and the equity markets (in which the borrower issues shares, or stocks, of ownership in the organisation to the lender, with possible dividend payments).

Clean Price
Full market value minus the accrued interest, expressed as a percentage of face value.

Collateral Trust Bonds
In the US markets, bonds secured by assets.

Convertible Bond
Usually a fixed rate instrument giving the holder the right, but not the obligation, to exchange the bond and all the remaining coupons for a predetermined number of ordinary shares or other debt instruments of the issuer at a pre-stated price and pre-stated date/s.

Convexity
The change in modified duration for a 1% change in yield.

Corporate Securities
Instruments issued by domestic organisations in the domestic currency. They are usually issued by a syndicate of domestic banks.

Coupon
The rate of interest, which can be fixed or floating, that the issuer agrees to pay the investor. Coupon payments are usually annual or semi-annual.

Covered Warrant
A security issued by a party other than the issuer or originator of the underlying asset, giving the holder the right to acquire a share or bond at a specific price and date.

Credit Risk
Risk that a counterparty will fail to honour its agreed obligations.

Currency Swaps
Agreement between counterparties in which one party makes payments in one currency and the other party makes payments in a different currency on agreed future dates until maturity of the agreement.

D

Debentures
In many Commonwealth money markets, is an acknowledgment of a debt and describes the amount which is secured by the assets of a corporation. Can be split into units and traded on an exchange or OTC as debenture stocks. In the US, debenture bonds are not secured and those bonds that are secured by assets are known as collateral or collateral trust bonds.

Debt Markets
Deal in financial instruments such as notes and bonds which represent loans to large organisations that investors believe will be able to honour their obligations to repay the loan and interest payments due. This market is most commonly referred to as the bond markets.

Derivative
An agreement between two counterparties in which they agree to transfer an asset or amount of money on or before a specified future date at a specified price. A derivative's value changes with changes in one or more underlying market variables, such as interest rates or foreign exchange rates.

Dirty Price
Full market value of a bond including accrued interest expressed as a percentage of its face value.

Dragon Bonds
Issued in any currency, usually US dollars, on at least two of the "dragon" exchanges – Hong Kong, Singapore or Taiwan. Trading takes place during the Asian time zone.

Dual Currency Bond
Involves a different currency for the coupon payments than that used for the repayment of the principal at maturity.

Duration
Duration, or Macaulay duration, is a way of comparing interest rate or market risk between two bonds with different coupon rates and different original maturities. Duration is a measure of the weighted average life of a bond which takes into account the size and the timing of each cash flow. In effect, it is a weighted average of the PVs of all cash flows.

E

EMU (European Monetary Union)
The joining of eleven European countries in 1999 to use a common currency, the Euro, and participate in joint monetary policy.

Equity Markets
Market for medium- to long-term borrowing in which the borrower issues shares, or stocks, of ownership in the organisation to the lender, with possible dividend payments.

Eurobonds
Instruments for unsecured debt issued by governments, banks, corporate entities and supranationals, which are issued outside the domestic market of the currency of denomination.

Ex-Dividend
This cccurs approximately a month before a bond interest payment is due and means that the buyer of a bond will not receive the payment, the seller will. This is built into the bond price.

F

Fixed Income Markets
See Debt Markets.

Fixed Rate (also called a Bullet, Plain Vanilla or Straight Bond)
Has no special features and pays a fixed rate of interest to investors throughout its maturity period. The bond has a final maturity date when the final interest payment is made and the principal of the loan is repaid.

Foreign Bonds
Issued by foreign borrowers in a domestic market denominated in that market's own currency. Issuing these bonds is regulated by the domestic market authorities. For example, a US company issuing bonds in Japan denominated in yen would be issuing samurai bonds and in Australia would be issuing Matilda bonds.

Forward Contract
A transaction in which the buyer and seller agree upon the delivery of a specified quality and quantity of asset (usually a commodity) at a specified future date. A price may be agreed on in advance or at the time of delivery.

Forward Rate Agreement (FRA)
An agreement between two counterparties which fixes the rate of interest that will apply to a specified notional future loan or deposit commencing and maturing on specified future dates.

Futures Contract
A firm contractual agreement between a buyer and seller for a specified asset on a fixed date in the future. The contract price will vary according to the market price but it is fixed when the trade is made. The contract also has standard specifications so both parties know exactly what is being traded.

G

GEMMs
Gilt-edged market makers.

Guaranteed Bonds
These are unsecured bonds that are guaranteed by a third party, usually the parent corporation of the issuer or another organisation in the same group as the issuing corporation.

Global Bonds
Traded simultaneously in the Euromarket and on one or more domestic markets.

Government Securities
Issued by sovereign states denominated in their own currency. The instruments are issued to raise capital to finance government projects, to repay maturing debt and to pay interest on existing debt.

H

Hedging
Hedgers seek to transfer the risk of future price or interest rate fluctuations by selling forward contracts which guarantee them a future price for their asset. Hedging reduces risk but also reduces the opportunity for reward. Hedging does not increase or decrease the expected returns for a market participant, it simply changes the risk profile of those expected returns.

I

ISMA
International Securities Market Association, based in Zurich, Switzerland. ISMA is the self-regulatory organisation and trade organisation for the international securities market. ISMA's principal role is to oversee this market by issuing rules and recommendations, designed to promote its orderly functioning. The Association also provides its member firms with a range of services, products and support.

Index-linked Bonds
Bonds whose interest and/or principal payments are linked to an index, such as the Consumer Price Index for all Urban Consumers (CPI-U) in the US or the Retail Price Index (RPI) in the UK.

Interest Rate Futures
Forward transactions with standard contract sizes and maturity dates which are traded on a formal exchange.

Interest Rate Option
Agreement by which the buyer of the option pays the seller a premium for the right, but not the obligation, to buy or sell a specified amount on or before an agreed date at an agreed price.

Interest Rate Swaps
Agreement between counterparties in which each party agrees to make a series of payments to the other on agreed future dates until maturity of the agreement. Each party's interest payments are calculated using different formulas by applying the agreement terms to the notional principal amount of the swap.

Issuer
The borrower of funds responsible for ensuring that interest and principal payments are made to bondholders, usually via a paying agent.

J

JGBs
Japanese government bonds.

L

Liquidity
Ease with which a security can be traded on the market.

Liquidity Risk
Assessment of the risk involved in trading an instrument quickly and in quantity without affecting its price significantly.

Long-term Interest Rate Futures
Contracts with settlement based on notional government bonds or notes with a coupon and maturity period specified by the exchange. The settlement price is based on the final futures contract price – the Exchange Delivery Settlement Price (EDSP). Also called bond futures.

M

MTN
Medium-term note. An unsecured note issued in a euro-currency with a maturity of three to six years.

Market Risk
Risk resulting from a change in the value of a bond caused by any movements in the level or volatility of the current market yields or cost of money.

Maturity
The date on which the issuer of a bond must repay the principal due and the final interest payment.

N

Note
A note is an agreement in which an issuer is required to repay to the investor the amount borrowed plus interest over a specified period of time. A note is in effect an IOU which can be bought and sold. A note is the same as a bond differing only in maturity; a note is a medium-term instrument, usually from one to ten years.

O

OATS (Obligations Assimilable du Tresor)
Long-term bonds issued by the French government with maturities of 6-30 years. Coupons are paid annually and the principal is repaid in bullet form.

Offer Price
The selling price for securities in a market.

Operational Risks
Risks arising from accurate settlement of a transaction and legal risk connected with contract settlement.

Option Contract
A contract conferring the right but not the obligation to buy (call) or sell (put) a specific underlying instrument or asset at a specific price – the strike or exercise price – up until or on a specific future date – the expiry date. The price to have this right is paid by the buyer of the option contract to the seller as a premium.

P

Par
One hundred percent of face value.

Paying Agent
The organisation that handles the repayment of interest and principal to investors on behalf of the issuer.

Perpetual Bond
Has a coupon but no final maturity date specified.

Plain Vanilla Bond (also called a Bullet, Fixed Rate or Straight Bond)
Has no special features and pays a fixed rate of interest to investors throughout its maturity period. The bond has a final maturity date when the final interest payment is made and the principal of the loan is repaid.

Principal
The amount denominated in a specific currency that the issuer wishes to borrow and the agrees to repay the investor. The face amount of a bond.

R

Repo
See Repurchase Agreement

Repurchase Agreement (repo)
An agreement for the sale of an instrument with the simultaneous agreement by the seller to repurchase the instrument at an agreed future date and agreed price.

Reverse Repo
See Reverse Repurchase Agreement

Reverse Repurchase Agreement (reverse repo)
An agreement for the purchase of an instrument with the simultaneous agreement by the seller to resell the instrument at an agreed future date and agreed price.

S

Short-term Interest Rate Futures
Interest rate futures contracts are almost exclusively based on Eurocurrency deposits and are cash settled based on an Exchange Delivery Settlement Price (EDSP) or the last price traded.

Sinking Fund Bond
A bond in which a part of the total principal amount of the bond is repaid according to an agreed schedule of dates, amounts and prices.

Speculator
Takes on the opposite position to a hedger and takes on the exposure in the hope of profiting from price changes to her advantage.

Straight Bond (also called a Bullet, Fixed Rate or Plain Vanilla)
Has no special features and pays a fixed rate of interest to investors throughout its maturity period. The bond has a final maturity date when the final interest payment is made and the principal of the loan is repaid.

Strategic Risk
Risk arising from the way in which trading is carried out by market players operating for their institutions.

Stripped Bond
Is one in which a conventional bond with coupons is separated into its component cash flows. Each payment of coupon and principal becomes a separate bond maturing on its particular date.
The stripped bond becomes a zero-coupon bond that can be traded in its own right.

STRIPS (Separate Trading of Registered Interest and Principal of Securities)
The US government's version of stripped bonds, originating in 1985.

Subordinated Bonds
These are unsecured loan stocks subordinated to other debt. In the event of liquidation these instruments are paid after the more "senior" debts have been settled.

Swaption
A financial derivative which grants the right, but not the obligation, to buy or sell an interest rate swap (IRS) on agreed terms of interest rate, maturity, fixed or floating rate payer, on or by an agreed date. In return for this right, the buyer of the swaption pays the seller a premium.

T

Turnover
The volume of shares traded as a percent of total shares listed during a specific period, usually a day or a year.

U

UK Gilts

Marketable securities issued by the UK government. Gilts is short for gilt-edged security. Gilts are classified according to the amount of time remaining until maturity, pay semi-annual coupons and are repaid in full at maturity as a bullet repayment. Gilts are issued in sterling and euros.

US Treasuries

Marketable securities issued by the US government that are classified according to maturity at issuance, pay semi-annual coupons and are repaid in full at maturity as a bullet payment.

Underwriting

A way of guaranteeing that the issuer gets its funds. In the unlikely event that they are unable to sell the whole of an issue, the underwriters of an issue undertake to provide the issuer with the necessary funds. It may be that after an issue is announced, interest rates rise, making the bond less attractive to investors. At this stage the bond's coupon is fixed, so the underwriters are forced to sell the issue at a lower price than they had expected.

Y

Yield

The annualised interest rate that makes the present value (PV) of a bond's future cash flows equal to its market value.

Z

Zero-coupon Bond

A bond that pays no coupon during its life.

Glossary of Bond Related Terms

Your notes

Directory of Futures & Options Exchanges

courtesy of Numa Financial Systems Ltd

The following directory is taken from the Numa Directory of Futures & Options Exchanges which can be found on the internet at the URL address, http://www.numa.com/ref/exchange.htm. The Publisher will not be responsible for any inaccuracies found in the listing below. Kindly address any queries Numa Financial Systems Ltd via their home page at http//www.numa.com.

Argentina

Buenos Aires Stock Exchange
(Bolsa de Comercio de Buenos Aires)
Sarmiento 299, Buenos Aires
Tel: +54 1 313 3334
Fax: +54 1 312 9332
Email: cau@sba.com.ar
URL: http://www.merval.sba.com.ar

Merfox
(Mercados de Futuros y Opciones SA)
Samiento 299, 4/460, Buenos Aires
Tel: +54 1 313 4522
Fax: +54 1 313 4472

Buenos Aires Cereal Exchange
(Bolsa de Cereales de Buenos Aires)
Avenida Corrientes 127, Buenos Aires
Tel: +54 1 311 9540
Fax: +54 1 311 9540
Email: bolcerc@datamarkets.com.ar

Buenos Aires Futures Market
(Mercado a Termino de Buenos Aires SA)
Bouchard 454, 5to Piso, Buenos Aires
Tel: +54 1 311 47 16
Fax: +54 1 312 47 16

Rosario Futures Exchange
(Mercado a Termino de Rosario)
Cordoba 1402, Pcia Santa Fe, Rosario
Tel: +54 41 21 50 93
Fax: +54 41 21 50 97
Email: termino@bcr.com.ar

Rosario Stock Exchange
(Mercado de Valores de Rosario SA)
Cordoba Esquina Corrientes, Pcia Santa Fe, Rosario
Tel: +54 41 21 34 70
Fax: +54 41 24 10 19
Email: titulos@bcr.com.ar

Rosario Board of Trade
(Bolsa de Comercio de Rosario)
Cordoba 1402, Pcia Santa Fe, Rosario
Tel: +54 41 21 50 93
Fax: +54 41 21 50 97
Email: titulos@bcr.com.ar

La Plata Stock Exchange
(Bolsa de Comercio de La Plata)
Calle 48, No. 515, 1900 La Plata, Buenos Aires
Tel: +54 21 21 47 73
Fax: +54 21 25 50 33

Mendoza Stock Exchange
(Bolsa de Comercio de Mendoza)
Paseo Sarmiento 199, Mendoza
Tel: +54 61 20 23 59
Fax: +54 61 20 40 50

Cordoba Stock Exchange
(Bolsa de Comercio de Cordoba)
Rosario de Santa Fe 231, 1 Piso, Cordoba
Tel: +54 51 22 4230
Fax: +54 51 22 6550
Email: bolsacba@nt.com.ar

Mercado Abierto Electronico SA
(Mercado Abierto Electronico SA)
25 de Mayo 565, 4 Piso, Buenos Aires
Tel: +54 1 312 8060
Fax: +54 1 313 1445

Armenia

Yerevan Stock Exchange
22 Sarian Street, Yerevan Centre
Tel: +374 2 525 801
Fax: +374 2 151 548

Australia

Australian Stock Exchange
Exchange Centre, 20 Bond Street, Sydney
Tel: +61 29 227 0000
Fax: +61 29 235 0056
Email: info@asx.com.au
URL: http://www.asx.com.au

Sydney Futures Exchange
SFE
30-32 Grosvenor Street, Sydney
Tel: +61 29 256 0555
Fax: +61 29 256 0666
Email: sfe@hutch.com.au
URL: http://www.sfe.com.au

Austria

Austrian Futures & Options Exchange
(Osterreichische Termin Und Optionenborse)
OTOB
Strauchgasse 1-3, PO Box 192, Vienna
Tel: +43 1 531 65 0
Fax: +43 1 532 97 40
Email: contactperson@otob.ada.at
URL: http://www.wtab.at

Vienna Stock Exchange
(Wiener Borse)
Wipplingerstrasse 34, Vienna
Tel: +43 1 53 499
Fax: +43 1 535 68 57
Email: communications@vienna-stock-exchange.at
URL: http://www.wtab.at

Bahrain

Bahrain Stock Exchange
P.O. Box 3203, Manama
Tel: +973 261260
Fax: +973 256362
Email: bse@bahrainstock.com
URL: http://www.bahrainstock.com

Bangladesh

Dhaka Stock Exchange
Stock Exchange Building, 9E & 9F, Motijheel C/A, Dhaka
Tel: +880 2 956 4601
Fax: +880 2 956 4727
Email: info@dse.bdnet.net

Barbados

Securities Exchange of Barbados
5th Floor, Central Bank Building, Church Village, St Michael
Tel: +1809/1246 246 436 9871
Fax: +1809/1246 246 429 8942
Email: sebd@caribf.com

Belgium

Brussels Stock Exchange
(Societe de la Bourse de Valeurs Mobilieres de Bruxelles)
Palais de la Bourse, Brussels
Tel: +32 2 509 12 11
Fax: +32 2 509 12 12
Email: dan.maerten@pophost.eunet.be
URL: http://www.stockexchange.be

European Association of Securities Dealers Automated Quotation
EASDAQ
Rue des Colonies, 56 box 15, 1000 Brussels
Tel: +32 2 227 6520
Fax: +32 2 227 6567
Email: easdaq@tornado.be
URL: http://www.easdaq.be/

Belgian Futures & Options Exchange
BELFOX
Palais de la Bourse, Rue Henri Mausstraat, 2, Brussels
Tel: +32 2 512 80 40
Fax: +32 2 513 83 42
Email: marketing@belfox.be
URL: http://www.belfox.be

Antwerp Stock Exchange
(Effectenbeurs van Antwerpen)
Korte Klarenstraat 1, Antwerp
Tel: +32 3 233 80 16
Fax: +32 3 232 57 37

Bermuda

Bermuda Stock Exchange
BSE
Email: info@bse.com
URL: http://www.bsx.com

Bolivia

Bolivian Stock Exchange
(Bolsa Boliviana de Valores SA)
Av. 16 de Julio No 1525, Edif Mutual La Paz, 3er Piso, Casillia 12521, La Paz
Tel: +591 2 39 29 11
Fax: +591 2 35 23 08
Email: bbvsalp@wara.bolnet.bo
URL: http://bolsa-valores-bolivia.com

Botswana

Botswana Stock Exchange
5th Floor, Barclays House, Khama Crescent, Gaborone
Tel: +267 357900
Fax: +267 357901
Email: bse@info.bw

Brazil

Far-South Stock Exchange
(Bolsa de Valores do Extremo Sul)
Rua dos Andradas, 1234-8 Andar, Porte Alegre
Tel: +55 51 224 3600
Fax: +55 51 227 4359

Santos Stock Exchange
(Bolsa de Valores de Santos)
Rua XV de Novembro, 111, Santos
Tel: +55 132 191 5119
Fax: +55 132 19 1800

Regional Stock Exchange
(Bolsa de Valores regional)
Avenida Dom Manuel, 1020, Fortaleza
Tel: +55 85 231 6466
Fax: +55 85 231 6888

Parana Stock Exchange
(Bolsa de Valores do Parana)
Rua Marechal Deodoro, 344-6 Andar, Curitiba
Tel: +55 41 222 5191
Fax: +55 41 223 6203

Minas, Espirito Santo, Brasilia Stock Exchange
(Blsa de Valores Minas, Espirito Santo, Brasilia)
Rua dos Carijos, 126-3 Andar, Belo Horizonte
Tel: +55 31 219 9000
Fax: +55 21 273 1202

Rio de Janeiro Stock Exchange
(Bolsa de Valores de Rio de Janeiro)
Praca XV de Novembro No 20, Rio de Janeiro
Tel: +55 21 271 1001
Fax: +55 21 221 2151
Email: info@bvrj.com.br
URL: http://www.bvrj.com.br

Sao Paolo Stock Exchange
(Bolsa de Valores de Sao Paolo)
Rua XV de Novembro 275, Sao Paolo
Tel: +55 11 233 2000
Fax: +55 11 233 2099
Email: bovespa@bovespa.com.br
URL: http://www.bovespa.com.br

Bahia, Sergipe, Alagoas Stock Exchange
(Bolsa de Valores Bahia, Sergipe, Alagoas)
Rua Conselheiro Dantas, 29-Comercio, Salvador
Tel: +55 71 242 3844
Fax: +55 71 242 5753

Brazilian Futures Exchange
(Bolsa Brasileira de Futuros)
Praca XV de Novembro, 20, 5th Floor, Rio de Janeiro
Tel: +55 21 271 1086
Fax: +55 21 224 5718
Email: bbf@bbf.com.br

The Commodities & Futures Exchange
(Bolsa de Mercadoris & Futuros)
BM&F
Praca Antonio Prado, 48, Sao Paulo
Tel: +55 11 232 5454
Fax: +55 11 239 3531
Email: webmaster@bmf.com.br
URL: http://www.bmf.com.br

Pernambuco and Paraiba Stock Exchange
(Bolsa de Valores de Pernambuco e Paraiba)
Avenida Alfredo Lisboa, 505, Recife
Tel: +55 81 224 8277
Fax: +55 81 224 8412

Bulgaria

Bulgarian Stock Exchange
1 Macedonia Square, Sofia
Tel: +359 2 81 57 11
Fax: +359 2 87 55 66
Email: bse@bg400.bg
URL: http://www.online.bg/bse

Canada

Montreal Exchange
(Bourse de Montreal)
ME
The Stock Exchange Tower, 800 Square Victoria, C.P. 61, Montreal
Tel: +1 514 871 2424
Fax: +1 514 871 3531
Email: info@me.org
URL: http://www.me.org

Vancouver Stock Exchange
VSE
Stock Exchange Tower, 609 Granville Street, Vancouver
Tel: +1 604 689 3334
Fax: +1 604 688 6051
Email: information@vse.ca
URL: http://www.vse.ca

Winnipeg Stock Exchange
620 - One Lombard Place, Winnipeg
Tel: +1 204 987 7070
Fax: +1 204 987 7079
Email: vcatalan@io.uwinnipef.ca

Alberta Stock Exchange
21st Floor, 300 Fifth Avenue SW, Calgary
Tel: +1 403 974 7400
Fax: +1 403 237 0450

Toronto Stock Exchange
TSE
The Exchange Tower, 2 First Canadian Place, Toronto
Tel: +1 416 947 4700
Fax: +1 416 947 4662
Email: skee@tse.com
URL: http://www.tse.com

Winnipeg Commodity Exchange
WCE
500 Commodity Exchange Tower, 360 Main St., Winnipeg
Tel: +1 204 925 5000
Fax: +1 204 943 5448
Email: wce@wce.mb.ca
URL: http://www.wce.mb.ca

Toronto Futures Exchange
TFE
The Exchange Tower, 2 First Canadian Place, Toronto
Tel: +1 416 947 4487
Fax: +1 416 947 4272

Cayman Islands

Cayman Islands Stock Exchange
CSX
4th Floor, Elizabethan Square, P.O Box 2408 G.T., Grand Cayman
Tel: +1345 945 6060
Fax: +1345 945 6061
Email: CSX@CSX.COM.KY
URL: http://www.csx.com.ky/

Chile

Santiago Stock Exchange
(Bolsa de Comercio de Santiago)
La Bolsa 64, Casilla 123-D, Santiago
Tel: +56 2 698 2001
Fax: +56 2 672 8046
Email: ahucke@comercio.bolsantiago.cl
URL: http://www.bolsantiago.cl

Bolsa Electronica de Chile
Huerfanos 770, Piso 14, Santiago
Tel: +56 2 639 4699
Fax: +56 2 639 9015
Email: info@bolchile.cl
URL: http://www.bolchile.cl

China

Wuhan Securities Exchange Centre
WSEC
2nd Floor, Jianghchen Hotel, Wuhan
Tel: +86 27 588 4115
Fax: +86 27 588 6038

China Zhengzhou Commodity Exchange
CZCE
20 Huanyuan Road, Zhengzhou
Tel: +86 371 594 44 54
Fax: +86 371 554 54 24

Shanghai Cereals and Oils Exchange
199 Shangcheng Road, Pudong New District, Shanghai
Tel: +86 21 5831 1111
Fax: +86 21 5831 9308
Email: liangzhu@public.sta.net.cn

China -Commodity Futures Exchange, Inc of Hainan
CCFE
Huaneng Building, 36 Datong Road, Haikou, Hainan Province
Tel: +86 898 670 01 07
Fax: +86 898 670 00 99
Email: ccfehn@public.hk.hq.cn

Guandong United Futures Exchange
JingXing Hotel, 91 LinHe West Road, Guangzhou
Tel: +86 20 8755 2109
Fax: +86 20 8755 1654

Shenzhen Mercantile Exchange
1/F Bock B, Zhongjian Overseas Decoration , Hua Fu Road,
Shenzhen
Tel: +86 755 3343 502
Fax: +86 755 3343 505

Shanghai Stock Exchange
15 Huang Pu Road, Shanghai
Tel: +86 216 306 8888
Fax: +86 216 306 3076

Beijing Commodity Exchange
BCE
311 Chenyun Building, No. 8 Beichen East Road, Chaoyang District,
Beijing
Tel: +86 1 492 4956
Fax: +86 1 499 3365
Email: sunli@intra.cnfm.co.cn

Shenzhen Stock Exchange
203 Shangbu Industrial Area, Shenzhen
Tel: +86 755 320 3431
Fax: +86 755 320 3505

Colombia

Bogota Stock Exchange
BSE
Carrera 8, No. 13-82 Pisos 4-9, Apartado Aereo 3584, Santafe de
Bogota
Tel: +57 243 6501
Fax: +57 281 3170
Email: bolbogot@bolsabogota.com.co
URL: http://www.bolsabogota.com.co

Medellin Stock Exchange
(Bolsa de Medellin SA)
Apartado Aereo 3535, Medellin
Tel: +57 4 260 3000
Fax: +57 4 251 1981
Email: 104551.1310@compuserve.com

Occidente Stock Exchange
(Bolsa de Occidente SA)
Calle 10, No. 4-40 Piso 13, Cali
Tel: +57 28 817 022
Fax: +57 28 816 720
Email: bolsaocc@cali.cetcol.net.co
URL: http://www.bolsadeoccidente.com.co

Costa Rica

National Stock Exchange
(Bolsa Nacional de Valores, SA)
BNV
Calle Central, Avenida 1, San Jose
Tel: +506 256 1180
Fax: +506 255 0131

Cote D'Ivoire (Ivory Coast)

Abidjan Stock Exchange
(Bourse des Valeurs d'Abidjan)
Avenue Marchand, BP 1878 01, Abidjan 01
Tel: +225 21 57 83
Fax: +225 22 16 57

Croatia (Hrvatska)

Zagreb Stock Exchange
(Zagrebacka Burza)
Ksaver 208, Zagreb
Tel: +385 1 428 455
Fax: +385 1 420 293
Email: zeljko.kardum@zse.hr
URL: http://www.zse.hr

Cyprus

Cyprus Stock Exchange
CSE
54 Griva Dhigeni Avenue, Silvex House, Nicosia
Tel: +357 2 368 782
Fax: +357 2 368 790
Email: cyse@zenon.logos.cy.net

Czech Republic

Prague Stock Exchange
PSE
Rybna 14, Prague 1
Tel: +42 2 2183 2116
Fax: +42 2 2183 3040
Email: marketing@pse.vol.cz
URL: http://www.pse.cz

Denmark

Copenhagen Stock Exchange & FUTOP
(Kobenhavns Fondsbors)
Nikolaj Plads 6, PO Box 1040, Copenhagen K
Tel: +45 33 93 33 66
Fax: +45 33 12 86 13
Email: kfpost@xcse.dk
URL: http://www.xcse.dk

Ecuador

Quito Stock Exchange
(Bolsa de Valores de Quito CC)
Av Amazonas 540 y Carrion, 8vo Piso
Tel: +593 2 526 805
Fax: +593 2 500 942
Email: bovalqui@ecnet.ec
URL: http://www.ccbvq.com

Guayaquil Stock Exchange
(Bolsa de Valores de Guayaquil, CC)
Av. 9 de Octubre, 110 y Pinchina, Guayaquil
Tel: +593 4 561 519
Fax: +593 4 561 871
Email: bvg@bvg.fin.ec
URL: http://www.bvg.fin.ec

Egypt

Alexandria Stock Exchange
11 Talaat Harp Street, Alexandria
Tel: +20 3 483 7966
Fax: +20 3 482 3039

Cairo Stock Exchange
4(A) El Cherifeen Street, Cairo
Tel: +20 2 392 1402
Fax: +20 2 392 8526

El Salvador

El Salvador Stock Exchange
(Mercado de Valores de El Salvador, SA de CV)
6 Piso, Edificio La Centroamericana, Alameda Roosevelt No 3107,
San Salvador
Tel: +503 298 4244
Fax: +503 223 2898
Email: ggbolsa@gbm.net

Estonia

Tallinn Stock Exchange
Ravala 6, Tallinn
Tel: +372 64 08 840
Fax: +372 64 08 801
Email : tse@depo.ee
URL: http://www.tse.ee

Finland

Helsinki Stock Exchange
HSE
Fabianinkatu 14, Helsinki
Tel: +358 9 173 301
Fax: +358 9 173 30399
Email : mika.bjorklund@hex.fi
URL: http://www.hse.fi

Finnish Options Exchange
(Suomen Optioporssi Oy)
FOEX
Erottajankatu 11, Helsinki
Tel: +358 9 680 3410
Fax: +358 9 604 442
Email : info@foex.fi
URL: http://www.foex.fi

Finnish Options Market
SOM
Keskuskatu 7, Helsinki
Tel: +358 9 13 1211
Fax: +358 9 13 121211
Email : webmaster@hex.fi
URL: http://www.som.fi

France

Paris Stock Exchange
(Bourse de Paris)
39 rue Cambon, Paris
Tel: +33 1 49 27 10 00
Fax: +33 1 49 27 13 71
Email: 100432.201@compuserve.com

MONEP
(Marche des Options Negociables de Paris)
MONEP
39, rue Cambon, Paris
Tel: +33 1 49 27 18 00
Fax: +33 1 9 27 18 23
URL: http://www.monep.fr

MATIF
(Marche a Terme International de France)
MATIF
176 rue Montmartre, Paris
Tel: +33 33 1 40 28 82 82
Fax: +33 33 1 40 28 80 01
Email : larrede@matif.fr
URL: http://www.matif.fr

Germany

Stuttgart Stock Exchange
(Baden-Wurttembergische Wertpapierborse zu Stuttgart)
Konigstrasse 28, Stuttgart
Tel: +49 7 11 29 01 83
Fax: +49 7 11 22 68 11 9

Hanover Stock Exchange
(Niedersachsische Borse zu Hanover)
Rathenaustrasse 2, Hanover
Tel: +49 5 11 32 76 61
Fax: +49 5 11 32 49 15

Dusseldorf Stock Exchange
(Rheinisch-Westfalische Borse zu Dusseldorf)
Ernst-Schneider-Platz 1, Dusseldorf
Tel: +49 2 11 13 89 0
Fax: +49 2 11 13 32 87

Berlin Stock Exchange
(Berliner Wertpapierborse)
Fasanenstrasse 85, Berlin
Tel: +49 30 31 10 91 0
Fax: +49 30 31 10 91 79

German Stock Exchange
(Deutsche Borse AG)
FWB
Borsenplatz 4, Frankfurt-am-Main
Tel: +49 69 21 01 0
Fax: +49 69 21 01 2005
URL: http://www.exchange.de

Hamburg Stock Exchange
(Hanseatische Wertpapierborse Hamburg)
Schauenburgerstrasse 49, Hamburg
Tel: +49 40 36 13 02 0
Fax: +49 40 36 13 02 23
Email: wertpapierboerse.hamburg@t-online.de

Deutsche Terminborse
DTB
Boersenplatz 4, Frankfurt-am-Main
Tel: +49 69 21 01 0
Fax: +49 69 21 01 2005
URL: http://www.exchange.de

Bavarian Stock Exchange
(Bayerische Borse)
Lenbachplatz 2(A), Munich
Tel: +49 89 54 90 45 0
Fax: +49 89 54 90 45 32
Email: bayboerse@t-online.de
URL: http://www.bayerischeboerse.de

Bremen Stock Exchange
(Bremer Wertpapierborse)
Obernstrasse 2-12, Bremen
Tel: +49 4 21 32 12 82
Fax: +49 4 21 32 31 23

Ghana

Ghana Stock Exchange
5th Floor, Cedi House, Liberia Road, PO Box 1849, Accra
Tel: +233 21 669 908
Fax: +233 21 669 913
Email : stockex@ncs.com.gh
URL: http://ourworld.compuserve.com/homepages/khaganu/
stockex.htm

Greece

Athens Stock Exchange
ASE
10 Sophocleous Street, Athens
Tel: +30 1 32 10 424
Fax: +30 1 32 13 938
Email: mailto:aik@hol.gr
URL: http://www.ase.gr

Honduras

Honduran Stock Exchange
(Bolsa Hondurena de Valores, SA)
1er Piso Edificio Martinez Val, 3a Ave 2a Calle SO, San Pedro Sula
Tel: +504 53 44 10
Fax: +504 53 44 80
Email: bhvsps@simon.intertel.hn

Hong Kong

Hong Kong Futures Exchange Ltd
HKFE
5/F, Asia Pacific Finance Tower, Citibank Plaza, 3 Garden Road
Tel: +852 2842 9333
Fax: +852 2810 5089
Email: prm@hfke.com
URL: http://www.hkfe.com

Hong Kong Stock Exchange
SEHK
1st Floor, One and Two Exchange Square, Central
Tel: +852 2522 1122
Fax: +852 2810 4475
Email: info@sehk.com.hk
URL: http://www.sehk.com.hk

Chinese Gold and Silver Exchange Society
Gold and Silver Commercial Bui, 12-18 Mercer Street
Tel: +852 544 1945
Fax: +852 854 0869

Hungary

Budapest Stock Exchange
Deak Ferenc utca 5, Budapest
Tel: +36 1 117 5226
Fax: +36 1 118 1737
URL: http://www.fornax.hu/fmon

Budapest Commodity Exchange
BCE
POB 495, Budapest
Tel: +36 1 269 8571
Fax: +36 1 269 8575
Email: bce@bce-bat.com
URL: http://www.bce-bat.com

Iceland

Iceland Stock Exchange
Kalkofnsvegur 1, Reykjavik
Tel: +354 569 9775
Fax: +354 569 9777
Email: gw@vi.is

India

Cochin Stock Exchange
38/1431 Kaloor Road Extension, PO Box 3529, Emakulam, Cochin
Tel: +91 484 369 020
Fax: +91 484 370 471

Bangalore Stock Exchange
Stock Exchange Towers, 51, 1st Cross, JC Road, Bangalore
Tel: +91 80 299 5234
Fax: +91 80 22 55 48

The OTC Exchange of India
OTCEI
92 Maker Towers F, Cuffe Parade, Bombay
Tel: +91 22 21 88 164
Fax: +91 22 21 88 012
Email: otc.otcindia@gems.vsnl.net.in

Jaipur Stock Exchange
Rajasthan Chamber Bhawan, MI Road, Jaipur
Tel: +91 141 56 49 62
Fax: +91 141 56 35 17

The Stock Exchange ñ Ahmedabad
Kamdhenu Complex, Ambawadi, Ahmedabad
Tel: +91 79 644 67 33
Fax: +91 79 21 40 117
Email: supvsr@08asxe

Delhi Stock Exchange
3&4/4B Asaf Ali Road, New Delhi
Tel: +91 11 327 90 00
Fax: +91 11 327 13 02

Madhya Pradesh Stock Exchange
3rd Floor, Rajani Bhawan, Opp High Court, MG Road, Indore
Tel: +91 731 432 841
Fax: +91 731 432 849

Magadh Stock Exchange
Industry House, Suinha Library Road,
Patna
Tel: +91 612 223 644

Pune Stock Exchange
Shivleela Chambers, 752 Sadashiv Peth, Kumethekar Road, Pune
Tel: +91 212 441 679

The Stock Exchange, Mumbai
Phiroze Jeejeebhoy Towers, Dalal Street, Bombay
Tel: +91 22 265 5860
Fax: +91 22 265 8121
URL: http://www.nseindia.com

Uttar Pradesh Stock Exchange
Padam Towers, 14/113 Civil Lines, Kanpur
Tel: +91 512 293 115
Fax: +91 512 293 175

Bhubaneswar Stock Exchange Association
A-22 Falcon House, Jharapara, Cuttack Road, Bhubaneswar
Tel: +91 674 482 340
Fax: +91 674 482 283

Calcutta Stock Exchange
7 Lyons Range, Calcutta
Tel: +91 33 209 366

Coimbatore Stock Exchange
Chamber Towers, 8/732 Avanashi Road, Coimbatore
Tel: +91 422 215 100
Fax: +91 422 213 947

Madras Stock Exchange
Exchange Building, PO Box 183, 11 Second Line Beach, Madras
Tel: +91 44 510 845
Fax: +91 44 524 4897

Ludhiana Stock Exchange
Lajpat Rai Market, Near Clock Tower, Ludhiana
Tel: +91 161 39318

Kanara Stock Exchange
4th Floor, Ranbhavan Complex, Koialbail, Mangalore
Tel: +91 824 32606

Hyderabad Stock Exchange
3-6-275 Himayatnagar, Hyderabad
Tel: +91 842 23 1985

Gauhati Stock Exchange
Saraf Building, Annex, AT Road, Gauhati
Tel: +91 361 336 67
Fax: +91 361 543 272

Indonesia

Jakarta Stock Exchange
(PT Bursa Efek Jakarta)
Jakarta Stock Exchange Building, 13th Floor, JI Jenderal Sudiman,
Kav 52-53, Jakarta
Tel: +62 21 515 0515
Fax: +62 21 515 0330
Email: webmaster@jsx.co.id
URL: http://www.jsx.co.id

Surabaya Stock Exchange
(PT Bursa Efek Surabaya)
5th Floor, Gedung Madan Pemuda, 27-31 Jalan Pemuda, Surabaya
Tel: +62 21 526 6210
Fax: +62 21 526 6219
Email: heslpdesk@bes.co.id
URL: http://www.bes.co.id

Indonesian Commodity Exchange Board
(Badan Pelaksana Bursa Komoditi)
Gedung Bursa, Jalan Medan Merdeka Selatan 14, 4th Floor, Jakarta Pusat
Tel: +62 21 344 1921
Fax: +62 21 3480 4426

Capital Market Supervisory Agency
(Baden Pelaksana Pasar Modal)
BAPEPAM
Jakarta Stock Exchange Building, 13th Floor, JI Jenderal Sudiman, Kav 52-53, Jakarta
Tel: +62 21 515 1288
Fax: +62 21 515 1283
Email: bapepam@indoexchange.com
URL: http://www.indoexchange.com/bapepam

Iran

Tehran Stock Exchange
228 Hafez Avenue, Tehran
Tel: +98 21 670 309
Fax: +98 21 672 524
Email: stock@neda.net
URL: http://www.neda.net/tse

Ireland

Irish Stock Exchange
28 Anglesea Street, Dublin 2
Tel: +353 1 677 8808
Fax: +353 1 677 6045

Irish Futures & Options Exchange
IFOX
Segrave House, Earlsfort Terrace, Dublin 2
Tel: +353 1 676 7413
Fax: +353 1 661 4645

Israel

Tel Aviv Stock Exchange Ltd
TASE
54 Ahad Haam Street, Tel Aviv
Tel: +972 3 567 7411
Fax: +972 3 510 5379
Email: etti@tase.co.il
URL: http://www.tase.co.il

Italy

Italian Financial Futures Market
(Mercato Italiano Futures)
MIF
Piazza del Gesu' 49, Rome
Tel: +39 6 676 7514
Fax: +39 6 676 7250

Italian Stock Exchange
(Consiglio de Borsa)
Piazza degli Affari, 6, Milan
Tel: +39 2 724 261
Fax: +39 2 864 64 323
Email: postoffice@borsaitalia.it
URL: http://www.borsaitalia.it

Italian Derivatives Market
IDEM
Piazza Affari 6, Milan
Tel: +39 2 72 42 61
Fax: +39 2 72 00 43 33
Email: postoffice@borsaitalia.it
URL: http://www.borsaitalia.it

Jamaica

Jamaica Stock Exchange
40 Harbour Street, PO Box 1084, Kingston
Tel: +1809 809 922 0806
Fax: +1809 809 922 6966
Email: jse@infochan.com
URL: http://www.jamstockex.com

Japan

Tokyo Commodity Exchange
(Tokyo Kogyoin Torihikijo)
TOCOM
10-8 Nihonbashi, Horidome-cho, Chuo-ku, 1-chome, Tokyo
Tel: +81 3 3661 9191
Fax: +81 3 3661 7568

Japan Securities Dealing Association
(Nihon Shokengyo Kyokai)
Tojyo Shoken Building, 5-8 Kayaba-cho, 1-chome, Nihonbashi, Tokyo
Tel: +81 3 3667 8451
Fax: +81 3 3666 8009

Osaka Textile Exchange
(Osaka Seni Torihikijo)
2-5-28 Kyutaro-machi, Chuo-ku, Osaka
Tel: +81 6 253 0031
Fax: +81 6 253 0034

Tokyo Stock Exchange
(Tokyo Shoken Torihikijo)
TSE
2-1 Nihombashi-Kabuto-Cho, Chuo-ku, Tokyo
Tel: +81 3 3666 0141
Fax: +81 3 3663 0625
URL: http://www.tse.or.jp

Kobe Raw Silk Exchange
(Kobe Kiito Torihiksho)
KSE
126 Higashimachi, Chuo-ku, Kobe
Tel: +81 78 331 7141
Fax: +81 78 331 7145

Kobe Rubber Exchange
(Kobe Gomu Torihiksho)
KRE
49 Harima-cho, Chuo-ku, Kobe
Tel: +81 78 331 4211
Fax: +81 78 332 1622

Nagoya Stock Exchange
(Nagoya Shoken Torihikijo)
NSE
3-17 Sakae, 3-chome, Naka-ku, Nagoya
Tel: +81 81 52 262 3172
Fax: +81 81 52 241 1527
Email: nse@po.iijnet.or.jp
URL: http://www.iijnet.or.jp/nse-jp/

Nagoya Textile Exchange
2-15 Nishiki 3 Chome, Naka-ku, Naka-ku, Nagoya
Tel: +81 52 951 2171
Fax: +81 52 961 6407

Osaka Securities Exchange
(Osaka Shoken Torihikijo)
OSE
8-16, Kitahama, 1-chome, Chuo-ku, Osaka
Tel: +81 6 229 8643
Fax: +81 6 231 2639
Email: osakaexc@po.iijnet.or.jp
URL: http://www.ose.or.jp

Tokyo Grain Exchange
(Tokyo Kokumotsu Shohin Torihikijo)
TGE
1-12-5 Nihonbashi, Kakigara-cho, 1-Chome, Chuo-ku, Tokyo
Tel: +81 3 3668 9321
Fax: +81 3 3661 4564
Email: webmas@tge.or.jp
URL: http://www.tge.or.jp

Tokyo International Financial Futures Exchange
TIFFE
1-3-1 Marunouchi, Chiyoda-ku, Tokyo
Tel: +81 3 5223 2400
Fax: +81 3 5223 2450
URL: http://www.tiffe.or.jp

Hiroshima Stock Exchange
KANEX
14-18 Kanayama-cho, Naka-ku, Hiroshima
Tel: +81 82 541 1121
Fax: +81 82 541 1128

Fukuoka Stock Exchange
KANEX
2-14-2 Tenjin, Chuo-ku, Fukuoka
Tel: +81 92 741 8231
Fax: +81 92 713 1540

Niigata Securities Exchange
(Niigata Shoken Torihikijo)
1245 Hachiban-cho, Kamiokawame-don, Niigata
Tel: +81 25 222 4181
Fax: +81 25 222 4551

Sapporo Securities Exchange
(Sapporo Shoken Torihikijo)
5-14-1 Nishi-minami, I-jo, Chuo-ku, Sapporo
Tel: +81 11 241 6171
Fax: +81 11 251 0840

Kammon Commodity Exchange
(Kammon Shohin Torihikijo)
1-5 Nabe-cho, Shimonoseki
Tel: +81 832 31 1313
Fax: +81 832 23 1947

Kyoto Stock Exchange
KANEX
66 Tachiurinishi-machi, Higashinotoin-higashiiru, Shijo-dori,
Shimogyo-ku, Kyoto
Tel: +81 75 221 1171
Fax: +81 75 221 8356

Maebashi Dried Cocoa Exchange
(Maebashi Kanken Torihikijo)
1-49-1 Furuichi-machi, Maebashi
Tel: +81 272 52 1401
Fax: +81 272 51 8270

Cubu Commodity Exchange
3-2-15 Nishiki, Naka-ku, Nagoya
Tel: +81 52 951 2170
Fax: +81 52 961 1044

Yokohama Raw Silk Exchange
(Yokohama Kiito Torihikijo)
Silk Centre, 1 Yamashita-cho, Naka-ku, Yokohama
Tel: +81 45 641 1341
Fax: +81 45 641 1346

Kansai Agricultural Commodities Exchange
KANEX
1-10-14 Awaza, Nishi-ku, Osaka
Tel: +81 6 531 7931
Fax: +81 6 541 9343
Email: kex-1@kanex.or.jp
URL: http://www.kanex.or.jp

Jordan

Amman Financial Market
PO Box 8802, Ammam
Tel: +962 6 607171
Fax: +962 6 686830
Email: afm@go.com.jo
URL: http://accessme.com/AFM/

Kenya

Nairobi Stock Exchange
PO Box 43633, Nairobi
Tel: +254 2 230692
Fax: +254 2 224200
Email: nse@acc.or.ke

Korea (South)

Korea Stock Exchange
KSE
33 Yoido-dong, Youngdeungpo-gu, Seoul
Tel: +82 2 3774 9000
Fax: +82 2 786 0263
Email: world@www.kse.or.kr
URL: http://www.kse.or.kr

Kuwait

Kuwait Stock Exchange
PO Box 22235, Safat, Kuwait
Tel: +965 242 3130
Fax: +965 242 0779

Latvia

Riga Stock Exchange
Doma Iaukums 6, Riga
Tel: +7 212 431
Fax: +7 229 411
Email: rfb@mail.bkc.lv
URL: http://www.rfb.lv

Lithuania

National Stock Exchange of Lithuania
Ukmerges St 41, Vilnius
Tel: +370 2 72 14 07
Fax: +370 2 742 894
Email: office@nse.lt
URL: http://www.nse.lt

Luxembourg

Luxembourg Stock Exchange
(Societe Anonyme de la Bourse de Luxembourg)
11 Avenue de la Porte-Neuve
Tel: +352 47 79 36-1
Fax: +352 47 32 98
Email: info@bourse.lu
URL: http://www.bourse.lu

Macedonia

Macedonia Stock Exchange
MSE
Tel: +389 91 122 055
Fax: +389 91 122 069
Email: mse@unet.com.mk
URL: http://www.mse.org.mk

Malaysia

Kuala Lumpur Commodity Exchange
KLCE
4th Floor, Citypoint, Komplex Dayabumi, Jalan Sulta Hishamuddin,
Kuala Lumpur
Tel: +60 3 293 6822
Fax: +60 3 274 2215
Email: klce@po.jaring.my
URL: http://www.klce.com.my

Kuala Lumpur Stock Exchange
KLSE
4th Floor, Exchange Square, Off Jalan Semantan, Damansara
Heights, Kuala Lumpur
Tel: +60 3 254 64 33
Fax: +60 3 255 74 63
Email: webmaster@klse.com.my
URL: http://www.klse.com.my

The Kuala Lumpur Options & Financial Futures Exchange
KLOFFE
10th Floor, Wisma Chase Perdana, Damansara Heights, Jalan
Semantan, Kuala Lumpur
Tel: +60 3 253 8199
Fax: +60 3 255 3207
Email: kloffe@kloffe.com.my
URL: http://www.kloffe.com.my

Malaysia Monetary Exchange BHD
4th Floor, City Point, PO Box 11260, Dayabumi Complex, Jalan
Sultan Hishmuddin, Kuala Lumpur
Email: mme@po.jaring.my
URL: http://www.jaring.my/mme

Malta

Malta Stock Exchange
27 Pietro Floriani Street, Floriana, Valletta 14
Tel: +356 244 0515
Fax: +356 244 071
Email: borza@maltanet.omnes.net

Mauritius

Mauritius Stock Exchange
Stock Exchange Commission, 9th Floor, SICOM Building, Sir
Celicourt Anselme Street, Port Louis
Tel: +230 208 8735
Fax: +230 208 8676
Email: svtradha@intnet.mu
URL: http://lynx.intnet.mu/sem/

Mexico

Mexican Stock Exchange
(Bolsa Mexicana de Valores, SA de CV)
Paseo de la Reforma 255, Colonia Cuauhtemoc, Mexico DF
Tel: +52 5 726 66 00
Fax: +52 5 705 47 98
Email: cinform@bmv.com.mx
URL: http://www.bmv.com.mx

Morocco

Casablanca Stock Exchange
(Societe de la Bourse des Valeurs de Casablanca)
98 Boulevard Mohammed V, Casablanca
Tel: +212 2 27 93 54
Fax: +212 2 20 03 65

Namibia

Namibian Stock Exchange
Kaiserkrone Centre 11, O Box 2401, Windhoek
Tel: +264 61 227 647
Fax: +264 61 248 531
Email: tminney@nse.com.na
URL: http://www.nse.com.na

Netherlands

Financiele Termijnmarkt Amsterdam NV
FTA
Nes 49, Amsterdam
Tel: +31 20 550 4555
Fax: +31 20 624 54l6

AEX-Stock Exchange
AEX
Beursplein 5, PO Box 19163, Amsterdam
Tel: +31 20 550 4444
Fax: +31 20 550 4950
URL: http://www.aex.nl/

AEX-Agricultural Futures Exchange
Beursplein 5, PO Box 19163, Amsterdam
Tel: +31 20 550 4444
Fax: +31 20 623 9949

AEX-Options Exchange
AEX
Beursplein 5, PO Box 19163, Amsterdam
Tel: +31 20 550 4444
Fax: +31 20 550 4950
URL: http://www.aex-optiebeurs.ase.nl

New Zealand

New Zealand Futures & Options Exchange Ltd
NZFOE
10th Level, Stock Exchange Cen, 191 Queen Street, Auckland 1
Tel: +64 9 309 8308
Fax: +64 9 309 8817
Email: info@nzfoe.co.nz
URL: http://www.nzfoe.co.nz

New Zealand Stock Exchange
NZSE
8th Floor Caltex Tower, 286-292 Lambton Quay, Wellington
Tel: +64 4 4727 599
Fax: +64 4 4731 470
Email: info@nzse.org.nz
URL: http://www.nzse.co.nz

Nicaragua

Nicaraguan Stock Exchange
(BOLSA DE VALORES DE NICARAGUA, S.A.)
Centro Financiero Banic, 1er Piso, Km. 5 1/2 Carretera Masaya
Email: info@bolsanic.com
URL: http://bolsanic.com/

Nigeria

Nigerian Stock Exchange
Stock Exchange House, 8th & 9th Floors, 2/4 Customs Street, Lagos
Tel: +234 1 266 0287
Fax: +234 1 266 8724
Email: alile@nse.ngra.com

Norway

Oslo Stock Exchange
(Oslo Bors)
OSLO
P.O. Box 460, Sentrum, Oslo
Tel: +47 22 34 17 00
Fax: +47 22 41 65 90
Email: informasjonsavdelingen@ose.telemax.no
URL: http://www.ose.no

Oman

Muscat Securities Market
Po Box 3265, Ruwi
Tel: +968 702 665
Fax: +968 702 691

Pakistan

Islamabad Stock Exchange
Stock Exchange Building, 101-E Fazal-ul-Haq Road, Blue Area,
Islamabad
Tel: +92 51 27 50 45
Fax: +92 51 27 50 44
Email: ise@paknet1.ptc.pk

Karachi Stock Exchange
Stock Exchange Building, Stock Exchange Road, Karachi
Tel: +92 21 2425502
Fax: +92 21 241 0825
URL: http://www.kse.org

Lahore Stock Exchange Po Box 1315, 19 Khayaban e Aiwan e Iqbal,
Lahore
Tel: +92 42 636 8000
Fax: +92 42 636 8484

Panama

Panama Stock Exchange
(Bolsa de Valores de Panama, SA)
Calle Elvira Mendex y Calle 52, Edif Valarino, Planta Baja
Tel: +507 2 69 1966
Fax: +507 2 69 2457
URL: http://www.urraca.com/bvp/

Paraguay

Ascuncon Stock Exchange
(Bolsa de Valores y Productos de Ascuncion)
Estrella 540, Ascuncion
Tel: +595 21 442 445
Fax: +595 21 442 446
Email: bolsapya@pla.net.py
URL: http://www.pla.net.py/bvpasa

Peru

Lima Stock Exchange
(La Bolsa de Valores de Lima)
Pasaje Acuna 191, Lima
Tel: +51 1 426 79 39
Fax: +51 1 426 76 50
Email: web_team@bvl.com.pe
URL: http://www.bvl.com.pe

Philippines

Philippine Stock Exchange
Philippine Stock Exchange Cent, Tektite Road, Ortigas Centre, Pasig
Tel: +63 2 636 01 22
Fax: +63 2 634 51 13
Email: pse@mnl.sequel.net
URL: http://www.pse.com.ph

Manila International Futures Exchange
MIFE
7/F Producer's Bank Centre, Paseo de Roxas, Makati
Tel: +63 2 818 5496
Fax: +63 2 818 5529

Poland

Warsaw Stock Exchange
Gielda papierow, Wartosciowych w Warszawie SA, Ul Nowy Swiat 6/
12, Warsaw
Tel: +48 22 628 32 32
Fax: +48 22 628 17 54
Email: gielda@kp.atm.com.pl

Portugal

Oporto Derivatives Exchange
(Bolsa de Derivados do Oporto)
BDP
Av. da Boavista 3433, Oporto
Tel: +351 2 618 58 58
Fax: +351 2 618 56 66

Lisbon Stock Exchange
(Bolsa de Valores de Lisboa)
BVL
Edificio da Bolsa, Rua Soeiro Pereira Gomes, Lisbon
Tel: +351 1 790 99 04
Fax: +351 1 795 20 21
Email: webmaster@bvl.pt
URL: http://www.bvl.pt

Romania

Bucharest Stock Exchange
BSE
Doamnei no. 8, Bucharest
Email: bse@delos.ro
URL: http://www.delos.ro/bse/

Romanian Commodities Exchange
(Bursa Romana de Marfuri SA)
Piata Presei nr 1, Sector 1, Bucharest
Tel: +40 223 21 69
Fax: +40 223 21 67

Russian Federation

Moscow Interbank Currency Exchange
MICEX
21/1, Sadovaya-Spasskay, Moscow
Tel: +7 095 705 9627
Fax: +7 095 705 9622
Email: inmicex@micex.com
URL: http://www.micex.com/

Russian Exchange
RCRME
Myasnitskaya ul 26, Moscow
Tel: +7 095 262 06 53
Fax: +7 095 262 57 57
Email: assa@vc-rtsb.msk.ru
URL: http://www.re.ru

Moscow Commodity Exchange
Pavilion No. 4, Russian Exhibition Centre, Moscow
Tel: +7 095 187 83 07
Fax: +7 095 187 9982

St Petersburg Futures Exchange
SPBFE
274 Ligovski av., St Petersburg
Tel: +7 812 294 15 12
Fax: +7 812 327 93 88
Email: seva@spbfe.futures.ru

Siberian Stock Exchange
PO box 233, Frunze St 5, Novosibirsk
Tel: +7 38 32 21 06 90
Fax: +7 38 32 21 06 90
Email: sibex@sse.nsk.su

Moscow Central Stock Exchange
9(B) Bolshaya Maryinskaya Stre, Moscow
Tel: +7 095 229 88 82
Fax: +7 0995 202 06 67

Moscow International Stock Exchange
MISE
Slavyanskaya Pl 4, Bld 2, Moscow
Tel: +7 095 923 33 39
Fax: +7 095 923 33 39

National Association of Securities Market Participants
(NAUF)
Floor 2, Building 5, Chayanova Street 15, Moscow
Tel: +7 095 705 90
Fax: +7 095 976 42 36
Email: naufor@rtsnet.ru
URL: http://www.rtsnet.ru

Vladivostock Stock Exchange
VSE
21 Zhertv Revolyutsii Str, Vladivostock
Tel: +7 4232 22 78 87
Fax: +7 4232 22 80 09

St Petersburg Stock Exchange
SPSE
274 Ligovsky pr, St Petersburg
Tel: +7 812 296 10 80
Fax: +7 812 296 10 80
Email: root@lse.spb.su

Saudi Arabia

Saudi Arabian Monetary Authority
SAMA
PO Box 2992, Riyadh
Tel: +966 1 466 2300
Fax: +966 1 466 3223

Singapore

Singapore Commodity Exchange Ltd
SICOM
111 North Bridge Road, #23-04/, Peninsula Plaza
Tel: +65 338 5600
Fax: +65 338 9116
Email: sicom@pacific.net.sg

Stock Exchange of Singapore
No. 26-01/08, 20 Cecil Street, The Exchange
Tel: +65 535 3788
Fax: +65 535 6994
Email: webmaster@ses.com.sg
URL: http://www.ses.com.sg

Singapore International Monetary Exchange Ltd
SIMEX
1 Raffles Place, No. 07-00, OUB Centre
Tel: +65 535 7382
Fax: +65 535 7282
Email: simex@pacific.net.sg
URL: http://www.simex.com.sg

Slovak Republic

Bratislava Stock Exchange
(Burza cenny ch papierov v Bratislave)
BSSE
Vysoka 17, Bratislava
Tel: +42 7 5036 102
Fax: +42 7 5036 103
Email: kunikova@bsse.sk
URL: http://www.bsse.sk

Slovenia

Commodity Exchange of Ljubljana
Smartinskal 52, PO Box 85, Ljubljana
Tel: +386 61 18 55 100
Fax: +386 61 18 55 101
Email: infos@bb-lj.si
URL: http://www.eunet.si/commercial/bbl/bbl-ein.html

Ljubljana Stock Exchange, Inc
LJSE
Sovenska cesta 56, Lbujljana
Tel: +386 61 171 02 11
Fax: +386 61 171 02 13
Email: info@jse.si
URL: http://www.ljse.si

South Africa

Johannesburg Stock Exchange
JSE
17 Diagonal Street, Johannesburg
Tel: +27 11 377 2200
Fax: +27 11 834 3937
Email: r&d@jse.co.za
URL: http://www.jse.co.za

South African Futures Exchange
SAFEX
105 Central Street, Houghton Estate 2198, Johannesburg
Tel: +27 11 728 5960
Fax: +27 11 728 5970
Email: jani@icon.co.za
URL: http://www.safex.co.za

Spain

Citrus Fruit and Commodity Market of Valencia
(Futuros de Citricos y Mercaderias de Valencia)
2, 4 Libreros, Valencia
Tel: +34 6 387 01 88
Fax: +34 6 394 36 30
Email: futuros@super.medusa.es

Spanish Options Exchange
(MEFF Renta Variable)
MEFF RV
Torre Picasso, Planta 26, Madrid
Tel: +34 1 585 0800
Fax: +34 1 571 9542
Email: mefrv@meffrv.es
URL: http://www.meffrv.es

Spanish Financial Futures Market
(MEFF Renta Fija)
MEFF RF
Via Laietana, 58, Barcelona
Tel: +34 3 412 1128
Fax: +34 3 268 4769
Email: marketing@meff.es
URL: http://www.meff.es

Madrid Stock Exchange
(Bolsa de Madrid)
Plaza de la Lealtad 1, Madrid
Tel: +34 1 589 26 00
Fax: +34 1 531 22 90
Email: internacional@bolsamadrid.es
URL: http://www.bolsamadrid.es

Barcelona Stock Exchange
Paseo Isabel II No 1, Barcelona
Tel: +34 3 401 35 55
Fax: +34 3 401 38 59
Email: agiralt@borsabcn.es
URL: http://www.borsabcn.es

Bilbao Stock Exchange
(Sociedad Rectora de la Bolsa de Valoes de Bilbao)
Jose Maria Olabarri 1, Bilbao
Tel: +34 4 423 74 00
Fax: +34 4 424 46 20
Email: bolsabilbao@sarenet.es
URL: http://www.bolsabilbao.es

Valencia Stock Exchange
(Sociedad Rectora de la Bolsa de Valoes de Valencia)
Libreros 2 y 4, Valencia
Tel: +34 6 387 01 00
Fax: +34 6 387 01 14

Sri Lanka

Colombo Stock Exchange
CSE
04-01 West Bloc, World Trade Centre, Echelon Square, Colombo 1
Tel: +94 1 44 65 81
Fax: +94 1 44 52 79
Email: cse@sri.lanka.net
URL: http://www.lanka.net/cse/

Swaziland

Swaziland Stock Market
Swaziland Stockbrokers Ltd, 2nd Floor Dlan'ubeka House, Walker
St, Mbabane
Tel: +268 46163
Fax: +268 44132
URL: http://mbendi.co.za/exsw.htm

Sweden

The Swedish Futures and Options Market
(OM Stockholm AB)
OMS
Box 16305, Brunkebergstorg 2, Stockholm
Tel: +46 8 700 0600
Fax: +46 8 723 1092
URL: http://www.omgroup.com

Stockholm Stock Exchange Ltd
(Stockholm Fondbors AB)
Kallargrand 2, Stockholm
Tel: +46 8 613 88 00
Fax: +46 8 10 81 10
Email: info@xsse.se
URL: http://www.xsse.se

Switzerland

Swiss Options & Financial Futures Exchange AG
SOFFEX
Selnaustrasse 32, Zurich
Tel: +41 1 229 2111
Fax: +41 1 229 2233
Email: webmaster@swx.ch
URL: http://www.bourse.ch

Swiss Exchange
SWX
Selnaustrasse 32, Zurich
Tel: +41 1 229 21 11
Fax: +41 1 229 22 33
URL: http://www.bourse.ch

Taiwan

Taiwan Stock Exchange
Floors 2-10, City Building, 85 Yen Ping Road South, Taipei
Tel: +886 2 311 4020
Fax: +886 2 375 3669
Email: intl-aff@tse.com.tw
URL: http://www.tse.com.tw

Thailand

The Stock Exchange of Thailand
SET
2nd Floor, Tower 1, 132 Sindhorn Building, Wireless Road, Bangkok
Tel: +66 2 254 0960
Fax: +66 2 263 2746
Email: webmaster@set.or.th
URL: http://www.set.or.th

Trinidad and Tobago

Trinidad and Tobago Stock Exchange
65 Independence Street, Port of Spain
Tel: +1809 809 625 5108
Fax: +1809 809 623 0089

Tunisia

Tunis Stock Exchange
(Bourse des Valeurs Mobilieres de Tunis)
Centre Babel - Bloc E, Rue Jean-Jacques Rousseau, Montplaisir, Tunis
Tel: +216 1 780 288
Fax: +216 1 789 189

Turkey

Istanbul Stock Exchange
(Istanbul Menkul Kiymetler Borasi)
ISE
Istinye, Istanbul
Tel: +90 212 298 21 00
Fax: +90 212 298 25 00
Email: info@ise.org
URL: http://www.ise.org

United Kingdom

The London Securities and Derivatives Exchange
OMLX
107 Cannon Street, London
Tel: +44 171 283 0678
Fax: +44 171 815 8508
Email: petter.made@omgroup.com
URL: http://www.omgroup.com/

International Petroleum Exchange of London Ltd
IPE
International House, 1 St. Katharine's Way, London
Tel: +44 171 481 0643
Fax: +44 l7l 481 8485
Email: busdev@ipe.uk.com
URL: http://www.ipe.uk.com

London International Futures & Options Exchange
LIFFE
Cannon Bridge, London
Tel: +44 171 623 0444
Fax: +44 171 588 3624
Email: exchange@liffe.com
URL: http://www.liffe.com

London Metal Exchange
LME
56 Leadenhall Street, London
Tel: +44 171 264 5555
Fax: +44 171 680 0505
Email: lsnow@lmetal.netkonect.co.uk
URL: http://www.lme.co.uk

The Baltic Exchange
Tel: +44 171 623 5501
Fax: +44 171 369 1622
Email: enquiries@balticexchange.co.uk
URL:http://www.balticexchange.co.uk

London Stock Exchange
LSE
Old Broad Street, London
Tel: +44 171 797 1000
Fax: +44 171 374 0504

Tradepoint Investment Exchange
35 King Street, London
Tel: +44 171 240 8000
Fax: +44 171 240 1900
Email: g171@dial.pipex.com
URL: http://www.tradepoint.co.uk

London Commodity Exchange
LCE
1 Commodity Quay, St. Katharine Docks, London
Tel: +44 171 481 2080
Fax: +44 171 702 9923
URL: http://www.liffe.com

United States

New York Stock Exchange
NYSE
11 Wall Street, New York
Tel: +1 212 656 3000
Fax: +1 212 656 5557
URL: http://www.nyse.com

Minneapolis Grain Exchange
MGE
400 S. Fourth St., Minneapolis
Tel: +1 612 338 6216
Fax: +1 612 339 1155
Email: mgex@ix.netcom.com
URL: http://www.mgex.com

Philadelphia Stock Exchange
PHLX
1900 Market Street, Philadelphia
Tel: +1 215 496 5000
Fax: +1 215 496 5653
URL: http://www.phlx.com

Kansas City Board of Trade
KCBT
4800 Main St., Suite 303, Kansas City
Tel: +1 816 753 7500
Fax: +1 816 753 3944
Email: kcbt@kcbt.com
URL: http://www.kcbt.com

Chicago Board Options Exchange
CBOE
400 S. LaSalle Street, Chicago
Tel: +1 312 786 5600
Fax: +1 312 786 7409
Email: investor_services@cboe.com
URL: http://www.cboe.com

Chicago Board of Trade
CBOT
141 West Jackson Boulevard, Chicago
Tel: +1 312 435 3500
Fax: +1 312 341 3306
Email: comments@cbot.com
URL: http://www.cbt.com

New York Mercantile Exchange
NYMEX
4 World Trade Center, New York
Tel: +1 212 938 222
Fax: +1 212 938 2985
Email: marketing@nymex.com
URL: http://www.nymex.com

Chicago Stock Exchange
CHX
One Financial Place, 440 S. LaSalle St, Chicago
Tel: +1 312 663 222
Fax: +1 312 773 2396
Email: marketing@chiacgostockex.com
URL: http://www.chicagostockex.com

MidAmerica Commodity Exchange
MIDAM
141 W. Jackson Boulevard, Chicago
Tel: +1 313 341 3000
Fax: +1 312 341 3027
Email: comments@cbot.com
URL: http://www.midam.com

Philadelphia Board of Trade
1900 Market Street, Philadelphia
Tel: +1 215 496 5357
Fax: +1 215 496 5653

The Cincinnati Stock Exchange
400 South LaSalle Street, Chicago
Tel: +1 312 786 8803
Fax: +1 312 939 7239

Boston Stock Exchange, Inc
BSE
38th Floor, One Boston Place, Boston
Tel: +1 617 723 9500
Fax: +1 617 523 6603
URL: http://www.bostonstock.com

Nasdaq Stock Market
1735 K Street NW, Washington DC
Tel: +1 202 728 8000
Fax: +1 202 293 6260
Email: fedback@nasdaq.com
URL: http://www.nasdaq.com

American Stock Exchange
AMEX
86 Trinity Place, New York
Tel: +1 212 306 1000
Fax: +1 212 306 1802
Email: jstephan@amex.com
URL: http://www.amex.com

New York Cotton Exchange
NYCE
4 World Trade Center, New York
Tel: +1 212 938 2702
Fax: +1 212 488 8135
URL: http://www.nyce.com

Pacific Stock Exchange, Inc
PSE
301 Pine Street, San Francisco
Tel: +1 415 393 4000
Fax: +1 415 393 4202
URL: http://www.pacificex.com

Chicago Mercantile Exchange
CME
30 S. Wacker Drive, Chicago
Tel: +1 312 930 1000
Fax: +1 312 930 3439
Email: info@cme.com
URL: http://www.cme.com

Coffee, Sugar & Cocoa Exchange Inc.
CSCE
4 World Trade Center, New York
Tel: +1 212 938 2800
Fax: +1 212 524 9863
Email: csce@ix.netcom.com
URL: http://www.csce.com

Venezuela

Maracaibo Stock Exchange
(Bolsa de Valores de Maracaibo)
Calle 96, Esq Con Avda 5, Edificio
Banco Central de Vene, Piso 9, Maracaibo
Tel: +58 61 225 482
Fax: +58 61 227 663

Venezuela Electronic Stock Exchange
(de Venezuela)
C·mara de Comercio de Valencia, Edif. C·mara de Comercio, Av.
BolÌvar, Valencia, Edo. Carabobo, Apartado 151
Tel: +58 57.5109
Fax: +58 57.5147
Email: set@venezuelastock.com
URL: http://www.venezuelastock.com

Caracas Stock Exchange
(Bolsa de Valores de Caracas)
Edificio Atrium, Piso 1 Calle Sorocaima, Urbanizacion, El Rosal,
Caracas
Tel: +58 2 905 5511
Fax: +58 2 905 5814
Email: anafin@true.net
URL: http://www.caracasstock.com

Yugoslavia

Belgrade Stock Exchange
(Beogradska Berza)
Omladinskih 1, 3rd Floor, PO Box 214, Belgrade
Tel: +381 11 19 84 77
Fax: +381 11 13 82 42
Email: beyu@eunet.yu

Zimbabwe

Zimbabwe Stock Exchange
5th Floor, Southampton House, Union Avenue, Harare
Tel: +263 4 736 861
Fax: +263 4 791 045